TERMINATING
PSYCHOTHERAPY

TERMINATING
PSYCHOTHERAPY

A CLINICIAN'S GUIDE

EDITED BY

WILLIAM T. O'DONOHUE & MICHAEL A. CUCCIARE

Routledge
Taylor & Francis Group
New York   London

BP53

Routledge
Taylor & Francis Group
270 Madison Avenue
New York, NY 10016

Routledge
Taylor & Francis Group
2 Park Square
Milton Park, Abingdon
Oxon OX14 4RN

Library of Congress Cataloging-in-Publication Data

Terminating psychotherapy : a clinician's guide / [edited by] William O'Donohue, Michael A. Cucciare.
    p. ; cm.
    Includes bibliographical references.
    ISBN 978-0-415-95436-5
    1. Psychotherapy--Termination. 2. Psychotherapist and patient. I. O'Donohue, William T. II. Cucciare, Michael A., 1976-
    [DNLM: 1. Psychotherapy--methods. 2. Professional-Patient Relations. 3. Treatment Outcome. WM 420 T3187 2007]

RC489.T45T45 2007
616.89'14--dc22
    2007019099

Visit the Taylor & Francis Web site at
http://www.taylorandfrancis.com

and the Routledge Web site at
http://www.routledge.com

7/19/10

Contents

Contributors

Nehami Baum
Bar Ilan University
Ramat-Gan, Israel

James X. Bembry
University of Maryland
Baltimore, Maryland

Anne Bonsall-Hoekstra
Minnesota State University
Mankato, Minnesota

Jeffrey A. Buchanan
Minnesota State University
Mankato, Minnesota

Brenda Bursch
University of California
Los Angeles, California

R. Blake Chaffee
TriWest Healthcare Alliance
Phoenix, Arizona

John Chiles
University of Washington
Sound Psychiatry Consulting Group
Port Townsend, Washington

Guina Cohen
Ben-Gurion University of the Negev
Beer-Sheva, Israel

Michael A. Cucciare
Veterans Affairs Palo Alto Health Care System
Stanford University
Palo Alto, California

Nicholas A. Cummings
University of Nevada
Reno, Nevada

Paula R. Danzinger
William Paterson University
Wayne, New Jersey

Deborah Davis
University of Nevada
Reno, Nevada

Rachel Dawson
University of Maine
Orono, Maine

Keith S. Dobson
University of Calgary
Calgary, Canada

Steven J. Ellman
City University of New York
New York, New York

William C. Follette
University of Nevada
Reno, Nevada

Douglas H. Frayn
University of Toronto
Toronto, Canada

Steven R. Graybar
University of Nevada
Reno, Nevada

Hiroaki Harai
Kikuchi National Hospital
Koushi-City, Kumamoto, Japan

Keith W. Harris
Veterans Affairs Palo Alto Health Care System
Palo Alto, California

Lauren C. Haubert
University of Calgary
Calgary, Alberta Canada

Holly Hazlett-Stevens
University of Nevada
Reno, Nevada

Netta Horesh
Bar-Ilan University
Ramat-Gan, Israel

Leah M. Leonard
University of Nevada
Reno, Nevada

Elaine McMillan
University of Maine
Orono, Maine

Dana Miller
University of Iowa
Iowa City, Iowa

Brie A. Moore
University of Nevada
Reno, Nevada

J. Christopher Muran
Beth Israel Medical Center
New York, New York

Peter E. Nathan
University of Iowa
Iowa City, Iowa

Elizabeth Ochoa
Beth Israel Medical Center
New York, New York

William T. O'Donohue
University of Nevada
Reno, Nevada

Miyo Okajima
Kikuchi National Hospital
Koushi-City, Kumamoto, Japan

Lindsay R. Owings
University of Maine
Orono, Maine

Candace Peters
University of Iowa
Iowa City, Iowa

Jennifer Pien-Wong
Veterans Affairs Palo Alto Health Care System
Palo Alto, California

James O. Prochaska
University of Rhode Island
Kingston, Rhode Island

Janice M. Prochaska
Pro-Change Behavior Systems
West Kingston, Rhode Island

John L. Rodman
Minneapolis Veterans Affairs Medical Center
Minneapolis, Minnesota

Andreea L. Seritan
University of California
Davis, California

Golan Shahar
Ben-Gurion University of the Negev
Beer-Sheva, Israel and
Yale University
New Haven, Connecticut

Anne Helene Skinstad
University of Iowa
Iowa City, Iowa

Kirk Strosahl
Mountain View Consulting Group, Inc.
Moxee, Washington

Geoffrey L. Thorpe
University of Maine
Orono, Maine

Patricia Walshaw
Temple University
Philadelphia, Pennsylvania

Elizabeth Reynolds Welfel
Cleveland State University
Cleveland, Ohio

INTRODUCTION

WILLIAM T. O'DONOHUE AND MICHAEL A. CUCCIARE

Introduction: General Issues Regarding Termination

Terminating psychotherapy is an interesting and complex phenomenon for several reasons. First, as will be seen in the chapters of this volume, there is a wide variety of claims about how termination should be thought of and correspondingly how it should be properly done. Second, and perhaps foremost, there are various views on how large an issue it is. At one extreme, the view seems to be that termination is an ending of an extremely important relationship—a bit of an exaggeration, but picture the runway scene in *Casablanca* between Humphrey Bogart and Ingrid Bergman. Due to the importance of the relationship, termination is a very delicate and very consequential matter. On the other end of the spectrum, termination of psychotherapy might be much like ending treatment with one's orthodontist—one is grateful to the extent one's goals were fulfilled, and one might have thought highly of the professionalism or the warmth of the good doctor, but all the while one is happy the somewhat unfortunate process is finally over. This latter view is not well represented in this book, possibly because this view is simply not as applicable to psychotherapy, but also because of the widespread existence of a bit of professional narcissism—we think relating to us is so important and meaningful that ending this must be a difficult, emotional process. The fact that the vast majority of patients self-terminate by simply not coming back for additional sessions might, if properly considered, lend some support to this latter view.

In addition, this book is mainly focused on what might be called therapist-involved termination. Much psychotherapy is terminated without the therapist's involvement—the client simply drops out. Therapists may attempt to contact these clients, who become voluntarily MIA, by writing a letter or making a phone call, in order to bring these cases to a more satisfactory resolution (at least from the therapist's perspective), but it is not this sort of one-sided, client-initiated ending of therapy that is the focus of this book. These endings are generally regarded as premature (at least by the therapist). The therapist feels that continued contact is warranted as there is more work, and hopefully more progress to be achieved. This book focuses on termination in which the therapist and the client are still active participants in some sort of ending or transition of therapy.

The Inherent Complexity of Termination

In addition, any model that captures the termination process needs to recognize that termination is not a simple unitary phenomenon. Variables that might affect what termination is like can include:

The success of the therapy. It is reasonable to hypothesize that terminating with a client whose problems have been completely resolved would be at least somewhat different from terminating with a client who has made no change or even become worse.

The nature of the problem addressed in therapy. It also seems reasonable to hypothesize that working on a quicker, easier, less "deep" problem like functional enuresis versus a deeper more involved problem like complicated bereavement or marital discord would likely result in a more complicated, nuanced termination.

The diagnostic status of the client. It is reasonable to hypothesize that terminating with someone with chronic schizophrenia would be different in at least some important ways than termination with someone with a simple phobia.

The therapeutic allegiance of the therapist. As we will see in the following chapters, different therapy orientations say quite different things about termination. They also make different claims about the substance of the therapy that precedes any termination, so termination can also differ because the entire experience differed for both the client and the therapist.

Length of therapy. Again, one might hypothesize that terminating with a client who has been seen for years would be different from terminating with a client seen for a few sessions.

Personality characteristics of client and therapist (and their interactions). One can speculate that a therapist who related to the client with considerable aloofness, for example, can expect a termination that is different from a therapist who related to the client with much warmth. Attachment styles might also influence the termination process. A therapist or client with borderline or histrionic personality disorder would also have some effect on what termination would be like. There are, in all likelihood, a variety of complex interactions between the personality styles of the therapist and client, which influence the termination process.

Significant events in therapy. Significant events that occur in therapy such as confrontation, "tough love," splitting, divorce, abuse, and so forth can all possibly have some influence on what termination is like.

The number of participants in therapy. Terminating with a single client may be different from terminating with a couple or terminating with a large group.

Logistical details. Things happen—individuals move, or lose insurance, or forget appointments—and these sorts of logistical events can make termination necessary and may influence what termination is like.

Other human variables. Sexual attraction, hostility toward a gender, the need to be liked—the list could go on and any of these variables might influence termination.

Thus it would be misleading to think of termination as a univocal phenomenon, and wrong to think of it as a homogeneous, simple event. Just as every marriage has many unique characteristics, every termination has its own uniqueness. There is some commonality, and the word *termination* is still viable, but it is a multifaceted process to be explained, and explanations of it must be equally nuanced and complex. Termination may be much like Wittgenstein's (1958) comments on what games are like.

Consider, for example, the proceedings that we call *games*. I mean board games, card games, ball games, the Olympic Games, and so on. What is common to them all? Don't say: "There must be something common or they would not all be called games." If we look carefully we do not find one thing that is common to all; instead we find similarities and relationships. Are they all amusing? Compare chess with noughts and crosses. Is there always winning and losing or competition between players? Think of patience. In ball games there is winning and losing, but when a child throws his ball against the wall and catches it again this feature is not present. Look at the parts played by skill and luck, and at the difference between skill in chess and skill in tennis. Think now of games like ring around the rosey; here there is the element of amusement, but how many other characteristic features have disappeared! We can go through the many, many other groups of games in the same way; we can see how similarities crop up and disappear. The result of this examination is that we see a complicated network of similarities overlapping and crisscrossing; sometimes overall similarities, sometimes similarities of detail (Wittgenstein, 31–32).

Termination, then, becomes a phenomenon of considerable complexity—a phenomenon that is really one in a series of events, and one that is, in important ways, dependent both on the details of the events that preceded it as well as variables present while it is occurring. It is in many ways a historically conditioned event.

We are in the relatively early stages of understanding the process of psychotherapy. It is easier, by their very nature, to understand some variables that may affect psychotherapy than others. Variables that affect the beginning of therapy are simpler to understand than variables that affect its end. Time series designs, which can tease apart the relative contributions of events in the flow of a larger process, are more suitable for studying termination, given all the complexities listed above.

The Economic Context of Termination

Termination is not economically neutral. Termination typically stops a revenue stream coming from someone (typically a third-party payer) to the therapist. Thus, there are competing financial interests—therapists, all things being equal, would like the revenue stream to continue; the payer would like it to stop. This financial state of affairs has raised a concern in healthcare economics—that therapists may have a financial incentive to overtreat (delaying appropriate termination) and third-party payers an incentive to undertreat (terminate prematurely). This is the negotiation between therapists and managed care. Failing to terminate when it is appropriate to do so is one response to this adverse financial incentive. It was one of the main functions of the behavioral managed care companies that came into existence in the 1980s (and are still with us) to make sure therapists were not delaying appropriate termination (particularly in inpatient settings). However, some have criticized managed care companies claiming that they are reducing their costs (particularly when they are at risk for these costs) by attempting to prematurely terminate therapy.

Healthcare plans design benefits that also have an influence on therapy termination. Some place limits on the annual number of sessions. A policy with an annual limit of twenty-four sessions creates a lot of pressure for the therapy to be terminated at or before twenty-four sessions are complete. This may be fine for some patients but not for others.

This is made more complex by the all too human responses to economic contingencies. Some programs or therapists "treat to the benefit." This was readily apparent in the 1970s and 1980s when there were thirty-day inpatient programs designed to treat all sorts of problems, from adolescent disobedience to substance abuse. There were no outcome studies showing that these thirty-day programs were effective and no dosage studies showing that thirty days were necessary, but the program designers knew that most policies covered thirty days of inpatient hospitalization and they designed the program to maximize the financial benefit.

On the other hand, the late Nobel Prize–winning economist Milton Friedman has pointed out that there are perverse incentives in most health insurance policies. Professor Friedman notes that we do not spend other people's money (the insurance companies) as we do our own. Because third-party payments make treatment "free" to the patient, we generally want more of it. A recent RAND study, for example, revealed that individuals paying for their own healthcare spent 40% less than individuals who had all their healthcare expenses paid by a third party. This can explain the healthcare crisis we now face. Healthcare expenses have ballooned from 10% of the GDP (gross domestic product) in 1960 to 15% in 2005.

Economists, politicians, and healthcare industry leaders are attempting to work out benefit designs in which the incentives are not so perverse. However, this is tough work as there are disagreements about what will work and vested interests in outcomes. The point to be made is that financial matters also have a very important role in any discussion of termination.

The Ethical Context

Termination also is not ethically neutral. There are "oughts" and "ought nots" associated with termination. The American Psychological Association's (APA) Ethics Code (2002), for example, states that the therapist ought to terminate when he or she sees that therapy is no longer helping the client and another therapist or therapy can benefit the client more. Therapists should also terminate when the therapy is harming the patient ("at least do no harm"). On the other hand, therapists should not abandon clients by terminating with them if such termination will cause them harm. Therapists must have good reasons for terminating therapy (and for not terminating therapy) and must make appropriate safeguards to ensure that any unfortunate termination (e.g., due to a therapist's move) minimizes harm to the patient.

One reason why therapy has these ethical proscriptions is due to the factors just discussed—money can drive therapists to make termination decisions that are not in their patients' best interests. Greed can affect the therapist's termination decisions. Therapists as human beings can also let other factors drive therapy termination decisions. Here's a quick rundown of ethically problematic decisions related to some of the Seven Deadly Sins (always a reasonable framework for understanding human behavior):

Sloth: The therapist can find the case too difficult and decide to prematurely terminate to find an easier case. This is sometimes called dumping. On the other hand, termination might itself be difficult and the therapist might continue as this is the path of least resistance.

Pride: The therapist can believe that he or she is the only good therapist for the patient and fail to terminate in situations in which another therapist's skills are actually more relevant for the patient. The therapist's pride can also be wounded by a client complaint or failure to cooperate or progress as the therapist would like, and the therapist, because of wounded pride, could terminate prematurely.

Lust: The therapist may be sexually attracted to the patient and fail to terminate because of this attraction. On the other hand, the APA Ethics Code states that psychologists should not terminate therapy so that they can have sexual relationships with "former" patients. In addition, though very vague, the circumstances of termination, among other factors, help determine whether a therapist can ethically have a sexual relationship with a former patient after two years.

Anger: The therapist could become angry at the patient for a variety of reasons and decide to terminate prematurely.

Greed: The therapist could fail to terminate due to financial reasons; continuing to see the patient means a continued revenue stream.

Gluttony and envy seem to be largely irrelevant. We are not attempting to put the termination question in a religious context, but rather believe that these "sins" can cover some common human failings that can impact the ethical quality of termination decisions.

Specifically, the most recent APA Ethics Code (2002) says the following about termination:

10.10 Terminating Therapy

(a) Psychologists terminate therapy when it becomes reasonably clear that the client/patient no longer needs the service, is not likely to benefit, or is being harmed by continued service.

(b) Psychologists may terminate therapy when threatened or otherwise endangered by the client/patient or another person with whom the client/patient has a relationship.

(c) Except where precluded by the actions of clients/patients or third-party payors, prior to termination psychologists provide pretermination counseling and suggest alternative service providers as appropriate.

The second stipulation is an interesting one, but fortunately one that does not often arise in therapy. The remainder of this book may be construed as an unpacking of what pretermination counseling might look like. Although, again, one can see that there is little unanimity on this issue.

Background and Significance

Over the last two decades, mental health service delivery has transitioned away from single providers dominating mental health delivery to psychotherapy occurring in the context of settings that track types and length of services (i.e., organized managed care and various medical settings). This transition has undoubtedly brought with it a new emphasis on the delivery of cost-effective mental health services. To function successfully in a system of increased accountability, mental health professionals need to be proficient in a wide variety of skills, such as the delivery of brief, cost-effective assessment strategies and psychotherapies, and perhaps most importantly, the skillful termination of psychotherapy treatment. To address this latter issue we have assembled a distinguished group of international experts to present and discuss the most important issues and controversies surrounding the concept of psychotherapy termination and to provide the reader with the most effective, state-of-the-art strategies for terminating treatment in the context of various treatment modalities, (e.g., cognitive behavioral treatment and psychoanalysis), populations (e.g., children and the elderly), and patient problems (e.g., depression, substance use, and psychotic disorders). In this volume, we have asked the authors to respond to a wide variety of issues concerning the termination of psychotherapy. Some of these issues are presented below:

- What are the most effective, evidence-based strategies available for terminating psychotherapy treatment in the context of various treatment modalities, client populations, and problems?
- When there is a lack of research and evidence supporting specific strategies, what does clinical experience tell us about terminating psychotherapy in these same domains?
- What are the common ethical dilemmas clinicians face when terminating treatment with clients from various populations and problems? How are these situations most effectively addressed from the standpoint of both research and clinical lore?
- How should mental health providers deal with issues such as premature and inappropriately delayed termination? What are specific steps providers should take in an attempt to avoid these situations or manage them when they arise?
- Where are there holes in research pertaining to terminating psychotherapy? What are the studies that need to be done in order to better elucidate this aspect of mental health services delivery? The chapter authors were asked to present explicit recommendations for further research with a particular aim at unresolved conceptual, methodological, ethical, or clinical issues.

Structure of the Present Volume

We have organized the present volume into two sections and twenty-four chapters. We have selected chapter authors who are internationally recognized experts in each chapter subject.

Section I is titled "Issues, Controversies, and Strategies" and includes the first eight chapters. Chapter 1 presents and discusses the concept of termination and how this skill set relates to the provision of cost-effective mental health services in the context of organized managed care. Understanding how termination relates to the psychotherapy process and having the skills necessary to successfully engage in termination are required to improve patient satisfaction, the cost-effectiveness of treatment, and to make mental health services delivery a viable financial endeavor. For example, therapists who continue to see clients for lengthy periods of time may be having difficulty discontinuing treatment for a variety of reasons, such as unrealistic expectations about how the client should be thinking or behaving before the end of treatment. This can lead to poor patient satisfaction and possibly iatrogenic effects. Chapter 2 presents the issue of forced termination in the context of training in mental health service delivery. A study is described along with recommendations for future research. Chapter 3 outlines specific key issues regarding premature termination. The author of this chapter defines the concept, presents contextual factors that can lead to these problems, discusses the impact of the factors on the therapist-client relationship, and presents practical suggestions and skills to help therapists both prevent and manage these problems.

Chapter 4, discusses ways in which the therapist can terminate psychotherapy therapeutically. The authors present their approach to treatment, some common approaches to termination, and conclude with case examples.

Chapter 5 is written by Dr. Nicholas Cummings, who discusses his well-known, cost-effective approach to psychotherapy. Dr. Cummings presents some of the key components of his approach, psychotherapy discontinuation, not termination, including a discussion of his philosophy of psychotherapy treatment delivery, which is focused on providing clients intermittent treatment throughout their lifetime as different issues and problems arise. This approach differs from that of many mental health practitioners in that Dr. Cummings encourages his clients to come back to therapy at various times during their lives, much like one would episodically seek a primary care physician. Other important skills are presented such as how to identify and therapeutically approach clients' hidden agendas to avoid unnecessary and costly treatment, and delays in termination when these have not be adequately addressed in therapy. Chapter 6 is written by the coeditors of this volume and presents a clinical strategy for understanding how to effectively and ethically terminate psychotherapy using clinical case conceptualizations. Key issues are discussed, such as: (a) how to identify treatment targets in the first session, (b) how to develop a clinical case conceptualization, which can help prescribe treatment, and help from the outset to guide how treatment is eventually terminated, and (c) how to monitor the effectiveness of psychotherapy using identified targets as benchmarks for success. Specific skills and techniques are provided in the context of each of the above issues.

Chapter 7 provides the reader with an understanding of factors that impact changes in therapist and client behavior over the course of treatment. Key questions are addressed including: What causes people to progress in therapy? What causes people to continue therapy? How does one most quickly and effectively influence change in therapy? Chapter 8 is designed to orient the reader to ethical issues and possible concerns in the context of terminating psychotherapy. It is important for mental health providers to clearly understand (a) some of the ethical dilemmas that may arise during termination, such as losing income or possibly a friend, (b) the consequences of making certain decisions (such as failing to terminate therapy to sustain a personal relationship with a client), which can be imposed by licensing boards such as the American Psychological Association, and (c) strategies for both avoiding and successfully navigating these potential pitfalls while terminating treatment.

Section II is titled "Termination in the Context of Various Treatment Models, Populations, and Patient Problems," and includes the remaining chapters, 9 through 24. Chapters, 9, 10, and 11 present the reader with an overview of three treatment models—cognitive behavioral therapy, psychoanalysis, and behavior therapy—and provide the reader with an understanding and some key clinical skills involved in terminating within the context of each treatment mode. These treatment models are among the most commonly used and supported by the literature as effective for various psychological problems and patient populations. Chapters 12 through 14 outline special issues concerning the termination of treatment involving children, adolescents, and the elderly. For example, practical suggestions for reducing unwanted effects of terminating with children who have become attached to the therapist will be provided and discussed. Chapters 15 through 20 provide the reader with an overview of common psychological problems such as: depression, anxiety, psychosis, commonly occurring personality disorders, substance abuse, and suicide, respectively. Each of these chapters provides a brief overview of specific disorder(s) and presents possible complications that may arise while terminating treatment and practical, effective suggestions on how to avoid or address these problems in the context of therapy. Chapter 21 focuses on issues specific to terminating psychotherapy in inpatient and residential settings. Chapter 22 provides an in-depth discussion of specific issues concerning termination of treatment when the combination of psychotherapy and psychopharmacology are involved. Chapter 23 focuses on terminating treatment with Japanese clients. This chapter covers the unique factors related to termination that depend upon a particular nation's healthcare system and culture.

References

American Psychological Association. (2002). Ethical principles and code of conduct for psychologists. —Retrieved July 4, 2007 from http://www/apa.org/ethics/

Wittgenstein, L. (1958). *Philosophical investigations.* Trans. G. E. M. Ansombe. New York: Macmillan.

Section I: Issues, Controversies, and Strategies

Managed Care and Termination

R. BLAKE CHAFFEE

Termination of psychotherapy services is central to most discussions—verbal or written—of managed behavioral healthcare. Specifically, the concerns of providers typically revolve around the restrictions in authorizations for psychotherapy services that managed behavioral healthcare organizations (MBHO) may impose vis-à-vis what the provider considers to be necessary care. This may seem oversimplified, but this disagreement—or the potential for disagreement—does appear to be a fundamental objection of providers to managed care. This paper will examine the issue of termination in psychotherapy from the perspective of the MBHO and the provider of services with the goal of analyzing the ethical, professional, and business issues involved from both perspectives.

The Provider Perspective

Providers have an ethical obligation to provide to their clients services that are appropriate to and effective for the issues their clients present, and not to terminate treatment abruptly or "abandon" their clients once they have initiated psychotherapy. Other authors have detailed the origins of these obligations and the differences between the codes of ethics of psychologists, social workers, and counselors (Welfel & Danzinger 2006). Providers generally take these obligations seriously and seek to render uninterrupted services in a continuous episode of psychotherapy.

Many providers, however, are members of provider networks and are reimbursed for their services by third-party employers, insurers, or health plans, which frequently require prior authorization and concurrent review of psychotherapy services. These third parties make their review decisions based on the client's benefit plan and their evaluation of the medical/psychological necessity of the services being rendered. These considerations may represent a completely different decision-making perspective from that of the provider on whether the client needs psychotherapy services, or at least a significant difference in priority and emphasis. The provider may therefore find him/herself in the position of having an ethical obligation to provide psychotherapy treatment services to a client:

- Whose benefit plan does not cover the particular services the provider believes are necessary and appropriate;
- Whose benefit plan covers only limited numbers of sessions of the required services;
- Whose MBHO determines that the services the provider is delivering are not medically/psychologically necessary.

At this point in the lifecycle of managed behavioral healthcare, most behavioral health providers who participate in MBHO networks are quite aware of these differences, acknowledge them (if they don't always agree with them), and take them into account in their own decision making, treatment planning, and the financial arrangements they make with their clients. Historically, these eventualities sometimes left the provider with the prospect of continuing to deliver services that were not reimbursed by the MBHO or risk violating ethical principles by terminating services for nonpayment (when the client could not/would not assume the financial obligation). This situation typifies the basis of the classic provider/MBHO argument since the advent of managed behavioral healthcare. Several of the provider professional organizations have since altered their codes of ethics to include clauses that do not require the provider to continue to provide services in such circumstances and allow the provider to refer the client to community-based organizations offering no-cost or sliding-scale services to preserve continuity of care. Such changes are a positive development because they offer a realistic alternative to psychotherapists given the reality of the current healthcare system and marketplace.

Third-party reimbursement of psychotherapy services has the potential to create a conflict of interest for the provider when his/

her financial income depends on reimbursement for psychotherapy services. Consciously or unconsciously, the provider's judgment of the level of care and frequency of services a client requires may be influenced. For example, in cases where the provider must decide whether the client requires outpatient or inpatient services, the provider's judgment may be influenced if the provider can render services to the client only in an outpatient setting (i.e., concluding the client requires inpatient care would require a referral to another provider). Similarly, third-party reimbursement may influence a provider's decision making about the frequency or duration of psychotherapy services in either direction. Faced with no longer being reimbursed by a third party for psychotherapy services to a client, a provider may be more likely to rationalize that the client is ready for termination, particularly with clients who are unable to pay for their treatment on an out-of-pocket basis. At the other end of the spectrum, the availability of third-party reimbursement may subtly influence the provider to provide services where the need is equivocal or nonexistent, or to continue treatment when a client might be ready for termination. Cummings has described this last scenario as continuation of treatment for the convenience of the provider (Cummings 2005). In these instances, the provider's business interest (personal income) may conflict with his/her ethical and professional obligations.

The Managed Behavioral Healthcare Organization (MBHO) Perspective

Health plan coverage of psychotherapy services was never intended to cover all of the reasons clients present to providers for psychotherapy or necessarily all of the services the provider and client may agree are necessary. The reason for this is fundamental to the healthcare system in the United States. Health plans in the United States offer benefits that are intended to reimburse for medical care for the disorders their subscribers may develop. In other words, health plans primarily cover acute disorders. Health maintenance organizations may offer some preventive care benefits, but these are usually limited to basic services such as immunizations, well-baby checks, patient education and annual physicals. Stress management training, weight loss programs or smoking cessation programs are frequently not reimbursed by health plans despite the growing body of information on their relationship to healthcare utilization and healthcare costs. Similarly, health plans have only recently begun to cover alternative medicine treatments. Within behavioral health, the benefits offered by health plans are typically restricted to services for the treatment of acute disorders, usually defined as mental or substance abuse disorders listed in the *Diagnostic and Statistical Manual of Mental Disorders* (DSM-IV-TR). In other words, to qualify for health plan reimbursement, a client must be suffering from a diagnosed mental disorder or substance abuse disorder that meets DSM-IV-TR criteria.

Psychotherapy services are applied across a much broader spectrum of issues than those that concern health plans and MBHOs. Psychotherapists typically work with clients on psychosocial problems such as occupational problems, parenting issues, communication issues, or other relationship issues, health, wellness, and preventive medicine issues (e.g., weight loss, smoking cessation, or habit change), and personal growth or self-actualization. Most health plans do not reimburse for such services, and they are consequently not the purview of most MBHOs. DSM-IV-TR includes some of the foregoing in the category of "V Codes," defined as issues or problems that are the focus of behavioral health consultation that are not the result of a mental disorder. Within managed behavioral healthcare, these issues are typically the province of employee assistance programs (EAP) rather than MBHOs.

MBHOs also do not cover psychotherapy services for personal growth and development, or self-actualization. While this hardly needs mentioning at this point because most providers are well aware of it, it is mentioned here solely to highlight the relatively limited segment of the psychotherapy client population that is the focus of MBHOs. Additionally, providers may understand and operate according to these distinctions, but their clients may not, and the client's expectations can become a factor in the process of termination for both the provider and the MBHO.

Providers sometimes express concern with the decision-making processes and decision makers MBHOs employ, for example, clerks or nonclinical personnel without any clinical training or qualifications issue denials in authorization decisions and decisions are made without consideration or understanding of the clinical evidence. The criteria that MBHOs utilize in determining the medical/psychological necessity of services they authorize are standard criteria sets designed to evaluate whether the client's presentation (as described by their provider) represents a level of dysfunction and distress that requires treatment. MBHOs accredited by any of the national accreditation organizations (e.g., URAC [Utilization Review Accreditation Commission] or JCAHO [Joint Commission of the Accreditation of Healthcare Organizations]) must comply with stringent criteria for their clinical decision-making, particularly in making denial determinations. Managed behavioral healthcare began in the early 1980s as a distinct industry, and MBHOs rival HMOs in the complexity and sophistication of their business and medical management processes. In accredited programs, denials can be issued only by qualified medical directors, and with medical necessity denials, providers and beneficiaries must be advised of their rights to appeal the determination. In other words, nonclinical MBHO staff cannot deny care. They may be able to advise beneficiaries about their benefit coverage, but decisions that a particular service, procedure, or medication is not a covered benefit must be confirmed by clinical staff, and all denial letters are signed by medical directors. Similarly, medical necessity determinations can be made only by medical directors or peer reviewers from the same discipline as the requesting provider.

The actual numbers of denials for medical necessity that most MBHOs issue is very small, typically only a few percentage points of the total number of cases authorized, and many of those are issued upon the initial request for authorization rather than as a result of concurrent review during the course of treatment. This would indicate that provider concern over the prospect of denials of continued stay authorizations is out of proportion to the actual probability of having an authorization request denied for clinical reasons. More often in commercial MBHOs and health plans, continued psychotherapy is likely to be limited by the annual maximum benefit, typically 20 visits per year. Historically, limiting the maximum number of reimbursable psychotherapy sessions per year gave health plans a way to control their costs for outpatient psychotherapy that required fewer healthcare management resources. The impact of parity laws on these parameters remains to be seen (Floyd, Melek, & Wirecki 2004).

The data available on the utilization of outpatient psychotherapy likewise indicate that provider concern with denials may be disproportionate. Kramer and Trabin (1997) surveyed 106 members of the Institute for Behavioral Healthcare's National Leadership Council. Among the 15 managed care organizations and 54 community mental health centers responding, the average number of outpatient psychotherapy sessions was four to six. While some commercial MBHOs consider their utilization data proprietary, the "rule of thumb" in the industry is that the average number of outpatient psychotherapy sessions per episode of care is between six and seven. Knowing this, MBHOs frequently allow a certain number of outpatient psychotherapy sessions before prior authorization is required. This policy encourages access to care at the lowest, least expensive level of care and allows the MBHO to devote its limited healthcare management resources to cases that continue beyond the initial set number of sessions. Such cases are typically more complex, and continued psychotherapy for those cases may be prior authorized. Welfel and Danzinger (2006) cite studies that indicate that the mean number of outpatient sessions that clients attend in university counseling centers is less than four, and the frequency with which clients terminate after the first session is up to 33%, or one-third.

These findings are partially corroborated in the TRICARE (military health system) population. As the Department of Defense contractor for the TRICARE West Region, TriWest Healthcare Alliance is responsible for the administration of the TRICARE Program in 21 states for 2.6 million beneficiaries. The TRICARE behavioral health benefit is exceptionally generous by current commercial health plan standards, especially for outpatient psychotherapy services. There is no maximum annual number of outpatient psychotherapy sessions, and the frequency and duration of sessions is subject to medical necessity. In order to encourage access to care, the TRICARE Program allows eight sessions of outpatient psychotherapy before prior authorization is required. We wanted to determine whether this "initial 8" policy was doing what it was designed to do, specifically: (1) reduce barriers to care; (2) encourage beneficiary access at the lowest, least expensive level of care; and (3) allow the contractor to focus its managed behavioral healthcare resources on the smaller number of cases that continued beyond the initial eight sessions. If the policy was having the desired effect, we expected to find: (1) a larger proportion of cases completing treatment in eight or fewer sessions; and (2) the smaller number of cases continuing beyond the eighth session would account for the larger proportion of total outpatient visits.

Method

We looked at over 12,000 cases of outpatient care initiated during the first six months of the TRICARE West Region contract from October 1, 2004 to March 30, 2005. Cases were identified from claims data, and all client age groups (child, adolescent, and adult) were included as long as the service received was an outpatient psychotherapy service determined by the "place of service" item on the claim and the CPT (*Current Procedural Terminology*) code billed.

We looked at West Region claims with dates of service between October 1, 2004 and March 31, 2005 (the first six months of FY05 [fiscal year 2005]) and processed through July 31, 2005. Claims for outpatient individual and group psychotherapy services were included with the following CPT codes: 90804 through 90815, 90830 through 90847, 90853 and 90857.

Results

- 17,276 beneficiaries received outpatient psychotherapy services.
- This sample represents 2.43% of the 711,317 eligible active duty family members.
- 12,775 (73.95%) beneficiaries had <8 psychotherapy visits.
- 4,501 (26.05%) beneficiaries had >8 psychotherapy visits.
- The range of visits for individual cases was 1 to 80.
- Beneficiaries with <8 visits accounted for 44,640 (40.18%) of total visits.
- Beneficiaries with >8 visits accounted for 66,453 (59.82%) of total visits.

- The mean number of visits per beneficiary was 6.43.
- The modal number of visits per beneficiary was 1.
- The median number of visits per beneficiary was 4.
- The average number of beneficiaries in treatment during any month was 2,879.
- The average number of monthly visits was 18,515.
- Number of monthly outpatient psychotherapy visits per thousand was 26.02.
- Number of monthly unmanaged outpatient visits per thousand was 10.45.
- Number of monthly managed outpatient visits per thousand was 15.57.

Discussion

TriWest's initial 8 policy does not require prior authorization for the initial 8 outpatient psychotherapy sessions a beneficiary receives in each fiscal year. The policy was developed in accordance with data from commercial managed behavioral health plans that indicated that most episodes of outpatient psychotherapy terminate before the eighth session. These data support that assumption. The average number of outpatient psychotherapy sessions in commercial behavioral health plans is 4 to 6, which is also consistent with our 6.43 average visits per beneficiary. Visits per thousand were also within the range (1 to 150) experienced by commercial behavioral health plans (Kramer & Trabin 1997).

Not only do the majority of TriWest cases terminate by the eighth visit (73.95%), but the remaining 26.05% of the cases account for nearly 60% of the total visits. The intent of the policy is not only to reduce barriers to access to care and encourage utilization at the lowest level of care, but also to make the most efficient use of care management resources. In this sample, TriWest's initial 8 policy avoided managing nearly three-quarters of the cases and devoted management attention to the remaining one-quarter, which accounted for 60% of the visits.

Mental health specialty providers for health maintenance organizations (HMOs) (in nonintegrated settings) see only 3% to 6% of covered members in any given year (Melek 2001). Extrapolating from this six-month sample, roughly twice the number of beneficiaries would be seen in a full year, which would represent 4.86% of the total eligible population, placing TriWest's program toward the upper limit of commercial HMO specialty mental health providers in proportion of population served (Kramer & Trabin 1997).

We found that the modal number of sessions was 1. Of the total 17,276 beneficiaries receiving outpatient services, 3,008 (17.4%) had only a single session. This finding is not consistent with the results Welfel and Danzinger (2006) report (up to 33% had only 1 session), and this may be due to differences between the university and TRICARE populations. Those authors suggest that their finding undermines the traditional notion of psychotherapy being a provider-driven venture. The TRICARE data indicate that either (1) TRICARE providers more successfully engage their clients in the first session, or (2) TRICARE beneficiaries are more motivated to continue treatment than Welfel and Danzinger's university population. In either case, Welfel and Danzinger's conclusion that providers do not control the delivery of their psychotherapy services to the degree the traditional notion suggests, that is, by successfully engaging clients during the initial session, applies here. Instead, these data indicate that a sizeable proportion of clients do not continue consultation for psychotherapy services after the first session. Reasons for this are probably as varied as the clients themselves, but probably include:

- Clients determining that psychotherapy consultation is not what they had anticipated;
- Clients deciding that the particular therapist is not someone they believe can help them;
- Clients "shopping" for a therapist;
- Clients achieving adequate resolution of their concerns as a result of the session.

The TRICARE sample's average number of outpatient sessions of 6.43 is consistent with MBHO industry standards. This result is particularly noteworthy given the TRICARE outpatient psychotherapy benefit limits: Our average number of sessions closely resembles that of commercial managed behavioral health plans, which have strict benefit limits. Benefit limit, therefore, does not appear to be a factor in determining the average length of outpatient psychotherapy episodes of care. If it were, the average number of outpatient psychotherapy sessions per episode of care in TRICARE would be longer than that of commercial MBHOs. If the available benefit is not a determining factor, what are the other factors that could possibly explain these results? The eight-session limit before preauthorization is required could function as a limiting factor if providers viewed it as requiring inordinate effort or unlikely to result in continued authorization. Our numbers of continued stay authorizations and actual clinical denials do not support the development or maintenance of such a provider perception. While 74% of outpatient episodes terminated in eight or fewer sessions, 26% of episodes continued and that 26% accounted for 60% of the total number of outpatient sessions. A more likely prospect is the industry standard six-session average for outpatient psychotherapy sessions. West Region TRICARE behavioral health providers represent a cross-section of the behavioral health provider community in TriWest's West Region, and the fact that their practice patterns reflect the industry standard is not surprising. In other words, at least among providers who participate in MBHO provider networks, the average of six psychotherapy sessions for an outpatient episode of care appears to reflect the manner in which these providers practice, at least with their MBHO clients. Managed behavioral healthcare may have shaped their typical practice pattern in some respects, but developments in treatment interventions may also account for these results. Additional data on the problems presented, treatment inter-ventions, and reasons for termination would help clarify how and why termination occurs in these treatment episodes.

Closer analysis of the TRICARE sample results is revealing. The modal number of sessions was 1, and 17.4% of the sample had one visit. The median number of sessions was 4, meaning that 50% of cases were completed in four or fewer sessions. This also means that approximately 33% of cases had two, three, or four visits. The fact that 74% of outpatient treatment episodes in the TRICARE sample terminated in eight or fewer sessions means that approximately 24% of cases had five to eight sessions. In other words, the length of treatment episodes appears to be fairly evenly distributed in this sample, and clinical management does not appear to be a major contributing factor in episode length. If clinical denials or clinical management were a major contributing factor, the distribution of cases with eight or fewer visits would look entirely different, most likely skewed toward seven and eight visits with many fewer episodes terminating in lower numbers of sessions. An additional 18.27% of cases were completed in nine to sixteen visits. This means that 92.2% of cases were completed in sixteen or fewer sessions.

MBHOs have both a utilization and quality management outpatient interest in outpatient psychotherapy services. From a utilization management perspective, the MBHO is concerned that the care rendered is delivered in an efficient and effective manner so that the benefits used are used appropriately. From a quality management perspective, the MBHO would be concerned that the services rendered were medically necessary, appropriate to the presenting problem and consistent with evidence-based industry standards of care, for example, cognitive behavioral therapy for the treatment of depression with consideration of antidepressant medication. In addition, MBHO credentialing, contracting, and quality monitoring processes are designed to ensure quality of care for the beneficiary/client. Early termination or rendering care that is insufficient in content or duration constitutes a quality concern for the MBHO. Likewise, termination that was problematic for the beneficiary would also be a quality concern. The MBHO's interest is really aligned with the provider's and the beneficiary's interests in this regard—adequate, appropriate treatment and termination are in the best interest of all parties. Beyond the quality issues, insufficient or inadequate services—outpatient psychotherapy that is "not enough"—can be problematic for the MBHO when the presenting problem is not resolved and additional, subsequent treatment episodes are required, particularly when those treatment episodes may involve more intensive services at higher levels of care.

In summary, while termination has been a contentious issue between providers and MBHOs, actual utilization data appear to indicate that the length of outpatient treatment episodes may be determined more by provider treatment approaches and beneficiary behavior than by MBHO clinical management. Further, the interests of beneficiaries, providers, and MBHOs align around appropriate treatment and termination.

References

Cummings, N. A. (2005). Resolving the dilemmas in mental healthcare delivery: Access, stigma, fragmentation, conflicting research, politics and more. In N. A. Cummings, W. T. O'Donohue, & M. A. Cucciare, M. A. (Eds.), *Universal healthcare: Readings for mental health professionals* (pp. 47–74). Reno, NV: Context Press.

Current procedural terminology. (2007). Standard edition. Chicago: American Medical Association.

Floyd, P., Melek, S., & Wirecki, T. (2004). The real costs of behavioral healthcare benefits. Presented at the Society of Actuaries Spring Meeting; May 19–21; Anaheim, CA.

Kramer, T., & Trabin, T. (1997). *Performance indicator measurement in behavioral healthcare: Data capture methods, cost-effectiveness, and emerging standards.* Portola Valley, CA: Institute for Behavioral Healthcare.

Melek, S. P. (2001). Financial risk and structural issues. In N. A. Cummings, W. O'Donohue, S. C. Hayes, & V. Follette (Eds.), *Integrated behavioral healthcare: Positioning mental health practice with medical/surgical practice* (pp. 257–272). New York: Academic Press.

Welfel, E. R., & Danzinger, P. (2007). *Terminating psychotherapy: A clinician's guide.* New York: Routledge.

2

FORCED TERMINATION: TRAINEES' TREATMENT TERMINATIONS WITH CLIENTS

NEHAMI BAUM

Introduction

Background: Forced Termination by Trainees

Every year tens of thousands of trainees in the helping professions terminate their therapeutic relations with their clients at the end of the training period. Such terminations are generally viewed in the literature as forced terminations, on par with treatment terminations by full-fledged professionals occasioned by such things as illness, promotion, or moving to another locale or workplace (Bostic, Shadid, & Blotcky 1996; Dewald 1965; Penn 1990). From the perspective of the client, in both cases the termination is a nonnegotiable ending, initiated by the therapist without consulting the client or considering the client's therapeutic needs (Mikkelsen & Gutheil 1979).

Most writers refer to forced termination without distinguishing between the departure of an experienced therapist and that by a student in training (Bostic et al. 1996; Penn 1990). In at least some respects, however, treatment termination at the end of the training period is a distinct experience, different from the forced terminations of full-fledged professionals. The time of the termination is always determined by the rules or requirements of the training institution, be it a university, clinic, or hospital department. From the perspective of the trainee, this may give the termination a particularly arbitrary character. In addition, there is an inherent conflict between trainees' short-term interventions with their predetermined endings and the long-term treatment philosophy and technique that many trainees in the helping professions learn and apply. Furthermore, as Penn (1990) briefly observes, while both professionals and trainees who terminate treatment before it has come to its natural end have been part of an intense and significant relationship that is ending prematurely, trainees, unlike professionals, often leave their first patients, "without yet seeing the fruits of their labor. Many are leaving not just the patient, but also familiar clinics, schools, supervisors, and friends" (381). Finally, by definition, trainees' professional experience is limited, their skills not yet honed, and their professional identity not well developed—factors that cannot but impact on both their handling and their own personal experience of the termination.

The Literature

The literature on forced termination, and especially on clinicians' responses to and coping with it, is scant. From Dewald's (1965) clinical study of professional psychotherapists, we know that forced termination can be a very difficult experience for the therapist. Dewald observed a range of countertransference reactions, including a sense of guilt at deserting and betraying the patient, a sense of leaving before the job is finished, concern that the patient would not be able to tolerate the separation, and hurrying to transfer the patient to another therapist in order to allay the therapist's own guilt feelings.

The few studies that have been conducted on trainees indicate that many experience emotional problems with terminations and find it difficult to carry them out in a way that is helpful to the client. De Bosset and Styrsky (1986) found that around two-fifths of the psychiatric trainees they studied felt frustrated that their work was incomplete and that many issues were left unresolved. About one-fifth of the trainees reported feeling sadness and one-fifth reported feeling anger. Only 16%, however, registered their clients' disappointment. Fair and Bressler (1992) found that most psychiatric interns in the final stage of their internship did not tell their clients about the forth-coming termination until near the end of the treatment, and that the trainees felt fear, guilt, and powerlessness in the face of the termina-tion, as well as discomfort about these feelings. Bostic et al. (1996), exploring countertransference reactions among psychiatric trainees, found that they tried to accelerate the treatment shortly before the termination and to rapidly resolve issues that had remained closed until then, while avoiding painful or distressing issues that the clients raised. These authors also observed that the trainees tended to deny their importance to their clients.

Gould (1977), in a qualitative study conducted on ten social work students in their second year of fieldwork, found that for most of them, treatment termination was an unpleasant experience, marked by feelings of guilt, rejection, disappointment, trepidation, and self-doubt. Most of the students said they were unsure when to inform the client of the termination, some noted that they did not know how to plan the termination, and most stated that they did not know how to manage the termination.

Brill and Nahmani (1993), who examined clients' perceptions of how their social work student therapists handled the termination, found that most clients viewed the students as having difficulty containing the clients' emotional reactions to the termination. As the clients described it, the students seemed to want to have a "nice" finish and found it difficult to conduct an open dialogue about termination and separation. They did not summarize the intervention or assess the therapeutic process and its consequences with the clients. The clients interpreted the students' behavior as reflecting their difficulties in coping with the emotional reactions to the separation.

The literature on forced termination by professional therapists indicates that therapists who find the termination emotionally difficult are likely to have difficulty ending the treatment in a way that meets their clients' therapeutic needs (Dewald 1965; Siebold 1991; Quintana 1993). They may avoid dealing with their own feelings at termination, and discourage clients from raising theirs (Anthony & Pagano 1998; Siebold 1991). They may not leave enough time or space for treatment summary and evaluation (Germain & Gitterman 1996). Some may pull away and emotionally detach, leaving the client feeling abandoned, while others may support clients' resistance to termination (Levinson 1977). Numerous writers argue that these and other therapist behaviors may not only leave the client with unresolved anger and other bad feelings, but may also undermine whatever therapeutic attainments had been achieved (Glenn 1971; Penn 1990; Johnson & Yanca 2001).

Focus of the Paper

In view of the paucity of literature on forced terminations by student trainees and on the impact that their own emotional experience of the termination could have on their clients, I decided that it was important to learn more about trainees' experiences of their end-of-year termination. The next two sections of this paper describe the study I carried out and its findings. The last two sections offer some practical suggestions for easing the distress of student trainees' forced end-of-year terminations and recommendations for further research.

The Study: Method and Questions

The study was conducted on 76 social work student trainees at a school of social work in Israel. All of them were in a special two-year program for persons with at least a B.A. in another field. Forty-two were in the first year of the program, 34 in the second year. The program awards its graduates with a B.S.W. degree, which enables them to work as licensed professionals. It resembles American M.S.W. degree programs in that students do fieldwork during both the first and second years of study.

The study participants ranged in age from twenty-five to fifty-three, with a mean of around thirty-four. Most were female, as is the case throughout the profession. They were doing their fieldwork in a variety of government and municipal social work agencies, and treated between five and eight clients each, in weekly one-hour sessions for about 7½ months from the beginning to the end of the academic year.

Because the purpose of the fieldwork is to develop long-term treatment skills, a long-term treatment approach is employed. As is generally the case in long-term therapy, the aims of the treatment are rather loosely defined, and the ending is mentioned at the beginning, but not emphasized throughout—hence the perception of "forced termination."

About two weeks before the end of the academic year, when most of the students had either terminated their treatments or were on the verge of doing so, they were asked to answer two questions in writing:

1. What issues concern you in your separation from your clients?
2. What do you feel in your separation from your clients?

Contrary to expectations, the students wrote of their emotions along with their concerns and of their concerns along with their emotions.

The analysis of their responses did not impose an artificial distinction.

The Findings

Untimely and Premature Ending

The overriding sentiment, which came through the vast majority of the responses, was that the treatment termination was untimely. This sense of untimeliness reflects the reality of the fieldwork training. It gave rise to many statements about the prematurity of the termination and underpinned frequently expressed concerns that the premature termination damaged the client.

With respect to the prematurity of the termination, the trainees stressed that the treatment was stopped artificially, in the middle, before it could be completed, or at the turning point, just when the clients were about to make a great "leap" forward and only a little bit more time was required for them to make significant progress. For example, one wrote: "I feel that the work has been stopped at the middle most artificially." Another wrote: "I feel that I need another two months of therapy . . . because I feel that I am right at the middle of it rather than at the end."

Quite a few students complained that the termination came just at the point when they had finally established the therapeutic bond that would enable them to realize the potential of the therapeutic work. The frustration in the following statement is clear: "I feel at the peak of the process. We've established trust and certain things have happened, and suddenly a termination is imposed because of the calendar."

Emotions and Concerns Stemming From a Sense of Untimely, Premature Termination

A few students expressed anger that the system forced them to terminate before completing the treatment. The dominant feelings that emerge from the trainees' statements about the untimeliness of the termination, however, were sadness, regret, and above all, frustration at not being able to finish the work they started—at not being able to bring it to fruition. Students wrote about feeling "sorry" that the therapy was ending in the way it was, and asked how they could leave their clients just when some openness and intimacy had finally been established.

The sense of premature truncation left students feeling anxious and uncertain about the quality of their work. Some expressed concern that important therapeutic issues were left unresolved. Many wondered whether they had accomplished the therapeutic aims and whether they had helped their clients. Although such self-doubts often trouble social work students throughout their training and are part of the learning process, they seem to be intensified by the forced, premature ending of the therapy.

Along with self-doubt related to the untimely terminations, the students also expressed a good deal of concern about the damage and injustice that the untimely termination inflicted on their clients. A repeated sentiment was that the timing of the termination meets the needs of the system and the students themselves, but not those of the clients. As one trainee put it: "[There's] an incongruity between the time of the separation and the needs of the client; that is, that the termination does not come at the right time, but rather because of constraints." The feeling that the untimely termination did not meet the needs of the students created uncomfortable dissonance in the students, expressed as a sense "incongruity" or "a lack of fit" between the student's needs and the client's, or as the student's own feelings being "not simple."

Many students expressed worry that one or another client would not be able to cope on his or her own. "Who will take care of them?" one asked. Another expressed concern that a client would "collapse." Some students went so far as to look for alternative therapists, though it was not required of them.

The predominant feeling, however, was guilt. Only a few students actually used the term "guilt" and explained the source of their feeling; most manifested their guilt feelings indirectly, in a variety of ways. Some students communicated feelings of guilt about leaving without having helped their clients enough (e.g., "How do you leave a client when you have the feeling that you didn't really help him?"). Some conveyed it through their concern that the premature termination would damage the client (e.g., "How much damage have I inflicted ... and how much have I helped?"). Several trainees focused on the pain or damage they would cause by inflicting yet another separation on clients who had already suffered separations (e.g., "How to leave the clients without making it yet another desertion for them?"). Many wrote of abandoning their clients just when they needed them: "It's hard to separate and leave everything and run away, to abandon [the client]." Another wrote of feeling that "we're abandoning him and leaving him with his problems on his own."

The sense that they were damaging, paining, or abandoning their clients made the treatment termination a particularly painful experience for some of the respondents, and also led some of them to question the morality of training on clients: "Is it moral and right to train on patients and to abandon them after a few months?" one asked.

In addition, quite a number of students voiced concerns about carrying out the treatment termination. About one-third of the students in both years reported the desire to separate "properly"—presumably, in a way that would not damage the client, would not undo the progress made in the therapy, and would leave both them and the clients with positive feelings. As one wrote: "It's important for me to separate from each of them properly, in a way that will leave me and them with a feeling of acceptance and not loss. I am afraid it will not be like that." The feeling that proper closure would elude her was also not uncommon.

Over three quarters of the first-year students expressed some sort of trepidation in anticipation of the termination. Although they were taught when and how to broach the termination, some wrote that they did not know when to start the phase and/or how to tell their clients about it. Some confessed that they were frightened or found it difficult to broach the subject: (e.g., "I was scared to begin talking about the termination"). Some worried that their clients would be angry at their leaving and that they would not know how to deal with their anger.

Summation

In summary, the students' responses paint a picture of considerable personal distress stemming from their sense of the untimeliness of the end-of-year treatment termination. As they see it, the timing of the termination prevented them from reaching the treatment goals, did not suit the needs of the clients, and raised serious ethical questions. From a personal perspective, they told of sadness and regret at separating from persons with whom they had forged bonds, anger and frustration about not being able to complete what they started, and uncertainty about their professional capacities. From the perspective of the clients, students expressed concern that the clients would not be able to manage on their own, anxiety that the premature separation might cause the clients harm, and above all, a great deal of guilt. With respect to the termination itself, they expressed trepidation in anticipation of clients' anger, disappointment, and accusations, as well as the desire to separate "properly," in a way that would leave both them and their clients feeling good.

Suggestions for Practice

The question that arises is: What can be done to help mitigate the great distress of student trainees at their forced end-of-year client treatment terminations?

In her chapter on treatment termination by social work students, Clow (1998) makes extensive suggestions for field supervisors and practice teachers in helping students manage the endings. The following pages offer several sets of suggestions. The first two are general suggestions: legitimizing the trainees feelings and helping them to take some control over the process. The next three stem from my understanding of the key sources of the students' distress, namely the social work education they receive, their stage of professional development, and the "role exit" nature of their terminations (Baum 2004). The last set is anchored in the notion of the trainees' forced end-of-year treatment termination as a transition in their professional development and refers to ways of easing the transition.

Along with these suggestions, it is argued that trying to totally eliminate their distress is unrealistic and undesirable.

Legitimization: To begin with, trainees should be made aware that their feelings at termination are fully normal and legitimate, and be encouraged to accept them as such. Trainees' feelings of sadness, loss, fear, anxiety, self-doubt, and so forth are usually recognized, but are viewed primarily as obstacles to optimal termination of the treatment for the benefit of the client. This perspective reinforces rather than alleviates the trainees' sense of inadequacy and uncertainty. Greater self-acceptance would enable trainees to make room for their feelings, which they otherwise try, not always successfully, to shunt aside or to overcome. It should also help them to terminate the treatment with greater sensitivity to their patients' feelings and greater capacity to contain them.

Control: Trainees should also be helped to take a measure of control over the ending. Although the ending is forced and its timing fixed, trainees can gain some sense of control, and give their clients some sense of control, by announcing the ending clearly at the beginning of the treatment and repeating the information at around the halfway mark and again a few weeks before the end. While these procedures are standard practice in clinical fieldwork and taught in class, they are often followed only perfunctorily. Fearing their clients' responses, trainees often convey the information in passing and in a vague and blurred fashion. To help their trainees gain some control over the ending, supervisors should query how they really convey the information and, where necessary, help them to overcome the impediments to presenting it clearly. This will not only improve the honesty of the therapist-client relationship, it will also enable the trainees to terminate the treatment with fewer feelings that they are abandoning and betraying their clients.

Social Work Education: There is often an inherent contradiction between the long-term treatment philosophy and skills that students are taught and apply in their fieldwork, and the reality of a relatively short-term intervention with a predetermined ending. In view of this contradiction, the students' perception that the treatment was truncated prematurely, only a short while after they succeeded in bonding with their clients and before the treatment goals could be attained, are reality based, and much of the students' distress and frustration grounded in that reality.

One way of helping the students may be to somewhat temper this reality for them through more careful assignment of cases and redefinition of their task. Considerable attention is given to assigning students cases that will allow suitable intervention for the clients' needs within the time allotted. Nonetheless, as often happens in treatment, new and unexpected issues may arise and the first assessment may prove incorrect. It may thus be helpful to try to give student trainees a range of cases, with at least some of them having specific, well-focused goals that are attainable within the time allotted. This will give the students an opportunity to experience a measure of accomplishment and competence along with the frustration inherent in their premature terminations.

In addition, consideration may be given to redefining their assignments: from therapeutic intervention, which implies the full process, to a segment of such intervention, which implies a part of the process. Such redefinition might help both the trainees and their clients to frame their expectations in accord with the time allotted.

Stage of Professional Development: Students, by definition, are not full-fledged professionals. Their experience in the field is limited, their skills not yet honed, and their professional identity not well developed. Several scholars have suggested that, in compensation, students are usually more strongly invested in their relationships with clients than professionals and that this investment makes breaking the news of the termination and implementing it especially traumatic for them (Pumpian-Mindlin 1958; Petts 1967). In addition, without an accumulation of successful interventions in the past, students would naturally be more likely than professionals to feel inadequate as a result of the incompleteness of premature forced termination.

The prevalence and intensity of students' guilt feelings may also be anchored in unrealistic expectations that student trainees, at the beginning of their professional development, tend to have of themselves. Professionally, these students may be said to be in an adolescent phase. As in adolescence, they tend to harbor fantasies of omnipotence and to perceive reality in black and white. They fantasize rescuing their clients and solving all their problems. They see, but do not appreciate or properly value, their clients' incremental changes. In their thoughts, either they save their clients or their clients founder; they are either omnipotent rescuers or worthless incompetents. Treatment termination at a predetermined date, before they feel that they attained the therapeutic goals, strikes a blow at their fantasies and leaves them feeling like failures. It is reasonable to assume that these various sources all play a role in the students' strong distress at the end-of-year treatment termination.

Students whose distress at their end-of-year terminations is intensified by their professional immaturity may be helped by developing greater professional maturity. To this end, classroom instructors and fieldwork supervisors may work to help their students/trainees to accept the limits of therapy in general, and of time-limited therapy in particular, and to internalize that even partial and incomplete changes in their clients are worthy achievements.

They may also try to help their students attain a better perspective on any lack of success on their part. Students who do not achieve what they think they should with their clients tend to attribute this to their professional inadequacy and to regard themselves as failures. Such students might be helped by learning to identify the many possible reasons for clients not attaining the therapeutic aims: their own lack of skills, unrealistic aims, or the client's own emotional unreadiness.

Most students can probably obtain sufficient help from their classroom teachers and field supervisors to deal with the realities of the end-of-year termination. Some students, however, would probably benefit from therapy as well, especially those with unresolved prior losses or separations, or with particularly strong tendencies to guilt, self-reproach, and feelings of inadequacy.

Temporary Role Exit: Trainees' end-of-year treatment termination entails a radical break and simultaneous losses. Within a short time, they leave all their clients, their supervisor and colleagues, and their place of training. In some respects, this all-encompassing termination resembles the departures of professionals who leave their agency for other places or other jobs. However, unlike full-fledged professionals, students have not yet formed a solid professional identity. This lack adds a distinctive dimension to the simultaneous endings.

Students are, and experience themselves as, students. In the course of their training, they gradually hone their professional skills and adopt professional behaviors, values, and ways of thinking. But identity formation is a long process. It is highly unlikely that students complete the process of forming their professional identity before the end of their studies, and perhaps not for several years after. To identify themselves as social workers, students need their work and their clients.

The incompleteness of their professional identity makes trainees' end-of-year treatment termination not only a forced termination, but also a temporary role exit (Baum 2004). A *role exit* is the departure from any role that is central to one's self-identity. By definition, it involves processes of disengagement and dis-identification. Disengagement refers to withdrawal from the socially defined rights and obligations of the role, and from the people around one who had been associated with the role. Dis-identification refers to ceasing to think of oneself in the former role (Ebaugh 1988). The process of role exit is thus a process in which the exiter ceases to be what he or she had been before. Put differently, role exit entails the loss of the previous identity associated with the role.

When students terminate treatment with all their clients within a short period of time at the end of the academic year, they lose these crucial anchors of identity. They cease to fulfill the obligations and to enjoy the privileges of social workers; they depart from the people and places associated with their professional role in the making. They also effectively cease to be and to perceive themselves as social workers for the interval until they resume their fieldwork with new clients or move on to their first posting as licensed professionals.

According to Ebaugh (1988), the threat to identity that is inherent to role exit may result in a "vacuum experience," in which the individual is suspended between a past role that he/she no longer possesses and a future that is still unknown. This suspension is marked by fear, anxiety, and being "neither here nor there" (p. 144). These feelings are similar to the all-encompassing anxiety that the students describe, not only about whether they did a good job, but also about whether they are social workers at all or suited to being social workers. Their anxieties have a variety of causes, including their uncertainties about their futures. But some of their anxiety seems to be the anxiety of the "vacuum experience that they undergo as they are about to lose the external anchor of professional identity before they have put together an adequate inner representation of themselves as therapists.

It is important that both the trainees and their supervisors and instructors recognize their end-of-year role exit for what it is: a strong experience that undermines the students' frail sense of professional identity and brings in its wake not only feelings of sadness, loss, and guilt, as does any forced parting, but also a sense of incompetence and professional uncertainty. Within the existing academic framework, it is difficult to see how the students' multiple end-of-year exits can be avoided or even reduced. However, instructors and field supervisors can and should draw the students' attention to the fact of their interlocking departures and help them to anticipate and to consider how to deal with them.

Along with helping the trainees to recognize the elements of role exit in their end-of-year treatment terminations, instructors and supervisors should emphasize that the exit is temporary. They should draw attention to the fact that the trainees are involved in a forward-moving process, in which the end-of-year role exit is actually a transitional phase, and encourage them to consider how to proceed to the next station in their professional careers.

Easing the Transition: Transitions from a known situation to a new and unknown one are inherently anxiety provoking (Golan 1981). Two measures may be suggested to ease the transition.

One is making the forced termination a process that the trainees experience with others. Clinical training is a largely individual experience, where trainees are alone with their clients and supervisor. With this, student trainees generally end their fieldwork at much the same time. The classroom instructor and, in some cases, the agency can help make the termination more of a shared experience by providing a forum for the trainees to discuss their experience and the feelings that arise from it.

The other measure is to mark the end-of-year treatment termination with a ritual. Gutheil (1993) highlights the utility of rituals in helping persons to cope with powerful emotions during treatment termination and other transitions. The most pertinent ritual would be having each trainee present a case or issue in class or, preferably, at an end-of-year agency staff meeting. This would help to mark the termination and to create a sense of closure. It may also help to reduce the trainees' anxiety about the impending change, make the change appear more manageable, and shore up their identity as professionals (Wolin & Bennett 1984).

These recommendations notwithstanding, it is unrealistic to expect the end-of-year treatment termination to be painless. Feelings of sadness, pain and loss, guilt, and rejection are inherent in the experience of parting from persons with whom one has been emotionally involved, whether for good or ill. Some of the most distressing feelings that the students reported are intensified by their instruction and socialization in the profession. Their sense that they were abandoning their clients and the guilt that accompanied it are probably anchored, at least in part, in the emphasis placed on the clients' needs in their class- and fieldwork, and in the teaching that their clients' needs is a major and essential element of their work. Some of the anxiety and guilt that the students feel may stem from the great importance that is attributed to the termination phase in the course of their instruction (Webb 1985). Virtually all the literature on termination emphasizes the sensitivity of the process and the critical importance of executing it properly lest the work of the therapy be undone or, worse, the client be harmed. Along similar lines, some of the fear that the first-year students feel in anticipation of their clients' anger and disappointment at the termination may be traced directly to their being taught that these emotions are expected at separation and that they must encourage their clients to express them.

It is of note that the great distress the students experienced at the treatment termination came despite efforts routinely made in the course of their instruction to prepare them cognitively and emotionally. Considerable attention was paid both to providing guidelines as to how to go about the treatment termination and to anticipating the problems that might arise for the students in the process. Moreover, in keeping with recommendations in the literature (e.g., Clow 1998), the students were encouraged to explore their own feelings about the ending process, their habitual responses to loss, and any feelings about leaving the placement, colleagues, and clients. The possibility of having bad feelings was raised and these feelings were legitimized.

However the intervention is framed, the sense of premature ending and unfinished business is unlikely to disappear. The trainees' sadness is a natural response to parting, their apprehension of their clients' responses to the news grounded in reality. Their concern for their clients and their guilt feelings have a solid basis in their commitment and sensitivity as professionals. The recommended measures may alleviate some of the difficulty or help the trainees to better cope with it. They cannot eliminate the discomfort altogether.

And it is not desirable that they do. The frustration and distress the trainees experience at the end-of-year treatment termination are part of the learning process. As professionals, they will have to be able to contain their frustration and distress, to accept their clients' pace even where it seems slow, to live with the incompleteness of most of their interventions, and to accept and work within all the limitations of reality that inevitably affect the "ideal" of psychotherapy.

Suggestions for Research

As noted in the Introduction, very little study has been carried out on treatment termination by trainees. Based on the findings reported above and on the questions left unanswered, I recommend further study of trainees' management and experience of forced termination.

Trainees' Management of Termination: Students are generally taught how to manage their forced terminations. They are instructed on how to prepare for the treatment termination of each of their clients in consideration of their past separations and losses and their current emotional state. They are instructed on when to raise the issue of termination, to encourage their clients to express their feelings about the termination, and to review with them what they attained and did not attain in the treatment. Study is recommended to examine whether and how trainees carry out these instructions, and the impediments that arise for them in doing so.

Trainees' Experiences of Termination: The study reported above merely scratched the surface of trainees' experience of termination. Many issues remain unexplored. These include associations between trainees' experience of the forced termination and their management of it, the impact of former separations and losses on their experience and management of the forced termination, and the roles of such variables as the nature of the clinical setting, the duration of the intervention, and the trainees' stage of professional development. In addition, I recommend empirical examination of the role exit theory of trainees' forced terminations and comparison of trainees' and professionals' experience and management of forced terminations.

Summary

In view of the special nature of forced termination of client treatment by trainees and the very limited literature on the subject to date, this chapter presents the findings of a study that examined the feelings and concerns of social work student trainees at their end-of year treatment terminations with their fieldwork clients. The findings show that almost all of them regarded the termination as untimely and premature and experienced considerable distress as a result. Their feelings included anger, anxiety, and self-doubt about their professional abilities, and worry and guilt about damaging, exploiting, or abandoning their clients. Recommendations are offered to help alleviate the distress, while arguing that trying to eliminate the distress altogether is unrealistic and undesirable. Suggestions are made for further research into trainees' experience and management of forced termination.

References

Anthony, S., & Pagano, G. (1998). The therapeutic potential for growth during the termination process. *Clinical Social Work Journal, 26* (3), 281–295.

Baum, N. (2004). Social work students treatment termination as a temporary role-exit. *The Clinical Supervisor, 23*, 165–178.

Bostic, J. Shadid, L., & Blotcky, U. (1996). Our time is up: Forced terminations during psychotherapy training. *American Journal of Psychotherapy, 50* (3), 347–359.

Brill, M., & Nahmani, N. (1993). Clients' responses to separation from social work trainees. *Journal of Teaching in Social Work, 7* (2), 97–111.

Clow, C. (1998). Managing endings in practice teaching. In H. Lawson (Ed.), *Practice teaching changing social work* (pp. 128–140). London: Jessica Kingsley.

De Bosset, F., & Styrsky, E. (1986). Termination in individual psychotherapy: A survey of residents' experience. *Canadian Journal of Psychiatry, 31* (7), 636–642.

Dewald, P. A. (1965). Reactions to the forced termination of therapy. *Psychiatric Quarterly, 39*, 102–126.

Ebaugh, H. (1988). *Becoming an Ex. The process of role exit.* Chicago: University of Chicago Press.

Fair, M., & Bressler, M. (1992). Therapist-initiated termination of psychotherapy, *Clinical Supervisor, 10* (1), 171–189.

Germain, C., & Gitterman, A. (1996). *The life model of social work practice. Advances in theory and practice* (2nd ed.). New York: Columbia University Press.

Glenn, M. (1971). Separation anxiety: When the therapist leaves the patient. *American Journal of Psychotherapy, 25,* 437–446.

Golan, N. (1981). *Passing through transitions.* New York: The Free Press.

Gould, R. (1977). Students' experience with the termination phase of individual treatment. *Smith College Studies in Social Work, 48,* 235–269.

Gutheil, I. (1993). Rituals and termination procedures. *Smith College Studies in Social Work, 63,* 163–176.

Johnson, L., & Yanca, S. (2001). *Social work practice, a generalist approach* (7th ed.). Boston; New York: Allyn & Bacon.

Levinson, H. (1977). Termination of psychotherapy: Some salient issues. *Social Casework, 58,* 480–489.

Mikkelsen, E., & Gutheil, T. (1979). Stages of forced termination: Uses of the death metaphor. *Psychiatric Quarterly, 51* (1), 15–27.

Penn, L. (1990). When the therapist must leave: Forced termination of psychodynamic therapy. *Professional Psychology: Research and Practice, 21* (5), 379–384.

Petts, D. (1967). *Supervision in social work.* London: George Allen & Unwin.

Pumpian-Mindlin, E. (1958). Comments on technique of termination and transfer in a clinic setting. *American Journal of Psychotherapy, 12,* 455–464.

Quintana, M. (1993). Toward an expanded and updated conceptualization of termination: Implications for short-term individual psychotherapy. *Professional Psychology: Research and Practice, 24,* 426–432.

Siebold, C. (1991). Termination: When the therapist leaves. *Clinical Social Work Journal, 19* (2), 191–204.

Webb, N. (1985). A crisis intervention perspective on the termination process. *Clinical Social Work Journal, 13* (4), 329–340.

Wolin, J., & Bennett, A. (1984). Family rituals. *Family Process, 23* (3), 401–420.

3

Premature Termination Issues Involving Psychoanalytic Therapy

DOUGLAS H. FRAYN*

It is well known that psychoanalytic therapies frequently terminate prematurely and often abruptly. This can be a traumatic and disillusioning experience for both the therapists (especially students) and their analysands.

An earlier study was done (Frayn 1992) looking at the characteristics of patients accepted for both intensive psychotherapy and psychoanalysis who were rated during their initial assessments. Twenty cases that terminated prematurely (most frequently within the first month) were compared with twenty cases that continued in therapy. While specific diagnosis, type of insight therapy, and gender of the patient or therapist were unreliable predictors of premature termination, it was found that psychodynamic and environmental assessment factors significantly differed between these two groups. In those patients who eventually dropped out, specific ego deficits, primarily introspection, frustration tolerance, impulse control, and motivation were rated as significantly more impaired. The therapists' negative feelings toward their prospective patients and the patients' hostility toward past caretakers and present life circumstances were also associated with premature termination.

* This paper includes excerpts from earlier papers published: Frayn, D.H. (1992). Assessment factors associated with premature psychotherapy termination. *Amer. J. Psychother.*, 46:250–261; and Frayn, D.H. (1995) Premature termination issues in psychoanalytic control cases. *Can. J. Psychoanal.*, 3; No. 1, 17–41.

A later study (Frayn 1995) was undertaken to survey the magnitude of this problem as well as to consider factors that might prove to be associated with early termination specifically in student analyst cases.

This project was a combined Toronto Institute of Psychoanalysis (TIP) and Institut Psychanalytique de Montreal (IPM) assessment and outcome study to determine the frequency and characteristics of control patients who drop out as well as to investigate some features of the candidate analysts involved. For the purpose of this study premature termination was defined as meaning any analysand unilaterally leaving psychoanalysis before a minimal treatment period, that is, after less than twelve months (approximately two hundred hours) of analysis.

The extent of patient dropout or analytic attrition provides a definitive and useful outcome focus that can be measured, along with relevant comparisons made concerning both patient and therapist characteristics at time of the analytic assessment and at termination. In psychoanalytic research, the terms premature termination, forced termination, unilateral termination, patient withdrawal, attrition, and dropout have been used interchangeably, although some analysts feel that the word termination should be reserved for the therapeutic end phase and its intricate resolutions rather than an analytic interruption.

The dropout rate is a major issue in all outcome investigations and should be assessed and reported, yet frequently the premature termination data is completely omitted. For instance, if very few study patients are able to tolerate a certain procedure, a clinician should have major reservations about undertaking such therapy even if it could be shown that significant improvement occurred in those patients who were able to complete the treatment. As an example, particularly high dropout rates have been consistently noted in psychopharmacological studies of even the most effective drugs, when the drug alone situation is attempted. Almost one-half of depressed patients drop out within five weeks when psychotherapy or counseling is not part of the study protocol (Fabre 1991).

Attempts to objectify therapeutic outcomes have become a necessity in contemporary research. The sociopolitical pressures of a universal healthcare scheme as well as the competition from a variety of other psychotherapies now available, have forced analysts to justify their approach and query their results. A critical literature review of psychoanalytic outcome research consistently reveals clinical and methodological limitations.

Part of the difficulty in assessing relevant past research is due to the fact that certain variables such as the degree of patient pathology, therapist experience, and the outcome criteria utilized when compiling results are often omitted.

Analyzability and therapeutic benefits have been the measures most commonly studied yet have proven to be relatively separate dimensions, and among acceptable psychoanalytic cases only marginally predictable from the perspective of the initial evaluation (Bachrach 1991). Psychoanalytic and psychotherapy outcome studies show a considerable variability in both patient improvement and satisfaction factors. The results derived and conclusions determined appear to depend significantly on the patient population studied, the technique of therapy offered, length of proposed therapy, therapist experience, treatment setting, and dyadic expectations. Most of the earlier research studies were primarily retrospective and focused on symptom relief rather than more significant dynamic changes such as self-understanding and relationship improvement. While some post-classical analysts continue to entertain enthusiasm for a wide range of patients, Freud himself was never therapeutically zealous. Contemporary analysts seek to compare and prove that major therapeutic behavioral changes can take place as well as analytic insight as a consequence of analytic therapy. On follow-up of analysands who had terminated, Pfeffer (1963) concluded that although neurotic conflicts and transferences are not obliterated by analysis, when recognized and dynamically explored they tend to lose their poignancy and are better regulated as a consequence of the analysis (Pfeffer phenomena). The apparent overall conclusion of recent psychoanalytic research is that a substantially greater proportion of analysands derive therapeutic benefit than develop an analytic process (e.g., transference neurosis and/or insight into core conflicts), one-third of analysands are judged as unanalyzable at termination, and supportive factors seem to play a much greater role than have been previously recognized (Bachrach 1991; Kantrowitz, Katz, & Paolitto 1990 a, b, c; Kernberg, Burstein, & Coyne 1972).

In order to more fully evaluate psychoanalytic outcomes, one should compare them with the results of other psychotherapeutic under-takings. In a recent large, mixed psychotherapy study, one-third of depressive patients accepted for time-limited psychotherapy dropped out before the agreed-upon four months of treatment (Shea, Pilkonis, & Beckham 1990; Elkin, Shea, & Watkins 1989). A Yale clinic study of open-ended, once-weekly psychodynamic psychotherapy with no fixed termination, yielded therapeutically discouraging results. In this study, Sledge and Moras (1990) found that about one-half of such patients had dropped out without mutual agreement or a termination phase, within the first three months of therapy. In contrast to the Yale study, a recently reported Clarke Institute insight psychotherapy study revealed that when closely supervised senior residents were utilized as therapists, only one-quarter of the twice weekly insight psychotherapy patients had dropped out by the ninth month (Frayn 1992). Depend-ing upon the patient population studied and the type and duration of the psychological treatment undertaken, the unplanned termination figure can vary from one-eighth of all analytic cases over two years with experienced analysts (Erle & Goldberg 1984) to greater than one-half of borderline cases in analysis or psychotherapy over a four-year period (Waldinger & Gunderson 1984).

Psychoanalytic and psychotherapy process and outcome studies have investigated both patient (Malan 1976; Kernberg, Burstein, & Coyne 1972; Reder & Tyson 1980) and therapist (Luborsky & Crits-Christoph 1988; Frayn 1968) factors as well as their interactional variables (Kan-trowitz, Katz, & Paolitto 1990c; Luborsky & Crits-Christoph 1988; Hartley & Strupp 1983) with the consistent finding that patient variables most highly correlate with the eventual outcome, although individual traits of both parties do contribute. Some of the significant patient variables (e.g., mistrust, hostility, denial, and increasing anxi-ety), which contribute to a negative outcome, can be reliably evaluated during the assessment and initial phases of psychotherapy, using speech units and interaction profiles from tape recordings, direct observa-tions, and patient reports. These negative patient alliance factors have a higher correlation with the final result than the positive patient fac-tors (e.g., motivation for insight) when attempts are made to predict therapeutic outcome (Marziali, Marmar, & Krupnick 1981). Patients with such characterological traits exhibit interpersonal difficulties that reduce the possibility for a meaningful, intimate, or trusting relationship including eventually the analytic dyad. It appears that most analysands who do poorly demonstrate negative dynamic issues that persist across hours of therapy rather than just episodic misunderstandings. These destructive qualities and early resistance factors may be intransigent to the analysts' efforts to alter the impending termination or resolve the stalemate. Regarding the analyst variables affecting outcome, the earlier findings of accurate empathy, positive regard, flexibility, and assertiveness, as well as the therapist's awareness of some initial anxiety, all suggest a higher probability of a positive outcome. It has been observed that patients have less positive attitudes toward inexperienced and remote analysts, and more patients decline therapy and eventually drop out earlier when confronted with such therapists (Weber et al. 1985). Luborsky (1976) concludes that there is no evidence that the therapist's theoretical orientation is directly related to the patient's global outcome. For some patients the decision to terminate is not a mutual one. This is particularly so for patients receiving therapy through public health delivery systems. Discussion and bilateral decisions to terminate are more likely to take place in private practice settings with nonstudent therapists (DeBerry & Baskin 1989).

During assessment of analyses, the findings of prolonged silences, inability to look at the analyst (Searles 1986), persistent transference resistances, and primitive defenses with predominant preoedipal conflicts (e.g., paranoid personality structure with malevolent maternal introjects) are particularly foreboding (Baker 1980; Wallerstein 1986). Other patient factors that have been previously identified and are associated with the likelihood of not completing analyses are active substance abuse, axis II diagnoses (dramatic-erratic, borderline, and sociopathic) (Shea, Pilkonis, & Beckham 1990), psychosomatic or somatizing symptomatology, and major situational crises (Erle & Goldberg 1984; Weber et al. 1985). Patient selection, therapeutic approach and setting, length of treatment, procedural and goal expectations, and therapist experience and attitude are all interactional factors that influence the potential for patients to terminate therapy prematurely.

Dropping out of therapy is usually a complex interaction involving the patient, analyst, and the existing situational factors (Roback &

Smith 1987). Early recognition by the analyst of significant assessment qualities should lead to a more sophisticated selection of patients and appropriate intervention strategies that can facilitate continuing analysis, and may help lead to an eventual positive therapeutic outcome. Initial findings of a negative reaction to the analyst and increasing anxiety and mistrust of the analytic situation have special significance that, if ignored, can lead to regression, distancing, and early termination. It can be noted, in retrospect, that many of the eventual destructive elements in the failed analyses were described at the time of analytic assessment but were naively considered to be secondary to spousal or previous therapist inadequacies.

Premature Termination Study

A total of 119 control case analysands who had been assessed by both candidate and supervisor analysts as being suitable, began analyses. All analytic patients studied were consecutive control cases taking place over a six-year period between 1985 and 1991. The only significant difference in assessment protocol between the two psychoanalytic institutes was that most of the patients accepted in Montreal had been seen in consultation by the candidate analysts' supervisors, while in Toronto the supervisors usually assessed suitability from the candidates' case presentations alone.

The TIP Assessment Questionnaire (see Appendix) was fully completed by the candidates and their supervisors on twenty-two patients at the time of the initial assessment and then after one year of analysis (or at the time the patient dropped out). It was hoped that through the use of a descriptive clinical questionnaire (which gave each quality a brief quantitative outline) the individual dynamic factors would be more understandable and reliably rated, particularly when having to be completed by relatively inexperienced analysts. The questionnaire was an expanded version of the original TIP assessment form. It consisted of a listing of the analysands' biographical and clinical data as well as a series of twenty-four patient qualities and dynamic factors; all of which had been implicated from previous studies and reports as probable dropout factors. These assessment factors were rated using a descriptive scale and numerical quantifying score.

Results

Table 3.1 shows that the 119 psychoanalytic assessments and subsequent analyses were done by a total of 53 supervised candidates in training (mostly psychiatrists or psychologists) from both TIP (n = 36) and IPM (n = 17). Of the 53 different analysts in training, 27 were female and 26 were male. (Data concerning the 15 Canadian Institute of Psychoanalysis Quebec East candidates and their 28 patients were not complete and therefore could not be reported.)

Ninety-three (78%) of the total of 119 analysands studied were in treatment with the Toronto Institute candidates and 26 (22%) were in analysis with IPM analyst-trainees. There was a total of 71 (60%) female and 48 (40%) male patients in analysis (Table 3.2). Fifty-five analysands, or 46% of all analysands studied, were first or A cases; 45 (38%) were second or B cases and 19 (16%) were C cases (Figure 3.3).

Of the 119 analysands who began their control analyses, the findings in Table 3.3 and Figure 3.1 show that 29 or 24% of cases prematurely terminated (PT) while 90 or 76% of analysands continued their analysis after the first year of therapy.

Table 3.1 Analytic Control Cases Studied

STUDY PERIOD	THERAPISTS	ANALYSANDS	DROPOUTS (PT[a])
1985–87	15	36	9
1987–91	38	83	20
Total	53	119	29 (24%)

[a] Premature termination.

Table 3.2 Premature Termination and Gender

ANALYSANDS	FEMALE	MALE
Total n=119	71 (60%)	48 (40%)
Terminators(PT) n=29	19 (66%)	10 (34%)

Table 3.3 Premature Termination and Analytic Duration

ANALYSANDS	DURATION (MONTHS)					
	0	1	3	6	9	12
Continuing (CT) n=	119	110	105	96	92	90 (75.6%)
Terminators (PT) n=	0	9	14	23	27	29 (24.4%)

Tables 3.3 and 3.4 and Figure 3.2 illustrate that 14 or 48% of the terminators left therapy during the first three months (p < .001) and that 9 or 31% of the total who eventually dropped out did so during the first month of analysis.

From Table 3.5 and Figures 3.3 and 3.4 it can be seen that the most inexperienced candidates had the highest frequency of analysand dropout. That is, 18 out of 55 first cases or 33% of their total A cases terminated prematurely. That also represents 62% (18/29) of the total number of dropouts (Figure 3.4).

The premature termination rate (16% of C cases) for the most experienced candidates (C cases) was less than one-half that of the beginners (33% of A cases) (p < .05) (Table 3.5).

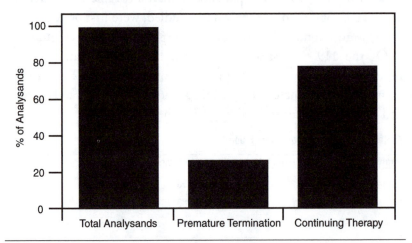

Figure 3.1   Premature termination dropouts (n = 29) compared to total analysands (1 year).

Table 3.4   Premature Termination (Quarterly) Rates

Duration (Months)	0–3	3–6	6–9	9–12
Terminators (PT) n = 29	14 (48%)[a]	9 (31%)	4 (14%)	2 (7%)

[a] p < .001 (KS test).

Table 3.5   Premature Termination and Specific Control Cases

CASE	A	B	C
Total Cases n =	55 (100%)	45 (100%)	19 (100%)
Continuing (CT)	37 (67%)	37 (82%)	16 (84%)
Terminators (PT)	18 (33%)[a]	8 (18%)	3 (16%)

[a] p < .05 (Pearson chi sq).

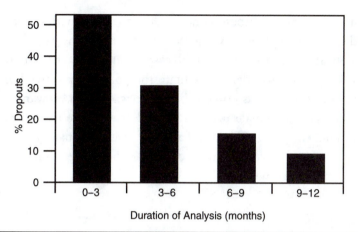

Figure 3.2   Dropout (premature termination) occurrences ($n = 29$) during the first year of analysis.

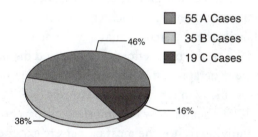

Figure 3.3   Control case ratios total analytic cases ($n = 119$).

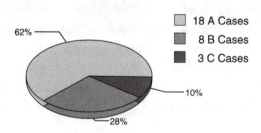

Figure 3.4   Total premature termination case ratios ($n = 29$).

Between the two institutes, there was no significant difference in the frequency of dropouts. The TIP had 23 early terminators out of 93 beginning analysands (24.7%) and IPM lost 6 of their initial 26 patients (23.1%).

Neither the gender of the patient nor therapist was significantly related to the subsequent occurrence of premature termination. There was a trend toward slightly higher dropout rates among patients who were with therapists of the same gender. This is an unexpected finding since more of these same gender cases were with experienced candidates. Perhaps this gives some credence to the institutes' original theoretical belief that the initial case should be a patient of the opposite gender in order to facilitate the potential positive libidinal transference. It was also noted that there was a trend toward higher dropout rates by female patients as well as in those psychoanalytic control patients under 25 years of age. Because age data was frequently omitted, a definitive statement could not be made about age and termination outcome.

Discussion

It is generally assumed that premature termination signifies a poorer therapeutic outcome than that which can be achieved by continuing analysis, although the differences may not be as significant as once believed. Because of the time, effort, expense, and disruption to both patients and their therapists, it is important to be able to identify those analysands most likely to terminate prematurely.

This sample of therapists was comprised of psychoanalytic students. These individuals (for the most part) were experienced professional clinicians with considerable therapeutic interest and clinical skills prior to their acceptance for training. The accepted control cases were outpatients without obvious contraindications for psychoanalysis. The analysands voluntarily made a verbal commitment to undertake analysis four or five times per week following the assessment interviews. Sometimes the analyst's supervisor directly took part in the assessment as well, although this was not a routine occurrence.

Previous outcome studies have shown that patients who drop out of therapy generally have higher pathology ratings and show significantly more relationship deficits (Gaston, Marmar, & Thompson 1988; Frayn 1992). Lower et al. (1972) found that both individual screening analysts and the group committee evaluation rated poor ego strength and social maladaptation as the most unfavorable qualities when judging analyzability potential. They also stressed that psychosexual phase pathology ratings were not as reliably related to outcome as ego functioning ratings (Huxster & Lower 1975).

In the earlier TIP study involving thirty-four psychoanalytic candidates as well as fifty-one senior psychotherapy residents (Frayn 1992), the patient characteristics that most highly discriminated for premature termination were higher total psychopathology scores and specifically poor motivation and frustration intolerance/impulsivity along with lack of introspection and more unsatisfactory present life circumstances. The analysts' awareness of negative feelings toward their prospective patients and patients' hostility toward past caretakers and present self-preoccupation were also more likely to be associated with premature termination. From that TIP pilot study, it was suggested that inadequate therapeutic alliance development is not only a major predictor of poor clinical outcome, but also of early psychoanalytic dropout. Surprising, perhaps, was the importance of positive life circumstances and support needed by those continuing in analysis. That the therapists' alliance (countertransference) turned out to be a more significant predictor than the assessed patients' alliance also probably reflects the therapists' difficulty in accurately assessing negative transferences. It has been previously noted that therapists naively rate the attitude of poorer outcome patients as being more positive than do the patients when rating themselves.

In this present analytic investigation, of the 29 prematurely terminated cases studied, 31% (9/29) dropped out during the first month while 48% (14/29) of the dropout total had discontinued treatment within the first three months of analysis. The final 21% or 6 dropouts were evenly distributed over the remaining six months of first year of therapy. This finding is similar to our earlier psychotherapy study where 50% of the terminators (10/20) dropped out during the first month of therapy (Frayn 1992). The NIMH (National Institute of Mental Health) Collaborative Study showed that 44% (35/77) of those who dropped out of brief time limited psychotherapy did so within the first month of treatment (Elkin, Shea, & Watkins 1989). The Yale psychotherapy study also revealed that 76% (32/42) of their dropouts had taken place by the first 12 sessions (Sledge & Moras 1990).

These findings suggest that there may be at least two distinct groups of premature terminators, excluding those nonstarters who leave during the assessment. The first and most predominant are the early terminators. Within this group there appears to be more of a wish for, rather than actual adequate motivation for, analysis. Retrospectively, both analyst and supervisor could frequently identify ominous factors that were overlooked during the assessment interviews. Some of these analysands experienced the emergence of an unexpected and sudden disorganizing negative transference and mistrustful resistance at a time before a significant therapeutic alliance was available. With the later terminators, seemingly a more heterogeneous group, dropping out was a manifestation of a variety of environmental and conflictive dynamic issues rather than their sharing a similar core conflict. When dropouts could be followed after treatment, these former patients frequently reported that they had left because the analysis did not help their situational difficulties or that they felt their therapist did not seem interested or understanding of them. It appears that patients' early predictions of their therapy outcome are more reliable than either their therapists' or the observers' initial impressions (Gurman 1977).

It should not be assumed that the outcome is unsuccessful just because a patient terminates earlier than the agreed upon date or prior to a delineated termination phase. Waldinger and Gunderson's borderline patient study (1984) found that the longer patients stayed in treatment, the more they improved, yet many of these longer term "successful" cases also eventually terminated against their therapists' advice. Although analysands are the obvious ones doing the leaving, sometimes termination seemed to be an intersubjective reflection of their analysts' ambivalence, as well. Less openly spoken about are the terminating patients' erotic fears, and envy of and disillusionment with their analysts, while more overt problems such as time limitations and family/work responsibilities are often cited as being the reason for not continuing in analysis. Some analysands say they don't want or need further therapy and seem satisfied to leave in spite of the analysts' pessimism over their apparent improvement or flight into health. As every experienced analyst knows, a surprising number of such early terminators with unresolved but certain idealizing transference features appear to maintain improvement as well as a positive attitude toward their "aborted" analysis. It is known that while therapists value insight as a necessary feature for lasting improvement, patients will rate feeling good about themselves and their improved life situation as more important factors in their decision. Kantrowitz,

Katz, and Paolitto (1990b, 1990c) found in post-termination interviews that analysands who believed that their analysis had been beneficial, consistently felt it to be due to one or a combination of two factors. Such patients believed that they had acquired a belief system or understanding of previously incomprehensible symptoms, thoughts and feelings. This insight was usually associated with the conviction that the patient had also developed a meaningful relationship with their analyst—someone who had tried to understand, to explore novel resolutions to old problems, and who could be made use of at times of stress, even if this occurred only in the analysand's fantasy.

Searles (1986) states that one of the most stressful aspects of practicing psychoanalysis is having to deal with feelings of impotence and rage following patients' sudden termination. Analysand dropout is a feared and frustrating situation for candidates, particularly so when initiated by the patient. This unexpected event can undermine a therapist's confidence in her developing identity as an analyst. The analyst may question her ability to be therapeutic while at the same time attempting to maintain a dynamically equidistant role and abstinent analytic stance. Frequently the terminating analysand is in a state of negative transference. More than half of the borderline disordered patients who discontinue their therapy early, do so in anger after confrontation by their therapist (Gunderson et al. 1989). Other patients with a history of repetitive impulsive "triumphant" separations may have an absence of grief or other feelings of loss, particularly when they feel in control of the separation. The dysphoric, vengeful feelings are then left for the therapist to experience. The departing analysands have actively reenacted that which they passively and helplessly had experienced in childhood, that is, they leave rather than being left.

A common observation made by supervisors is that once a candidate has received the required credit for the control of patient analysis and its supervision, the analysand's transference threats to leave often "magically" diminish. This may take place following the completion of the training requirement without the therapist's awareness of his own subtle but significant countertransference shift. Another form of forced termination is that which is primarily initiated by the analyst. This usually occurs after the supervision and credit for training hours have been completed. Such interrupted cases are often unreported and, if mentioned, tend to arise in the candidate's personal analysis rather than within formal supervision. Unilateral therapist termination may represent an acting out of suppressed negative countertransference. Usually a hostile yet mutually dependent relationship has developed centering around training issues that are never openly discussed yet eventually contribute to a destructive outcome. It has been suggested that this type of outcome would be more likely to occur when control cases pay a smaller fee than usual or when analysis is not covered by insurance. In our study the fee structure did not appear to be a significant predictor of dropout. There was a similar dropout rate with medical and nonmedical therapists as well as with their Toronto and Montreal analysands even though most patients from Ontario were insured for unlimited analysis.

We have not statistically reported on the independent ratings done by the supervisors and their candidates on twenty-two of the control cases at time of assessment. Based on the two different institutes' practices, there was not a significant difference in dropout between those cases seen in consultation by the candidate analysts' supervisors and those assessed from the candidate's presentation alone. We found, as in the earlier TIP study (Frayn 1992), that invariably the candidates initially overestimated their patients' strengths as compared to their supervisors' ratings of the same patients. After one year of analysis, these same analysts and their supervisors were much closer in their reevaluations of the patients. There was a consistent finding that the supervisors rated the control patients initially as having higher impairment scores than their supervisees and after the first year of analysis these same supervisors usually saw improvement and this was reflected in their ratings. Among the candidate supervisees (particularly the less experienced), ratings for the patient's immediate transference and therapist's countertransference (alliance) items, as well as the patient's manifest object relatedness and capacity for self-inquiry, seemed unduly optimistic and frequently unreliable when compared to their supervisors' assessments.

It has been previously reported and confirmed that agreement among experienced supervisors concerning trait and ability ratings is highly correlated (Malan 1976). Further patient ratings done by these same therapists-in-training after twelve months usually reflected a higher awareness of their patients' pathology, even when there had been obvious clinical improvement. This finding confirms the Menninger conclusion that the analysand's pathology was underestimated in almost half of accepted cases (Kernberg, Burstein, & Coyne 1972). In Erle and Goldberg's (1984) New York Institute study, Erle states that the final diagnosis (at termination) differed from the initial impression in nearly half of the cases, all in the direction of more severe pathology. Our findings suggest that after one year's analytic experience, student analysts tend to be optimistic about their patients, yet in contrast with their initial assessments, rate more pathology. Regardless of their patients' clinical status, candidates' later evaluations tend to be more objective and approximate that of their supervisors.

Unfortunately the hope that the best-rated therapists should be able to salvage the most difficult cases is generally unfounded. Results show that the more likely outcome is repeated failure, which could have been reliably predicted from the patient assessment factors alone. It has also been noted that the analyst who consistently experiences and/or exhibits negative reactions to the analysand is unlikely to be successful with that patient. Wallerstein's (1986) clinical retrospective of the Menninger Project states that the patients who had been taken into analysis on the basis of "heroic indications" had all failed to improve. The importance of the analytic "match" between analysand and analyst includes but goes beyond interpersonal similarities in gender, cognitive styles, sociocultural experiences, shared transferences, or existential views of the past and present. A fundamental undertaking in further contemporary psychoanalytical research should include the identification of significant interactive matching factors and the exploration of the subsequent impact on analyses and their outcomes (Kantrowitz, Katz, & Paolitto 1990c).

One can speculate about the need for and unconscious use of denial, show of optimism and expectant faith that both analysts and patients require in order to undertake an intensive, regressive, and intimate therapeutic relationship, particularly without specific time limitation. It is our impression that after analysis has progressed, these same therapists are not only more understanding of their patients' pathology but also more aware of their own countertransference. With developing therapeutic confidence, additional personal analysis, and a manageable dyadic situation, trainee-analysts appear to become more empathic and less defensive in identifying these problematic areas (Easser 1974). The significance of the interaction between the patient factors and the candidate/supervisor rating discrepancies at the time of initial evaluation are of interest. Further study of these findings may lead to more objective assessments without unduly discouraging the beginning analyst. It should be recognized that difficulties between the supervisee and supervisor can be influenced by and lead to disruptions in the empathic process within the analysis. In six out of the eight unanalyzable cases quoted from the later Boston Institute study, Kantrowitz et al. (1987) noted that definite supervision conflicts had occurred.

The interest in identifying patient factors that are associated with early termination is not meant to ignore or exonerate poor therapists who because of lack of skill, character conflicts, empathic failure, or untimely interventions can drive away even the most motivated patients. Psychoanalysis is increasingly perceived as an intersubjective, two-person situation in which the personalities, conflicts, and cognitive styles of both participants play a major role in determining the ultimate outcome of the analysis. Termination may occur when there is an impasse or hindrance due to conflicts in the patient-analyst match. If initially there is intense transference and/or countertransference resistances, analysis may prove to be impossible due to the primitive libidinal and oppositional effects on free association and therapeutic alliance development. Patients see mismatching as the most significant factor in non-therapeutic terminations. In over half the cases where matching was evaluated as playing a central role, similarity or complementarity was deemed to have hindered the analytic process. Even in the follow-up of cases where there was a mutually agreed-upon termination, as many patients have continuing intense and unresolved negative feelings (even after ten years) toward their former analysts as those who maintain an idealized image. It was felt that a facilitating (compensatory) match was more likely to develop with older, more experienced analysts. "For (some) patients, analysis reinforced earlier painful experiences, rather than enabling them to understand and come to some resolution in relation to the past. We cannot be sure how much the analysts' inexperience contributed to the failure of these cases, but we suspect it was a relevant factor." (Kantrowitz, Katz, & Paolitto 1990, 664).

There should be encouragement and opportunity for student analysts to take part in supervisory and peer group experiences relating to analytic assessment and termination issues. Unlike the U.S. Institute curricula, most Canadian candidates finish their formal didactic lectures and supervision prior to any of their control cases coming to a scheduled therapeutic termination. This unfortunately leaves the very important termination phase of an analysis with its issues of separation, identification, and transference/countertransference resolution to take place without supervision. It also appears that many candidates need to continue or seek further personal analysis during regressive transference and countertransference periods, particularly with their initial and unstable control cases.

It is unlikely that any one type of analyst can be equally effective with all types of patients. There were dropout differences among individual candidate analysts but the numbers were too small to make any definitive comments. Some trainees were well aware of having to assess many patients before finding one willing to start an analysis with them. Some of these same therapists were worried that more of their patients seemed to discontinue analyses, but were unsure if or why that was so, and were too fearful to explore the implications in their supervision (or analyses for that matter). A few of the student analysts in this study no longer practiced psychoanalysis following graduation. The supervisors felt that as a rule the candidates who took part in this project were not only adequate, interested, and experienced, but had been successful with patients in the past using other forms of psychotherapy.

In beginning an analysis it is necessary that the analyst have an adequate assessment of the patient's regressive potential and some understanding of his previous modes of acting out. The analyst must also be prepared to be innovative using active, interpretive, and empathic strategies in attempting to deal with an impending early dropout situation. The importance of assessing not only the patient's potential analyzability but also evaluating those mismatching factors that impede the analysis and bring about premature termination is essential and requires considerable supervisory input. The first three months of an analysis with a control patient is crucial and frequently the most unstable period of that analysis. This is particularly so with the psychoanalytic candidate's initial case. The premature termination of an analytic control case is a disrupting influence on a beginning analyst-trainee's developing analytic identity. It is essential that inexperienced analytic candidates be closely supervised during the assessment and the initial phase of analysis with their control cases. The introductory phase of an analysis is the most vulnerable time for both parties. It requires the analyst to be therapeutically adept at dealing with sudden regressive conflicts concerning trust, dependency, intimacy, and separation both within the analyst as well as the analysand. Further research into improved analysand/analyst matching and more effective analytic supervision and support systems for beginning trainee-analysts is required.

Summary

A psychoanalytic assessment and outcome study was undertaken in an effort to determine the frequency and characteristics of control analysands who drop out, as well as to identify some of the therapist and supervision factors that may be associated with premature termination.

Premature termination during the first year of analysis takes place in about one-quarter of all accepted and commenced psychoanalytic control cases. One-half of all those terminating prematurely drop out within the first three months. It is suggested that there may be important similarities within this earliest dropout group. Frequently they exhibited unstable and regressive transferences and/or problematic motivation from the outset of the analysis.

There were significantly more female than male analysands in therapy, while there were equal numbers of male and female candidate-therapists. There were no significant differences in the subsequent dropout rates associated with the patient/analyst gender match, nor the psychoanalytic training institute involved.

The most inexperienced candidates have the highest dropout rate, with more than one-third of their first cases leaving prematurely and often precipitously. During the initial assessment, supervisees appear to consistently underestimate the degree of their analysands' psychopathology.

Acknowledgments

I wish to acknowledge the help of the candidates of the Canadian Institute of Psychoanalysis and their supervisors for their ongoing contributions to this project, as well as Cathy Spegg, Jean Bowlby, Nadia Gargour, and Michael Frayn for their editorial assistance.

References

Bachrach, H., Galatzer-Levy, R. Skolnikoff A., & Waldron S. (1991). On the efficacy of psychoanalysis. *Journal of the American Psychoanalytic Association, 39,* 871–917.

Baker, R. (1980). The finding of "not suitable" in the selection of supervised cases. *International Review of Psychoanalysis, 7,* 353–358.

DeBerry, S., & Baskin, D. (1989). Termination criteria: a comparison of private and public practice. *American Journal of Psychotherapy, 43,* 43–53.

Easser, B. R. (1974). Empathic inhibition and psychoanalytic technique. *Psychoanalytical Quarterly, 43,* 557–580.

Elkin, I., Shea, M. T, Watkins, J., et al. (1989). N.I.M.H. Treatment of depression. Collaborative research program: general effectiveness of treatment. *Archives of General Psychiatry, 46,* 971–982.

Erle, J., & Goldberg, D. (1984). Observations on assessment of analyzability by experienced analysts. *Journal of the American Psychoanalytic Association, 32,* 715–737.

Fabre, L., & Scharf, M. (1991). Comparative efficacy and safety of nortriptylene and fluoxetine in the treatment of major depression. *Journal of Clinical Psychiatry, 52,* 62–67.

Frayn, D. H. (1968). A relationship between related ability and personality traits in psychotherapists. *American Journal of Psychiatry, 124* (9), 1232–1237.

Frayn, D. H. (1992). Assessment factors associated with premature psychotherapy termination. *American Journal of Psychotherapy, 46,* 250–261.

Frayn, D. H. (1995). Premature termination issues involving psychoanalytic control cases. *Canadian Journal of Psychoanalysis, 3* (1), 17–41.

Gaston, L., Marmar, C. R., & Thompson, L. (1988). Relation of patient pretreatment characteristics to the therapeutic alliance in diverse psychotherapies. *Journal of Consulting and Clinical Psychology, 56,* 483–489.

Gunderson, J. G., Frank, A. F., Ronningstam, E. F., et al. (1989). Early discontinuance of borderline patients from psychotherapy. *Journal of Nervous Mental Disorders, 177,* 38–42.

Gurman, A. S. (1977). The patient's perception of the therapeutic relationship. In A. S. Gurman & A. M. Razin (Eds.), *Effective psychotherapy* (pp. 503–543). New York: Pergamon Press.

Hartley, D., & Strupp, H. H. (1983). The therapeutic alliance and its relationship to outcome in brief psychotherapy. In J. Masling (Ed.), *Empirical studies of the psychoanalytic theories* (Vol. 1; pp. 1–38). Hillsdale, NJ: Lawrence Erlbaum.

Huxster, H., & Lower, R. (1975). Some pitfalls in the assessment of analyzability in a psychoanalytic clinic. *Journal of the American Psychoanalytic Association, 23,* 90–106.

Kantrowitz, J., Katz, A., & Paolitto, F. (1990a). Follow-up of psychoanalysis 5–10 years after termination. I. Stability of change. *Journal of the American Psychoanalytic Association, 38,* 471–496.

Kantrowitz, J., Katz, A., & Paolitto, F. (1990b). Follow-up of psychoanalysis 5–10 years after termination. II. Development of the self-analytic function. *Journal of the American Psychoanalytic Association, 38,* 637–654.

Kantrowitz, J., Katz, A., & Paolitto, F. (1990c). Follow-up of psychoanalysis 5–10 years after termination. III. Relation between the resolution of the transference and the patient-therapist match. *Journal of the American Psychoanalytic Association, 38,* 637–654.

Kantrowitz, J., Katz, A. L., Paolitto, F., Sashin, J., & Solomon, L. (1987). The role of reality testing in the outcome of psychoanalysis: follow-up of 22 cases. *Journal of the American Psychoanalytic Association, 35,* 367–386.

Kernberg, O., Burstein, E., Coyne, L., et al. (1972). Psychotherapy and psychoanalysis: Final report of the Menninger Foundation's psychotherapy research project. *Bulletin of the Menninger Clinic, 36,* 87–275.

Lower, R., Escoll, P., & Huxster, H. (1972). Bases for judgement of analyzability. *Journal of the American Psychoanalytic Association, 20,* 610–621.

Luborsky, L. L. (1976). Helping alliances in psychotherapy. In James L. Claghorn (Ed.), Successful psychotherapy. Proceedings of the Ninth Annual Symposium; November 19–21, 1975; Texas Research Institute of Mental Sciences. New York: Brunner\Mazel.

Luborsky, L. L, & Crits-Christoph, P. (1988). Measures of psychoanalytic concepts. *International Journal of Psychoanalysis, 69,* 75–86.

Malan, D. H. (1976). *The frontier of brief psychotherapy.* New York: Plenum Publishing.

Marziali, E., Marmar, C., & Krupnick, J. (1981). Therapeutic alliance scales. *American Journal of Psychiatry, 138,* 361–364.

Pfeffer, A. Z. (1963). The meaning of the analyst after analysis. *Journal of the American Psychoanalytic Association, 11,* 229–244.

Reder, P., & Tyson, R. (1980). Patient dropout from individual psychotherapy. *Bulletin of the Menninger Clinic, 44,* 229–252.

Roback, H., & Smith, M. (1987). Patient attrition in dynamically oriented treatment groups. *American Journal of Psychiatry, 144,* 426–431.

Searles, H. F. (1986). *My work with borderline patients* (pp. 318–319). London: Jason Aronson.

Shea, M. T., Pilkonis, P. A., & Beckham, E. (1990). Personality disorders and treatment outcome in the N.I.M.H. Treatment of depression. Collaborative research program. *American Journal of Psychiatry, 147,* 711–718.

Sledge, W., & Moras, K. (1990). Effect of time-limited psychotherapy on patient dropout rates. *American Journal of Psychiatry, 147* (10), 1341–1347.

Waldinger, R., & Gunderson, J. (1984). Completed psychotherapies with borderline patients. *American Journal of Psychotherapy, 38,* 190–202.

Wallerstein, R. S. (1986). *Forty-two lives in treatment: A study of psychoanalysis and psychotherapy.* New York: Guilford Press.

Weber, J., Bachrach, H., & Solomon, M. (1985). Factors associated with the outcome of psychoanalysis (III). *International Review of Psychoanalysis, 12,* 251–262.

4

TERMINATING PSYCHOTHERAPY THERAPEUTICALLY

STEVEN R. GRAYBAR AND LEAH M. LEONARD

Introduction

A deeper understanding of psychotherapy would certainly include a longer look at termination. By terminating psychotherapy therapeutically we mean ending therapy with thoughtfulness and care. That is, taking advantage of the possibilities and avoiding the pitfalls often present at termination. From our perspective, therapeutic terminations involve planning, conducting, and concluding treatment with termination in mind. It means providing a treatment and a termination that accounts for the emotional and interpersonal impact that ending therapy may hold for a given client. A therapeutic termination brings closure to treatment and prepares the client for life without therapy or the therapist. For many clients, termination is a relatively minor step. It involves a quick jump from the consulting room back into the rush of the rest of their lives. For others, termination is powerfully reminiscent of days past, relationships lost, and opportunities missed. As such it brings with it deep pain and confusion. Still other clients experience termination like many other life transitions. For them it is a time of joy mixed with sadness, success tinged with defeat, hope colored by anxiety. Regardless of how a given client approaches the end of his/her treatment, it is incumbent upon the clinician to respond effectively to the needs of each client at termination. While many of these client concerns will be familiar and relate clearly to concerns discussed earlier in treatment, some issues raised at termination will be unique to the termination process itself.

Throughout this chapter we will present our perspective on how we conceptualize psychotherapy and facilitate therapeutic terminations. Our thoughts about termination come from our experience providing and supervising individual psychotherapy. Our discussion is meant to serve as an introduction and an outline to our approach to termination. It is not intended (or believed) to be a definitive treatise on the topic. We begin by describing our approach to treatment, considering three prevailing approaches to termination and reviewing the associated clinical literature. We then address the central issues of termination as they are incorporated into treatment, and consider two related concerns: the termination- and loss-dominated client and the de-idealization of the therapist and the therapy during termination. We conclude with a case example that highlights the clinical potential of a therapeutic termination in an integrated treatment of a bereaved and traumatized client. The case example highlights the potential therapist reactions (countertransference) can play in treatment and at termination. It is our hope that clinicians from any school of thought will read this chapter and experience a renewed appreciation for their work as psychotherapists, for the deep and ongoing impact they have in the lives of their clients and for the need to end their work in deliberate, thoughtful, and clinically informed ways. It is the thesis of this chapter that when meaningful therapies are accompanied by meaningful terminations a therapeutic termination occurs and a successful therapy has been completed.

Termination and Treatment

The importance of termination in our work stems from our belief that human beings are relationship-driven creatures and psychotherapy a relationship-driven process (Yalom 2002). Regardless of its content, psychotherapy is interpersonal in its delivery, impact, and implications. From this interpersonal perspective, we have come to view all of life's transitions—beginnings and endings, rifts and ruptures, attachments and separations, losses and the threat of loss—as critical factors in the development of personality and psychopathology. For many clients it is the stress of these transitions that drives their initial decision to seek psychotherapy. As we begin treatment we are very interested in why the client has decided to seek psychotherapy at that time and place in his/her life. Often they will cite difficulty with one of the above transitions, such as the end of, or a significant change in, an important relationship, the loss of a job, a move to a new another city, and so forth. We pay special attention to how our clients have navigated autonomy, intimacy, and conflict across the lifespan, in their contemporary relationships, and in their subsequent interactions with us. In addition, we believe the need to maintain self-esteem by managing fears of ridicule, rejection, or failure abounds in life and in psychotherapy. For our clients, these fears and their attendant defenses operate throughout treatment, within the treatment relationship, and can become prominent at termination. If not addressed empathically, early, and often, these fears operate beneath the surface of therapy, haphazardly pushing treatment in confused and confusing directions and potentially toward premature termination.

Within this interpersonal framework, we function in therapy as participants/observers (Sullivan 1952). As participants we are willing to get involved, deeply involved with our clients. We believe that as therapists we must be willing to leave the safety of dry land and professional objectivity and wade out into the swirling waters of our clients' emotional lives. By getting in and getting wet (as distinguished from getting in and getting drowned), we allow ourselves to be pushed by our clients' pain, pulled by the current of their interpersonal impact, and moved by the depth of their suffering. The willingness to be participants allows us greater access to our own empathy and ultimately a greater understanding of our client's confusing choices, self-defeating behaviors, and polarizing conflicts. As observers, we use our experience and training to climb out of the white water and examine, from the relative calm of shore, the content and process of our clients' difficulties. From our position as observers we can offer our clients different perspectives and alternative views of themselves and their problems. Often, from the vantage point of a participant/observer, we acquire a degree of credibility that participants or observers alone do not have. From this therapeutic stance we develop very personal yet clearly professional relationships with our clients. In sum, as participant/observers, we are in a unique position to provide new information, new insights, and new experiences, all in the context of a unique relationship.

Within our approach to psychotherapy, termination is a transition that functions as a bridge across time and treatment. It is a bridge that carries clients and their progress out of psychotherapy and into the rest of their lives. If included in the treatment plan, the expanse of this bridge stretches from the initial session and presenting problem, across the evolving therapeutic relationship, through each clinical issue, a final good-bye, and beyond. A therapeutic termination facilitates the internalization of what was good, helpful, and important in therapy and the clinical relationship. At the same time, if done well, termination brings greater balance to the therapy relationship and promotes client self-confidence. Further, a therapeutic termination can deal with regrets as well as resentments by acknowledging what fell short or was simply never possible in the therapy or therapeutic relationship. Such emotional honesty underscores the resilience of the gains made during treatment and the treatment relationship.

We fear, in practice, and in its most common or basic form, that termination often involves a simple and sometimes awkward expression of "good-bye and good luck" from the therapist to the client. Basic terminations, like brief therapy in general, frequently just happen. Often they sneak up on clinicians who, under the pressure of time, are left scrambling to mine something therapeutic from unexpected or premature terminations, which occur at an alarming 36% to 51% of the time (Prevkarik & Wolf 2002). Though it is certainly an empirical question, we believe that avoiding discussions of termination early in treatment may lead to premature terminations later. Further, leaving these discussions until the very end of therapy may result in awkward or confusing endings and possibly to iatrogenic terminations, which actually damage or take away from the therapy itself. We are concerned that unplanned terminations, or terminations in their most basic form, represent a series of misunderstandings and missed opportunities. Simply stopping treatment with little or no planning or preparation involves a failure to recognize the relational nature of psychotherapy. Further, it fails to capitalize on a multitude of therapeutic possibilities. Ironically, a basic termination brings a superficial end to what we presume was a substantive professional relationship. Basic terminations can leave the clinician colluding with a part of the client that wishes to avoid the meaning and impact of treatment and its end. We believe such half-hearted terminations function to diminish the therapy and subsequently decrease the likelihood that clients will draw from their therapy experiences after treatment has concluded.

The most important step in avoiding a basic termination is clinician awareness of the combined and cumulative power psychotherapy and the psychotherapy relationship hold for most clients. For a majority of clients, entering psychotherapy is a courageous step, as are staying in treatment, working through difficult or painful material, acting on therapeutic conversations by taking risks in one's personal life, and eventually leaving a relationship where one feels accepted and understood. Once the therapist grasps the interpersonal importance of treatment, he/she can use the end of treatment as an additional opportunity to understand and intervene with the client. In its totality, a therapeutic termination is the culmination of a series of interventions and itself can serve as a last and lasting intervention. A therapeutic termination can be a final intervention that connects and solidifies previous interventions. The power and potential of ending psychotherapy therapeutically will be the focus of the remainder of this chapter.

The Termination Literature

There are three general approaches to termination. The first is primarily psychodynamic. Its emphasis is on termination as a period of grief and bereavement. The second is a more contemporary perspective and has some empirical support. It views termination as a period of transition, consolidation, and growth. Quintana (1993) described these two perspectives of termination, referring to them as the "termination as loss" and "termination as transformation" approaches. The third approach to termination is what we refer to as the "termination as accessory" or the "basic" approach to termination. It views termination as an afterthought. Such a perspective seems to assume that good therapy stands on its own, and does not require much in the way of planning or preparation for termination. We will begin by reviewing the termination as accessory approach first.

Approaching termination as an accessory or afterthought is of course no approach at all. No school of psychotherapy advocates neglecting or avoiding termination. In practice, sins of omission not commission surround the termination as accessory approach. Yet avoiding full discussions of termination and saving what discussions do occur for the very end of therapy devalues the end of treatment as well as the end of the therapeutic relationship. As a result, therapists who neglect or avoid termination do not engage in a termination phase of treatment, but more typically a termination session, if not a termination comment. While the issue of termination should not dominate treatment, neither should it be relegated to an awkward endpoint or an uncomfortable "so long" in the closing moments of a concluding psychotherapy. As stated above, this approach to termination often stands in stark contrast to the thoughtful work that preceded it. It treats termination like an island, completely disconnected from the rest of psychotherapy, as an after thought or social nicety.

The notion that we can safely neglect termination, or that good psychotherapy can stand alone, is not supported by the clinical literature. In their review, Pakarik and Wolf (1998) found that regardless of overall progress, client evaluations of therapy were largely based on how they felt at termination or follow-up. This finding alone seems to justify a longer look and a more careful approach to the end of treatment and its termination. It suggests that clients appear to use their experience of termination as a lens through which they view the whole of their psychotherapy experience. Pakarik and Wolf's findings suggest that termination may play a very significant role in treatment outcome and client satisfaction. Additional research is consistent with Pakarik and Wolf (1998). It suggests that unplanned or poorly planned terminations tend to negatively affect treatment outcome (Fox et al. 1969; Hiat 1965; Martinez 1982; Holden 1983). These unplanned terminations are particularly detrimental for clients who have a history of loss, or where loss was an important issue in the therapy (Marx & Gelso 1987). Unplanned terminations are also detrimental when clinicians avoid discussing at termination difficult feelings or negative events that occurred earlier in therapy (Holden 1983); a finding consistent with (and one that appears to extend) the work of Safran and McDougal (2006) and their investigations into ruptures in the therapeutic alliance.

Though limited, the above literature is still quite clear. Neglecting or ignoring termination is a mistake. We believe minimizing or ignoring termination is experienced by the client as a process comment on the importance of therapy and can leave some clients hurt, confused, or otherwise doubting the importance of treatment and/or the treatment relationship. Clients invest a good deal of time, effort, and money in their treatment. A therapeutic termination acknowledges and underscores these investments. Ignoring or minimizing termination invalidates them.

The "termination as loss" approach is strongly influenced by psychoanalytic and psychodynamic theorizing. Given the prominence of trauma, separation, and loss in Freud's thinking, it is not surprising that his views on termination would place a heavy emphasis on grief and bereavement. According to Freud (1895), successful treatment relieves patients of their neurotic suffering and allows them to enter the world of "ordinary human unhappiness." By maintaining such a perspective on life, it is understandable that Freud's view of termination would emphasize a certain degree of pain and suffering, but Freud and his followers believe it is pain and suffering with a purpose. According to psychodynamic theorizing, the approaching loss of the therapist and the therapy resurrect repressed feelings around previously disavowed losses (Freud 1937). These past losses are believed to have left the patient vulnerable to the many neurotic and self-defeating compromises they are experiencing in the present. As a result, Freud (1937) saw separation and loss as core issues in psychological suffering, and overcoming loss as crucial in the client's march toward psychological freedom. He came to view termination as the last opportunity to liberate the client's psyche from his/her destructive attachments to the past. Strupp and Binder (1984) echo these sentiments and suggest that psychotherapy's primary objective is to help patients make peace with their personal history of bereavement. The authors state, "many patients enter psychotherapy because they failed to resolve reactions to earlier traumas and losses. Symptoms and complaints often embody a plea to return to earlier lost objects (significant others/caretakers) with whom the patient has unfinished business. The patient unconsciously wishes to reinstate the earlier relationship, perpetuate it, and/or bring it to a more satisfactory close" (Strupp & Binder 1984, 260).

From the termination as loss point of view, termination is seen as a critically important and potentially difficult period of therapy. It is characterized by challenges and opportunities. Given that termination reawakens past losses, it is anticipated to be a sad and painful time for the neurotic client and a distressing if not disorganizing time for the more characterologically disturbed client. In either case, as the end of treatment approaches, the therapist is encouraged to be prepared for potential changes in client affect and interpersonal relatedness. There can be a flattening of client emotion and a corresponding interpersonal distancing from the therapist. Conversely there may be a rise in emotional distress and an increase in conflict in the therapeutic relationship. In the wake of these client (transference) reactions to termination, there is believed to be an increased potential for impulsive acting out, return of old symptoms, development of new problems, and/or flight from therapy. Despite these challenges, the termination as loss perspective values termination and treats it as a unique and powerful opportunity for additional growth. As stated above, from this perspective, termination is seen as an opportunity for the client to revive, reexperience, and rework losses of the past within the safety of therapeutic relationship. Thus, a successful termination is an experiential reworking of the client's history of separation and defenses against loss expressed through difficulties with independence and commitment. Ultimately, termination provides the client a chance to experience an emotionally honest, nontraumatizing good-bye with significant others of the past, as well as with therapy and the therapist in the present. In addition, the termination as loss perspective acknowledges that therapists are not immune to their own emotional reactions to termination (i.e., countertransference), and these reactions can help or hinder the client's transition through this phase of treatment (Boyer & Hoffman 1993). Therapists who have not worked out their own difficulties with separation and loss may ignore the significance of termination or prematurely terminate clients from therapy in order to avoid the personal discomfort associated with losing a particular client. Other therapists may attempt to avoid such discomfort by unwittingly fueling client dependency and keeping their clients in treatment for personal rather than professional reasons. Those therapists who have dealt with their own issues involving loss can use this self-awareness to appreciate their client's emotional experiences during the ending of treatment. In sum, the termination as loss model sees the end of therapy (for better and for worse) as a time of unlimited complexity and potential for client and clinician alike. In the ideal, termination is where past losses are mourned, distortions of the therapist and therapy are addressed, and where previous gains are consolidated, internalized, made accessible to the client, and remain accessible long after treatment has ended (Malan 1979; Mann 1982; Weiner 1998).

Despite the theoretical detail associated with this perspective of termination, no explicit studies testing the ideas of the termination as loss approach have been conducted. Given the importance the termination as loss approach places on the therapeutic relationship, data supporting this approach to termination would contribute to the mounting evidence of the power of the therapeutic relationship, and the need to give it central importance when planning for and engaging in termination with clients.

A third approach to termination is what Quintana (1993) refers to as the "termination as transformation" perspective. Proponents of this approach take issue with the assumption that grief and loss are inevitable at termination. From the transformation perspective, termination is a period of therapy characterized by positive rather than negative emotion. Termination is not seen as qualitatively different from the rest of treatment. Instead, it is viewed as maintaining and building upon the positive trajectory of psychotherapy.

Termination is a time of celebrating, not grieving. From this perspective, the therapist's primary role at termination is to applaud and appreciate client risks and achievements all while nurturing optimism for the future. Termination is not a time of bereavement, but "a critical transition that can promote transformations in the therapist-client relationship and in how clients view themselves, their therapists, and their therapies" (Quintanna 1993, 431). Thus, the termination as transformation perspective views ending treatment as a period of validation of client efforts at change and growth. This validation is provided by the therapist and reflected in the therapist's recognition and support for what the client has accomplished. Building on this recognition is the therapist's increased use of self-disclosure and explication of the therapeutic process. Self-disclosure is believed to bring balance and equality to the therapy relationship. Explaining and discussing the process of therapy is believed to facilitate de-idealization of the therapist and demystification of the treatment. These therapeutic efforts are intended to solidify client successes and support client confidence about a future outside therapy.

The termination as transformation perspective has received significant empirical support. The notion that termination is a positive rather than negative experience for a majority of clients finishing treatment has held up empirically. Marx and Gelso (1987) report 65% of their study's clients held very positive feelings about termination, while only 10% were dissatisfied with their termination experience. Other studies of termination report similar findings. Clients are consistently satisfied with their experience of termination and regularly report ending therapy with a sense of pride, personal well-being and accomplishment (Quintana & Holahan 1992; Mohr 1995; Gelso & Woodhouse 2002). What is stressed by the termination as transformation perspective is that termination is not a loss but a transition—a developmental phase where the client has outgrown the need for psychotherapy (Quintana 1993). Again, providing some additional support to this perspective is the work of Wierzbicki and Pekarik (1998) and their study of psychotherapy dropout rates. Given that one third to one half of all clients drop out of treatment early, clients who actually complete therapy and make it through to a planned termination may represent a unique subset of individuals. As such, they might be expected to value termination and view it more positively than clients who terminate prematurely.

Termination at the Beginning, Middle, and End of Treatment

In our clinical work, we find the divide that separates the termination as loss and termination as transformation literatures unnecessary. Neither perspective is antithetic to the other. Both frequently dovetail in our practice. Each informs nearly every termination we conduct. As such, our approach to termination reflects our integrated approach to psychotherapy. We listen to what the client is "asking" for from their treatment and their termination and do our best to provide a flexible series of integrated interventions consistent with these "requests." By starting with a termination as transformation approach, and remaining sensitive to issues of separation and loss, we believe we can promote a more complete termination. Through this integrated approach, the overall termination experience tends to be a three-dimensional one for the client. One that is positive, affirming, and hopeful, while at the same time open to and validating of any feelings of sadness related to ending this significant experience. Thus, we have come to see the termination as transformation and termination as loss approaches as complementary and mutually informative, rather than mutually exclusive.

We will discuss termination in terms of how we end treatment in our briefer therapies. We use the word *briefer* because defining brief psychotherapy is difficult and somewhat subjective. Often brief therapy and its definition depends on who is doing the defining—the clinician, the client, the researcher, or the third-party payer. We believe brief treatment is best defined by its structure and corresponding therapeutic values, not the number of sessions. Budman and Gurman (1988, 34), wrote of their desire to see brief therapy understood and conducted "by design rather than by default." They view brief therapy by default as one where therapy is initiated without a clear therapeutic focus, and is allowed to lose momentum and subsequently fade away in an average of 8 to 10 sessions. The authors' sense of brief therapy by design recognizes that most therapies are brief and therefore need to be focused and conducted with parsimony, pragmatism, and termination in mind. We couldn't agree more. In fact, this chapter is grounded in our desire to see all therapies and their terminations occur by design rather than by default. Thus, the defining features of our approach to brief therapy avoids a specified number of sessions but focuses instead on the development of a clear therapeutic focus, an active and collaborative therapeutic relationship, the judicious use of time, an integrative approach to therapeutic interventions, and of course a planned therapeutic termination.

In the course of a brief therapy, termination should be listened for throughout the treatment and specifically raised at three different times. We introduce it near the end of the initial interview or evaluation period, near a perceived midpoint in therapy, and of course to usher in the termination phase. In a brief therapy we begin the termination phase near the end of the third to the last session. Unless loss is the focus of therapy, a central theme for the client, or at the center of the client's feelings about ending treatment, we initiate termination from a termination as transformation perspective. As hypothesized above, if a client has stayed with treatment and is committed to completing it, the odds are in favor of him/her approaching the close of treatment as a time of transformation, personal success, and accomplishment. In addition to acquiring some empirical support, the transformation approach offers the greatest number of therapeutic options at termination. It is inherently flexible and allows the therapist to respond to the clinical material shared throughout the termination phase. As mentioned above, approaching termination as a positive transition, while remaining open to subtle or obvious expressions of anxiety, anger, sadness, and/or loss, is a natural extension of the listening and sensitivity that characterizes all good therapy. It is also easier to shift from the termination as transformation approach to a termination as loss approach, rather than the other way around. Starting with and then backing away from a termination as transformation approach is relatively straightforward. It requires the clinician to be responsive to what the client is communicating and to attend to these communications mindfully. Starting with and then backing away from a termination as loss approach can be more difficult. When the therapist begins termination with the presumption of grief or is invested in finding feelings of sadness or loss, he/she risks suggesting or imposing an emotional experience that may not be present for the client. Such a tack can leave the client feeling confused, inadequate or deficient for not having a stronger or "deeper" reaction to the end of treatment. As such, it is preferable to start from a termination as transformation perspective and stay with it until proven otherwise. Thus, we begin the termination phase looking for opportunities to affirm, applaud, and empower. These terminations are often very enjoyable and very rewarding. They allow successes to be acknowledged, the future to be embraced, and both the treatment and the therapist to be *largely* demystified.

Termination at the Beginning

We begin the initial interview by inquiring about the client's presenting concern, history of the problem, and the efforts made trying to change or modify the situation. In addition, we listen for conflicts and relationship difficulties and note repetitive interpersonal scenarios. We also attend to losses and themes of loss in the client's description of his/her concerns that when present, often impact the development of the therapeutic alliance, the course of therapy, and the process of termination. At the same time, we remain open to the client's interpersonal impact on us. We do this by attending to our own thoughts, feelings, and internal reactions to the client and his/her story. Frequently, certain images, interpersonal pressures, and feelings come up as we listen. These experiences are very subjective, yet very instructive. They often give us a sense of how the client consciously and unconsciously goes about making first impressions, impacts other people, asks for help, and essentially choreographs his/her entrance into and exit from new relationships.

Near the end of the first session (which in our work is usually an hour and twenty minutes) we share our understanding of the client and his/her concerns. We attempt to convey our clinical impressions as impressions rather than facts. We also try to create a mutual sense of the problem by building upon what the client has shared and using some of his/her words and descriptions in the process. We also acknowledge the client's efforts to cope with and change the problem. We then offer a tentative focus and discuss our criteria for success and termination. A straightforward conversation about treatment goals and termination seems to facilitate, but does not a guarantee, an uncomplicated termination. For some clients there is no softening the blow. For others there is barely a need to discuss termination in this first interview.

Our discussion of treatment goals does not involve healing or cures, unchecked happiness, or soaring self-esteem. It does include substantial improvement in a few key areas of difficulty described by the client within the time constraints in which we must work. We do not wait to terminate treatment until all life's problems are solved or when the client's allotted number of sessions is up. We look to end therapy when the client is largely functioning as his/her own therapist.

That is, when he/she is demonstrating an increased ability to recognize and respond to life's difficulties with little or no input from the therapist. Thus, we value and strive for increased self-understanding, significant symptom relief, and improved relationships with family, friends and/or coworkers. We expect the client to make significant progress, yet in some ways expect this progress to be incomplete. As Weiner (1999) points out, the most important and robust achievement of psychotherapy, worked toward throughout all of therapy, is in teaching clients new and useful ways of observing and relating to themselves (i.e., their thoughts and feelings) and subsequently to significant others. By using these new capacities during and after treatment, clients can meet new and familiar challenges with a greater sense of perspective, proportion, and historicity. Stepping back, observing, and accepting (rather than judging or avoiding) aspects of one's self or one's experiences are powerful therapeutic outcomes. Engaging in self-reflection and recalling or calling on past therapeutic conversations often oppose impulses to engage in self-defeating or self-destructive behaviors. The capacities of self-acceptance, self-observation, and soothing self-talk are lifelong tools acquired in therapy, facilitated by the therapeutic relationship and consolidated by a therapeutic termination. By becoming their own therapists, we hope our clients become the center and source of their own self-confidence, courage, compassion, and calm.

After our discussion of what would constitute a successful treatment, we then ask the client about his/her sense of the length of treatment. We literally ask, "Have you thought about how long we might meet?" or "How long do you feel it might take to help you with your depression, difficulties with your boss, anger problem, and so on?" We assist the client who responds, "I don't really know," and attempt to match the length of treatment to the expectations of clients who feel they do. If the client's expectations seem unworkable, we try to understand their feelings that we should meet for "two sessions" or "two years." We then negotiate a time frame that approximates our experience working with clients with similar problems.

A small but important intervention during the initial evaluation concerns discussing with the client our intentions with respect to termination. We discuss our intentions in order to assuage any fears of being abandoned or otherwise dumped, and ultimately plant a seed that may inhibit the need to flee treatment prematurely. We tell each client that we will check in with him/her regularly to ensure we are on track and that he/she is satisfied with the direction of treatment. We share that we have found it helpful to save the last few sessions to "review our work, plan for the future and say good-bye." If a client signals that the issue of time or termination is a concern for him/her, we may make an observation about their reaction and ask a question we typically save for the termination phase of treatment. Such as, "I noticed when I mentioned ending therapy you (smiled, looked away, rolled your eyes, took a deep breath, etc.). Can you share your thoughts about ending therapy?" We may also ask, "Can you see a pattern in how you've ended or felt about ending important relationships in the past?" Depending on the client's response, we try to build on it by stating our hope to end our relationship differently, better, or just as well as they have ended previous relationships.

Termination in the Middle

After the first or second session of a planned brief therapy, where a focus has been developed, length of treatment agreed upon, and termination discussed, termination and the end of therapy tend to fade into the background. Often it will not be mentioned again until we reach an approximate midpoint of treatment. When clients make references to termination or stopping therapy prior to this time, we consider these references in the context in which they are made. First, we consider such comments directly with the client. We ask if they are thinking about stopping treatment. We also consider these comments in relation to the clinical focus. If appropriate we inquire about the client's feelings about his/her progress, satisfaction with treatment, comfort with the therapist, and/or feelings about change or overcoming his/her problems. Any or all of these issues may be behind such references to termination and are explored in terms of their potential to hinder or help move therapy ahead. Often, clients deny the significance of their allusion to termination. Just as often, something important about treatment or the treatment relationship will be revealed by these discussions.

Whether or not there have been any prior discussions of termination, we use the approximate midpoint of therapy (session six of twelve, or thirteen of twenty-five, etc.) to check in with our clients. This is the first proactive intervention dealing with termination since we began treatment. We ask the client if they share our sense that we are at the halfway point. We ask about progress made and progress still to be achieved. After listening to the client's responses, we clarify what we've heard and extend the conversation to our goals for the remainder of treatment. We discuss and renegotiate any issues that have changed since our goal setting was originally conducted. Finally, we ask for any thoughts or feelings about ending therapy in the not too distant future, and if we have not already agreed to a specified number of sessions, use this hour to state exactly how many sessions we have left.

It is also from the midpoint on that both our termination as transformation and termination as loss antennae are active. We listen for, but typically do not introduce, issues related to ending therapy. We follow up on any references to ending, such as client sentiments about "not having enough time" or "needing to move on." We also watch for changes in attitude toward treatment or us as therapists. These attitudes can be reflected in words or actions, such as arriving late for sessions, "forgetting" sessions, or rescheduling or canceling appointments. It is important to note that while we listen for these attitude shifts, we do our very best not to impose issues of separation or loss on the client. As mentioned above, a valuable contribution by Quintana (1993) and others suggests there is a danger when imposing issues of grief and loss in a therapy where such feelings do not exist or are not accessible to the client. Such an imposition can tug at and undermine the positive momentum and progress accomplished to that point in treatment. At the same time, ignoring or avoiding changes in attitude may be tacitly approving moves toward premature termination by the client.

These midpoint conversations are not perfunctory. Even among successful and satisfied clients, we have received many powerful suggestions during these conversations. We have also been surprised and even embarrassed by some of these check-in sessions. A number of clients have suggested that we needed to "get back on track," for example, back to his/her substance use, public speaking anxiety, marriage, work conflicts, or some other issue we've wandered from or neglected. These check-ins have righted many listing treatments, turned some treatments around, and simply strengthened others.

A subset of clients (more than is commonly believed) can't let go of the specter of therapy's end. If their concerns about termination were not apparent earlier in treatment, they become very clear at these midpoint conversations. We refer to them as termination-dominated clients. In more traditional psychodynamic circles they are viewed as transference-resistant clients. These are clients who are so afraid of being rejected, abandoned, or otherwise retraumatized in or by the treatment relationship, that they cannot commit to working within it. As a result they often remain emotionally distant and interpersonally disconnected. We see termination-dominated clients across diagnostic categories and clinical presentations. The termination-dominated client often lives under the shadow of termination from the first session onward. For these clients, the thought of another new relationship reawakens fears of yet another failure experience, another loss, interpersonal rejection, or humiliation. Such fears prevent these clients from opening up in therapy or getting close to the therapist. These clients resist engaging in treatment just as they resist engaging in their lives. They are bound by their fears and often transform treatment into a sterile, lifeless, evasive, highly intellectualized, and at times frustrating or painfully boring exercise. Therapist boredom is often a sign that emotion is absent in treatment and the treatment relationship. Such emotionally barren therapies need to be explored interpersonally and in very gentle ways. The odds are great that the therapist is not the first person wishing to flee from this person's stiflingly cautious approach to other people.

Sometimes these client's fears are obvious. They are apparent at the outset of treatment, if not at the introduction in the waiting room. At other times these fears are subtle and not easily uncovered. They can be hidden by a variety of sociable, thoughtful, intellectual, and/or ingratiating interpersonal presentations. These clients are skilled at disguising their lack of interpersonal involvement. They are skilled in the way many functionally illiterate adults are able to avoid, disguise, and distract from their illiteracy. When we encounter such clients, we attempt to address their fears gently but directly. It is not a great clinical feat to connect the client's fears to the presenting problem, clinical focus, the therapeutic relationship, and/or to termination. For example, for the client struggling to let go of an estranged spouse, an addiction, dead-end job, or some other self-defeating relationship, the prospect of getting involved in yet another, less familiar, less predictable relationship is daunting, and we share this awareness. The same is true of clients whose histories are colored by unpredictable, overwhelming, or otherwise traumatic losses. With these clients, we share our appreciation that opening themselves up and allowing a relationship to develop feels foolish and even reckless to them. "Why," we ask, "would he/she knowingly get involved in another relationship that might leave them so exposed and vulnerable?" At a preconscious level these clients live with an ongoing dialogue that reminds them, "Given that this relationship must inevitably end, why even begin?" Their thinking seems to go, "If the relationship goes well, either I will ruin it or it will end badly and I will be left feeling abandoned and alone." Further, they seem to believe, "If therapy fails it will be my fault and I will once again be left feeling humiliated, ashamed, and worthless." This dynamic and these core beliefs surface in many high- and low-functioning clients alike.

Yet many therapists, for reasons of time, training, or temperament roll over the top of this clinical issue. They deny or ignore the client's deep ambivalence about therapy and plow full speed ahead with their therapeutic agendas. By doing so they damage, if not doom the treatment. Not only is the treatment endangered by such an approach, if it actually falters, it will confirm the client's fears and he/she will be forced to absorb and endure yet another interpersonal failure. In order to avoid another humiliating psychological defeat, these clients often leave treatment early in order to maintain a semblance of self-control and self-cohesion.

Empathically communicating this "damned if you do, damned if you don't" dynamic to these clients is a powerful first step toward actually engaging them in treatment. Frequently they need thoughtful accommodations to the brief treatment format, including time extensions, spacing between sessions before and during the termination phase, and a flexible open-door policy to return to therapy if needed. With such accommodations in hand, the therapist can respectfully acknowledge these fears and underscore their reasonableness. In response, many of these clients can begin to sit still for the offer of a different kind of relationship with a different kind of ending.

Unlike the people in past relationships, we as therapists will not require the client to sell his/her soul in order to receive our help. He/she will not have to prop us up or dumb him/herself down to be treated respectfully. She/he will not have to trade sex or titillation for our compassion, or passivity for our concern. We will applaud their successes instead of forcing them to applaud ours. In addition, we can offer an ending that will be different from previous endings. Our ending will be mutual. It will be planned, anticipated, and gradual. As such, it does not have to leave the client hurt, helpless, confused, and alone. Our ending will not be an abandonment because it will not be abrupt, absolute, or done in anger. This is why therapy and therapeutic endings can be reasonably offered as different and less overwhelming than endings of the past. For the majority of these clients, termination will inevitably be experienced as a loss. In response, our efforts are directed toward making it less traumatic, less overwhelming, and if possible, empowering.

Termination at the End

As stated above, we approach the termination phase of psychotherapy as a period of transformation, as a time to celebrate success while remaining open to it as a period of loss for certain clients. In our work, a majority of clients experience termination as a positive transition punctuated by moments of reflection about this important ending. We introduce this final phase of treatment by asking a series of questions. Through these questions we hope to elicit client thoughts and feelings about ending therapy and therein determine how they are feeling about termination, that is, as a transformation, as a loss, or some of both. The questions we ask are both generic and client specific. They are generally loaded toward promoting client awareness of their accomplishments. There is no set of questions we always ask every client. However, we do have our favorites and we include some in our discussion below.

Several overt changes in our behavior signal the introduction of the termination phase of treatment. We tend to direct, lead, initiate, and modify (Greenberg 2002) more in the termination phase than anywhere else in treatment other than the initial interview. During the termination phase we replace a certain therapeutic reserve with a more active and open approach. This shift is not wild or dramatic, but certainly noticeable to the client. In the termination phase, which in our briefer therapies lasts approximately 2½ sessions, we shift gears and become more directive, actively encouraging and more self-disclosing than we have been previously. In keeping with the termination as transformation perspective, we are generally more content than process focused. (Though there is room for process comments that notice how confidently a client is approaching termination, dealing with a less than perfect therapy outcome, and/or preparing for the future.)

In an uncomplicated brief therapy, we typically save approximately the last 15 minutes of the third to last session to introduce the termination phase. We refer to termination as "bringing our work to an end." We do not use the word termination with clients because it has too many negative, as well as cold and mechanistic, connotations. Our request for the final portion of this session is a significant change, because by this point in therapy, sessions are primarily initiated and led by the client. In these last fifteen minutes we mention the obvious—that our work together is nearly up and we have just two sessions left. Recall that we have been gathering information in the initial interview and throughout treatment to gauge how this client may approach ending therapy. Still, we wait expectantly for the client to respond to this observation. Some clients respond directly about how they are feeling about stopping therapy. Many share their excitement and optimism. Others joke. Still others become sad, reflective, or quiet. Within the context of each client response, we remind them that they have "come a long way" from where they began. We ask them to look back on our work and bring to the next session their thoughts and feelings, any questions or concerns they may have about our work and its conclusion. Remarking that the client "has come a long way" and sometimes referring to therapy as a "journey" are definite attempts by us to frame termination as a developmental transition. Again, if we or our clients do not feel there has been much movement or progress, we do not make such statements and follow a different tack as discussed below. If there is a mutual sense of progress, we suggest that the client consider where they were when we began versus where they are now. We ask them to think about how they feel about their progress, especially progress in relation to their initial concerns, relationships with significant others, and ability to recognize, respond, even avoid stumbling blocks of the past. We also ask our clients to consider any doubts or reservations they may have about ending therapy. This process and these questions are intended to elicit client thoughts and feelings about termination while leaving room for responses related to feelings of transformation or loss.

In the second to last session we are vigilant about client concerns related to feelings of separation or loss. We take pains to ensure this vigilance does not mean foisting issues of loss onto the client, but we do not want to empathically fail a client who may feel hurt, angry, or confused by a pending termination. We listen to and expand on our clients' responses to questions posed at the end of the previous session. We also directly answer any questions or concerns they raise. Whether or not we engage in a termination as loss or transformation, ending is in large part determined by connecting what was worked on in the therapy with what the client brings to the termination phase. We may consider these responses at great length, taking much of the hour, or consider them quite briefly, depending on the client. Often we use a portion of this second to the last session tying up loose ends. We discuss concerns about potential setbacks or future relapses in terms of past successes. In discussing anticipated problems, we ask our clients specifically about challenges that may be made more difficult without therapy or the therapist. We acknowledge the loss of therapy as a complication of, but not necessarily as a barrier to, successful coping. We remind our clients that setbacks are to be expected, planned on, and prepared for. By doing so, we hope to put clients in a position to use any setbacks as opportunities to apply what they've learned in therapy and to continue the therapeutic relationship on their own. We also discuss circumstances under which a return to therapy for a "tune-up" or "booster" session is appropriate.

The backdrop of this second to last session is that while we are open to addressing a variety of topics, we begin and end this session around the issue of termination. Further, we reinforce what was learned and accomplished in treatment and how these accomplishments can be used now and after therapy has ended. A potential trouble spot in the termination phase in general is allowing for, or chasing after, seemingly new client concerns. Though ostensibly "new," very often these concerns are related to those discussed earlier in treatment or are concerns triggered by termination. As such, they are frequently amenable to the skills clients have been working on or already acquired. In addition, we sometimes wonder aloud about these new concerns and how they might be related to our ending. If the bringing up of new problems, symptoms, or worries can be gently steered back to termination, we move ahead toward ending treatment. If these concerns are substantial, even monumental, as is sometimes the case, we reconsider and renegotiate termination. If all is well in this penultimate session, clients will have been inspired to think about termination in ways they had not considered previously. Again, we like to end this session with a series of requests. We ask clients to think about and bring to our last session all of their thoughts and feelings about their therapy and our work together. We prompt them by asking them to think about what they imagine our (the therapist's) thoughts or feelings might be about their leaving. We may also ask them, as we described above, to look at patterns they may have followed when ending important relationships in the past (Bruckner-Gordon et al. 1988). We ask them to consider how ending treatment is similar or dissimilar to this earlier pattern. Very gently, we end this session by reminding them that the next session will be our last.

The last session is more tightly connected to termination. Initially, we begin with very open-ended questions about clients' thoughts and feelings about ending. Often clients use this time to address our questions from the previous session. We listen empathically, join with them, expand on their thoughts, and offer examples of what we hear them saying. We remain committed to underscoring clients' sense of accomplishment and pride. If there are openings, we ask if there were any particular moments in therapy that stand out for them. We wonder if there were any turning points in treatment—points where an interaction occurred or an issue was discussed that clicked or made a difference for them. We often ask clients about what they valued most in our work together. Similarly, we ask about what they will take with them, and why and how they anticipate this aspect of our relationship or our work will help them in the future. Again, we might ask about what changed from the start to the finish in our work and in our relationship. We like to ask if their first impression of us was correct and what about this impression was off or even wrong, and tie client responses directly to the clinical focus. Client answers to these questions almost always afford us an opportunity to point out how hard they've worked, how much they learned, and how far they have come. We also listen for and inquire about regrets, rough patches in treatment, frustrations, or disappointments. By doing so we are not borrowing trouble, but continuing to model our faith in the client and the therapeutic relationship to discuss and deal with important issues.

For certain clients, and in keeping with the termination as transformation approach, we sometimes extend the termination process by meeting every other week. In brief therapies we may do this for the last three sessions prior to ending. In longer treatments we may do this over the final three to six months of therapy. In addition, we leave the door open for nearly all of our clients to return if they feel the need. An open-door policy, alongside the gradual reduction of the frequency and subsequently the intensity of meetings, can prevent therapy from feeling as if it is ending abruptly. Such endings provide clients with opportunities to experiment outside of therapy without having the therapist in their lives on such a regular basis. These experiments and the vicissitudes of a client's newfound independence are considered and discussed from a termination as transformation perspective. Again, spacing the last three sessions over a period of weeks or months allows for experimentation and tends to dampen the intensity of ending therapy. Emotional reactions such as sadness or worry are dealt with empathically. Our focus is on acknowledging and attempting to normalize such feelings, though only if they strike us as normal. To normalize or reframe more intense or overdetermined reactions is disingenuous and potentially harmful, especially to clients who have come to expect a level of integrity and emotional honesty from their therapist.

If the therapy itself has been an intensive brief therapy (or an in-depth, long-term treatment for that matter), we frequently intermix the termination as transformation and termination as loss approaches. We almost always do so when: (1) a client has presented for treatment with a history of significant losses, (2) separation and loss have been the focus of treatment, (3) we have become a prominent figure in the client's life and/or safe, meaningful, or intimate relationships have been few and far between for the client, or (4) the client begins presenting material that calls for such a shift. This shift often involves a resurgence, rather than a mild return of previous symptoms. Such a resurgence may involve a dramatic emotional turn ranging from client anxiety and panic about ending therapy to client confusion or anger about being "forced" out of treatment.

In such instances, combining the two approaches to termination involves being positive and optimistic while at the same time considering the very real feelings of ending therapy and the therapeutic relationship. We consistently draw from previous successes and previously obtained skills acquired earlier in treatment. If helpful, we make comparisons and draw parallels between the client's past and present life circumstances and the intensity of the feelings they are experiencing as therapy draws to a close. We often find that the clients who begin to experience termination as an overwhelming loss are those who lost a parent in childhood, a way of life in childhood, or their childhood period.

In addition to exploring the similarities between old and new losses, it is equally important in these "combined" terminations that the therapist and client examine the differences between past and present losses. As noted by Quintana (1993), the end of therapy is a transition, a step taken by an adult, applauded and encouraged by a supportive and approving significant other. As therapists, we are the approving and encouraging other. We are not threatened, diminished, or damaged by our clients outgrowing and no longer needing us. In fact, we are pleased and share in the client's accomplishments. There are no issues of competition or envy between our clients and us as therapists. Therefore there is no need for guilt, fear, apology, or undoing by clients for having achieved their goals and wanting to end therapy. In this therapeutic termination, every step taken by the client is a step taken with emotional and interpersonal resources that were not present in his/her childhood, and may not have been present at the outset of treatment. The end of this relationship is not being forced upon an ill-prepared and overwhelmed child. Instead, this relationship is ending because the client no longer needs or requires it (Quintana

1993). In this synthesis of the loss and transformation models, both grieving and transformation occur, and combine to strengthen what was gained from treatment with what is possible in the rest of the client's life.

In sum, we introduce termination in the first session, at or near a perceived midpoint, and to usher in a 2½-session termination phase. Part or all of the last three sessions are used to: (1) elicit client reactions to termination, (2) review and recognize treatment gains, (3) acknowledge treatment limitations or difficult periods in the therapy or therapeutic relationship, (4) plan for future challenges, and (5) balance the therapist-client relationship through a change in our activity level, directiveness, and self-disclosure. Our clients typically experience this approach as very hopeful and encouraging. They often respond with a mix of self-reflection, appreciation, apprehension, and humor. This flexible approach allows the clinician to draw from the strengths of both the termination as transformation and loss perspectives. It is flexible enough to allow for an integrative stance or for one approach or the other to prevail given a particular client's needs at termination. It is an approach to termination very similar to one advocated by Marx and Gelso (1987). Twenty years ago, the authors broke termination down into its most basic form, a looking back, a looking ahead, and a final good-bye.

Idealization in Treatment and De-idealization at Termination

We hold the view and share it with others that idealization is an essential process in psychological development and in psychotherapy (Kohut 1984; May 1972; Baum 1900). For the developing child the need to feel safe, secure and attached to someone bigger, stronger, and wiser allows for the healthy maturation of the self, cognitively and emotionally. The idealized "object" or parent functions as both a safety net and as a source of inspiration. The protective function allows for the growing child to take risks and develop budding competencies, goals, ideals, values, and ambitions. In a similar fashion, the client entering psychotherapy often requires that his/her therapist be, in some ways, "bigger, stronger, and wiser" than he or she.

By standing in as an idealized figure, the therapist serves as a source of safety, understanding, and strength for the psychotherapy client. Such an idealized relationship allows the client to share his/her difficulties, to take risks and dare to dream of a better life without drugs, a demeaning job, crippling anxiety, or paralyzing depression.

Many therapists we've spoken to are uncomfortable with the notion of idealization. They seem uncomfortable with being or allowing themselves to be idealized by their clients. We see these clinicians as confusing therapeutic idealization with adulation, self-aggrandizement, and the subsequent exploitation of clients. On the surface such discomfort seems to be born of a very egalitarian approach to treatment. Our colleagues seem to believe that it is some how devaluing, even degrading to allow a client to think so highly of the therapist. Further, many psychoanalytically informed clinicians believe that idealization is little more than a client defense against their own hostility or aggression. From this perspective, idealization is a form of resistance and the idealizing client is viewed as simply waiting for an opportunity to knock the therapist and his/her interventions of his/her therapeutic pedestal.

To be blunt, we believe both the egalitarian and psychoanalytic perspectives are wrong. Both deny or distort the developmental and therapeutic process that promotes healthy risk taking and personal growth. These perspectives overlook the need for the client entering therapy, or the client in crisis, to temporarily merge with the cohesive self and cohering interventions of the therapist. Further, we see the egalitarian assumption as one potentially born of false therapeutic modesty and therefore as a form of countertransference. Such modesty appears tied to therapist discomfort with client expressions of admiration or perhaps therapist anxiety around client expressions of dependency. We find it ironic that therapists are trained and become adept at working with client rage, resistance, even psychosis, but squirm in the face of client approbation. We have been struck by how unavailable outstanding clinicians have become when faced with client gratitude, appreciation, and admiration. We believe it is personal and professional discomfort with expressions of client esteem that is at the heart of many therapists' concerns about idealization in therapy and are at the root of de-idealization at termination.

Transforming the therapeutic relationship at termination, often referred to as the leveling, balancing, or equalizing of the therapist-client relationship, is a very important issue. Bringing greater balance to the therapeutic relationship at termination is discussed throughout the literature and across theoretical orientations (Quintana 1993). We interpret many of these discussions of leveling at termination as advocating for de-idealization of the therapy and therapist. The idea behind leveling at termination is to empower the client and support self-efficacy upon the client's leaving therapy. From this perspective, therapists are encouraged to demystify therapy by discussing the therapeutic process and offer more revealing self-disclosures during termination (Quintana 1993). At the same time, and under the auspices of empowerment, it is also recommended that the de-idealized therapist refuse or redirect credit for most if not all of the client's successes in therapy. By doing so, it is believed that clients can accrue more self-confidence and pride in the work they have done and the progress they have made.

Though we believe in empowering clients and attempt to do so throughout treatment, we are concerned that by denying or disavowing the significance of their contributions at termination, clinicians are committing a grave error at a critical time in therapy. This approach to termination brushes up against what we consider to be a serious therapeutic mistake, that of therapist duplicity via false modesty. No therapist or client for that matter seriously believes that the client is entirely responsible for the progress of therapy. Psychotherapy is interactive. It is the therapeutic relationship that facilitates and often catalyzes client efforts at change. From our perspective, it makes no sense for the therapist, at the end of treatment, to deny the reality of this mutually influential process or for the therapist to deny or distort his/her level of involvement in the success of such work.

Thus, in theory we agree with the function and intent of de-idealization; however there is a danger of going too far. It is just a stone's throw from de-idealizing the therapist to de-idealizing and devaluing the therapy. Idealization is harmful if it leads the client to overvalue the clinician and devalue him/herself and subsequently attribute the success of treatment to the therapist. It is equally harmful for the client to deny or distort the therapist's value in his/her treatment. Therapist-client trust and collaboration is an important therapeutic outcome in and of itself. Denying the mutuality of the therapeutic endeavor is unhelpful and unnecessary. If this occurs, the client may no longer take his/her progress, accomplishments, and newly acquired skills seriously. Further, in times of distress, he/she may not turn to or draw from his/her therapy experience because this experience no longer holds the meaning and power it deserves. The process of de-idealization is a delicate one. It must be done with a purpose and balance. Therapists must be prudent when leveling the therapeutic relationship. Specifically, it is crucial that therapists acknowledge their contributions to their clients' work and accept their clients' appreciation. Therapists must acknowledge and accept their client's praise and of course temper it if it goes too far. Tempering a client's overidealization is done with a gentle reminder that it was the client who took the risks and made the strides. Thus it is the client who has ultimate ownership of the treatment's successes. Disavowing or deflecting client appreciation is hurtful and confusing. It wounds our clients, invalidates the collaborative effort, damages and diminishes treatment. Frequently such deflection by the clinician is the result of professional training or more typically, personal discomfort fielding praise or compliments (countertransference by any other name). It is not our clients' "issue" that we cannot comfortably take on or take in a compliment. By accepting a client's gratitude, we are not being narcissistic, but modeling maturity.

Striking the delicate balance between idealization and de-idealization requires therapists to be circumspect in their self-disclosures. A conservative approach to self-disclosure protects the therapeutic relationship and the gains made in therapy. At termination, it is appropriate for the therapist to reveal his/her genuinely held admiration and feelings for the client and anchor these feelings in observations and experiences acquired through the course of therapy. If the therapist has been successful in gradually turning the therapy over to the client, then a sincere and mutually respectful good-bye is more likely. In such instances, the therapist is idealized for having provided a safe and accepting relationship that was devoted solely to the client and his/her needs. This type of idealization, the type we are advocating, is not harmful or devaluing, but more akin to a deep respect and a heartfelt appreciation won through hard work, collaboration, and yes, a hint of mystery. We believe that such an approach is sustaining to many clients and their future "conversations" with their internalized therapist. Together, we believe a solid course of therapy and a touch of idealization will allow these conversations to carry more weight and stand the test of time after treatment has concluded.

Termination in Less Than Successful Therapy

Before presenting our case example, we believe it is valuable to discuss a category of terminations that can easily be overlooked—therapeutic terminations in less than successful therapies. Of our lesser therapies, a number have been rescued, some even transformed by an emotionally honest and therapeutic approach to termination. These terminations acknowledged the shortcomings of the therapy, the therapist, and/or the therapeutic relationship. While we attend to the quality of the work throughout therapy, sometimes it becomes clear near the end of treatment that things have not gone as well as we would have hoped. At these times, there is no other choice but to acknowledge to the client that, "I have a feeling that our work has not been as helpful as either of us would have liked." If there is subtle or obvious agreement, we then ask, "What could I have done differently or better?" Leaning into a lukewarm treatment during the termination phase of therapy is a personally and professionally threatening move, especially when it occurs late in the game, say in the last one or two sessions of a managed care driven treatment! Yet as humbling as these conversations have been, many have been very therapeutic. They have been particularly meaningful to certain clients, such as those who have lived with and grown to expect every form of interpersonal invalidation imaginable. The relief for these individuals came from naming the elephant in the room, which was the lack of clinical improvement or lack of interpersonal connection between themselves and the therapist. There was no attempt by the therapist to place blame or dodge responsibility in these discussions. There were no attacks, no defensiveness, no denials, and no martyrdom. Just the simple recognition, initiated by a person in power (the therapist), that he/she had not been as helpful or as close to the client as he/she wanted to be. These conversations remain productive as long as our questions are sincere, and as long as we are able to restrain our need to interpret, reframe, clarify, or otherwise defend our personal or professional self-esteem.

In response to our inquiries, there have been three distinct client responses, with a significant majority responding with kindness and grace (solid clinical outcomes in and of themselves). A first group of clients seemed handcuffed by the constraints of social etiquette or their own interpersonal fears. They tended to shoulder the blame or downplay their disappointment. With gentle nudging, many of these clients could be encouraged to explore their less than stellar therapy experience. Often, these conversations provided the client with a sense of relief as they were allowed to share rather than bear this disappointing outcome. At this point, an important intervention is the therapist's ability to point out to the client his/her clear commitment to treatment and personal growth despite such disappointing results. Such an observation is important for those clients who have been accused in the past of not wanting to get better, lacking motivation, not having a commitment to change, and so forth.

A second group of clients just flat out agree with us that their therapy fell short or was simply not useful to them. Many of these clients have offered very reasonable advice about what we could have done better. After having their advice taken seriously, a number of these clients returned to themselves and their role in their disappointing treatment. Some acknowledged that it may have been helpful to have shared their frustrations earlier in our work. A few (and we make an effort not to make these connections for our clients during these discussions) spontaneously recounted similar failures in other therapies or important relationships. Without the benefit of clinical jargon, they described their reluctance to get close and are now seeing firsthand the consequences of their need to remain at a safe distance. Some clients were able to see that yet another relationship had been avoided and possibly another meaningful experience missed. It is important to note that the therapist must not use these moments of self-reflection to turn the tables on the client or subtly blame him/her. Genuine and empathic listening is all that is needed here. As sad (and as uncomfortable) as many of these termination sessions have been, many were ultimately therapeutic and empowering. At times they led to intimate conversations and honest good-byes. For some clients they fostered emotionally charged and experientially lived insights to take with them, perhaps into their next therapy.

Finally, there has been a third group of clients who simply felt vindicated by our disclosures about their less than successful treatments. They had "known" all along that therapy wouldn't work, that we were incompetent or were simply not to be trusted. Despite these hurtful interpretations of our work and ourselves, we still held out hope— hope that for these clients our honesty, concern, and nondefensiveness so late in the game afforded them a different kind of good-bye, that our refusal to defend, deny, or blame left some doubt in their minds about our motives if not our skills.

Case Example

I (Steven Graybar) presented this case to the Society for Psychotherapy Integration many years ago. At the time I was a young clinician hopeful about the inclusive and all-encompassing possibilities of psychotherapy integration. I still believe that good psychotherapies have more in common than not. Yet significant barriers persist and in some ways these barriers are more formidable than ever before. Though it may not be readily apparent from the case example, the treatment below used an interpersonal stance with cognitive-behavioral and experiential techniques to provide an integrated psychotherapy. The treatment lasted six months and was increased from one to two sessions per week for a significant portion of the treatment. In this regard, the case example may not meet the practitioner's idea of "brief" therapy. Still, we hope the case stands as a reasonable example of our approach to termination.

"Eve" presented for treatment six months after the murder of her husband "Tom." She was in her early thirties, a bright, attractive, professional woman with two small children. She and her husband had been married for ten years. Both were successful in their careers, as well as active members of their local church and community. One afternoon, Tom was accosted by an intoxicated ex-employee whom he had fired previously. The ex-employee used a revolver to shoot him several times in the chest. Tom was pronounced dead at the scene. His assailant was arrested hours later at a local bar.

Eve sought therapy on the advice of her physician. She was confused and irritated by a return of insomnia, headaches, and the realization that she had no appetite. She reported experiencing these symptoms immediately following her husband's death, but recalled that these difficulties had stopped after only a few weeks. Eve presented for her initial interview on time and smartly dressed. She had a no-nonsense approach that indicated she was all business. Despite her hypernormal presentation, I experienced Eve as extremely brittle. She seemed to be just barely hanging on. She looked exhausted. She was emotionally constricted and task oriented, yet easily perturbed by my questions. Initial efforts to engage Eve were rebuked. She had no patience for small talk or the exchange of pleasantries. Together her impatience, frequent eye rolling, and terse responses to questions triggered such countertransference responses as checking the clock and silently wondering if a full hour and twenty-minutes was necessary for this initial meeting.

Eve ignored nearly all of my requests for specific details. Inquiries into thoughts and feelings that accompanied particular events or interactions were avoided completely or steered back to more general topics. By her own assessment, Eve was "over" her grief. She stated that she had accepted her husband's death, mourned his loss, and had been quite self-sufficient for the past five months. As such, Eve was angry about the return of her symptoms and annoyed by my suggestion that they may be related to additional feelings about Tom's death. Futhermore, Eve was committed to a biological explanation of her current state. In this first meeting she made it clear that she had little faith in "talking cures" and kept her appointment with me out of respect for her physician.

The first hint of termination concerns came as a result of Eve's powerful interpersonal impact on me in this first interview. She stirred in me competing fantasies that included a wish and a fear that she would fire me sometime prior to the end of this first meeting. My conflicted feelings toward Eve were in large part due to my divided reaction to her story and her behavior. The tragedy of her husband's death drew me in and had me feeling great empathy for Eve and her children. At the same time, Eve's treatment of me left me defensive and put off. Such an entrance left me wondering if we could ever get this therapy off the ground and if we did, would we make it through to a full termination. Further, if Eve did commit to treatment, termination would be a very significant issue given the prominent role loss would play in our work together. Finally, Eve's initial presentation made it clear that she expected little in the way of help, hope, or understanding. On the contrary, her interpersonal stance suggested that she anticipated attack, condemnation, or some other form of retraumatization.

There were a number of empathic failures in this first session that Eve would have to endure. Yet this session was typical of many that followed. Early on in treatment we would have to repair many misunderstandings on our way to a better and more successful working relationship. In our first meeting, Eve made it clear she was not a big fan of psychotherapy. She was not taken with me, or my perception of her current difficulties as being grief related. She experienced moments of silence during the session as opportunities for her to be judged. She also felt my empathic reflections were attempts to embarrass her by making her tear up or cry. I apologized for these offenses and clarified that I simply wanted to understand her better. I tried to explain that I paused to allow her and myself time to think, and that my reflections were my way of checking out my thoughts. While uncomfortable with my explanations, Eve seemed open to my apologies.

Late in the first session I actually thought we might be making progress. As a result, near the end of the interview, which had gone beyond the planned hour and twenty minutes (another indication of the role countertransference would play in this treatment), I mistakenly offered my thoughts on termination and treatment duration. As we were ending, I mentioned that our therapy might be affected, even shortened by the fact that I would be leaving in six months to take a position in another city. Eve was mortified.

While she might be willing to give me two to three weeks to work with her, and only then if I brought my "A" game, she had no intention of seeing me for six weeks let alone six months. Nor did she care "where I would be in six months." I had wrongly assumed that my apologies, explanations, and therapeutic acumen had won her over.

I assumed that in the space of 1½ hours she had come to accept me and trust my intentions. My only defense of such a move was that she appeared more relaxed and less agitated at the end of the session than at the beginning. Further, since she had suffered such a devastating loss and appeared to be in so much pain, I believed we'd be working together for a significant period of time. I was wrong. I did not, and looking back, could not have convinced her of my value, let alone the value of ongoing treatment in one meeting.

Despite my "six month" blunder, we were able to make a deal. Given that I struck Eve as generally harmless, she agreed to work with me on a week-by-week basis with the requirement that she "get something" from each session. If she found something helpful in one session, she would return for the next. While Eve did not mention what she "got" from our first session, I suspect that seeing me as mostly benign and malleable was significant, as was her sense that it was she and not I who was in control of treatment and its termination.

This therapy took many interesting turns. Eve's deep fears, extreme beliefs, and ultimate need to be in control were at times very challenging. Predictably, themes of helplessness, hopelessness, anger, and sadness were prominent throughout our time together. Eve held deep convictions that she was needy, and therefore unworthy and flawed. As a result, many transference tests, which are basically client tests of the therapist's commitment and understanding, left me feeling helpless, out of control, frustrated, and doubting myself. At times I labored under Eve's scrutiny, suspicion, and explicit criticism. For the first several sessions, I never knew how she felt about our work, about me, or whether or not she would return for her next appointment. Scheduling of a next appointment was always left until the very end of the current session. Leaving and not coming back was ever present and very symbolic, but an interpretation I did not share until much later in treatment. Passing these transference tests was essential. Eve "did to me" what she experienced significant others and life as having done to her. As a result I, like her, often felt anxious, confused, frustrated, of little value, and regularly out of control in the therapy. I frequently felt judged, misunderstood, and taken for granted, just as Eve had felt growing up and since her husband's death. What became clear was that all her life Eve was admired for her hard work and

independence. Growing up, Eve frequently found herself parenti-
fied, taking on many adult responsibilities and often feeling "in over
her head." Eve accepted these responsibilities and often succeeded in
dealing with them. However, this dutiful approach to life often left
her feeling alone, overmatched, misunderstood and resentful. Thus,
despite receiving extensive support from family, friends, and the community following Tom's death, Eve still felt angry and alone. Over the
course of therapy, Eve came to see that her personal strength (and her
corresponding suppression of her needs and feelings) allowed others
to wrongly assume that she was fine. It facilitated their misperceiving
her needs and her feeling taken for granted.

As Eve allowed our relationship to grow, she took more risks and
her treatment expanded. It expanded beyond her grief and included
some issues from her childhood that had been triggered by Tom's
murder. We explored these issues in detail and in relation to Tom's
death. In addition, one of Eve's greatest fears, a common fear among
bereaved and traumatized clients, was that if she felt her loss in full,
she would begin crying and never stop, that she would essentially
"go crazy." Going crazy was not an option for a number of reasons,
not the least of which was Eve's maternal responsibilities. When her
tears finally came, they were powerful and gut wrenching. This was a
woman who played by the rules, a "good" person by any measure. She
had a successful career, a solid marriage, a happy family, and a faith in
God, all of which were pointlessly shattered in a matter of seconds.

As the intensity of her grieving began, Eve's subtle and not so subtle threats to end treatment stopped. Further, the need to control the
therapy and the therapeutic relationship softened but did not totally
disappear. As she grieved, Eve seemed to experience a sense of timelessness about her therapy. Given my awareness of our limited time,
I reacted to Eve's sense of timelessness with significant anxiety. Though
it was not easy, it was important for me to manage this anxiety and
allow Eve a respite from the pressures of time while she was engaged
in this intensive period of her therapy.

With Eve's grief came additional feelings of being out of control. In
response we agreed to increase our meetings from once to twice per
week. This therapeutic adjustment was another passed transference
test; it refuted Eve's long-standing fear that I would be disgusted and

compelled to reject her if I saw the depth of her emotions, particularly the depth of her fear, anger, and outrage. This too is a common fear among traumatized individuals, but in Eve's case it was compounded both by family of origin issues of the past and interpersonal fears being enacted in the present. She reported that while growing up, her family's stance toward "dark" emotions was that they should not be experienced let alone expressed. Thus, the expression of intense and negative feelings was forbidden in the past, and left her feeling extremely vulnerable in the present. Eve believed she had to protect others from her feelings, and that expressing such feelings would expose her as bad or defective. As our work and relationship deepened, her vulnerability grew. She feared becoming too dependent and also feared that these "negative" feelings would somehow harm me, diminish my feelings for her, and/or end our work together.

My role during this period was to hold steady and remain empathically present. I was serving as what Alice Miller (1980) has eloquently termed, an enlightened witness for Eve. The extent of my "enlightenment" was anchored in my understanding of grief, and my faith in the healing potential of both empathic listening and a therapeutic relationship. While I was never appalled or disgusted, bearing witness to such pain was not easy.

There were times when Eve's pain was so great that I nearly felt overwhelmed myself. At a very personal level, this therapy shook my naïve, but nonetheless enduring conviction, that the world was basically a safe place. Eve's tragedy threatened my own sense of physical safety and the safety of my loved ones. Though fleeting, these thoughts left me feeling rather pathetic, selfish, and ashamed. Some good consultation helped me see the parallels between what I was experiencing and what Eve was experiencing. She too felt selfish and pathetic for worrying about herself and her future given her husband's fate.

I have come to view my reactions to Eve and her tragedy as a not uncommon experience when treating survivors of trauma. These reactions are what Kahn (2001) refers to as objective countertransference. Objective countertransference includes internal reactions experienced by nearly anyone exposed to such a tragic story and terrible suffering. Of course, many of my reactions were quite neurotic, uniquely mine, and based in what Kahn refers to as subjective countertransference.

That is, countertransference born of our own histories, fears, blind spots and imperfections. It is the therapist's responsibility to understand his/her reactions to a client's material and use these reactions to more thoroughly understand the client's experience. My countertransference, that is, my own emotional reactions to Eve's pain, allowed me to appreciate how difficult it was for Eve to maintain positive feelings about herself, the world, and God. This was especially difficult given her investment in being good, in control, not having certain feelings on the inside, and showing no signs of weakness on the outside.

As her grieving slowly subsided, Eve was able to acknowledge how much she relied on me and appreciated therapy. The passing of Eve's most intense grief came after three months of work, leaving just six weeks to bring therapy to an end. Recall that it took over a month for her to agree to discuss her deceased husband. Though we had passed the midpoint of therapy, the point at which termination is reintroduced, I felt it would have been disruptive to bring up termination any sooner. When I finally did mention termination, I was surprised by Eve's reaction, actually by her lack of a reaction. She seemed unaffected by the thought of ending soon. After mentioning ending therapy, Eve seemed fairly neutral about stopping. For the next two or three visits she was generally optimistic about her future and spontaneously brought up Tom and life without him. Eve was able to acknowledge that she had made significant gains and significant changes in her life since Tom's death. Her approach to treatment and termination were very positive. To be honest, I was surprised and somewhat hurt (more countertransference and more information). Despite my confusion, I followed Eve's lead and stayed with her in a termination as transformation approach. I applauded Eve as she recounted her efforts and significant successes. Each of these sessions seemed to pass easily and quickly. Eve sounded good and appeared to be ready to leave therapy in excellent shape. After getting over my initial confusion and disappointment, I was relieved and very happy for Eve and her family.

Eve presented for her second to last session with an eerily familiar coolness. She had no reason for her change in mood or reserve toward me. She explained her distance by suggesting that she was "tired." In response to Eve's defense of her return to supernormal behavior (i.e., no thoughts or feelings for us to discuss, issues or concerns to consider), I recall sitting silently and looking back at her expectantly. Eve had long since convinced me that she could tolerate and utilize such an intervention. In response to my silence, Eve was able to thoughtfully share her feelings about ending therapy. She spoke of her sadness about losing her "special place each week." She also shared some frustration about not being "completely cured." As she spoke, we were also able to discuss that ending this treatment and our relationship, like so many things in life, felt out of her control. She left this session quietly.

In our last session, Eve confessed that she had some fears about "making it, on her own." We examined this fear and she quickly realized that she would not be alone. She had plenty of support and through therapy she had learned how to access genuine support from others in her life. Yet I did not want to invalidate the other half of Eve's sentiments. I suggested that our relationship was different from others in her life, and that she would be without me and her "special place." (My comfort with some idealization allowed me to avoid an invalidating response to her strong feelings about me and her therapy.) I asked her what she would miss most. She shared a number of things that she would miss about me, about our work, and about our time together. After a good deal of sharing and yes, some additional idealizing, Eve made a joke about all this going to my head when she "had done all the work." We both laughed because we each knew the truth of what she was saying. While Eve did not do all the work, she did most of it and all of the heavy lifting. We also reviewed how far our relationship had come, from the many struggles and open conflicts to the respect and affection we currently felt toward one another.

In this last session Eve was thoughtful, articulate, and cautiously optimistic. She reiterated that in the last few weeks she was beginning to wonder whether or not she could make it without her therapy. She feared that ending therapy might initiate an intense downward spiral similar to the one she experienced after her husband's death, and six months later when she presented for treatment. I empathized with, rather than refuted, these fears. As often happens after having one's fears validated, Eve went on to refute them herself.

Regardless of my leaving the area, Eve knew it was time for her to stop therapy. She had made many gains and felt she needed to spread her wings. She was different now. She felt stronger, wiser, and healthier. She felt she had some tools, resources, and self-awareness that she did not have six months earlier. She and her children had found comfort in the solid routine she had established for them, one that included school, church, family, and friends. In addition, I offered that it was she, not me, who had developed such a solid support system. It was she who had patiently cultivated professional opportunities until one came along that offered a schedule and a salary that fit her needs. Eve concluded that while still sad, she was not overwhelmed. We ended tearfully but not sadly. We both knew that Eve was ready to end treatment and possessed the skills and abilities to care for herself and her family. She was capable of seeking support as well as additional psychotherapy if she needed it.

Though conducted a number of years ago, this case is an example of a blended termination. While I had my own biases and preconceptions toward termination as loss, I believe I was flexible enough not to impose such a bias on Eve. Her termination, like the rest of her therapy, would be done at her pace and on her terms. Initially, Eve seemed destined to experience her termination as a transformation only. She had come a long way. She had grown a great deal, and had outgrown her need for continued treatment. Despite my suspicions (and hurt feelings), we focused on her many accomplishments, which solidified her optimism for the future. As her actual termination date approached, however, Eve's manner changed and signaled that she had something more on her mind.

Eve began to experience her termination as less of a transition and more as a loss. I believe that to have stayed the course and ignored this change in behavior would have been a significant mistake. As we began to examine Eve's sense of loss, she openly discussed her feelings about losing the safety and sanctity of her therapy. It was a special place for Eve, a place where she could experience and express forbidden thoughts and feelings. It allowed her to relinquish her defensiveness, trust another human being, share her deepest feelings, and move through Worden's (1985) stages of grief in earnest. Eve had accepted the reality of Tom's death, felt the full impact of his loss, made the needed adjustments to life without him, and had begun to consider the possibility of other intimate relationships. Similarly, she grieved the loss of her therapy and took steps to obtain support and close personal contact from others outside treatment. Finally, while termination was mentioned after the perceived midpoint of therapy, given the nature and focus of Eve's treatment, more time was allowed for termination to occur, six sessions over six weeks. If we had the time, I would have preferred to taper the end of this therapy to every other week, but looking back, this might have been an unnecessary adjustment.

Countertransference was a prominent issue in this therapy, and is a potentially powerful factor in many terminations. If we conceptually separate countertransference from Freudian meta-psychology, it can be appreciated as the range of emotional reactions a therapist has to a client and a client's clinical material. Over the course of therapy, a relationship develops for two people, not just one. The therapist develops a level of attachment to the client and the therapy, just as the client becomes attached to the therapist and the treatment process. The emotional attachment a therapist develops need not be "bad," unethical, neurotic, or otherwise inappropriate. In fact, we suspect that a positive emotional attachment to a client is a healthy prerequisite for most good therapy.

It goes without saying that it is useful, if not essential, for a therapist to care about his/her clients and look forward to their work together. Countertransference is merely a construct we use to organize and understand our reactions to the attachment process, to our clients, their difficulties, and the end of therapy.

As briefly mentioned above, countertransference comes in at least two forms. Kahn (2002) refers to one source of countertransference as objective and useful, the other as subjective and ultimately obstructive. Useful countertransference is often grounded in empathy and allows the therapist to resonate to his/her clients' thoughts, feelings, and experiences. Useful countertransference allows the therapist to use his/her emotional reactions to understand a client more clearly and intervene with him/her more effectively. For instance, my feelings of being devalued, judged, and controlled by Eve early in treatment were very instructive. Had I simply reacted to these pressures and defensively disabused Eve of her misperceptions of me and the practice of psychotherapy, I would have confirmed her worst fears and lost her as a client. Instead, I weighed my own feelings of hurt and annoyance and used them to guide my understanding of, and approach to, Eve and her problems entering treatment. Given her criticisms of me and my chosen profession, I assumed that Eve expected me to criticize, judge, and devalue her. I avoided this mistake by not criticizing or correcting her. Given her controlling stance toward me, I assumed she felt out of control and expected me to control her and colonize her emotional life perhaps like others had in the past. In response, I did my best to allow her as much room as she needed to feel comfortable. For example, I did not insist that grief be the focus of our work together. I did not confront her need to avoid overly emotional topics. I did not require a commitment to ongoing therapy. I apologized for my missteps and other transgressions. I changed my therapeutic approach dramatically in that I often led where I was accustomed to following, and followed where I would have been more comfortable leading. I essentially let Eve run the show for the first several weeks of therapy. All of these interventions were culled from my emotional reactions to Eve and my empathy for what I imagined she felt and required. Without this appreciation of countertransference and transference tests, I doubt I would have been so willing to make these accommodations. Yet had I not allowed Eve this latitude, I believe I would have lost her very early in treatment.

On the potentially obstructive side was my reaction of hurt and disappointment when Eve responded so cavalierly to my mention of termination. Had I acted on these feelings I may have been tempted to embarrass or shame Eve (all in a very professional way of course). Instead, I reflected on my feelings, shared them with a trusted colleague, and came to understand them as a function of the therapeutic relationship and my own countertransference. While approaching the end of such a demanding treatment, I was unconsciously seeking validation for my efforts. At the same time, Eve was defending against the pain of ending this work by invalidating it and denying its significance to her.

Transforming obstructive countertransference into useful countertransference is often a function of time, self-reflection, patience, and good consultation. Allowing disturbing feelings to settle, sifting through them, sorting out one's own emotional history from the client's, and looking deeply into the therapeutic relationship/transference are all very useful. When these feelings are particularly sharp or unsettling, seeking consultation is invaluable. Sharing one's emotional reactions to a client with a colleague can bring clarity to confusing moments in treatment and decrease the likelihood of an impulsive intervention such as an abrupt or hurtful comment. In this particular instance, a colleague provided the validation I was seeking for my hard work, thus relieving my client of the responsibility of having to take care of me in this manner. Further, once my feelings were untangled from Eve's, I could see more clearly how she was returning to old behaviors—behaviors she typically used to avoid difficult feelings, and distance herself from others while repeating a painfully familiar pattern where she would feel unheard and unseen, unappreciated, and in many ways unknown to others in her life.

Closing Thoughts

Termination, like therapy in general, can and should be a collaborative process that emphasizes and promotes client self-efficacy. Ultimately, the decision to end therapy rests with the client. Ideally, it is a mutual decision that is introduced early in treatment by the therapist, tracked by him or her, and planned for long before discussions of termination begin. While we emphasize termination as a time of transformation (Quintana 1993), and work from this perspective to review previous successes and chart a positive course for the future, we remain open to termination as a time of separation and loss as well. To bring a successful treatment to an end, termination must be used to applaud and ultimately empower, to bring greater balance to the therapeutic relationship, to prepare the client for disappointments and setbacks and set a hopeful course for life after therapy. Termination is not only a time to review gains in treatment but also to consider the limits of what has been accomplished. In addition, if there have been difficult sessions, issues, or periods of therapy, reviewing these challenging times with an eye toward underscoring client mastery is often very helpful. If separation and loss have been significant themes in treatment or in the life of the client, special attention to a reemergence of these issues at termination is essential.

Clients whose clinical concerns or personality structures leave them vulnerable to anxiety or dysphoria during transitions must be handled with special sensitivity and care at termination. Such sensitivity might include bringing up termination early and often in treatment, tapering sessions over a greater period of time and taking on a more active and directive stance in treatment overall. Further, greater therapist activity level and use of therapeutic self-disclosures over a greater period of time can decrease the intensity of the therapeutic relationship and consequently decrease painful feelings at termination for these clients. Finally, emphasizing therapy as an ongoing process and opportunity to be accessed as needed and deemphasizing termination as an absolute endpoint (Greenberg 2002) are also helpful to these clients.

It is imperative that therapists be mindful of the numerous issues inherent in the ending of therapy and the therapeutic relationship. We have highlighted several of these issues throughout this chapter including (1) approaching termination as a period of transformation, loss, or a blend of both, (2) the delicate balance involved in the de-idealization of the therapist, (3) an appreciation of the termination-dominated client, and (4) attending to countertransference during termination. Accounting for these issues will help provide clients with a meaningful ending to treatment, honor the risks they have taken, and applaud the gains they have made.

Suggested Readings

Anchin, J. C., & Kiesler, D. J. (1982). *Handbook of interpersonal psychotherapy.* New York: Pergamon Press.

Kahn, M. (1997). *Between therapist and client: The new relationship.* New York: W.H. Freeman.

Mann, J. (1986). The core of time-limited psychotherapy: Time and the central issue. In S. H. Budman (Ed.), *Forms of brief therapy* (2nd ed.; pp. 48–55). New York: Guilford Press.

Strupp, H. H., & Binder, J. L. (1984). *Psychotherapy in a new key: A guide to time-limited psychotherapy.* New York: Basic Books.

Weiner, I. B. (1998). *Principles of psychotherapy.* New York: John Wiley & Sons.

References

Boyer, S. P., & Hoffman, M. A. (1993). Counselor affective reactions to termination: Impact of counselor loss history and perceived client sensitivity to loss. *Journal of Counseling Psychology, 40,* 271–278.

Bruckner-Gordon, F., Kuerer-Gang, B., & Urbach-Wallman, G. (1988). *Making therapy work.* New York: Harper & Row.

Budman, S. H., & Gurman, A. S. (1988). *Theory and practice of brief therapy.* New York: Guilford Press.

Fox, E. F., Nelson, M. A., & Bolan, W. M. (1969). The termination process. A neglected dimension in social work. *Social Work, 14,* 53–63.

Freud, S. (1900). *The interpretation of dreams.* London: Hogarth Press.

Freud, S. (1937). *Analysis terminable and interminable.* London: Hogarth Press.

Gelso, C. J., & Woodhouse, S. S. (2002). The termination of psychotherapy: What research tells us about the process of ending treatment. In G. S. Tyron (Ed.), *Counseling based on process research: Applying what we know* (pp. 344–369). Boston: Allyn & Bacon.

Greenberg, L. S. (2002). Termination of experiential therapy. *Journal of Psychotherapy Integration, 12,* 358–363.

Hiat, H. (1965). The problem of termination of psychotherapy. *American Journal of Psychotherapy, 19,* 607–615.

Holden, M. (1983). The use of negative transference in a follow-up session: Its impact on short-term psychotherapy. Dissertation, University of California, Berkeley, Wright Institute. In T. A. Kupers (Ed.), *Ending Therapy.* New York: New York University Press.

Kahn, M. (1997). *Between therapist and client: The new relationship.* New York: W.H. Freeman.

Malan, D. H. (1992). *Individual psychotherapy and the science of psychodynamics.* Oxford, UK: Butterworth-Heinmann.

Mann, J. (1986). The core of time-limited psychotherapy: Time and the central issue. In S. H. Budman (Ed.), *Forms of brief therapy* (2nd ed.; pp. 25–44). New York: Guilford Press.

Martinez, A. C. (1982). The termination of counseling and psychotherapy: A review and critique. Presented at the American Psychological Association 90th Annual Convention; August 23–27, 1982; Washington, DC.

Marx, J. A., & Gelso, C. J. (1987). Termination of individual counseling in a university center. *Journal of Counseling Psychology, 34,* 30–39.

Miller, A. (1981). *The drama of the gifted child.* New York: Basic Books.

Mohr, D. C. (1995). Negative outcome in psychotherapy: A critical review. *Clinical Science: Science and Practice, 2,* 1–27.

Quintana, S. M., & Holohan, W. (1992). Termination in short-term counseling: Comparison of successful and unsuccessful cases. *Journal of Counseling Psychology, 39,* 299–305.

Safran, J. D., & Muran, J. C. (1996). The resolution of ruptures in the therapeutic alliance. *Journal of Consulting and Clinical Psychology, 64,* 447–458.

Strupp, H. H., & Binder, J. L. (1984). *Psychotherapy in a new key: A guide to time-limited psychotherapy*. New York: Basic Books.

Sullivan, H. D. (1953). *The interpersonal theory of psychiatry*. New York: W.W. Norton.

Wierzbicki, M., & Pekarik, G. (1993). A meta-analysis of psychotherapy dropout. *Professional Psychology: Research and Practice, 24*, 190–195.

Worden, W. J. (1982). *Grief counseling and grief therapy*. New York: Springer Publishing.

Yalom, I. D. (2002). *The gift of therapy*. New York: Harper Collins Publisher.

5

INTERRUPTION REPLACES TERMINATION IN FOCUSED, INTERMITTENT PSYCHOTHERAPY THROUGHOUT THE LIFECYCLE

NICHOLAS A. CUMMINGS

Much has been written regarding the difficulties surrounding termination, not the least of which is the frequent return of the presenting symptoms that initially brought the patient to psychotherapy. Faced with termination and fearing the consequences of severing a dependency on the psychotherapist, the patient unconsciously responds with a resurgence of symptoms that had disappeared during the course of treatment. Another consequence not often discussed is the implication that the patient has overcome all difficulties, and it would be a betrayal of the therapeutic process to seek treatment again at some future time. Thus, there is a reluctance to resume treatment, and if necessity drives the patient, often a new therapist is sought to avoid the embarrassment. Treatment may be unnecessarily prolonged in one instance, and needed treatment may be avoided in the second. In the model discussed in this chapter, the patient is apprised that treatment is being interrupted, not terminated, and is encouraged to contact the psychotherapist if the vicissitudes of one or more of the future stages of life require assistance (Cummings 2001).

A model in which psychotherapy is seen as a continuous process, even between intermittent episodes of treatment, renders termination, with all its attendant problems, unnecessary. Pioneered by me and my colleagues a half century ago, hundreds of psychotherapists have received hands-on training in focused, intermittent psychotherapy throughout the lifecycle, and much has been written on the subject (see, for example, Bloom 1991; Cummings, 1990, 1991; Cummings & Cummings, 2000; Cummings & Sayama, 1995; Cummings & VandenBos, 1979). It is not within the scope of this chapter to describe the entire model; only those aspects that pertain to the substitution of interruption for termination are addressed. This substitution would seem to be a simple procedure until one confronts all the complexities involved. Performed correctly, psychotherapy becomes a continuous process throughout one's life. It is resumed whenever problems in life's cycle make it necessary, while progress continues within the patient between episodes of treatment. For some patients the initial episode of treatment is sufficient; others return once, twice, or more; while still others may be seen for a session or two once every two or three years for the rest of their lives. In any case, the problems of termination are eliminated because the patient sees therapy to be open and available even if she or he never returns.

The problems of termination are only slightly ameliorated by the therapist's exhortation that the patient is free to resume treatment any time in the future. Termination by definition refers to a discrete episode of treatment that has a beginning and end; thus, resuming treatment means to the patient that she is beginning a second episode and that something was missed the first time around. Furthermore, she has not been given silent ways of continuing the therapy without the psychotherapist, a procedure that clearly defines psychotherapy as a continuous process that may reinvolve the psychotherapist at any time the self-process bogs down. Thus, the strength of the treatment experience carries over and continues during periods of interruption, whether they are six months or twenty years. The patient continues the therapy, talking to the therapist and finding the answers in his or her head whenever difficulties arise. When the answers are not forthcoming, the patient knows it is time to make a return appointment. Psychotherapists are mobile and over a life span one's therapist may have moved or retired. Experience demonstrates that a patient easily relates to a new psychotherapist as long as the successor psychotherapist is skilled in this model.

It is usual, but nonetheless startling, to see a patient after several years who begins talking as if the last session was two weeks ago. This attests to the continuous nature of the treatment, and reflects a different type of transference than that fostered in traditional psychotherapy. The patient has learned to be her own therapist, and one who knows when she needs the psychotherapist. Return appointments, no matter how many months or years may intervene, are usually comprised of one to three sessions, demonstrating a learned self-reliance that only occasionally needs tweaking.

To substitute interruption for termination successfully, the strength of the transference must be diminished, while the intensity of the therapy is increased. This seems contradictory inasmuch as the intensity of the psychotherapy often parallels the depth of the transference. However, the patient's attachment and dependency are variables that can complicate and delay termination. It was Freud (1933) who first postulated that a neurosis is treated by substituting a "transference neurosis" (i.e., attachment and dependency in the treatment situation). The problem, then, was to work through and resolve the transference neurosis—a process that was seen as protracted, making psychotherapy a long-term undertaking not because of the nature of the presenting symptoms, but because of the necessary way of addressing them. Stated in another way, the cure was worse than the disease.

Depending upon the type of psychotherapy, the approach of the psychotherapist, and the personality of the patient, all psychotherapy more or less fosters dependency. In our model, the fear of losing the therapist is eliminated by a prescription to return to psychotherapy as needed. In addition, the patient has learned techniques that continue the therapeutic process. As in the intervening week between sessions when the patient is assigned homework and has been taught to talk to the therapist in her head, after interruption the patient continues this procedure, assigning her own homework and carrying on an imaginary conversation with the therapist. Surprisingly, most of the time answers or solutions to her problems will be forthcoming. When an answer is not forthcoming, she is encouraged to resume sessions with the psychotherapist.

The concept of medical necessity is irrelevant in this model, because years of experience and research have shown that focused, intermittent psychotherapy administered before there is absolute necessity prevents later serious episodes that would require much more intensive treatment (Cummings & Cummings 2000). Thus, early intervention is not only therapeutically desirable, sparing the patient prolonged and even increased distress, but it is also cost-effective in that it prevents the need for more costly interventions at a future time. In summary, the model eliminates unnecessary sessions prompted by the threat of termination by creating a therapeutic process that continues in the absence of the psychotherapist. Returning to see the psychotherapist is only an aspect of this continuous process. Furthermore, returns to treatment are brief and are usually one to three sessions, resulting in a life span of therapy that is most often less in session totals than the usual traditional therapy followed by termination.

There are clinical strategies for implanting continuous psychotherapy throughout the lifecycle, each of which is part of a well-defined series of three steps.

Step 1: Diminishing the Transference Through a Therapeutic Partnership

The key to diminishing the transference is the establishing of a true partnership between the therapist and the patient, and then unrelentingly implementing it despite any dependency on the part of the patient. That this is accomplished for the benefit of the patient is reflected in the psychotherapist's empathy, understanding, and patience in the process, all of which do not detract from its determination. The cornerstones of this partnership are the therapeutic contract, homework, and fostering resiliency.

The Therapeutic Contract

At the appropriate time in the first session the psychotherapist presents the therapeutic contract, which makes clear that the therapy is primarily the responsibility of the patient, whereas the therapist acts as a catalyst. The language is varied in accordance with the patient's socioeconomic status and level of education, but the message is always the same. The appropriate time is after the psychotherapist has skillfully and rapidly fostered bonding and other aspects of the therapeutic alliance. In its succinct form, the therapeutic contract states the following:

> I shall never abandon you as long as you need me, and I shall never ask you to do something until you are ready. In return for this, I ask you to join me in a partnership to make me obsolete as soon as possible.

This contract is not presented in a perfunctory manner; rather, it is discussed until the patient fully understands and accepts its impact. It is made clear that although the patient will not be asked to do something for which he is not ready, it is made clear that once patient and therapist determine readiness, the patient is required to move forward. This is the essence of the partnership, and differs markedly from the model in which the therapist more or less passively waits for the patient to initiate the next step comfortably.

Homework

It is the homework, more than anything else, that results in the patient's realization that this is, indeed, a partnership. Homework is assigned after the first session and every session thereafter, and is enforced in a variety of ways. When the patient has agreed to the therapeutic contract and the homework is in keeping with the three characteristics described in the next paragraph, enforcing the homework is not an issue. In the rare instances when the homework is not completed, the session first addresses the reasons and their implications, with a revisit to the therapeutic contract.

There is no cookbook from which homework is arbitrarily assigned. Rather, the homework is tailored to be meaningful to each patient's goals and therapeutic contract, and three requisites must be fulfilled in each and every homework assignment: (1) the patient must be capable of doing it, but (2) it must be difficult enough so that the patient achieves a sense of accomplishment, and (3) it represents the next step in this patient's goal in therapy. (For a more comprehensive discussion of homework, see chapter 12.)

Learning Resiliency

Promoting resiliency in the patient is a certain way to diminish the transference, while at the same time increasing appreciation of the therapist as catalyst rather than a person upon whom to rely unduly. It must be emphasized that in this role, all the characteristics of compassion and understanding that are the hallmarks of a good psychotherapist are present, but this is coupled with decisiveness in insisting the patient proceed to the next step in spite of fears and objections. The focused psychotherapist must possess a set of qualities that encompasses an understanding of when the patient is ready as well as the reasons for the patient's reluctance, and then have the ability to inspire the patient to move forward. Misjudging a patient's readiness is a sign the therapist lacks empathy and understanding, and excusing a patient when the optimum time to move forward has come is a sign that the therapist lacks skill as well.

Self-esteem must be achieved; it cannot be handed to the patient by well-intentioned but overblown praise. This may make the patient feel good, but only temporarily. As patients overcome their learned helplessness (Seligman 1975) and achieve self-efficacy (Bandura 1977), a therapeutic excitement develops that facilitates success in the next discrete therapeutic task. Patients discover their resiliency and enjoy exercising and enhancing it. Much of the excitement has to do with the mutual appreciation that this was accomplished by the patient, while the therapist acted as catalyst. The confidence that ensues not only adds to the vitality of the therapeutic experience, it also creates the platform upon which the patient will continue the therapy alone after interruption of the formal sessions. In this way therapy is continuous, even though the presence of the therapist is intermittent throughout the life span.

Step 2: Raising the Intensity of the Treatment Experience

A strong transference can enhance therapy, but it can also prolong it because the attachment to the therapist must be resolved before the patient has the courage to terminate. On the other hand, diminishing the transference to avoid protracted treatment without increasing the intensity of the therapeutic experience can result in a lowering of expectation and lack of progress. Enforcing the therapeutic contract and the homework raises the intensity of the therapy, as will promoting the excitement that comes with newfound resiliency. Increasing the intensity of therapy must compensate for the diminished transference to the degree that it not only accelerates treatment, but it is also sufficient to carry the individual through a number of hiatuses in therapy throughout the life span. The following additional techniques can only be briefly described, and the reader is referred to textbooks for a fuller exposition of the methodology (Cummings & Cummings 2000; Cummings & Sayama 1995).

The First Session Must Be Therapeutic

By making the first session therapeutic, the therapist is hitting the ground running. It enables the patient to see that help is not only possible, but probable. The concept that the first session must be devoted solely to taking a history or getting acquainted is outmoded, and often results in the patient feeling so overwhelmed he does not return for the second session. History taking is important, but the therapist can always glean and then respond to something useful during the first session so that the patient experiences a therapeutic benefit. For example, after the patient concludes a litany of what, to her, is a monumental problem, the therapist can recall that he saw a woman with a similar problem several years ago and the outcome was very positive. By making certain the demographics of the previous patient fit the current one, the troubled patient not only identifies with her, but also immediately experiences hope, the therapeutic alliance is strengthened, and the intensity of the therapy is increased. Such a patient will eagerly return for the second session.

Perform an Operational Diagnosis

The reason most often proffered by the patient regarding why he is seeking therapy is seldom, if ever, the actual one. The operational diagnosis asks one thing: Why is the patient here today instead of last month, last year, or next year? If the patient responds that he is an alcoholic, this is not the real reason, because he has been an alcoholic for more than ten years. What is it about his alcoholism that brings him in today instead of ten years ago? The real reason might be that he has just received his third DUI (driving under the influence) arrest and is facing six months in jail. Skillfully discerning the operational diagnosis, along with the implicit contract that accompanies it, remarkably intensifies psychotherapy.

Elicit the Implicit Contract

Although the operational diagnosis tells the therapist why the patient is there, the implicit contract reveals what the patient actually wants out of psychotherapy. In the example of the alcoholic with his third DUI arrest, this might be to enlist the therapist as an ally toward getting probation instead of jail time. All the while, however, the patient is offering an explicit (rather than implicit) contract—ostensibly that he wants help in quitting drinking. Skillfully bringing out into the open the implicit contract will cut through the resistance and manipulation; clarify the therapist's role as a healer, not an advocate, and solidify the therapeutic goal as abstinence.

Performing the operational diagnosis and eliciting the implicit contract will markedly intensify the therapeutic process. Misjudging either or both will equally diminish the intensity. Patients want to impress the therapist and will say the right things or whatever they believe the therapist wants or needs to hear. Missing the real reason why the patient is there, or inadvertently accepting the explicit rather than the implicit contract, results in the therapist having feet of clay. The intensity of the therapy is lowered accordingly. Experience has shown that therapists are prone to accept the explicit contract and miss the implicit contract along with the operational diagnosis. A certainty that the implicit contract has been elicited often results in the later discovery that it was, in actuality, the explicit contract. (For further discussion and more examples see chapter 9.)

Do Something Novel in the First Session

In this "era of psychology," patients are seldom completely naive about psychotherapy. They come to the first session with certain expectations derived from watching movies or television, their reading, friends who have been in treatment, or from their own previous psychotherapy. Patients who have seen a number of psychotherapists with only a modicum of success are no longer a rare phenomenon, especially among those with personality disorders. Thus, the first session has been preceded by a number of rehearsals within the patient's mind, all of which are easily discernible to the skilled and experienced therapist based on how the patient presents himself. Doing something therapeutic that is both unexpected and novel often catapults a wishy-washy patient into intensity. A well-timed and nicely crafted paradox may quickly change the attitude of a patient who was expecting the therapist to "do it all for me." A well-delivered opinion that the unmotivated or manipulative patient need not continue in therapy will not only turn a patient around, but will result in an impressive surge of motivation. (There is more discussion of this in chapter 9, but for a wide range of novel and innovative interventions for the first session, see Cummings & Cummings (2000) and Cummings & Sayama (1995).)

Enforce the Homework

More than anything else, enforcing the homework amplifies the intensity and drives home the realization that the therapeutic process is, indeed, a partnership. As part of the therapeutic contract that makes therapy a partnership, the patient upholds her side of the agreement by doing her homework, and forfeits the session if she comes in without having completed it satisfactorily. Timid therapists have difficulty sending a patient home, especially if she is cleverly screaming for help, saying, "Today I need you more than ever and you are not letting me have my appointment." The appropriate response from the therapist is, " If you need these sessions so much, do your homework so you can derive benefit from them. Remember, this is a partnership. You do your work and I'll do mine."

Experience has demonstrated that about 40% of patients will test the rule and be sent home once for not completing the homework. Once the patient is sent home, there is rarely the forfeiture of a second session; rather, it is the patient who was excused the first time who is likely to repeat the behavior. If care has been taken to assign the homework properly in accordance with the aforementioned three requirements, there is no reason to excuse the patient. The same timid therapist will fear the patient will quit treatment if the rule is enforced. To the contrary, it is the patient who is excused who is likely to drop out of treatment. Enforcing well-designed and appropriate homework increases the intensity of the treatment and motivates the patient to continue.

Step 3: Clinical Strategies for Implementing the Interruption

In traditional therapy the subject of termination is usually first brought up by the patient, who then quickly backs away when the therapist seems to concur. The therapist's response has been premature, awakening fears of separation and prompting barriers to ending treatment. As previously mentioned, the most frequent is the resurgence of initial symptoms that had long disappeared. The message is clear: The patient is frightened. The dependency is threatened. A similar, although somewhat less intense fear may arise in approaching interruption, even though all along the attachment to the therapist has been deemphasized and self-reliance has been cultivated. Nonetheless, interruption requires that it be approached skillfully so the patient is prepared for the continuation of treatment in the absence of the psychotherapist.

Paramount is the requirement that interruption is understood so that its impetus always comes from the patient. This does not mean the therapist is not active in the process, but that she is obliquely so. There is therapeutic guidance analogous to that of the homework, completed by the patient, but assigned by the therapist, who anticipates the next level of therapeutic progress. Just as, ultimately, it is the patient who decides the future by determining the outcome and direction of the completed homework, similarly the therapist is guiding the interruption, but the patient sees it as his decision to interrupt. The patient who is comfortable with the ongoing nature of therapy without the psychotherapist manifests no resurgence of symptoms or other difficulties.

Augmenting the Readiness

Generally it can be expected that psychotherapy will progress rapidly, because self-reliance has been a major consideration from the onset of treatment. The patient will signal a readiness, actually not yet embraced by the patient, by musing how long she might need to continue coming. The therapist is careful not to jump on this; rather, with jocularity says, "I think you may be getting ready to fire me." The patient may seem surprised, but usually laughs along with the therapist, who then ignores the aside and recapitulates the therapeutic contract, "I shall never abandon you as long as you need me." This is the apparent emphasis, while the therapist then muses seemingly with another aside about the characteristics of continuous psychotherapy, reflecting on how the patient continues to grow after interruption, and that the patient is encouraged to resume the sessions with the therapist at any time. It is pointed out to the patient that there will be future times, following unforeseen events and unexpected complexities of life, when the patient may need the therapist again, and the promise in the therapeutic contract includes such future eventualities, whether this is in two months or twenty years. Then the therapist abruptly drops this seeming tangent and attends, with the patient, to other matters.

Augmenting the Decision

If the timing and sequence are as described, invariably in the following session the patient suggests there seems to be no need to keep coming in and she will ask if the therapist agrees. The therapist must, at this point, throw it back to the patient. However, the therapist must take time to point out that it has been the patient who has made all the progress and the patient can continue the problem solving in the absence of the therapist. "Many patients find it helpful when there is a problem to talk to me in their heads. You know by now what I am likely to say, and you will be pleased by how you come to your own conclusions just as you have here. My patients tell me they always get an answer, and when they do not, they know it is time to call and make an appointment to come in." If the therapist has read the patient correctly, and has appropriately augmented both the readiness and the decision to interrupt, the typical patient will nod assent. Interruption usually results after such a session. The patient is satisfied that the goal has been reached, has the security of knowing that returning to psychotherapy is an encouraged option, and has a modus operandi for continuing the problem solving on her own. The word termination has never been uttered.

Overcoming the Occasional Glitch

Occasionally there will be a patient who, after showing readiness, does not take the second step in the following session, but in the one after that. In such instances the therapist must exercise restraint and not try to augment the decision prematurely. There are some patients who are uncertain and do not want to interrupt yet, even though they had expressed what is defined here as readiness. Again, if the therapist has read the patient correctly, this occasional balking can be addressed by assigning a specific kind of homework. The patient is asked to write down five reasons therapy should be interrupted, and five reasons why it should not. Almost invariably the patient will relate in the next session that the five reasons to interrupt came easily, but he could come up with only two or three reasons why the sessions should continue, and then only after much thought over several days.

The Hiatus

During periods of interruption it is common for most patients to write to the psychotherapist. Most often it is a holiday card with a greeting and a brief message that things are going well. At other times it may be a letter, sometimes a very long letter, describing a difficulty and how it was overcome. Still other patients will ask for advice or reassurance that they did the right thing. The psychotherapist responds to all communications, indicating how pleasant it is to hear from the patient, but carefully avoids any advice, admonition, or therapeutic insight. The patient is complimented for continuing to solve life's problems, but if help is asked for in the letter, the response should be to merely ask the patient if she thinks it is time to come in. More often than not, the next written communication will report that the problem has been solved.

Half a Century of Experience

I began using this model in 1950, and began actively teaching it a few years thereafter in clinical case conferences at the psychiatry department at Kaiser Permanente in San Francisco, where I was chief psychologist. It became the model used in the government's Hawaii Project and with the thousands of psychotherapists working with American Biodyne nationally, as well as with hundreds of psychotherapists in independent practice who attended training sessions. Unfortunately most data are scattered, essentially incomplete, and usually impossible to access. As a follow-up, I surveyed 243 patients I had personally treated using this model, and who had their initial sessions between 1961 and 1965.

Table 5.1 Tabulation of 243 patients initially seen by me in focused psychotherapy from 1961 to 1965 by episodes and number of sessions per episode, with follow-up tabulation for 40 years

	AVERAGE NUMBER OF SESSIONS PER NO. OF EPISODES		*n*	% OF TOTAL
	8.1	0.0	56	23
2	6.2	3.4	39	16
3–5	6.4	3.5	17	7
6–12	6.1	2.9	131	54
Total			243	100

These are all the patients I had seen in my own independent practice during this time period, and whose records were readily available. Their records were surveyed for up to four decades following the initial session (Cummings 2001).

You will note from Table 5.1 that 56 patients (23%) were never seen again beyond the initial episode, which averaged 8.1 sessions. Another 39 patients (16%) had one return episode, with the initial episode averaging 6.2 sessions and the second episode averaging 3.4 sessions. The smallest group of 17 patients (7%) had 3 to 5 return episodes, with the first episode averaging 6.4 sessions and the return episodes averaging 3.5 sessions. The largest group of 131 (54%) availed themselves of 6 to 12 return episodes, with the sixth episode averaging 6.1 sessions and subsequent episodes averaging 2.9 sessions.

It is clear from these results that more than half the patients seen availed themselves of the model of focused, intermittent psychotherapy throughout the lifecycle throughout a 35- to 40-year period. It is clear also that in this model there is considerable generalization of therapeutic effect, for subsequent episodes average only about 3 sessions for all patients returning for more than 3 episodes. In succeeding episodes often only one session is needed. By adding the average number of sessions per episode for those in the 12-return-episode group, the total number of sessions is only 40.9 over a 35- to 40-year span. This model is not only responsive to the needs of these patients, but also meets the most stringent standards of cost-effectiveness imposed by third-party payers today.

Case Illustrations

Two cases are described here because they illustrate the two extremes of the model. The first is the case of Gregory (Cummings 2001), who was seen twice, had a 22-year hiatus, after which there was just one more session. It startled even the therapist with its degree of success. The second is Steve, a physician who was first seen as an undergraduate, and continued intermittent sessions throughout medical school, his marriage, divorce, remarriage, the birth of his children, and his career over a 39-year period, with a total of 43 sessions to date.

Gregory: Sorry I Am Back So Soon

This twenty-six-year-old-man was openly distraught during the first session because his wife was leaving him. He said he would do anything to hold the marriage together, but he was vague and evasive when asked, "If your wife were here, what would she say was her reason for leaving you?" His explicit contract, which stated he was here to save the marriage, did not seem to reflect the whole story, and repeated probing eventually revealed that his wife had been complaining for some time that he was gambling too much. He attempted to dismiss this by jocularity, asking, "What is wrong with placing a little wager once in a while?" It soon became apparent, however, that Greg was a compulsive gambler whose addiction had not only deprived the family of necessities, but had plunged them into debt. Nonetheless, the patient persisted in his denial, and repeatedly asked the psychotherapist to intercede with his wife and ask her to postpone the divorce while they both sought marital counseling. The implicit contract was "save my marriage without interfering with my gambling." Greg's homework assignment was to give the therapist no less than five valid reasons why his wife should not leave him now, and to list five additional reasons why he should be allowed to continue gambling for an indefinite period while the couple is in marital counseling.

Greg returned for his second session stating he was unable to do his homework as assigned. He came up with more than 30 reasons why he should quit gambling now, accept the fact that he was a compulsive gambler, and do whatever necessary never to gamble again. The therapist intimated that although Greg's newfound resolve was commendable, he needed help and discussed with him Gamblers Anonymous and a group program available in the current treatment setting. Greg said he would think about it, left, and never called for a third appointment. In my mind, the therapy was a failure, and I made a note in the chart to that effect.

Twenty-two years later Greg called for his third appointment. His nineteen-year-old son was involved in a fatal auto accident, and the patient feared that in his severe emotional upset he might weaken and gamble. He felt and recognized the craving, which was disguised as, "What the hell? What did being clean get you?" He described in the session how ashamed he had been with his own behavior two decades before, but even more ashamed of his rationalizations, which attempted to justify his continued gambling in the face of his inability to provide basic necessities for his spouse and children. "You said just the right thing to me, and I'm back for a refresher that will get me through the next twenty-two years." Greg had not even made as much as a so-called innocent wager in the twenty-two years following his first appointment. During those years when he was tempted, he would talk in his head to the therapist, and indicated, "I always got the right answer." One such time he asked what would be the harm if he bought a lottery ticket? He heard the therapist reply, "You want me to say it's okay, but you know the real answer to your question." He did not buy the ticket. Another time he was tempted to enter the Publishers Clearinghouse Sweepstakes, and laughed when he heard me say, "Now your denial is approaching the absurd." After we discussed his bereavement and he received encouragement to grieve, Greg left satisfied he was good for another 22 years, and subsequent holiday cards confirm he has remained abstinent and has worked through his mourning.

Steve, the Reluctant Physician

A midday panic phone call from Steve resulted in my giving him an appointment during what would have been my dinner hour, because I was booked that day until midnight. He had first spoken with my secretary, learned my schedule was full, and surmised how I had accommodated the urgency of his request. He began the session expressing gratitude. Steve was a tall, handsome, but somewhat obsequious twenty-year-old man who was a junior in college and had aspirations of going to medical school. He was taking the appropriate premedical courses and had an almost straight-A grade-point average until the last academic quarter, in which his performance in two of his physical science courses had fallen precipitously. His presenting complaint was that he suddenly was unable to concentrate on his studies, especially his science courses, and suggested that he probably did not really want to go to medical school after all. His father was a construction worker and Steve was the first in his family to go to college. "My family is all blue collar; what makes me think I can be a doctor? I'm not smart enough." His almost three-year history of excellent grades, plus the sudden onset of his inability to concentrate, made me doubt the etiology he so readily proffered. Probing got us nowhere until I asked about the man who referred him to me, a university professor and my casual acquaintance of several years. Steve broke out into a sweat. With difficulty he spoke of this man's sexual interest in him, his own capitulation to sexual encounters in which he passively submitted, but did not reciprocate. Shaking and sweating, he confessed, " I'm afraid I might be queer," and went on to say that if his burley father knew what he was doing he "would beat me to death with a cement shovel." Steve was also afraid of the professor, in whose class he was doing poorly, and opined that if he broke off the sexual relationship the professor might well give him the failing grade he deserved. A number of issues were discussed: It is not the end of the world to be gay, but rather a lifestyle choice for many men and women. The professor would not be forcing himself on the patient, and would have no right to do so, were Steve to say no. If the professor used the threat of poor grades he would be guilty of sexual harassment and would thus be more vulnerable than Steve. The therapist discerned that Steve was ready to confront the issue and was given a choice for homework: either stop submitting to the sexual encounters or continue them as an active, willing participant. Expressing considerable fear, the patient accepted the assignment. Recognizing the danger, this intervention was undertaken with a great deal of forethought. It catapulted the therapy into a remarkable intensity, and it was successful.

During the second session Steve described, without embarrassment, how he participated in the next sexual encounter with the professor, and found out to his amazement that he did not enjoy it, it was somewhat repugnant, but he did not fear it. He realized that all his attraction since his earliest memory was for girls and women. The professor accepted without animosity the decision that Steve would no longer have sex with him. The therapist asked about masturbatory fantasies because these are psychologically more definitive than verbalizations. He reported these were entirely heterosexual, as were his earlier nocturnal emissions, and it had never even occurred to him that he might have a homosexual fantasy. Yet like a lot of shy men who are awkward with women, he thought this meant he might be gay. His poor concentration had abated, and Steve's homework was to catch up on the late lab assignments that were contributing to his poor grades. This might mean burning the midnight oil for a time. As for Steve's professor (who referred him), he never asked about Steve and, because of the complicated relationship, the therapist did not contact him to acknowledge the referral.

The next six sessions involved rather emotional discussions of Steve's strong ambivalence to his sometimes bullying father whom he both feared and admired, and of a rather cold mother whom he could never really please. He feared that with his humble background if he should graduate with his medical degree he would look like "a blue collar worker in a white coat," be scorned by his colleagues, and avoided by patients. Steve was doing well, and at the ninth session the treatment was interrupted.

Steve was not seen again until he had graduated, had applied to medical schools, and was experiencing an excruciating wait to hear whether he would be admitted. His father had finally not only accepted Steve's decision to go to medical school, but had been crowing to everyone that there would soon be a doctor in the family. During the wait, many of Steve's insecurities had returned, and were now coupled with the fear of possibly having to disappoint his father. He was in near panic. His inability to concentrate had returned, and he doubted he could succeed in medical school even if he were accepted. During the third session of this second episode, Steve learned he had been accepted by the University of California at San Francisco medical school, just down the street from the therapist's office. He was ecstatic, because he could continue to have access to the therapist. Steve was given homework designed to help him understand his panic state and how to handle it in his future life because he might again be overwhelmed with self-doubt. Treatment was interrupted after the fourth session.

Steve was seen again in the middle of his second year in medical school. He was doing very well in his studies, but his life was now complicated by his swift marriage to a nurse. Lenora was an aggressive borderline personality disorder who decided she wanted to marry a doctor, and shy Steve did not have a modicum of a chance to object. His wife was a difficult, unpredictable, and volatile woman, but Steve was enjoying the torrid sex and he decided not to disrupt his studies with what would be a nasty separation. During the next two years he was seen occasionally for a total of nine sessions, as required to help him make the best of a bad marriage. Eventually Lenora did herself in by a series of turbulent extramarital affairs and Steve divorced her shortly before embarking on his residency. Having found an established and far more exciting surgeon, Lenora did not contest the divorce.

Steve accepted a residency in internal medicine in a prestigious northeastern hospital, but he kept in touch with an occasional letter that indicated he was doing well and was also dating. Four years elapsed, Steve had completed his residency, and he returned to the San Francisco Bay Area to join a large group practice in an upscale suburb. He came in for one appointment, mainly to update the psychotherapist and reestablish a connection. Although this episode was limited to one session, episode five two years later consisted of six sessions, two of them conjointly with his fiancée, whom he married shortly thereafter. In accordance with their intention, Steve's spouse bore three children in rapid succession, two girls and one boy. She had interrupted her career as a business executive to become a stay-at-home mom.

Seven years after Steve had joined his group practice, troubles emerged among the physician partners. Managed care was beginning to take its toll, the cost of malpractice insurance was skyrocketing, and competition was keen. The Bay Area had become a very desirable place to practice, resulting in too many physicians with not enough patients. The group practice members annually rated each other's performance, and the emerging score determined how much of the divisible profit each physician member would receive at the end of the year. Steve was always rated at the bottom, which he accepted, but now that the practice's revenue had dropped, there was talk of drastically restructuring the group, with the senior physician arguing that they should let Steve go because of his poor performance. Steve, now a husband and father of three children, was shaken and reinstated his psychotherapy sessions. He manifested the same kind of lack of concentration that he had shown on his very first visit. The senior physician was somewhat of a bully, and reminded Steve of his father. It readily became apparent that Steve's performance in practice did not match his scholastic achievements. He was unsure of himself, wishy-washy with patients, and would say to them upon prescribing a medication or a regimen, "We'll try this, and if it doesn't work we'll try something else." Patients shunned Steve, seeing him as poorly trained, where in actuality he was more highly trained than most of his colleagues. It became clear that Steve felt inferior to his partners, all of whom came from upper-middle-class, educated families. He had become the blue-collar worker in a white coat. We spoke of many things, not the least of which was that the placebo effect accounts for 30% of successful medical treatment, augmenting the pharmacological benefit. A skilled physician strives to strengthen the placebo effect by presenting a positive demeanor. During the course of eleven sessions, Steve not only became a confident physician, but a favorite with the patients. He worked through his fear of the managing physician, and within a few months became his right hand in the partnership, and as serendipity he found himself reconciled with his father. He remembered how hard his father worked in heavy construction, always putting food on the table, even in lean times. He had feared he would never be a breadwinner like his father. The last few years of his father's life were a joy to Steve, and he only regretted that no matter what he did he could not break through his mother's coldness and aloofness. She took these to the grave, but long before she died, Steve discovered that much of his shyness with women had been a result of the belief that he could no more please them than he could his mother. He also realized that a great deal of his father's anger was displaced from his cold wife, yet he never raised his voice to her and was loyal to the end.

A little more than a decade passed before Steve was seen again. His children were doing well in school and he had been named the managing partner of the group, which had expanded considerably in size. His wife and children were complaining that he spent all his time at work, almost totally neglecting the family. At Steve's request, he was seen along with his wife and three children. The latter were not shy about voicing their disappointment with their father, who acknowledged they had a right to complain. Steve was seen alone for two more sessions, during which he was able to liken his behavior to that of his mother, who was always too busy with her own activities to spend time with the family. He changed his behavior rapidly and markedly. Steve was seen once two years ago. He had no complaints, and just came in to bring the therapist up to date and to express his gratitude for the very happy life he had with his family and his work. In almost four decades Steve was seen 43 times, including the sessions with his wife and with the children.

This is an average of a little more than once a year, a parsimonious number in light of the excellent outcome. It is doubtful that the same outcome would have been possible without the model of focused, intermittent psychotherapy throughout the forty years of Steve's life, addressing a number of vexing problems as they unfolded over time.

Summary

By replacing termination with interruption, psychotherapy is spared the difficulties that result in needless sessions on the one hand, and a reluctance to seek future treatment when new problems arise. It is facilitated by a model of focused, intermittent episodes of psychotherapy as needed throughout the patient's life span, which is the way all healthcare is dispensed (Cummings & VandenBos 1979). The physician does not continue to see the patient after the pneumonia is cured, but it is understood that the patient returns to treatment in the future should she break a leg or become ill with influenza. Half a century of experience has demonstrated that patients like this model and utilize it accordingly. In addition, tracking these patients reveals that the approach is cost-effective and meets the requirements of even the most stringent rules of third-party payers. The model may seem deceptively simple, and some training and experience are required before the psychotherapist who is used to the termination model is able to correctly implement the interruption sequence (Pallak et al. 1994).

References

Bandura, A. (1977). Self-efficacy: Toward a unifying theory of behavioral change. *Psychological Review, 84,* 191–215.

Bloom, B. (1991). Planned short-term psychotherapy. Boston: Allyn & Bacon.

Cummings, N. A. (1990). Brief, intermittent psychotherapy throughout the life cycle. In J. Zeig & S. Gilligan (Eds.), *Brief therapy: Myths, methods, and metaphors* (pp. 169–184). New York: Brunner/Mazel.

Cummings, N. A. (1991). Brief, intermittent psychotherapy throughout the life cycle. In C. Austad & W. Berman (Eds.), *Psychotherapy in managed healthcare* (pp. 35–45). Washington, DC: American Psychological Association.

Cummings, N. A. (2001). Interruption, not termination: The model from focused, intermittent psychotherapy throughout the life cycle. *Journal of Psychotherapy in Independent Practice, 2,* 3–16.

Cummings, N. A., & Cummings, J. (2000). *The essence of psychotherapy: Reinventing the art in the era of data.* San Diego, CA: Academic Press.

Cummings, N. A., & Sayama, M. (1995). *Focused psychotherapy: A casebook of brief, intermittent psychotherapy throughout the life cycle.* New York: Brunner/Mazel.

Cummings, N. A., & VandenBos, G. (1979). The general practice of psychology. *Professional Psychology, 10,* 430–440.

Freud, S. (1933). *Collected papers.* London: Hogarth Press.

Pallak, M., Cummings, N. A., Dorken, H., & Henke, C. (1994). Medical costs, Medicaid, and managed mental health treatment: The Hawaii Study. In N. A. Cummings & M. Pallak (Eds.), *Managed care quarterly* (Vol. 2) (pp. 3–23). Frederick, MD: Aspen Publishers.

Seligman, M. (1975). *Helplessness: On depression, development, and death.* New York: Alfred A. Knopf.

6

CLINICAL CASE CONCEPTUALIZATIONS AND TERMINATION OF PSYCHOTHERAPY

MICHAEL A. CUCCIARE AND WILLIAM T. O'DONOHUE

Introduction

The use of clinical case conceptualizations in mental health practice has become increasingly popular over the last decade (Sperry 2005a), and its growing popularity is due to a wide variety of factors ranging in scope from economic (e.g., managed care's demand of accountability) to clinical (e.g., to determine the most appropriate/effective treatment[s]) (Haynes & O'Brien 2000; Scamardo, Bobele, & Biever 2004; Sperry 2005b). Clinical case conceptualizations are a way to organize information about a client's presenting problems, identify treatment targets, and specify intervention strategies. One of the biggest advantages of using the clinical case conceptualization in practice is to keep the therapy process on track and to prepare for one of the perhaps most imprecise aspects of the therapy process—termination. There is little to no empirical research supporting strategies for preparing the therapy for termination; thus it is the focus of this chapter to present and discuss the concept of the clinical case conceptualization and to integrate its use into preparing for the termination of psychotherapy. In doing so, this chapter will (a) define the clinical case conceptualization, (b) discuss some of the factors leading to its recent popularity, (c) present and discuss the general components and types of clinical conceptualizations, followed by a more detailed discussion of (d) specific models and components of clinical case conceptualizations from different theoretical perspectives (e.g., cognitive-behavior therapy, problem-solving approaches). This chapter concludes with specific recommendations for using a clinical case conceptualization to prepare for termination of psychotherapy.

Defining Clinical Case Conceptualizations

A clinical case conceptualization is an approach to summarizing a wide variety of clinically relevant case information into a brief, coherent outline that provides at least a preliminary understanding of a client's pattern of behaving, thinking, and feeling with respect to the presenting problem or set of problems (Sperry 2005a). The ultimate purpose of clinical case conceptualizations is to help clinicians organize relevant information about their clients' presenting problem(s) so that they may prescribe effective treatment(s). That is, clinical case conceptualizations can help link numerous pieces of assessment data (at the preintervention level) to the design of an individualized treatment program (Haynes & O'Brien 2000). An important part of this organizing is to take pieces of idiographic information expressed in informal terms ("I have been crying every day") into linguistic categories used in scientific regularities ("client is depressed") so that these regularities can be utilized for the client's benefit ("depression can be ameliorated by treatment x"). Clinical case conceptualizations can integrate a vast array of intervention-related clinical judgments, important variables related to the presenting problem, data from relevant research, and hypotheses about potentially relevant client characteristics into a single conceptual framework.

Why Use Clinical Case Conceptualizations?

As a result of recent economic forces, practicing clinicians have become increasingly interested in understanding the basic features of clinical case conceptualizations. One such economic force is the requirement of many managed care companies for clinician's to construct treatment plans for each patient. Managed care companies want to gain some idea of the scope of the bill and some other related specifics that they are buying. This requirement has not only impacted practitioner behavior, but has also impacted the state of California's requirements for some types of mental health licensure. For example, to be licensed as a marriage and family therapist, prospective practitioners are currently required to pass an oral examination concerned with both case conceptualizations and treatment planning (Sperry 2006).

In addition to the current economic forces that are contributing to the growing popularity of case conceptualizations, learning to construct a conceptualization of a client's psychological problems can be clinically useful in terms of obtaining, interpreting, and organizing information thought to be related to the onset and/or maintenance of psychiatric disorders and involved in making well-informed treatment decisions. This is particularly the case as one begins to acquire greater amounts of information about a client's presenting problems. Furthermore, a clinical case conceptualization should assist the clinician in focusing on what information still needs to be acquired to make valid treatment decisions, and then ultimately guide the clinician toward choosing the appropriate intervention(s) to implement. Moreover, it is argued that clinical case conceptualizations can limit or help reduce mistakes of bias and error often noted in clinical judgment (Haynes & O'Brien 2000). A final major reason to construct and implement a clinical case conceptualization is to help the clinician and client prepare for the termination process. For example, accurate and thoughtful clinical case conceptualizations may make the process of termination easier, as it is easier to terminate the therapy process with a client who has resolved their presenting problems or reached their treatment goals than with one who has not.

The following sections briefly discuss how clinical case conceptualizations can be useful in organizing information collected during the clinical assessment process, fitting assessment data into one unifying theoretical framework, and preparing the therapy process for termination.

Deductive Reasoning in Clinical Assessment

Assessment, and particularly the process of arriving at a diagnosis, involve the use of deductive reasoning. Deductive reasoning is generally considered logic that moves from generals to specifics. That is, arguments based on rules, principles, or laws are generally considered to be deductive (Russell 1972). "Mr. Brown is a man, all men are mortal, therefore Mr. Brown is mortal," is an example of deductive reasoning. In clinical assessment, the process of deductive reasoning takes place when clinicians collect data about a client's symptoms (or history of symptoms) and degree of functional impairment and use that information to arrive at some conclusion about symptom severity (e.g., degree of depression and/or anxiety) and/or the presence of a psychiatric disorder(s) (Sperry 2005a, 2005b). A therapist might reason, "This client is depressed, and if the client is depressed, then she/he should be given either CBT or interpersonal therapy. Thus, this client will be treated with one of these therapies." This is an example of deductive reasoning. In general, as additional data are collected about a client's history and current level of symptomatology/functioning, clinicians are better able to both arrive at a possible DSM-IV diagnosis and to generate increasingly accurate hypotheses about precipitating and/or maintaining factors involved in a client's presenting problem(s).

O'Donohue (1991) has depicted how key components of case conceptualization can be construed as deductive arguments.

Argument 1: What assessment methods should be used in this case?

1. Therapist T wants information $I1$ to In.
2. Information $I1$ to In is potentially relevant to the treatment of Client C.
3. Gathering information $I1$ to In is morally permissible.
4. Gathering information $I1$ to In is practically feasible.
5. Information $I1$ to In is sufficiently complete and comprehensive information about the principle dimensions of the case.
6. Assessment methods $A1$ to An are reliable and valid methods for gathering information $I1$ to In.
7. Assessment methods $A1$ to An are cost-effective methods for gathering information $I1$ to In.
8. The client is fully informed regarding alternatives to gathering this information and these assessment methods and consents to the gathering of this information by the use of these methods.
9. If 1, 2, 3, 4, 5, 6, 7, 8, and ceteris paribus, then assessment methods $A1$ to An are the proper assessment methods to use in this case.

10. Ceteris paribus.

11. Therefore, assessment methods $A1$ to An are the proper methods to use in this case.

The deductive argument for treatment methods:

1. Treatment goal G entails the realization of states of affairs $S1$ to Sn.

2. $F1$ to Fn are all factors that are known to be or have the best evidence to be causally related to $S1$ to Sn.

3. $F1$ to Fn are cost-efficient methods to obtain $S1$ to Sn.

4. $F1$ to Fn are the least restrictive methods to obtain $S1$ to Sn.

5. Client C is fully informed concerning alternative methods, the costs, and the benefits of these methods and consents to the use of $F1$ to Fn.

6. If 1, 2, 3, 4, 5 and ceteris paribus, then $F1$ to Fn are the proper treatment methods to use in this case.

7. Ceteris paribus.

8. Therefore, $F1$ to Fn are the proper treatment methods to use in this case.

Inductive Reasoning in Clinical Case Conceptualizations

One potential pitfall of collecting large amounts of data about a client's presenting problem is that as more data are collected, it becomes more complicated to organize and conceptualize the information into a clinical case conceptualization (Sperry 2005a). Thus, developing a clinical case conceptualization requires the process of inductive reasoning, which is essentially logic that moves from specifics to generals (Russell 1972). Inductive reasoning is a logical argument in which the premises of an argument support the conclusion but do not ensure it. "These pieces of ice are all cold; therefore all pieces of ice are cold," is an example of inductive reasoning. When developing a clinical case conceptualization, clinicians must synthesize various pieces of seemingly unrelated data about a client's present (and historical) symptoms, various levels of functioning, family history, and medical history into a single integrated conceptual framework that *starts* the process of explaining why a particular patient is experiencing the particular problems he or she is presenting with at the present moment (Sperry 2005a). It should be noted that case conceptualizations are dynamic documents that are constantly changing as new information relevant to the patient's presenting problem(s) become available.

Fitting Assessment Data Into One Unifying Theoretical Framework

Fitting together various pieces of seemingly unrelated data points may be a daunting task for some individuals; thus, having a theoretical framework (or clinical formulation) that guides what pieces of data one might attend to can be helpful in discerning which particular pieces of data can be more helpful in making treatment decisions. A clinical case conceptualization is most commonly a theoretical rationale for the development of presenting symptoms and dysfunctional life patterns (Sperry 2005a), which is more than describing symptoms or arriving at a conclusion about DSM-IV diagnostic criteria. Furthermore, clinical case conceptualizations can help inform the process of specifying treatment recommendations and can help guide the course of treatment based on the information gathered during the pretreatment assessment and throughout the therapeutic process. Moreover, having a theoretical framework about a patient's presenting problems can help focus the clinician on certain (or perhaps more important) pieces of information that are needed during the assessment process. Sperry (2005a) provides an example of how clinical case conceptualizations are helpful in guiding the attention of the clinician:

> For instance, let's say that the theoretical framework of Therapist A (an acknowledged master therapist) would have her elicit four pieces of data: parents, child, car, and map for which the linking theme is "family trip." Compare this to Therapist B (a beginning counseling practicum student) who, guided by no theoretical framework, collects all 50 pieces of data in no particular order. As is often the case, students and therapist with little or no training and experience in deriving clinical formulations tend to engage in premature closure. Thus, in the illustrated exercise, they might take the first three pieces of data presented and arrive at "things that entertain" as their formulation. (73)

The Clinical Case Conceptualization and Termination of Psychotherapy

An additional reason to consider the use of clinical case conceptualizations is to get clients on board with the treatment process, and similarly to address any assumptions and/or misconceptions they may have at pretreatment about the various components of psychotherapy, such as termination. For example, recent research shows that clients often come into the therapy process with a sense of how many sessions they will require to adequately address their presenting problem(s), and this can influence how long they stay in therapy (Scamardo, Bobele, & Biever 2004).

To better understand clients' decision processes regarding how long they feel they will require psychotherapy, Scamardo, Bobele, and Biever (2004) designed a qualitative study to examine how clients: (a) determine how long they should stay in therapy, (b) choose when to self-terminate the therapy process, and (c) change their expectations about therapy from start to finish. The investigators used a qualitative methodology to examine nine participants—seven women and two men (ranging in age from twenty-three to forty-five). A client was considered "terminated" when formal termination paperwork was completed by the therapist or the client's file was inactive for six weeks. Presenting problems consisted of difficulties with mood (e.g., depression), sexual and physical abuse, relationship problems, and occupational or academic difficulties. Before entering treatment, participants were asked to estimate the number of sessions they thought they would need to adequately address their presenting problems. This number was later compared to their actual records, which indicated the total number of sessions attended. All participants were contacted by phone to complete a thirty- to sixty-minute, semistructured interview designed to gain information about (a) how they predicted the number of sessions they would require prior to the first appointment, (b) how they decided to end treatment, and (c) how their expectation about treatment changed over its course. Results of the study showed that:

Predicting Number of Sessions

- Clients who had previous therapy experience were more likely to have given thought to the number of sessions they would need, but were no more accurate at predicting actual session length than those without prior therapy experience.

- Neither ethnicity nor gender played a significant role in making predictions about session length.
- In general, participants based their predictions about number of sessions needed by their perceptions of their problems (e.g., less serious problems would require fewer sessions).

Termination Decisions

- The majority of participants (67%) perceived therapy to be useful and decided to discontinue treatment without discussing this decision directly with their therapist.
- The remaining participants terminated treatment due to personal reasons.
- None of the participants reported any negative experiences while in therapy; conversely, all reported that therapy was helpful in addressing their presenting problems.

Changing Expectations

- There was clear evidence (by self-report) that participants' views of therapy changed over the course of treatment.
- Prior to treatment, participants reported that they assumed therapists would be authoritative, judgmental, ask many questions, and tell participants what to do. Furthermore, participants reported that this view of treatment prior to therapy was heavily influenced by the media.
- After treatment, participants described therapists as understanding, easy to talk to, empathic, and helpful in problem solving.

The authors of this study integrate these results into several clinical recommendations (Scamardo, Bobele, & Biever 2004). First, clients tend not to bring up the issue of termination, but in many cases enter treatment with an assumed number of sessions they feel will best address their presenting problem(s). Therefore, it is suggested that mental health practitioners discuss the process of termination with their clients early within the treatment process. Second, consistent with the finding that clients often want fewer therapy sessions and desire problem-focused interventions (Pekarik 1985), 67% of the participants in this study reported that they (not the therapist) were best suited to judge the number of sessions needed to address their presenting problem(s). Therefore, it is recommended that therapists discuss client's expectations about therapy and explore (and perhaps define) what will be sufficient gains to warrant the termination of treatment. It was shown through qualitative methods that clients can have negative views of therapy prior to starting treatment. Thus, it is important to address any misconceptions about therapy early in the treatment process to enhance rapport and ease any client concerns or fears about the treatment process.

Clinical case conceptualization can help facilitate the process of implementing each of the recommendations stated above. Specifically, a clinical case conceptualization should be produced in written form and shared with the client early in the treatment process (i.e., first or second session). The clinical case conceptualization should contain elements (which will be discussed in greater detail in later sections) such as: an identified behavior problem (or set of problems), specific treatment targets and/or what improvements of a behavior problem might look like (e.g., increased intimacy with others, improved ability to manage aversive emotional experiences), and the use of the most effective treatment components for addressing those problems. In addition, during this session clinicians can ask the client for their perspective on the number of sessions they feel they will require in order for their presenting problems to be adequately addressed, and can cover any misconceptions about the termination process, length of treatment, treatment goals/foci, and expectations regarding the client's and therapist's roles during the treatment process and termination. It is recommended that the clinical case conceptualization not be handed directly to clients for them to interpret, but instead explained to them during a regularly scheduled session as the possibility of misinterpretation of information exists.

Recently there has been a questioning of whether psychotherapy should be considered a "one shot" project. Instead, researchers and theorists have suggested that therapy may be looked at as having three components:

1. Assessing readiness to change, treatment interfering behaviors
2. Therapy
3. Relapse Prevention

This tripartite model would suggest both that cases need to be conceptualized in terms of these three components and termination questions arise in all three.

Stage 1: Lessons From Motivational Interviewing and Dialectical Behavior Therapy   Building patient motivation for behavior change is now recognized as an important task of psychotherapists, and research and development efforts in this area have been fruitful (O'Donohue & Levensky 2006). In particular, the communication style of motivational interviewing (MI), introduced in 1983 by psychologist William Miller, Ph.D., has shown great promise as a brief counseling method to enhance behavior change. Its developers describe MI as a directive, patient-centered style for promoting behavior change by helping patients explore and resolve ambivalence regarding change efforts and change targets (Miller & Rollnick 2002). Initially developed for the treatment of addictions, MI has been widely adapted to facilitate change across a range of psychotherapy targets. Motivational interviewing is well suited for use in many settings, as it can be applied in very brief (ten to fifteen minute) patient encounters (Resnicow et al. 2002). A recent meta-analytic review (Hettema et al. 2005) evaluated seventy-two published clinical trials of MI. At least modest effects were replicated across a variety of behavioral domains, including alcohol and drug use, dual disorders, treatment adherence, HIV-risk reduction, diet and exercise, and health safety practices, thus showing promise in addressing some of the more difficult behavior change challenges in routine healthcare.

There are four counseling principles that are core to the practice of MI. These are to express empathy, develop a discrepancy, roll with resistance, and support self-efficacy. Correspondingly, there are four basic therapeutic skills or methods used in MI: reflective listening, asking open questions, affirming, and summarizing.

Dialectical behavior therapy (DBT; Linehan 1993) suggests that clients can bring with them "treatment interfering behaviors." They include, for example, failure to attend sessions reliably, failure to keep to contracted agreements, or behaviors that overstep therapist limits. An assessment of these behaviors should be part of case conceptualization and strategies developed for dealing with them, as these can result in either client termination (chronic failure to attend) or force the therapist to terminate prematurely (overstepping therapist limits).

However, it is always possible that a client is not ready to participate in therapy, that he or she is insufficiently interested in working to change. When this is the case and when MI has failed, it is reasonable to consider termination or interruption of therapy until such time when the client is ready and committed to participate in therapy.

Stage 2: Therapy Most of the remainder of the book will cover this component and we will make no additional comments on it.

Stage 3: Relapse Prevention There is a plethora of evidence that therapy gains do not always endure. This is true for many problems, but particularly for problems such as substance abuse and the paraphilias. This caused G. Alan Marlatt (1980) to develop a cognitive-behavioral strategy called *relapse prevention*. In this strategy, therapists don't terminate after initial treatment gains, but work with clients to develop a relapse prevention plan to increase the likelihood of having treatment gains endure. Part of the implication of this is that the therapy is never really terminated, but the therapist continues to help the client deal with lapses and relapses. This model identifies high-risk situations related to lapses or relapses (fishing again with drinking buddies) as well as lifestyle imbalances, cognitive distortions (including the abstinence violation effect), dealing with urges, seemingly irrelevant decisions that can contribute to moving away from treatment gains.

Thus, in this tripartite model, case conceptualization would cover three stages: (1) issues in starting therapy (ambivalence, treatment interfering behaviors, readiness to change), (2) therapy proper (what techniques are best for what goals), and (3) maintaining gains by constructing a supportive relapse prevention plan.

In the following sections, specific components of clinical case conceptualizations are presented and discussed along with a brief review of specific models of clinical case conceptualizations. A special emphasis will be placed on how to use the clinical case conceptualization to prepare for termination of psychotherapy.

Components of a Clinical Case Conceptualization

According to Sperry (2005ab), a clinical case conceptualization consists of three general components—a diagnostic, clinical, and treatment formulation. The next section includes a brief discussion of each component, followed by a review of specific models of clinical case conceptualization.

Diagnostic Formulation

A diagnostic formulation is a descriptive statement about the nature and severity of the client's presenting psychiatric problem(s). The diagnostic formulation is clinically helpful because it can provide the clinician with information as to the etiological nature of the psychiatric presentation. Because our knowledge as a field is often stored using diagnostic labels (etiology of major depression, assessment of panic disorder, etc.), diagnostic formulations are also helpful as they provide us with the links to evidence that can help us understand various issues and make predictions about outcomes ("If patient is experiencing a major depressive episode and is given Treatment T, then the p of this outcome is x"). In addition, is the patient's presenting psychiatric problem of a psychotic, characterological, and/or neurotic nature? Is the problem primarily organic or psychogenic? Is this a long-standing, chronic problem or acutely severe requiring immediate treatment? In summary, the diagnostic formulation can provide the clinician with preliminary information as to "what happened" to the patient and provide information to begin generating hypotheses about a DSM diagnosis.

Clinical Formulation

A clinical formulation is more explanatory than the diagnostic formulation by emphasizing a theoretical rationale for the development of presenting symptoms and dysfunctional life patterns. Many different types of theories can be used for this component of the clinical case conceptualization. Some of these might include: cognitive-behavioral, psychodynamic, family systems, and biological theories of personality and behavior. The clinical case formulation is focused on answering the question "why did it happen" regarding a client's presenting psychiatric problem(s). Furthermore, the clinical formulation stresses a clinically meaningful explanation (regardless of the theory used to explain the presentation) of the client's current and long-standing ways of behaving, thinking, and feeling. In this manner, the clinical formulation serves to bridge the diagnostic and treatment formulations in the clinical case conceptualization.

Treatment Formulation

The treatment formulation follows the diagnostic and clinical formulations and has its main purpose in providing specific treatment recommendations and guiding the course of treatment. Following the questions, "what happened?" and "why did it happen?" the treatment formulation attempts to provide recommendations based on the question, "How can it [dysfunctional ways of behaving, thinking, and feeling] be changed?" Treatment formulations can consist of many components, such as environmental variables that are related to the behavioral problem, "triggers" that give rise to dysfunctional ways of behaving and thinking, treatment goals, and examples of improved ways of behaving. It is important to note that like the diagnostic and clinical formulation, the treatment formulation is a dynamic, ever changing part of the clinical case conceptualization that changes as new information is made available to the clinician.

All three types of clinical case conceptualization can be useful in preparing for termination due to their focus on specific variables affecting the behavior(s) of interest and/or developing treatment targets. Both pieces of information can serve as important foundations for determining when termination of treatment is most appropriate. For example, a clinician and client can agree early during the treatment process about what gains will constitute "therapeutic success," and then make a tentative decision about when to terminate treatment.

Specific Clinical Case Conceptualization Models

Many clinical case conceptualization models have been presented in recent years (Eells 1997; Haynes & O'Brien 2000; Sperry 2005a, 2005b). For example, there are edited volumes on the topic that go into great detail regarding the components and varieties of clinical case conceptualizations (e.g., Eells 1997). The purpose of this section is not to provide an exhaustive review of clinical case conceptualization, but to provide an overview of some specific models of psychotherapy (e.g., symptom focused, problem solving, behavioral therapy, cognitive-behavioral therapy, and dialectical behavior therapy). It may be useful to note that despite the apparent variety of clinical case conceptualizations, the reader may become aware quite quickly of the apparent similarity between the components of clinical case conceptualizations presented. The following section begins with more general types of clinical case conceptualization and ends with clinical case conceptualizations for specific presenting problems.

Sperry (2006) describes three general types of clinical case conceptualization. These include symptom, theory, and client-focused case conceptualizations. The following is a brief description of each type.

Symptom-Focused Conceptualizations

Symptom-focused conceptualizations have their foundation in medical and biological models of human behavior and tend to be the preferred form of case conceptualizations by third-party payers such as managed care organizations. The emphasis of this type of clinical case conceptualization is on identifying symptoms (e.g., depressive symptoms) and specific measurable objectives, such as functional impairment (e.g., missed work). Once symptoms or behavioral objectives are identified, treatment goals and interventions for reducing symptoms and/ or improving behavioral outcomes are specified. Symptom-focused clinical case conceptualizations emphasize the "what" (diagnoses) and "how" (treatments and interventions) questions regarding patient presentations and tend to regard the "why" (clinical understanding) question as unimportant. Furthermore, symptom-focused clinical case conceptualizations are thought to promote accountability and positive health outcomes, as symptoms and treatment goals are relatively easy to identify, measure, and monitor.

There are some limitations to the symptom-focused clinical case conceptualizations, which may be particularly evident in individual therapy cases where interpersonal psychodynamics are thought to contribute significantly to the understanding and changing of specific behaviors. For example, family therapy perspectives have little interest in individual symptoms and tend to understand symptoms and behaviors as occurring in a larger interpersonal context. However, despite these limitations, symptom-focused clinical case conceptualizations are commonly used in many mental health clinics and inpatient and residential treatment programs.

Theory-Focused Conceptualizations

Theory-focused conceptualizations concentrate on providing theory-based explanations for psychiatric symptoms and impaired functioning. This type of clinical case conceptualization uses a practitioner's therapeutic orientation or understanding of patient symptoms or problem behaviors as the basis for setting treatment goals and identifying appropriate interventions. Theory-focused clinical case conceptualizations can be based on any theoretical model of human behavior, such as cognitive, behavioral, psychodynamic, existential, humanistic, and family systems.

Theory-focused clinical case conceptualizations focus on the "why" question and consider it the most important of the three previously mentioned questions relevant to the construction of a case conceptualization. This is because the "why" question can provide information about a psychiatric presentation beyond that of purely describing symptoms and behavioral functioning. Moreover, theory-focused clinical case conceptualizations are considered by some to more fully capture complex variables (and interactions among important variables) thought to contribute to causing human behavior such as family, cultural, and interpersonal dynamics, as well as biological factors (e.g., physical health status) through a theory-focused explanation.

There are clinical advantages to using the theory-focused clinical case conceptualizations. First, many mental health professionals are trained in using a specific theoretical orientation and framework for understanding and conceptualizing human behavior. This framework may be useful in communicating to other professionals about why the patient is presenting with certain symptoms and some of the potential contributors (e.g., interpersonal, cultural, familial, and biological). Second, having a theoretical orientation or framework can be helpful in guiding the practitioner through the process of identifying valid treatment goals and efficacious intervention techniques. This is perhaps the most important clinical advantage of using the theory-focused clinical case conceptualization.

One potential disadvantage to the theory-focused clinical case conceptualization is the potential for incongruence between the practitioner's theoretical understanding of a patient's presenting problem(s) and a patient's own conceptualization of the same concern(s). This can lead to limited client commitment to the therapist, treatment plan, and process since the treatment goals and plan of intervention may be more meaningful to the practitioner than to the patient.

Client-Focused Conceptualization

Client-focused conceptualizations are developed primarily from the patient's experiences, needs, and expectations as opposed to the practitioner's therapeutic framework. The focus of this type of clinical case conceptualization is tailored treatment and maximizing the fit between the client's needs and expectations with the interventions provided.

One type of client-focused clinical case conceptualization is pattern analysis (Sperry 2005a, 2005b). Pattern analysis is focused on understanding the "what" and "why" of a client's current situation or presentation in order to answer the "how" question (i.e., to make treatment recommendations). For example, a pattern analysis involves collecting information and developing a conceptual framework for understanding patterns of behavior including triggers to specific symptoms and ineffective ways of interacting with others.

Sperry (2005) defines a *pattern* as a consistent and predictable style of thinking, feeling, and engaging in overt behavior. There are four elements of a pattern analysis that are used to describe and better understand a client's ways of behaving—precipitating, predisposing, perpetuating, and presenting factors. A *precipitating factor* might include any triggers or stressors that activate a pattern of behaving. *Predisposing factors* include any intrapersonal or interpersonal factors, such as having a family history of mental illness and/or trauma, which may make the client vulnerable to engaging in a particular pattern of behavior at present. *Perpetuating factors* are those factors that reinforce or strengthen patterns of behavior, such as self or social confirmation regarding particular ways of behaving. And finally, *presenting factors* include such information as severity of symptoms, course of illness (e.g., etiology of psychological problems and/or specific symptoms), diagnosis, and degree of well-being.

Sperry (2005a) suggests that a client's particular ways of behaving and functioning in the world are best understood by examining the interrelationships among precipitating, predisposing, perpetuating, and presenting factors. Specifically, while it may appear that a client's predisposing factors, such as a history of trauma or abuse, maladaptive ways of thinking, and/or personality characteristics, may primarily contribute to how he or she thinks, feels, and acts, it is argued that environmental and intrapersonal triggers, history and course of psychological problems, and how he or she interacts with the environment be considered when developing a case conceptualization.

Problem-Solving Approach to Clinical Case Conceptualizations

One problem-solving approach to developing a clinical case conceptualization, which is grounded in behavior therapy, was developed by Nezu and Nezu (1989) and involves what is called a "superordinate" problem. This can be summarized as "what intervention strategy is likely to be most effective for this client with this specific problem?" (Nezu et al. 1997). This approach to clinical case conceptualization development has two main components—the clinician's *problem orientation* and *problem-solving skills*. The former involves the clinician's beliefs, values, and expectations regarding a client and his or her presenting problem(s). It is argued that these processes form the paradigm of psychological assessment that the clinician utilizes and helps guide he or she toward the problem-solution strategies the clinician will ultimately utilize (Haynes & O'Brien 2000). The latter component, the clinician's problem-solving skills, involves the behaviors in which the clinician engages in an attempt to solve (or lessen the functional impact of) the client's presenting problem. Problem-solving skills include formulating and defining the problem, generating possible solutions to the presenting problem(s), deciding on potential solutions, and implementing chosen solutions.

Nezu and Nezu (1989) suggest three sequential judgments, related to the superordinate problem of deciding on the most effective treatment. Furthermore, these three judgments need to be solved in order. They are: (1) identifying the client's problem and determining if treatment is possible, (2) analysis of the client's problem and determining intervention goals, and (3) determining the best intervention strategy (see Haynes & O'Brien 2000).

Step 1: Identifying the client's problem and determining if treatment is possible. This process involves the assessor collecting information about the client's presenting problem(s) and translating that information into specific and clear treatment goals. Treatment goals can be immediate (e.g., client safety), intermediate (e.g., learn coping skills), and/or ultimate (e.g., learn effective ways to build intimacy). The first step involves collecting information about the client's problems by using a "funnel approach," which involves beginning with a broad-based assessment across several domains relevant to the client's concerns and eventually focusing the assessment on more specific factors, such as antecedent events, specific behavioral responses, and response consequences.

Step 2: Analysis of the client's problems and deciding on intervention goals. Analyzing the client's problem requires identification of specific, instrumental outcomes for the client. These outcomes (e.g., avoidance of intimacy) are often identified as causal variables for behavior problems (e.g., isolation from interpersonal interactions) and can therefore be the target of the behavioral intervention(s). It is assumed that variables contributing to similar behavioral problems across patients may differ; that is, clients may have similar behavioral problems for different reasons. Thus, it is important during this step of the process to identify specific variables that may trigger and/or maintain a client's behavioral problems.

Step 3: Determination of the best intervention strategy. The decision on what will be the best intervention strategy is based on the outcome of steps 1 and 2, along with familiarization of the research on important issues such as the efficacy and cost-effectiveness of a particular intervention approach or set of approaches. All of these pieces of information should be taken into account when choosing intervention strategies. It is also important to note that this process is dynamic, and that new pieces of assessment data may be acquired during the intervention process requiring adapted changes to the intervention approach.

Cognitive–Behavioral Clinical Case Conceptualizations

Like other approaches to clinical case conceptualizations, cognitive-behavioral (CB) clinical case conceptualizations are designed to help the clinician decide on the best treatment approach for the client. This approach to clinical case conceptualization uses assessment data that includes information about the client's problem behavior (e.g., topographical features such as symptom severity and structure of the behavior problem), causal/maintaining factors (e.g., work-related stress), and identification of functional relations. The term *functional relations* refers to a situation where "two or more variables have shared variance. Some dimension (e.g., rate, magnitude, length, age) of one variable is associated with some dimension of another" (see Haynes & O'Brien 2000, 302).

Cognitive-behavioral clinical case conceptualizations parallel cognitive theories of behavioral problems in that they focus on the role of core beliefs, unhelpful thinking patterns, and life events as important contributors to behavior problems (Persons & Tompkins 1997). Furthermore, CB clinical case conceptualizations of client problem behavior can help the clinician develop working hypotheses about factors contributing to the presenting problem(s). CB clinical case conceptualizations have four components: (a) behavior problems list, (b) core beliefs list, (c) activating events and situations, and (d) working hypotheses (see Haynes & O'Brien 2000):

a. *Behavior problems list.* This is an exhaustive, specific list of the client's behavior problems.

b. *Core beliefs list.* This list includes a client's set of beliefs about him or her and/or the surrounding world. This list would include beliefs that are thought to be influencing the problem behavior in some way. In this type of case formulation, these are the primal causal variables. One common approach to assessing the client's beliefs about themselves and/or the world is thorough a *thought record*—a method of self-report by which clients write down specific situations and the behaviors, emotions, thoughts, and other responses they might have to the these situations.

c. *Activating events and situations.* These are external events that activate or trigger core beliefs about oneself and/or the world, which lead to behavior problems.

d. *Working hypotheses.* These are dynamic models of interrelations among variables (e.g., core beliefs, activating events) thought to contribute to the behavior problems.

In addition to the four components of a CB clinical case conceptualization discussed above, there are also three other important components—the origins of core beliefs, the intervention plan, and predicted intervention obstacles. These seven components form the basis for the CB variant of a clinical case conceptualization, and guide the clinician toward a treatment plan.

Dialectical Behavior Therapy Clinical Case Conceptualizations

Dr. Linehan (1993) has developed a model of clinical case conceptualizations to be used when working with clients presenting with borderline personality disorder (BPD). This approach to clinical case conceptualization development integrates such factors as a stage theory of intervention, a biopsychosocial theory of precipitating and maintaining factors contributing to the development of BPD, learning principles, and potential barriers to the success of the intervention, all within the context of a dialectical approach to change (Koerner & Linehan 1997).

One important feature of the DBT model of clinical case conceptualizations is that it is contextual in nature, meaning that a client's problem behavior is examined within the context of the setting in which the behavior occurs. Moreover, this type of clinical case conceptualization takes into account the client's interactions with the therapist and any variables that might affect the therapist, and it makes the assumption that there are many factors affecting the client's behavior and that this process is dynamic.

The DBT model of clinical case conceptualization emphasizes the importance of preintervention assessment and the development of a clinical case formulation to guide treatment recommendations. This emphasis is highlighted in the following points (adapted from Haynes & O'Brien 2000):

- The development of BPD can occur as a result of multiple interacting factors. Perhaps some of the most important factors are a biological vulnerability and high sensitivity to emotional stimuli, which can result in high reactivity and slow recovery. High emotional reactivity followed by the client's difficulty returning to baseline emotional experience is moderated by the client's social environment. For example, an environment that is invalidating or teaches a client that his or her emotional reactions are incorrect or problematic can trigger intense, dysfunctional emotional responses.

- Intervention strategies are chosen based on identified functional relations, particularly important to this decision are antecedent and consequence relationships, which are hypothesized to contribute to the problem behavior (i.e., causal chains). Causal chains consist of any thoughts, overt behaviors, emotional reactions, and environmental activities (such as responses by others) that may precipitate and/or maintain the client's problem behavior. Furthermore, identifying causal chains, and specifically factors that may influence a client's behavior, is important in helping the client choose potential places on the chain to engage in perhaps new, more adaptive ways of behaving.

- The client's ability to behave effectively varies across contexts. For example, clients' emotional reactivity may be higher in those situations where they are sleep deprived or facing a life stressor.

- The client plays an active role in influencing how the environment (e.g., other persons) responds to their actions.
- Clients can interact with the environment in dysfunctional ways for a wide variety of reasons, including having insufficient skills, a history of being reinforced for dysfunctional behavior, difficulty managing aversive emotional experiences, and faulty or irrational beliefs.
- DBT employs a task analysis model for improving client problem behavior. For example, the therapist might use information gathered from the causal chains to find points on the chain where the client might engage in new, more effective ways of responding to his or her environment. The task analysis will include a step-by-step sequence of behaviors leading up to a more effective way in which to respond to an environmental stressor.
- In addition, DBT does not assume that the client will always act like he or she is supposed to. Linehan has developed an important construct—*therapy interfering behaviors*. These are behaviors that impede the progress of therapy (e.g., missing sessions, not doing homework, tangential discussions in therapy, etc.). These are also important to consider in one's case conceptualization. The therapist should ask, "What tendencies can I discern in the client that might cause him or her to terminate therapy prematurely, and how can I prepare for and handle these?"

Commonalities Between Models of Clinical Case Conceptualizations

Several models of clinical case conceptualizations have been presented in this chapter. It is important to note that despite the apparent difference in these approaches (e.g., model of psychotherapy), there are many similarities that can be extracted from a careful review of their components. For example, similarities include: the importance of pretreatment assessment and specification of the client's problem behavior(s); using pretreatment assessment data to identify the most effective intervention strategies, and, perhaps similarly, a focus on teaching the client new, more effective ways of interacting with the environment, whether the focus is on changing negative thoughts, managing aversive emotional experiences, or changing overt behavior; and the assumption that client's problem behavior is influenced by many factors.

Using Clinical Case Conceptualizations to Prepare for the Termination of Psychotherapy: Some Final Clinical Recommendations

Unfortunately there is a lack of empirical research on the most effective ways to engage in the process of termination. However, several recommendations for using clinical case conceptualizations with clients to prepare for the process of termination can be deduced from the review presented in this chapter. The following section is broken down into three subsections concerning the development of a clinical case conceptualization, how to present and discuss this information with the client, and, finally, how to use the clinical case conceptualization to prepare for the termination process.

Development of a Clinical Case Conceptualization

- Develop a clinical case conceptualization so that it contains at least the following elements: identified problem behaviors, specified improvements (or treatment goals), the client's therapy-interfering behaviors, and planned intervention strategies to be used over the course of treatment. It is important to note that the contents of a clinical case conceptualization are expected to change as new information becomes available about variables contributing to a client's problem behavior. This is especially the case for treatment strategies that should be changed, added, or discarded contingent on new information about a client's problem behavior.
- Have a preliminary draft of the clinical case conceptualization completed early in the therapy process, preferably after initial assessment is complete and before treatment begins. Share this information with the client during a regularly scheduled session. As stated earlier, a clinical case conceptualization

should not be given directly to a client (due to the potential for misinterpretation of the information presented), but instead it should be discussed in the context of the therapy session, whereby any questions and/or misconceptions can be addressed directly by the therapist.

*How to Present and Discuss the Clinical Case
Conceptualization With the Client*

- The clinician should present the behavior problems that have been identified and compare this information with the client's perceptions of their presenting problem. The clinician and client should generally be in agreement as to what the presenting problems are that will be targeted in therapy.
- The clinician should inform the client of his/her general approach to treatment and secure "informed consent" (e.g., advise the client what treatment will consist of and secure the client's consent) and address misconceptions about the treatment process at that time.
- Once treatment targets and interventions are presented, discussed, and agreed upon, the clinician should inform the patient that "the clinical case conceptualization will help guide us through the treatment process; specifically, it will help inform us of the impact of treatment on these identified problems."

*Using the Clinical Case Conceptualization to
Prepare for the Termination Process*

- Periodically it may be useful to review the clinical case conceptualization with the client to inform him or her of any changes in your perspective regarding treatment targets, goals, and intervention strategies. This is also a useful way to check in with the patient every session or couple of sessions to discuss treatment progress (e.g., does the client feel he or she is getting better?).
- Ideally, the clinical case conceptualization should guide the clinician toward the termination process. As the treatment

goals are addressed, the treatment process moves closer to the termination phase. The client is always informed of what the treatment targets, goals, and strategies are, and is viewed as a partner in the treatment and termination process.

Summary and Conclusion

Clinical case conceptualizations are arguably becoming a standard component of many psychotherapies and treatment delivery contexts, and this trend will most likely continue. One of the main advantages of using a clinical case conceptualization is that it can help guide the process of psychotherapy and help the practitioner identify when it may be in the client's best interest to terminate psychotherapy (e.g., when the most important goals of therapy have been addressed successfully). In sum, this chapter provided an overview of the concept of clinical case conceptualization, its main components, and most common models for developing clinical case conceptualizations while working in various treatment modalities. Specific recommendations are made where applicable and were designed to provide readers with practical suggestions for employing clinical case conceptualizations in their practice.

References

Eells, T. D. (Ed.). (1997). *Handbook of psychotherapy case formulation*. New York: Guilford Press.

Eells, T. D., & Lombart, K. G. (2003). Case formulations and treatment concepts among novice, experienced, and expert cognitive-behavioral and psychodynamic therapists. *Psychotherapy Research, 13* (2), 187–204.

Falvey, J. E. (2001). Clinical judgement in case conceptualization and treatment planning across mental health disciplines. *Journal of Counseling & Development, 79*, 292–303.

Haynes, S. N., & O'Brien, W. H. (2000). *Principles and practice of behavioral assessment*. New York: Kluwer Academic.

Hettema, J., Steele, J., & Miller, W. R. (2005). Motivational interviewing. *Annual Review of Clinical Psychology, 1*, 91–111.

Koerner, K., & Linehan, M. M. (1997). Case formulation in dialectical behavior therapy. In T. D. Eells (Ed.), *Handbook of psychotherapy case formulation* (pp. 340–367). New York: Guilford Press.

Linehan, M. M. (1993). *Cognitive-behavioral treatment for of borderline personality disorder.* New York: Guilford Press.

Marlatt, G. A. (1980). Relapse prevention; a self control program for the treatment of addictive behaviors. Unpublished manuscript, University of Washington, Seattle.

Miller, W. R. & Rollnick, S. (2002). *Motivational interviewing: preparing people for change* (2nd. Ed.). New York: The Guilford Press.

Nezu, A. M., Nezu, C. M., Friedman, S. H., & Haynes, S. N. (1997). Case formulation in behavior therapy: Problem-solving and functional analytic strategies. In T. D. Eells (Ed.), *Handbook of psychotherapy case formulation* (pp. 368–401). New York: Guilford Press.

Nezu, A. M., & Nezu, C. M. (1989). *Clinical decision making in behavior therapy: A problem solving perspective.* Champagne, IL: Research Press.

O'Donohue, W. T. (1991). Normative models of clinical decisions. *Behavior Therapist, 14,* 70–72.

O'Donohue, W. T., & Levensky, E. (2006). *Promoting treatment adherence: A practical handbook for health care providers.* Thousand Oaks, CA: Sage.

Pekarik, G. (1985). Coping with dropouts. *Professional Psychology: Research and Practice, 16,* 114–123.

Persons, J. B., & Tompkins, M. A. (1997). Cognitive-behavioral case formulation. In T. D. Eells (Ed.), *Handbook of psychotherapy case formulation* (pp. 340–367). New York: Guilford Press.

Resnicow, K., DiIorio, C., Soet, J. E., Ernst, D., Borelli, B., & Hecht, J. (2002). Motivational interivewing in health promotion: It sounds like something is changing. *Health Psychology, 21*(5), 444–451.

Russell, B. (1972). *The history of western philosophy.* New York: Simon & Schuster.

Scamardo, M., Bobele, M., & Biever, J. L. (2004). A new client perspective on client dropouts. *Journal of Systematic Therapies, 23* (2), 27–38.

Sperry, L. (2005a). Case conceptualizations: a strategy for incorporating individual, couple and family dynamics in the treatment process. *American Journal of Family Therapy, 33,* 353–364.

Sperry, L. (2005b). Case conceptualizations: The missing link between theory and practice. *Family Journal: Counseling and Therapy for Couples and Families, 13* (1), 71–76.

7

TERMINATION AT EACH STAGE OF CHANGE

JAMES O. PROCHASKA AND JANICE M. PROCHASKA

Psychotherapy does not equal change. Change typically starts before therapy begins and change should continue after therapy ends. Change can occur without therapy and sometimes change fails to occur with psychotherapy. Given these facts, how therapy begins and ends is very important to whether change occurs and continues. This chapter will explore different types of change in therapy and different types of termination from the theoretical and empirical perspective of the stages of change. We will close with recommendations for optimizing change and termination from psychotherapy.

Types of Change

Figure 7.1 presents the four most common types of changes that occur as a result of psychotherapy. No treatment effect is the most disappointing result, in which no significant changes compared to no treatment are found during therapy and after therapy has terminated. An example of a *no effects* trajectory has been found with batterer intervention programs. A recent meta-analysis of 22 outcome studies found effect sizes of $d. = 09$ and $d. = .12$ for studies relying on partner reports of recidivism and criminal justice records (Babcock, Green, & Robie 2004). The report concluded that current interventions have a minimal impact on reducing recidivism beyond the effect of being arrested. Therapies that produce no significant effects are particularly problematic for both the starting and ending of treatment. The first question is

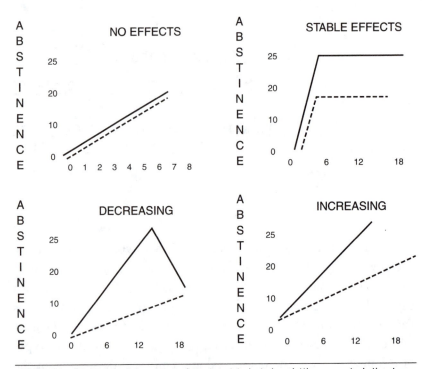

Figure 7.1 Illustration of four types of treatment trajectories plotting percent abstinent over time: no effects, stable effects, decreasing effects, and increasing effects with a solid line representing treatment groups and a dashed line for control groups.

should therapies be started, and in an age of evidence-based therapies many would argue that they should not. But given the seriousness of a problem like partner violence, a case can be made that the best that is available should be offered, even if it is not good enough.

When should such a treatment be terminated? If a treatment is producing no significant effects, then premature termination is likely to be a serious problem. In batterer's treatment, dropouts are all too common, even though there are likely to be serious legal consequences for dropping out of mandated treatment. In cases where treatment is not working and no significant changes are occurring, then termination of that treatment is clearly indicated. Either referral to another type of treatment or changing to an alternative therapy would be appropriate if the therapist is skilled in an alternative treatment.

Decreasing effects have often been found with more intensive treatments where patients may become dependent on the services for social support, social monitoring, and other social controls and assistance. Treatments for obesity are examples of where decreasing effects are the norm. In one of our most intensive population-based, smoking cessation interventions combining tailored interventions with proactive telephone counseling, we found that this condition was outperforming tailored interventions alone in the first assessment after treatment ended. But over time, the more intensive treatment effects decreased, while the tailored treatment effects increased and the two conditions ended up tied (Prochaska et al. 2001a). Therapies that lead to decreasing effects with particular behaviors produce special termination problems for both patients and practitioners.

In contrast, in their comprehensive meta-analyses of motivational interviewing (MI), Burke et al. (2003) analyzed the pattern of treatment effects over time. *Stable effects* were found with alcohol abuse and drug addiction with the significant effects at the end of MI remaining stable over longer-term follow-ups. Also, in a stress management study, a national sample of 1,085 adults was recruited by mail and telephone in the pre-action stages for stress management. The treatment group received a stage-based manual at baseline, and individualized tailored reports in the mail at baseline, at three months, and at six months. At twelve and eighteen months follow-up, significantly more treatment-group than assessment-only participants were in the action or maintenance stage for stress management (62 percent vs. 45 percent, respectively) (Evers et al. forthcoming). Therapies that produce stable effects with particular behaviors can make termination much easier for both patients and psychotherapists.

With transtheoretical model tailored interventions, *increasing treatment effects* is the trajectory that has been produced most often. Here the further out the follow-ups occur, the more the treatment groups improved compared to controls (e.g., Prochaska et al., 2001 a, b). Increasing trajectories are found with each demographic group we have analyzed. For example, the trajectories of male and female smokers are essentially identical at each assessment over two years (Velicer et al. 2007). This trajectory can be particularly important for therapy services, where the treatment continues to have increasing impacts long after the treatment ends. Here the client is more self-reliant and keeps improving after treatment has terminated. Termination should be the easiest for therapists and therapies that produce increased self-reliance and increasing changes long after the treatment ends.

Types of Termination

The quickest termination, which should be most troubling, is the *no show*. Ken Howard, the noted psychotherapy researcher, used to say that the modal or most common number of sessions in psychotherapy was not one session. It was –1; call and no show. With female patients who are in the hospital and are prescribed cardiac rehabilitation for free, what percentage are no shows? Nationally the percentage is over 80 percent (Beckie 2002). The recovery movement claims that people must have a crisis before they will be motivated to change. Even with a life-threatening crisis like a heart attack, a large majority do not show up for free behavioral therapies that can save lives. Ken Howard encouraged therapists to recognize that therapy begins at the very first contact, such as the first phone call. We shall see how therapists can use the stages-of-change model to keep therapy from terminating before it barely begins.

Premature termination is when therapy ends quickly and against the therapist's advice. Premature termination is a major concern due to its remarkable prevalence. In mental health agencies 20 percent to 57 percent of outpatients terminate against their therapist's advice after the first session (Deane 1991; Waller 1997). Reviews of the literature revealed that 30 percent to 60 percent of psychotherapy outpatients drop out of treatment prior to completing their therapeutic goals (Clinton, 1996; Pekarik 1992). Meta-analyses of 125 studies (Wierzbicki & Pekarik 1993) found that a mean of 47 percent of clients drop out of psychotherapy prematurely.

Premature termination also receives much attention due to its high cost to patients, therapists, healthcare systems, and employees. Patients' personal losses include the disservice clients impose upon themselves for terminating against the clinician's advice. Therapists may interpret early termination as a personal failure as well as rejection. Financial losses disrupt the effective provision of psychotherapeutic services.

With the goal of reducing the high costs of dropping out, research has been aimed at identifying predictors of premature termination. Wierzbicki and Pekarik (1993) found only four variables that yielded significant effect sizes. Three of these were client demographic variables. Clients with low education and low income, and who were identified as ethnic or of a racial minority dropped out more often. The fourth variable was definitional–lower dropout rates were found when dropouts were defined by therapist judgments rather than by number of sessions or by number of sessions and judgments combined.

The range of variables that were not significantly related to dropout was striking. Therapy modality (individual vs. family, couple, and group), therapy setting (university clinic vs. private clinic vs. public clinic vs. others), and developmental status of clients (adults vs. children vs. mixed) were not significantly related to dropout status (Wierzbicki & Pekarik 1993). Therapist variables that did not correlate significantly with dropout included gender, minority status, experience, and type of academic degree. The type of treatment problem, such as emotional, behavioral, or psychotic, as well as substance abuse and health and developmental disorders, also did not relate significantly to dropout status, nor did prior treatment or waiting period. Wierzbicki and Pekarik (1993) concluded that variables that are measured most often and most simply, such as client, therapist, and problem characteristics, are not strongly associated with dropout. We shall see how variables, such as stage of change from the transtheoretical model, have been able to predict premature termination, and how the same variables can be used to prevent premature termination.

Delayed termination is when therapy continues even though additional benefits from therapy do not continue. Delayed termination can occur with therapies that have no treatment effects, but both the therapist and the client believe that effects can be found if they just keep trying. Delayed termination can also occur when decreasing treatment effects are anticipated, and both the therapist and client are afraid to stop lest they face a future of decreasing benefits. We shall see how delayed termination can also occur when both the therapist and client are stuck in a favorite stage of change.

Rapid but appropriate termination is when therapy ends sooner than anticipated, but appropriately, as judged by the therapist. Here the therapist and client should both have confidence that the relatively quick changes in therapy are at least stable and perhaps even likely to increase. We shall see which stages of change predict such termination.

Planned and appropriate termination is when therapy ends in the number of anticipated sessions and as appropriately planned by both the patient and practitioner. Here they both should have confidence that the changes are likely to be stable or increase after therapy ends.

Stages of Change and the Transtheoretical Model

The dominant approach to behavior change has been an action paradigm that construes change as an event, such as when someone quits using cocaine or stops battering his or her partner. The transtheoretical model (TTM) construes behavior change as a process that unfolds over time and involves progress through six stages of change: precontemplation, contemplation, preparation, action, maintenance, and termination (Prochaska, Norcross, & DiClemente 1994). We shall briefly review the stages of change and other TTM constructs, and then see how they can be applied to help many more people begin therapy and complete therapy appropriately.

Precontemplation is the stage in which people are not intending to take action in the foreseeable future, usually measured as the next six months. Historically, these patients were labeled noncompliant, resistant, unmotivated, or not ready for our therapies. We now know that *we* were not ready for *them,* and that we were not motivated to match our interventions to their needs rather than demand that they match the needs of our therapies. People in precontemplation underestimate the pros of changing, overestimate the cons, and are usually not conscious of making such mistakes. If they are not consciousness of making such mistakes without our help, they are likely to stay stuck in this stage for long periods of time, doing considerable damage to themselves or others.

When people progress to the *contemplation* stage, their appreciation of the pros of changing increase, but the cons often increase as well. If they are seriously intending to quit drinking alcohol for good in the next six months, they can be more acutely aware that they may be more stressed, they may have to let go of a "good friend," and they certainly have to risk failing. We shall see that their evaluations of the pros and cons of changing are about equal, producing profound ambivalence. "Is change worth it? Should I keep progressing? Should I put it off?" The rule of thumb for contemplators is "When in doubt, don't change!"

As people progress into *preparation*, their pros of changing pass up the cons. They are convinced that the benefits of changing outweigh the costs. The number one concern is "When I act, will I fail?" This is a realistic anxiety since the rule for chronic behavior on a single action attempt is relapse rather than sustained action. Those in preparation need to be adequately prepared before they take action.

Action is the busiest stage in which change is now overt and clearly observable, such as when the person exercises to reduce depression or takes their medications as prescribed. Here people need to be prepared for how long action lasts. Many think the worst is over in a few weeks or a few months. We prepare people for a six-month concerted effort where they need to be prepared to work hard to keep from relapsing.

After about six months, people progress into the *maintenance* stage, where they do not have to work nearly as hard to keep from relapsing. What do they need to be prepared for? What is the most common cause of relapse across most chronic conditions? Stress is what many guess, but it is distress. Times of depression, anxiety, loneliness, boredom, anger, and stress are the times in which people are at their weakest, psychologically and emotionally.

How do average Americans cope with distress? They drink more alcohol, eat more junk food, smoke more cigarettes, and take more over-the-counter and under-the-counter drugs to cope with distress. Americans cope most often with some form of oral behavior. What is a healthy oral behavior that many can use to cope with distress? Talking, of course. We have known for decades that talking and social support is a major buffer for stress and distress. Distress is the number one reason why people seek healthcare. And how long do they get to talk before their physician interrupts them? About thirty seconds.

Termination is the stage in which the problem is over and the person does not have to work to keep from relapsing. The criteria we use to measure this stage are 100 percent confidence and zero temptation to return to the pathological pattern. No matter whether they are depressed, anxious, lonely, celebrating, or stressed, they have total confidence they will not return to the bottle and they have no temptations to return. Of alcoholics in the maintenance stage, we found that about 20 percent had reached termination of their problem (Snow, Prochaska, & Rossi 1994). The problem for patients and providers is

that psychotherapy always has to terminate before the problem terminates, if it ever does.

Pros and Cons of Changing Across the Stages of Change

Figure 7.2 represents a meta-analysis of the pros and cons of changing across five stages of change for over forty behaviors (Hall & Rossi
2003). These behaviors include mental health problems like depression, anxiety, eating disorders, cocaine and heroin use, and health
behaviors like smoking, inactivity, unhealthy diets, and obesity. The
same pattern is found for physician's stages of change for counseling
smokers. The same pattern is also found for patients' pros and cons
of being in therapy and for patients' stage of change when starting
psychotherapy.

Figure 7.2 clearly shows that people in precontemplation see the
cons of changing as clearly more important than the pros. But this is
true only when we use standardized scores, which control for ease of
responding. Raw scores, which would reflect more conscious responding, almost always have the pros of changing as more important than
the cons for people at each stage of change.

The pros of changing clearly increase from precontemplation to contemplation, where the pros and cons are tied. In preparation, the pros

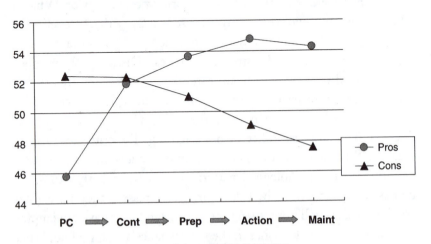

Pros and cons (in T scores) across stages of change for 43 health behaviors

Figure 7. 2   Meta-analysis of the pros and cons across five stages of change.

clearly outweigh cons and the difference increases in action and maintenance. Let's apply the TTM variables to predicting termination.

TTM and Termination Data

Figure 7.3 shows the stage profiles of three groups of patients in psychotherapy for a variety of mental health problems. The 40 percent of the patients who were premature terminators had a group profile of people in precontemplation at the start of treatment. The 15 percent of the patients who were rapid but appropriate terminators had a group profile of people in the action stage when they started. Those who continued in long-term treatment were a mixed group, with most in contemplation (Brogan, Prochaska, & Prochaska 1999).

When professional audiences of therapists and counselors are asked about their clinical strategy or plan with patients who have recently taken action to quit an addiction, a quick consensus is reached about relapse prevention. But would relapse prevention make sense with patients starting in precontemplation? Of course not, is the consensus. But what would be their clinical strategy? Here there is mostly silence

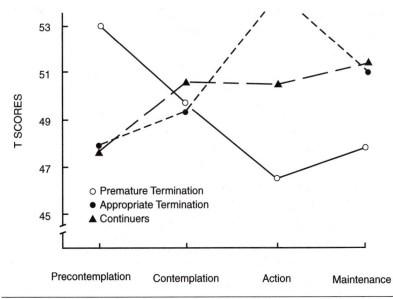

Figure 7.3 Pretherapy stage profiles for premature terminators, appropriate terminators, and continuers.

and struggling. When asked to identify their number one concern, they quickly concur—dropout or premature termination. So our strategy needs to be dropout prevention or premature termination prevention.

First, we need to assess what stage the patient is in to determine their risk of dropping out. Second, we need to set a realistic goal for the start of therapy. Is it realistic to get the patient in precontemplation to take immediate action? If we try, they are likely to drop out. That doesn't mean we cannot help them to begin changing if we understand changing as equaling as progressing. So a starting goal that can raise their sense of self-efficacy and ours is to first help them progress to contemplation. How do we accomplish that? By helping them to increase their appreciation of the pros of changing.

Here is an example with a client in precontemplation who had a serious cocaine addiction, marital conflicts, career crisis, and anger that at times burst into abuse. First, I (Jim) provided the patient with a diagram of the stages of change and where he was (precontemplation). I let him know that I could work with that, but my major concern was that he would drop out before I had a chance to make a significant difference in his life. I shared with him my understanding that he was more likely to stay with therapy if he appreciated all the pros or benefits that came from therapy. So I asked, "Do you think therapy could help you with your cocaine problem?"

"Yeah, I believe that."

"Do you think it could help you to be less defensive about yourself?"

"Yeah, I see that."

"Do you believe it could help you with your wife?"

"Yes, she sent me here."

"Good. Do you think it could help you to make more money?"

"It will help you make more money!"

"That's true, and I appreciate that."

I told him that as far as I knew, there is only one thing he could do for an hour a week that could give him more benefits.

"What's that?" he asked.

"I'm not going to tell you because you might leave for that," I joke, "but I will tell you when you are done."

At another point I asked him, "If you feel I am pressuring you to do things you are not ready to do, will you let me know?"

"You'll know!" he blurted.

"How will I know?"

"I'll get angry as hell!" he asserts.

"That's O.K., I can work with that. What I can't work with is your not coming back."

Stages of Change and Types of Termination

No Show

Unfortunately, we know the least about people who need the most help when starting therapy—the no shows. We do know that individuals who are least likely to start an intervention program without special efforts are those in the precontemplation stage. Think of their denial, defensiveness, and demoralization. Remember that intervention begins at the initial contact, and we need to let those people know that wherever they are in the process, we can work with that. We share our understanding that some people are ready to take action—some are not ready. Some people are determined, some are demoralized, some are defensive, and some are in doubt. Wherever you are, we can be of help. Since the dominant paradigm of behavior change is still action, the naïve public is likely to believe that if they are not ready to take action, therapy will be a waste of time, effort, and money.

With our population-based programs for a variety of health and mental health behaviors, like alcohol abuse, partner abuse, depression, stress, and smoking, our outreach methods with such messages result in a majority of the population participating, and the majority of the participants are in precontemplation or contemplation (e.g., Prochaska et al. 2001 a, b; Evers et al. forthcoming; Laforge forthcoming).

Premature Termination

As seen in Figure 7.3, the stage profile of the whole group of patients who terminated psychotherapy quickly, and prematurely as judged by their therapists, was of people in precontemplation. The general principle of helping these patients complete therapy is to match our treatment to their stage. In our population programs, where the expert system intervention is matched to their stage and tailored to each TTM variable that can help them progress to the next stage, we find that participants in precontemplation complete the programs at the same high rate as those in preparation.

Here is another method for influencing premature termination. Connors et al. (2001) compared two interventions to reduce their rates of 75 percent premature termination in their psychotherapy program for alcohol problems. Role induction has been the most studied method, and it is designed to prepare people for the unusual role of being a patient in therapy. They found that this intervention had no significant effect. However, a single session of motivational interviewing based on a stage paradigm reduced dropout rates from 75 percent to 50 percent.

Delayed Termination

In the era of managed care, seriously delayed termination is much less common than in earlier eras. This issue has mainly come under the social control of managed care. We do joke at times, that in the old days if you had a patient in contemplation with a therapist who loved to contemplate, you had interminable therapy. We do empathize, however, with the anxiety that can be raised as patients are prepared to take action. Here, achievement anxiety can occur for clients and clinicians since relapse is the rule for most chronic problems rather than successful action. With contemplation, the anxiety can be avoided, so action can be delayed as can termination.

More challenging is the issue of termination when it is clear that decreasing treatment effects will occur, like with obesity. A case can be made that obesity should be treated as a chronic, lifetime disorder, like diabetes. On the other hand, if a significant amount of weight loss can be maintained, then much of diabetes could be prevented or reversed. One of the problems has been that healthy weight management typically involves multiple behavior changes, such as exercise, diet, calorie control, and control of emotional eating. Until recently, we had no evidence-based programs for multiple behavior change. The general rule was to change only one behavior at a time, lest you overwhelm patients. But that rule was based on an action paradigm. In populations with four behavior risks, less than 10 percent are prepared to take action on two or more behaviors, so people won't be overwhelmed with too much action. A growing body of research is demonstrating that stage-based interventions can produce significant changes in multiple behaviors treated simultaneously (Jones et al. 2003; Prochaska et al. 2004; Prochaska et al. 2005). Further, the results are the same as treating a single behavior like smoking (Prochaska, J. J., 2006). Finally, with all behaviors there are either stable or increasing treatment effects long after intervention has ended. Currently, we have population and stage-based multiple behavior change programs for weight management in clinical trials for both adults and adolescents.

As seen in Figure 7.3, the 15 percent of patients who terminated quickly but appropriately had a stage profile of people in action. These patients benefit from all the progress (change) they had made prior to starting therapy and did not need longer therapy. A serious concern in the managed care era is that clinicians will feel pressure to get their clients to take rapid action so they can terminate within the tight time constraints under which they must work. The consequences are likely to be predictable: either rapid but inappropriate termination or decreasing treatment effects once the pressured treatment has ended.

Planned and Appropriate Termination

The types of planned and appropriate termination should be related to the predicted type of treatment effect. With decreasing treatment effects, for example, our primary concern is that the patients have become dependent on their clinicians in the same way they can become dependent on substances. Therapists provide social support, social monitoring, and other social controls that complement self controls. One way to assess how much change during therapy is under social control is to determine when patients do their therapy homework. If they do it the night before or the day of therapy, it is a sign of their therapeutic behavior being more under social than self-control. If patients are dependent on their clinician, then one strategy that can be used is to fade out the therapy the way we at times fade out nicotine. Our typical practice was to see patients once a week until they were progressing, then go to every two weeks, monthly, and then as needed for a couple of sessions. Another alternative for those with greater needs is to transfer some of the dependency to a social support group, like AA (Alcoholics Anonymous) or Weight Watchers.

With stable treatment effects, patients are most likely to have progressed to the action stage by the time our brief treatments end. We can communicate with more confidence that they are likely to experience stable effects of the action they have taken to date. In regular psychotherapy, we would want to see if the patient would feel free to call us if the stable effects were not occurring. Then, with recycling, we would determine to what stage they had regressed. Fortunately, only about 15 percent regress all the way back to precontemplation. The others are already contemplating or preparing to take action in the near future. We would review what they did right, what mistakes they made, and what they would need to do differently as they take action again.

With increasing treatment effects, patients are most likely to have progressed, but without taking action by the time our brief treatment ends. With such patients, we encourage them to build on the progress to date and what they have learned about how to change. They learn, for example, that if they have progressed two stages with brief treatment, they have about tripled their chances of taking effective action in the next six months. While therapy may terminate, change can continue as they build on a stronger foundation and attribute progress primarily to their own competencies rather than those of the clinician.

Types of Termination by Stages of Change

Figure 7.4 presents an integration of the five types of termination and five stages of change. What is clear is that the most common and problematic types of termination (no shows, premature, and delayed termination), typically occur most often with patients who begin therapy in the precontemplation or contemplation stages of change. As we have learned more empirically and clinically about these important populations, we have developed strategies for engaging many more of those individuals in therapy. As these patients begin to progress through the stages, we can then engage in appropriate termination strategies that need not be problematic. A key factor is to respect where they are in the process when they finish therapy. One of the values that TTM can add

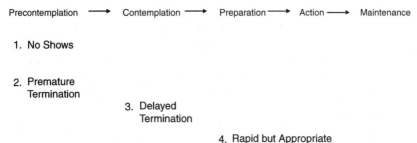

Figure 7.4 Types of termination by stages of change.

is to help clients appreciate that change is a process that typically begins prior to therapy, continues after therapy, and involves progression and often recycling through the stages of change. This approach can help clients and clinicians to be realistic about what can be accomplished in brief therapy and to terminate therapy knowing that important stages in their journey of change are still to come.

References

Babcock, J. C., Green, C. E., & Robie, C. (2004). Does batterers' treatment work? A meta-analytic review of domestic violence treatment outcome research. *Clinical Psychology Review, 23,* 1023–1053.

Beckie, T. (2002). A women's-only phase II cardiac rehabilitation program. Grant application. U.S. Department of Health and Human Services.

Brogan, M. M., Prochaska, J. O., & Prochaska, J. M. (1999). Predicting termination and continuation status in therapy using the transtheoretical model. *Psychotherapy, 36,* 105–113.

Burke, B. L., Arkowitz, H., & Mechola, M. (2003). The efficacy of motivational interviewing: A meta-analysis of controlled clinical trials. *Journal of Consulting and Clinical Psychology, 71,* 843–861.

Clinton, D. (1996). Why do eating disorder patients drop out? *Psychotherapy and Psychometrics, 65,* 29–35.

Connors, G., Donovan, D., & DiClemente, C. C. (2001). *Substance abuse treatment and the stages of change.* New York: Guilford Press.

Deane, F. (1991). Attendance and drop-out from outpatient psychotherapy in New Zealand. *Community Mental Health in New Zealand, 6,* 34–51.

Evers, K. E., Prochaska, J. O., Mauriello, L. M., Padula, J. A., Prochaska, J. M. (In press). A randomized clinical trial of a population and transtheoretical-based stress management intervention. *Health Psychology.*

Hall, K. L., & Rossi, J. S. (2003). Informing interventions: A meta-analysis of the magnitude of effect in decisional balance stage transitions across 43 health behaviors. *Annals of behavioral Medicine, 25* (Suppl.), S180.

Jones, H., Edwards, L., Vallis, T. M., Ruggiero, L., Rossi, S. R., Rossi, J. S., et al. (2003). Changes in diabetes self-care behaviors make a difference in glycemic control: The Diabetes Stages of Change (DiSC) study. *Diabetes Care, 26,* 1468–1474.

Laforge, R. G. (In press). A population based individual alcohol harm reduction program feedback intervention: Preliminary results from the college-based alcohol risk reduction (CBARR) trial. *Alcoholism: Clinical and Experimental Research.*

Pekarik, G. (1985). Coping with dropout. *Professional Psychology: Research and Practice, 16,* 114–123.

Pekarik, G. (1992). Post treatment adjustment of clients who drop out vs. late in treatment. *Journal of Clinical Psychology, 48,* 378–395.

Prochaska, J. J., Velicer, W. F., Prochaska, J. O., Deluschi, K. I., & Hall, S. M. (2007). Comparing treatment outcomes in smokers with single versus multiple behavior risks. *Health Psychology, 25,* 380–388.

Prochaska, J. O., Norcross, J. C., & DiClemente, C. C. (1994). *Changing for good.* New York: Morrow.

Prochaska, J.O., Velicer, W.F., Redding, C.A., Rossi, J.S., Goldstein, M., Depue, J., Greene, G.W., Rossi, S.R., & Sun, X. (2005). Stage-based expert systems to guide a population of primary care patients to quit smoking, eat healthier, prevent skin cancer and receive regular mammograms. *Preventive Medicine, 41,* 406–416.

Prochaska, J.O., Velicer, W.F., Rossi, J.S., Redding, C.A., Greene, G.W., Rossi, S.R., Sun, X., Fava, J.L., Laforge, R.G., & Plummer, B. (2004). Multiple risk expert systems for smoking, high-fat diet, and sun exposure in a population of parents. *Health Psychology, 23,* 503–516.

Prochaska, J. O., Velicer, W. F., Fava, J., Ruggiero, L., Laforge, R., Rossi, J. S., et al. (2001a). Counselor and stimulus control enhancements of a stage matched expert system for smokers in a managed care setting. *Preventive Medicine, 32,* 23–32.

Prochaska, J. O., Velicer, W. F., Fava, J. L., Rossi, J. S., & Tsoh, J. Y. (2001b). Evaluating a population-based recruitment approach and a stage-based expert system intervention for smoking cessation. *Addictive Behaviors, 26,* 583–602.

Snow, M. G., Prochaska J. O., & Rossi, J. S. (1994). Processes of change in alcoholics anonymous: Issues in maintaining long-term sobriety. *Journal of Studies on Alcohol, 55,* 362–371.

Velicer, W. F., Redding, C. A., Sun, X., & Prochaska, J. O. (2007). Demographic variables, smoking variables and outcomes across five studies. *Health Psychology, 26,* 278–287.

Waller, G. (1997). Drop-out and failure to engage in individual outpatient cognitive behavior therapy for bulimic disorders. *International Journal of Eating Disorders, 22,* 35–41.

Wierzbicki, M., & Pekarik, G. (1993). A meta-analysis of psychotherapy dropout. *Professional Psychology: Research and Practice, 24,* 190–195.

8

ETHICAL ISSUES IN TERMINATION

ELIZABETH REYNOLDS WELFEL
AND PAULA R. DANZINGER

When clinicians think of termination they tend to conceive of it as a therapist-driven and emotionally charged issue. In reality, nearly half the people who enter therapy decide the timing of termination independent of therapist input, at points in treatment that their therapists define as premature. In a meta-analysis of 125 studies of early termination from therapy, Wierzbicki and Pekarik (1993) reported that nearly 47 percent of clients who entered treatment ended it before their therapists believed the therapy was complete. Early termination from services is not limited to community mental health settings; at university counseling centers the rate also nears 50 percent of clients (Hatchett 2004). The mean number of outpatient sessions that clients attend is less than four (Clarkin & Levy 2004; Draper et al. 2002), and the frequency with which clients terminate after a single session is high, up to 33 percent (Garfield 1994; Hansen, Lambert, & Forman 2002). Research also suggests that clients' estimations of the length of therapy or its benefits are significantly more accurate than their therapists' judgments (Hunsley et al. 1999; Mueller & Pekarik 2001) and that the predominant emotions clients experience at termination are relief and satisfaction rather than loss and anxiety (Marx & Gelso 1987). Even psychoanalytic clients terminating from this extended form of treatment report significantly positive experiences at termination (Roe et al. 2006).

The ethical implications of these therapist misconceptions about termination are the first major focus of this chapter. If clinicians are to act responsibly regarding termination, we must first revise our view of the therapeutic process as a therapist-driven, top-down endeavor, and instead adopt a collaborative construction of therapy that confers on the client a central and explicit role in decisions about the duration and structure of the therapeutic process. Such a perspective is rooted in the ethical values underlying the codes of ethics and in their specific provisions. These values include respect for the dignity and autonomy of the client, acknowledgment of one's own strengths and limitations as a professional, and a commitment to place the welfare of the client ahead of one's own interests.

The second major focus of the chapter is a discussion of the ethical implications of external factors that accelerate the timing of termination, including financial limitations imposed by third-party payers, especially managed care organizations, restrictions imposed by agency administrators, or arbitrary events such as the end of an academic year or the resignation or illness of the professional that force an early or unexpected ending to treatment. The third focus of the chapter centers on the ethical issues of termination when its cause is referral to another professional, either for more specialized services or to accommodate changes in the life circumstances of the client, such as relocation or enrollment with a new insurance carrier. Lastly, the chapter addresses issues related to the ethics of accepting gifts at termination and post-termination contacts with former clients.

A Collaborative Model of Psychotherapy Process and Termination

The central premises of all ethical standards are that professional service aims to benefit and avoid harm to clients, and that clients are to be treated as autonomous individuals to the fullest extent possible. The mandate to benefit and not harm means that therapy that is persistently ineffective, that is, benefit-neutral, or that results in client deterioration should be ended. The ethics codes are consistent in their statements on this matter.

The Ethical Principles and Code of Conduct for Psychologists (American Psychological Association [APA] 2002)

10.10 Terminating Therapy

(a) Psychologists terminate therapy when it becomes reasonably clear that the client/patient no longer needs the service, is not likely to benefit, or is being harmed by continued service.

Code of Ethics (National Association of Social Workers [NASW] 2000)

1.16 Termination of Services (a) Social workers should terminate services to clients and professional relationships with them when such services and relationships are no longer required or no longer serve the clients' needs or interests.

Code of Ethics (American Counseling Association [ACA] 2005)

A.11.b Inability to assist clients

If counselors determine an inability to be of professional assistance to clients, they avoid entering or continuing counseling relationships. Counselors are knowledgeable about culturally and clinically appropriate referral resources and suggest these alternatives. If clients decline the suggested referrals, counselors should discontinue the relationship.

Implicit in these statements is the responsibility of the therapist to monitor client progress and to make efforts to explore client reactions to therapy at regular points during treatment. Without such deliberate actions, therapists do not seem to accurately gauge whether clients are at risk for failing to benefit or for dropping out. Lambert and colleagues (Hansen, Lambert, & Forman 2002; Harmon et al. 2005; Whipple et al. 2003) have developed methods to assess client views of therapy effectiveness early in treatment, and have organized clinical support tools to help therapists become more efficacious in treatment. Such interventions are not only clinically useful to improve therapy effectiveness and efficiency, they also have ethical merit in increasing professional awareness of emerging problems or discrepancies between therapist and client views of progress. The latter is especially important since evidence suggests that clients from culturally diverse populations are more likely to end therapy prematurely (Sue & Sue 2003).

Statements in the codes about informed consent derive from respect for the autonomy of the client, and support a collaborative and patient-focused approach to decisions about treatment duration. The standard in the APA and the NASW codes read as follows:

APA *Ethical Principles* (APA 2002) 10.01 Informed Consent to Therapy

When obtaining informed consent to therapy as required in Standard 3.10, Informed Consent, psychologists inform clients/patients as early as is feasible in the therapeutic relationship about the nature and anticipated course of therapy, fees, involvement of third parties, and limits of confidentiality and provide sufficient opportunity for the client/patient to ask questions and receive answers.

NASW *Code of Ethics* (NASW 2000) 1.03 Informed Consent

(a) Social workers should provide services to clients only in the context of a professional relationship based, when appropriate, on valid informed consent. Social workers should use clear and understandable language to inform clients of the purpose of the services, risks related to the services, limits to services because of the requirements of a third-party payer, relevant costs, reasonable alternatives, clients' right to refuse or withdraw consent, and the time frame covered by the consent. Social workers should provide clients with an opportunity to ask questions.

This language clearly places the duty on the psychologist or social worker to disclose what he or she views as therapy's anticipated course or duration. Unfortunately, this wording assumes a therapist-driven process since it seems to limit client involvement to the opportunity to ask questions and get answers. The ACA standard is more explicit about a collaborative approach to treatment planning:

ACA *Code of Ethics* (ACA 2005) A.1.c. Counseling Plans

Counselors and their clients work jointly in devising integrated counseling plans that offer reasonable promise of success and are consistent with the abilities and circumstances of clients. Counselors and clients regularly review counseling plans to assess their continued viability and effectiveness, respecting the freedom of clients.

Abandonment

At the other extreme from failing to be alert to client expectations about the length of therapy is the problem of abandonment—therapist-initiated ending of therapy without appropriate attention to the risks to the client. Both the NASW and ACA standards address this issue directly.

NASW *Code of Ethics* (NASW 2000) 1.16(b) Termination of Services

Social workers should take reasonable steps to avoid abandoning clients who are still in need of services. Social workers should withdraw services precipitously only under unusual circumstances, giving careful consideration to all factors in the situation and taking care to minimize possible adverse effects. Social workers should assist in making appropriate arrangements for continuation of services when necessary.

ACA *Code of Ethics* (ACA 2005) A.11.a. Abandonment Prohibited

Counselors do not abandon or neglect clients in counseling. Counselors assist in making appropriate arrangements for the continuation of treatment, when necessary, during interruptions such as vacation, illness, and following termination.

Interestingly, the 2002 revision of the APA standards removed the language of abandonment, allowing for termination even if services may be needed or beneficial as long as pretermination counseling takes place.

APA *Ethical Principles* (APA 2002) 10.10 (c) Terminating Therapy

Except where precluded by the actions of clients/patients or third-party payors, prior to termination psychologists provide pretermination counseling and suggest alternative service providers as appropriate.

This standard permits termination because a third-party payer or client rejects payment for additional sessions and stands in contrast to earlier versions of the code (APA 1992) that cautioned professionals against ending therapy for nonpayment if the client needed additional services. Thus, psychologists are freed from claims of misconduct based on termination of services for nonpayment even if clients are in significant distress, as long as they are counseled prior to termination. The APA code does not specify the content of pretermination counseling, but a reasonable person may assume it refers to a discussion of access to alternative services. Similar statements are included in the codes of the other professions, although in Standard 1.16c the NASW Code specifically prohibits termination for nonpayment if the client represents a "an imminent danger to self or others." Fisher (2003) also advises that under this section of the APA standards, psychologists may terminate therapy if they "find therapy with a particular client/ patient stressful in a manner that risks compromising professional services" (APA 2002, 233). In other words, psychologists may end treatment if the therapy raises issues for the professional that place him or her at risk for providing substandard care. For example, a psychologist working with a client on combat-related posttraumatic stress may be permitted to terminate services if the professional is having difficulty separating the client's concerns from her own because her own spouse is currently serving in combat. Section 2.06 of the APA code also addresses this issue.

APA *Ethical Principles* (APA 2002) 2.06 Personal Problems and Conflicts

(b) When psychologists become aware of personal problems that may interfere with their performing work-related duties adequately, they take appropriate measures, such as obtaining professional consultation or assistance, and determine whether they should limit, suspend, or terminate their work-related duties.

The APA code also provides more explicit language regarding the therapists' responsibility when clients present a threat of harm to them, "Psychologists may terminate therapy when threatened or otherwise endangered by the client/patient or another person with whom the client/patient has a relationship" (APA 2002, 10.10(b)). Fisher (2003) suggests that this standard can be invoked when clients make direct threats or when there is other evidence of danger. She goes on to state that it allows psychologists to obtain protective orders against the person making the threats and to breach confidentiality to obtain such an order. The ACA *Code of Ethics* is equally direct about this matter.

ACA *Code of Ethics* (ACA 2005) A.11.c Appropriate Termination

Counselors terminate a counseling relationship when it becomes reasonably apparent that the client no longer needs assistance, is not likely to benefit, or is being harmed by continued counseling. Counselors may terminate counseling when in jeopardy of harm by the client, or another person with whom the client has a relationship or when clients do not pay fees as agreed upon. Counselors provide pretermination counseling and recommend other service providers when necessary.

The more general wording of the NASW standard 1.16(b) that permits withdrawing services in "unusual circumstances" appears to address situations in which social workers feel threatened by clients or others connected to clients.

De Facto Abandonment   Knapp and VandeCreek (2006) comment on another aspect of abandonment usually overlooked in the literature— *de facto abandonment*. They define this form of abandonment as the circumstance in which the client feels abandoned because the therapist is not consistently available and has not arranged reliable backup service. De facto abandonment may be intentional (a therapist refusing to respond to messages or requests to schedule another session because he or she finds the client difficult to work with), or it may be unintentional (a therapist getting overwhelmed with work and failing to respond to messages in a timely fashion). In either situation, the therapist has failed to meet his or her ethical responsibilities to follow through on the commitment to service offered when therapy was initiated.

Ethics and Outside Pressures to Terminate

Consider the following situation:

> Janette is a client who presented with adjustment disorder with anxious mood. Her managed care organization (MCO) authorized four sessions for her. After three sessions, Janette shared with her therapist that she thought she might have been sexually abused as a child along with other symptoms of more significant and persistent anxiety. The therapist contacted the MCO and requested additional sessions for Janette based on this information. The MCO denied more sessions, and Janette does not have the financial resources to self-pay for therapy.

This scenario is all too typical in a world of managed care insurance. Practitioners find themselves confronted with the possibility of early termination (i.e., before either party wishes treatment to end) based on the MCO endorsement of brief therapy models and limitations of managed care payments. These limitations may come from MCO policy restricting services for a particular diagnosis, or from the financial hardship a client may face for out-of pocket-payments once the yearly or lifetime cap for services is reached. Mental health practitioners have found managed care to be a hindrance to ethical practice, influencing the extent of informed consent, the content of therapy, the accuracy of diagnosis, and the timing of termination (Danzinger & Welfel 2001; Murphy, DeBernardo, & Shoemaker 1998; Phelps, Eisman, & Kohout 1998). For example, clinicians have reported that they have given clients diagnoses that are at least partially inaccurate in order to obtain reimbursement, and have failed to communicate the nature of their contracts with payers and the extent of communication with payers in order to ensure client continuance in treatment.

Several ethical obligations emerge at this point, as well as several options for the therapist. The therapist's first duty is to advocate for the client with the MCO (Acuff et al. 1999; Appelbaum 1993). An MCO denial of additional sessions is not the end of the process. It is the therapist's ethical and legal responsibility to appeal the denial, contacting the MCO and reiterating the rationale for continued services. The therapist is obligated to take this process as far as reasonable within the MCO in spite of the difficult, time-consuming, and confusing appeal processes MCOs often use (Appelbaum 1993). This situation is also complicated by the use of untrained or undertrained reviewers at the MCO (Sanchez & Turner 2003). The practitioner is likely to have more knowledge and experience in assessing client needs than the reviewer denying service. Because the appeal process necessitates the disclosure of additional client information not ordinarily provided to the MCO, the client must be informed of the extent of information being released prior to these disclosures.

If the MCO refuses to reconsider additional sessions for a client like Janette, the therapist's next duty is to offer appropriate alternative services for the client. If appropriate services cannot be found, professionals have an ethical obligation not to abandon the client if the client is at substantial risk of harm to self (Welfel 2006). Even after such services are found, the therapist must take care to make the transition to another therapist as smooth and as comfortable for Janette as possible.

Managed care organization contracts and policies may make finding alternative services for clients like Janette difficult. Transferring the client to another therapist under the MCO's coverage poses the same limitations of services faced by the original therapist (Acuff et al. 1999). Referring the client to an agency that offers reduced rates or pro bono services may also be complicated, since many of these agencies have waiting lists and may not offer the specific services needed.

A comprehensive informed consent process initiated at the start of therapy can help when MCO policy and client finances necessitate termination (Cooper & Gottlieb 2000). By including information on MCO policies in informed consent, the therapist is preparing the client for the possibility that these policies may force premature termination or self-payment. Alternate payment arrangements can be discussed and agreed upon before treatment begins and alternatives to therapy can also be reviewed. Presenting this information at the beginning of therapy can assist the client in coping with termination, and can also help the therapist plan for possible transfer of services.

Underlying these ethical duties is the reality of divided loyalties (Koocher & Keith-Spiegel 1998). In a world in which an increasing proportion of a clinician's income depends on the availability of reimbursement from MCOs, clinicians may be hesitant to challenge payers too frequently, lest they be dropped from the very provider panels they rely on for referrals. They also have legal obligations to abide by the contracts they have signed with MCOs and other third-party payers. As understandable as these concerns may be, professionals have an obligation to place the welfare of the client ahead of their own financial interests and to advocate on behalf of clients.

Sometimes managed care can affect termination even if the MCO is agreeable to continuation of services. For example:

> David has been seeing his therapist for six months. David has been diagnosed with obsessive compulsive disorder, and with the help of medication and continued therapy he has been able to engage in normal life activities. David has been offered a higher-paying job in the same city. He wants to continue with his therapist because he feels he has been able to cope with his disorder much better since starting therapy. Unfortunately, David's new MCO does not pay for services from this particular therapist, who is not on their preferred provider list.

If a client changes jobs or the client's employer changes managed care companies, the therapist may be faced with prematurely terminating the client. Even though the client is ostensibly initiating the termination, the client and therapist may not be ready for the relationship to terminate. While this presents a different type of ethical dilemma for the therapist, it is a dilemma nonetheless. Practitioners must be prepared to arrange alternate payment, offer free service, or find the best way to terminate with the client and arrange a proper transfer.

The issue of divided loyalties is highlighted when practitioners are directly employed by the MCO, for example, in an employer assistance program or a health maintenance organization. The practitioner's employment may be predicated on his/her ability to restrain costs, and limiting services is the primary means of controlling those costs. The practitioner may be tempted to terminate with a client earlier than appropriate in order to keep his or her employment, but the same principle applies—practitioners may not jeopardize the safety of the client in their own self-interest. Consequently, professionals who accept these positions should clarify their employers' expectations and their own ethical obligations prior to acceptance of the position. They should also be clear with clients at the initiation of services about the limitations of care necessitated by the program or institution.

Ultimately, clinicians have a social responsibility to influence public policy regarding the accessibility and funding of mental health services (Cooper & Gottlieb 2000). The healthcare delivery system is in crisis, and this systemic issue is at the root of the ethical dilemmas that clients and therapists face daily in deciding treatment duration. Those dilemmas will not be effectively resolved until the flaws in the system are addressed. Therefore, a portion of the profession's and the professional's energy should be directed toward suggesting modifications in the funding system and in access to care for clients without insurance. This is a matter of the integrity of practice and the most fundamental ethical issue related to termination of services.

Ethics and Interruptions in Service

Interruptions in service may occur unexpectedly or are anticipated. The former occurs when a therapist or client becomes too ill to continue therapy, and the latter happens when retirement occurs or the end of training experiences is reached. The end of an internship, fellowship, or training rotation is also referred to as a *forced termination* because neither the client nor the therapist has any control over the timing of the termination (Zuckerman & Mitchell 2004). Clinicians are responsible for preparing for the possibility of an unexpected interruption of service by arranging for another qualified professional to provide coverage and have access to client information. In fact, many licensing boards require clinicians to identify a responsible professional who would have access to client data in the event of their disability or death. The professional so designated should be given all the information needed, such as computer passwords for access to files and keys to the office to carry out this responsibility. Pope and Vasquez (1998) advise that the following questions be addressed during a therapist's unexpected illness:

- Who will provide ongoing care and crisis intervention during the therapist's absence?
- Who will notify clients about the therapist's absence?
- How can clients and others obtain information about the therapist's recovery during the absence?
- How will the therapist's records be handled and who will have access?

If the interruption is anticipated, as it may be for an elective surgery or an extended vacation, the clinician is bound to inform the client about the duration of the absence and the arrangements for alternative care in the interim. Again, this discussion should be a collaboration, with the client having an equal role in determining the type of service to occur in this period.

Ethics and Referral

Professionals make referrals to alternate services for a myriad of reasons—client requests, client need for more specialized service, client failure to benefit from the current treatment, limitations in ability to pay for current care, or changes in the availability of the therapist, to name the most common factors. The codes of ethics speak to the responsibilities of the current therapist when referral is occurring in Section 1.16 of the NASW Code and Section 10.10 of the APA Ethical Principles (see above), and in the following section of the ACA *Code of Ethics*.

ACA *Code of Ethics* (ACA 2005) A.11.d Appropriate Transfer of Services

When counselors transfer or refer clients to other practitioners, they ensure that appropriate clinical and administrative processes are completed and open communication is maintained with both clients and practitioners.

The APA standards also mention the need for referral if the professional lacks sufficient training and background to work competently with diverse populations. It is important to note that this standard suggests that obtaining such training is a more appropriate resolution to this limitation in competence over the long run.

APA *Ethical Principles* (APA 2002) 2.01(b) Boundaries of Competence

Where scientific or professional knowledge in the discipline of psychology establishes that an understanding of factors associated with age, gender, gender identity, race, ethnicity, culture, national origin, religion, sexual orientation, disability, language, or socioeconomic status is essential for effective implementation of their services or research, psychologists have or obtain the training, experience, consultation, or supervision necessary to ensure the competence of their services, or they make appropriate referrals, except as provided in Standard 2.02, Providing Services in Emergencies.

Embedded in the statements about the ethics of terminating clients who are to be referred to other professionals is the assumption that the clinician is informed about the competence or availability of the referral source. Professionals have an ethical duty to have some basis in fact to believe that the alternate source of care is appropriate for the client's need and is reasonably available. Ideally, clients should be provided with multiple options for referral and information about contacting each source (Welfel 2006). Instructing clients to look in the telephone directory for local mental health centers or offering a single name of a professional in private practice is not likely to meet the standards for competency or avoiding abandonment in the ethics codes. Needless to say, when clients are in significant distress, the care with which the referral is made is especially important. Clinicians ought to discuss with the client the advisability of consenting to allow the therapist to have communication with the referral source prior to contact to smooth the transition. Although contact with a referral source without express client permission is not clearly prohibited by the codes or HIPAA (The Health Insurance Portability and Accountability Act) standards as long as the client has signed the Notice of Privacy Practices, and the purpose is to provide needed services (APA Ethical Standards 4.05b), it is an unwise to make contact without expressed permission.

Ethics and Post-Termination Contact With Clients

Multiple relationships with current clients, whether sexual or nonsexual, constitute the largest single group of ethics complaints to professional associations and licensing boards (Welfel 2006). The codes of ethics address the issue of sexual contact with former therapy clients. Both the APA and ACA standards establish criteria under which such a sexual relationship may be appropriate. These include a two-year to five-year waiting period (in the ACA standards) and several other criteria related to the conditions of therapy and its termination. The language in the APA code is illustrative:

> APA *Ethical Principles* (APA 2002) 10.08 Sexual Intimacies with Former Therapy Clients/Patients
>
> (a) Psychologists do not engage in sexual intimacies with former clients/ patients for at least two years after cessation or termination of therapy.
>
> (b) Psychologists do not engage in sexual intimacies with former clients/ patients even after a two-year interval except in the most unusual circumstances. Psychologists who engage in such activity after the two years following cessation or termination of therapy and of having no sexual contact with the former client/patient bear the burden of demonstrating that there has been no exploitation, in light of all

relevant factors, including (1) the amount of time that has passed since therapy terminated; (2) the nature, duration, and intensity of the therapy; (3) the circumstances of termination; (4) the client's/patient's personal history; (5) the client's/patient's current mental status; (6) the likelihood of adverse impact on the client/patient; and (7) any statements or actions made by the therapist during the course of therapy suggesting or inviting the possibility of a post termination sexual or romantic relationship with the client/patient.

Unfortunately, the codes are largely silent on the ethics of other types of contact with former clients. The statements in the codes on avoiding harm and exploitation and the principles of integrity and beneficence are applicable, but the specific ethical responsibilities of therapists after termination are not specified. Not surprisingly, mental health professionals are strongly divided about the ethics of nonsexual relationships with former clients, as summarized by Kitchener (2000). Because every code uses the term *client* in these sections, the question arises: Are individuals who have terminated services still defined as clients? May a therapist become friends, enter into a business partnership, or become a former client's employer or supervisor?

Anderson and Kitchener (1998) encourage professionals to assess four major aspects of the therapeutic contact to determine the ethics of nonsexual contacts with terminated clients. The first aspect to consider is the nature of the therapeutic services offered and their complexity, including the clarity of termination and its recency, the degree of achievement of therapeutic goals, a satisfactory mutual agreement about how confidentiality of services will be handled, and the level of client understanding of the implications of the nonprofessional contact on the availability of future services. Former clients who meet Pipes's (1997) definition of terminated clients, "clients for whom there has been a responsible and appropriately documented termination process, who do not anticipate returning for therapy, and who have in no way been led to believe that they are free to return to therapy" (28) seem to be the only individuals with whom nonprofessional contacts are possible after termination. The second feature to consider is the strength of the therapeutic bond. The more intense the relationship, the less capable the client of autonomous behavior with the therapist, the greater is the likelihood that the post-termination relationship will be problematic. The degree of change in social roles, and the extent of the parties' understanding of the degree to which the roles of client and therapist may influence their roles in the new connection comprise the third consideration. The final important point is the therapist's motivation—the degree to which the therapist is likely to benefit and the potential for exploitation of the client. This is reminiscent of the question asked to ferret out conflicts of interest: Whose needs are being met by this action? The ideal ethical action of therapists is to take a risk-avoidant stance, as advocated by Sonne (1994), and to consult with colleagues before engaging in any ongoing and close contact with terminated psychotherapy clients. In fact, all ethical standards strongly advise professionals to seek out advice from colleagues when they have questions about the ethics of an action. Even when professionals have concluded that a social or business relationship with a former client is ethically permissible or even potentially beneficial to a client, professionals should monitor the appropriateness of the contact on an ongoing basis and continue consultation with colleagues on a periodic basis (Younggren & Gottlieb 2004).

Ethics and Gifts

Clients often feel great relief and gratitude for the help that therapists provide in improving their life satisfaction and reducing their symptoms. Sometimes clients offer their therapists gifts to express their appreciation. The ACA *Code of Ethics* (2005) addresses this issue directly, while the other codes suggest it in their comments about cultural sensitivity, the avoidance of exploitation, and promotion of client welfare over personal interests.

ACA *Code of Ethics* (ACA 2005) A.10e. Receiving Gifts

Counselors understand the challenges of accepting gifts from clients and recognize that in some cultures, small gifts are a token of respect and showing gratitude. When determining whether or not to accept a gift from clients, counselors take into account the therapeutic relationship, the monetary value of the gift, a client's motivation for giving the gift, and the counselor's motivation for wanting or declining the gift.

In situations in which clients are inclined to offer gifts of significant monetary value, professionals are well advised to suggest that the client offer the gift to a charity anonymously or to an agency that provides mental healthcare to indigent clients. With this strategy the client is able to find an expression for being helped without direct benefit to the therapist personally.

Summary

Ethical termination of services requires competence, compassion, and to some degree, altruism. Clinicians must possess the knowledge and skill to monitor client progress and to engage in frank discussions of client satisfactions and frustrations in therapy so that an unexpected client-initiated ending does not occur. If external pressures or therapist circumstances force an early termination, professionals should be diligent in assisting the client in finding appropriate alternative care, and should place the welfare of the client ahead of any personal considerations. Clinicians are also well advised to avoid post-therapy contact with clients that may exploit a former client and should be aware of any state regulations restricting such nonsexual post-therapy relationships. Similarly, therapists should refrain from accepting anything but token gifts from clients at termination, balancing respect for the client and his or her intentions and cultural background against the appearance of self-interest.

References

Acuff, C., Bennett, B. E., Bricklin, P. M., Canter, M. B., Knapp, S. J. Moldawsky, S, & Phelps, R. (1999). Consideration for ethical practice in managed care. *Professional Psychology: Research and Practice, 30*, 563–575.

American Counseling Association. (2005). *ACA Code of ethics*. Retrieved April 11, 2006, from http://www.counseling.org/Resources/CodeOfEthics/TP/Home/CT2.aspx

American Psychological Association. (1992). *Ethical principles of psychologists and code of conduct*. Retrieved April 11, 2006, from http://www.apa.org/ethics/code1992.html

American Psychological Association. (2002). *Ethical principles of psychologists and code of conduct*. Retrieved April 11, 2006, from http://www.apa.org/ethics/

Anderson, S. K., & Kitchener, K. S. (1998). Nonsexual posttherapy relationships: A conceptual framework to assess ethical risks. *Professional Psychology: Research and Practice, 29,* 91–99.

Appelbaum, P. S. (1993). Legal liability in managed care. *American Psychologist, 48,* 251–257.

Clarkin, J. F., & Levy, K. N. (2005). The influence of client variables on psychotherapy. In M. J. Lambert (Ed.), *Bergin and Garfield's handbook of psychotherapy and behavior change* (pp. 194–226). New York: Wiley.

Cooper, C. C., & Gottlieb, M. C. (2000). Ethical issues with managed care. *Counseling Psychologist, 28,* 179–236.

Danzinger, P. R., & Welfel, E. R. (2001). The impact of managed care on mental health counselors: A survey of perceptions, practices, and compliance with ethical standards. *Journal of Mental Health Counseling, 23,* 137–150.

Draper, M. K., Jennings, J., Baraon, A., Erdur, O., & Shankar, L. (2002). Time-limited counseling outcome in a nationwide college counseling center sample. *Journal of College Counseling, 3,* 26–38.

Fisher, C. B. (2003). *Decoding the ethics code: A practical guide for psychologists.* Thousand Oaks, CA: Sage.

Garfield, S. L. (1994). Client variables in psychotherapy. In A. E. Bergin & S. L. Garfield (Eds.), *Handbook of psychotherapy and behavior change* (pp. 72–113). New York: Wiley.

Hansen, N. B., Lambert, M. J., & Forman, E. M. (2002). The psychotherapy dose-response effects and its implications for treatment delivery services. *Clinical Psychology: Science and Practice, 9,* 329–343.

Harmon, C., Hawkins, E. J., Lambert, M. J., Slade, K., & Whipple, J. L. (2005). Improving outcomes for poorly responding clients: The use of clinical support tools and feedback to clients. *Journal of Clinical Psychology, 61,* 175–185.

Hatchett, G. T. (2004). Reducing premature termination in university counseling centers. *Journal of College Student Psychotherapy, 19,* 13–27.

Hunsley, J., Aubry, T. D., Verstervelt, C. M., & Vilo, D. (1999). Comparing therapist and client perspectives on reasons for psychotherapy termination. *Psychotherapy: Theory/Research/Practice/Training, 36,* 380–388.

Kitchener, K. S. (2000). *Foundations of ethical practice, research and teaching in psychology.* Mahwah, NJ: Lawrence Erlbaum.

Knapp, S. J., & Vandecreek, L. D. (2006). *Practical ethics for psychologists: A positive approach.* Washington, DC: American Psychological Association.

Koocher, G. P., & Keith-Spiegel, P. C. (1998). *Ethics in psychology: Professional standards and cases.* New York: Oxford University Press.

Marx, J. A., & Gelso, C. A. (1987). Termination of individual counseling in a university counseling context. *Journal of Counseling Psychology, 34,* 3–9.

Mueller, M., & Pekarik, G. (2001). Treatment duration prediction: Client accuracy and its relationship to dropout, outcome, and satisfaction. *Psychotherapy: Theory, Research, Practice, Training, 37,* 117–123.

Murphy, M. J., DeBernardo, C. R., & Shoemaker, W. E. (1998). Impact of managed care on independent practice and professional ethics: A survey of independent practitioners. *Professional Psychology: Research and Practice, 29,* 43–51.

National Association of Social Workers. (2000). *Code of ethics.* Retrieved April 11, 2006, from http://www.socialworkers.org/pubs/code/default.asp

Phelps, R., Eisman, E. J., & Kohout, J. (1998). Psychological practice and managed care: Results of the CAPP practitioner survey. *Professional Psychology: Research and Practice, 29,* 31–36.

Pipes, R. B. (1997). Nonsexual relationships between psychotherapists and their former clients: Obligations of psychologists. *Ethics and Behavior, 7,* 27–41.

Pope, K. S., & Vasquez, M. J. T. (1998). *Ethics in psychotherapy and counseling* (2nd ed.). San Francisco: Jossey-Bass.

Roe, D., Dekel, R., Harel, G., Fennig, S., & Fennig, S. (2006). Clients' feelings during termination of psychodynamically oriented psychotherapy. *Bulletin of the Menninger Clinic, 70,* 68–81.

Sanchez, L. M., & Turner, S. M. (2003). Practicing psychology in the era of managed care: Implications for practice and training. *American Psychologist, 58,* 116–129.

Sonne, J. L. (1994). Multiple relationships: Does the new ethics code answer the right questions? *Professional Psychology: Research and Practice, 25,* 336–343.

Sue, D. W., & Sue, D. (2003). *Counseling the culturally different: Theory and practice* (4th ed.). New York: Wiley.

Welfel, E. R. (2006). *Ethics in counseling and psychotherapy: Standards, research, and emerging issues* (3rd ed.). Belmont, CA: Wadsworth.

Whipple, J. L., Lambert, M. J., Vermeersch, D. A., Smart, D. W., Nielson, S. L., & Hawkins, E. J. (2003). Improving the effects of psychotherapy: The use of early identification of treatment failure and problem solving strategies in routine practice. *Journal of Counseling Psychology, 50,* 59–68.

Wierzbicki, M., & Pekarik, G. (1993). A meta-analysis of psychotherapy dropout. *Professional Psychology: Research and Practice, 24,* 190–195.

Younggren, J. N., & Gottlieb, M. C. (2004). Managing risk when contemplating multiple relationships. *Professional Psychology: Research and Practice, 35,* 255–260.

Zuckerman, A., & Mitchell, C. L. (2004). Psychotherapy interns' perspectives on the forced termination of psychotherapy. *Clinical Supervisor, 23,* 55–70.

SECTION II:
TERMINATION IN THE CONTEXT OF VARIOUS TREATMENT MODELS, POPULATIONS, AND PATIENT PROBLEMS

9

A RELATIONAL TAKE ON TERMINATION IN COGNITIVE-BEHAVIORAL THERAPY

ELIZABETH OCHOA AND J. CHRISTOPHER MURAN

Cognitive-behavior therapy (CBT) is often conducted in a time-limited format. Treatment goals initially include symptom relief and schema change, although the overarching goal of CBT is relapse prevention (Nelson & Politano 1993; A. T. Beck, 2005; Antony, Ledley, & Heimberg 2005). Much work in CBT involves therapists teaching patients techniques that will allow them to preserve the gains they have made beyond termination. While the influence of the therapeutic alliance on treatment effectiveness and change processes in CBT is generally acknowledged (Persons 1989; Goldfried & Davila 2005), how the patient-therapist relationship influences the process of termination has been relatively unaddressed. We believe that a core component of the termination process in CBT is the successful resolution of the ultimate alliance rupture, that is, saying good-bye to the therapist and the therapeutic relationship. By negotiating issues of loss and separation that emerge as the therapy ends, individuals find a balance between independence and relatedness, which is a key developmental milestone (Muran & Safran 2002; Stevens, Muran, & Safran 2003). We maintain that striking this balance during termination promotes self-efficacy and mastery, which can, in conjunction with other treatment gains, inoculate the patient against relapse.

This chapter serves as a guide for CBT clinicians as they negotiate the complexities of terminating treatment. It is our goal to bring the importance of the therapeutic relationship to the forefront as it impacts upon the process of ending treatment. Our chapter is comprised of three sections. In the first section, existing literature on the process of treatment termination in CBT is reviewed. Key principles (generalization, maintenance and relapse prevention, and negotiation of the therapeutic relationship) that pertain to treatment termination are discussed. In the second section, specific techniques that we believe promote generalization and maintenance are presented. In the final section, practical treatment considerations and obstacles to termination are presented.

Literature Review

The Process of Terminating CBT

There is an accumulating body of data from empirical outcome studies that suggests that CBT can produce lasting changes after treatment, which reduce the risk of relapse, and may even prevent the initial expression of disorders in vulnerable individuals (Hollon & Beck 2005). However, little empirical research has specifically examined the process of treatment termination from within a cognitive-behavioral framework. This is surprising given widespread agreement by CBT clinicians of its centrality as a focus throughout the course of treatment (Beck 1995; Nelson & Politano 1993; Antony, Ledley, & Heimberg 2005). Nelson and Politano (1993) suggested that the striking lack of empirical research studies or conceptual articles on the termination process in CBT stems in part from the historical minimization of the importance of the therapist-client relationship, difficulties in conducting empirical research of process variables, and a focus on measurement of observable behaviors.

In our subsequent review of the literature from the past decade on treatment termination in CBT, we too were surprised by the lack of recent empirical research on the topic. However, there are a number of conceptual articles and book chapters on conducting CBT, which include discussion of treatment factors that affect termination (J. Beck 1995; Goldfried 2002; Ledley, Marx, & Heimberg 2005; Nelson & Politano 1993). For example, in their 1993 article, Nelson and Politano maintained that there are three "structural aspects" of CBT that directly impact on termination: duration of treatment, specification of goals, and phases of treatment. They stated that each structural element keeps central the desired endpoint of treatment, which is the attainment of "independent functioning through generalization and maintenance" (254).

We have restated the phases of treatment, as described by Nelson and Politano (1993), in order to anchor the process of termination in the context of an overall CB treatment. Termination is conceptualized as an ongoing process that begins during the first session and continues as a focal point of each phase of treatment (J. Beck 1995; Nelson & Politano 1993). Throughout each phase, the primary aim is to "assure that the treatment effects transfer to the client's natural environment and endure over time" (Nelson & Politano 1993, 253). The initial phase focuses on assessment and goal setting, which defines the desired changes. Goals are operationalized so that progress toward meeting the goals can be monitored. The intervention phase is aimed at producing changes in behavior that accomplish the goals specified in the assessment phase. Choice of appropriate treatment strategies is crucial at this juncture to maximize the likelihood that goals will be met and a positive treatment outcome attained. Monitoring treatment gains during the intervention phase allows for goals to be adjusted as needed to obtain the desired changes. The next phase involves generalization, whereby change is encouraged in real-life situations and the patient utilizes the coping skills learned in therapy to resolve dilemmas independently. The fourth phase of treatment involves the maintenance of gains made during treatment and the explicit negotiation of the process of termination (Nelson & Politano 1993). The focus is on furthering the patient's sense of self-efficacy. Decreased reliance on the therapist for help is established. A review of problem-solving strategies, coping skills, and treatment gains, as well as preparing the patient for future conflicts and symptom recurrence, are among the issues typically examined during the termination process in order to mitigate or prevent relapse (Beck 1995; Linehan 1993).

Therapeutic Relationship and Its Role in Termination

There has been a lack of empirical research historically on which process factors, including the therapeutic relationship, facilitate or hinder the development of generalization and maintenance (Nelson & Politano 1993). Nelson and Politano (1993) suggested that in the cognitive-behavior therapy field there has been an ambivalence about "finding common ground with more dynamic or humanistic orientations at methodological, philosophical, conceptual or implementational levels" (252), as one explanation for the lack of relative significance attributed to the role of the patient-therapist relationship in termination. No known article has provided an elaborated discussion of the role of the therapeutic relationship in termination within CBT, until that of Nelson and Politano (1993), although others, including Klein, Dittman, Parloff, and Gill (1969), Bornstein and Rychtarik (1983), and Garfield (1983) have noted that the therapeutic relationship may be critical to generalization and maintenance of gains and positive outcome (Nelson & Politano 1993). Beck et al. (1979) implied that the therapeutic relationship affects the process of termination when they acknowledged that patients may have feelings about the end of treatment, as might the therapist, and that these feelings should be clarified, reflected, and discussed.

The effect of the therapeutic relationship on termination is an issue that has recently received heightened attention in the literature, signaling a shift by clinicians and researchers in their views of its relevance in CBT (Ledley, Marx, & Heimberg 2005; J. Beck 1995, 2005; Stevens, Muran, & Safran 2003; Rowa, Bieling, & Segal 2005). For example, Nelson and Politano (1993) maintained that it is important to explore "how the therapeutic relationship effects cooperation, truthful feedback from the client, therapist as model, etc., and how this then influences the client's perceptions of self-efficacy, benefits of therapy, etc., all of which can interactively, impact on generalization and maintenance of therapeutic gains" (255).

The therapeutic relationship in CBT is usually conceptualized as active and collaborative, where the patient's eventual independence from the therapist is understood as inevitable if treatment is successful. As cognitive-behavioral therapists teach patients how to perform the tasks of therapy independently, and the patient demonstrates progress in this regard, the therapists withdraw from the treatment in a "fading out" process. Fading out is gradual and occurs as the patient develops mastery and competence in problem solving, which support the generalization and maintenance of the behavioral changes attained during treatment (Nelson & Politano 1993).

Goldfried (2002) referred to the role of the therapeutic relationship in CBT termination in his article in the psychotherapy integration literature. He considered excerpts from Freud's "Analysis Terminable and Interminable" (1937/1953) to highlight root similarities and differences between the psychoanalytic and cognitive-behavioral orientations. Goldfried (2002) commented that the issue of loss and the ending of the therapist-patient relationship are not emphasized as explicitly in strict CBT as they are in psychodynamic approaches. Rather, termination from a CBT perspective is centered around the patient having opportunities to test new coping skills (mastering techniques) as they are weaned from treatment (the number of sessions is cut back), rather than on the farewell (the loss of the relationship), which is emphasized more directly in psychodynamic approaches. He did indicate, however, that there are some patients for whom it is appropriate to directly highlight issues of loss around the ending of the therapeutic relationship, namely those who have complex presentations where CBT is modified to allow increased attention to patient-therapist interactions. Linehan (1993), who treats personality disordered patients using dialectical behavior therapy (DBT), has supported the idea that generalization and maintenance is bolstered by negotiating the therapeutic relationship during treatment and by processing the meaning of its loss with patients.

Stevens, Muran, and Safran (2003) underscored the importance of the therapeutic relationship for successful outcome in CBT in their chapter on negotiating ruptures in the alliance, although they did not specifically address the relevance of rupture resolution to the process of termination. They stated, "the traditional cognitive-behavioral therapy approach to the alliance does much to implicitly promote ongoing negotiations with patients about the goals and tasks of therapy and to promote the alliance as an agent of positive change" (283). They put forth the alliance as "a process of ongoing negotiation rather than as a static backdrop to therapy" (276), and suggested that clinicians confront and work through alliance ruptures as a pivotal part of the treatment process (Safran & Segal 1990; Safran 1998; Safran & Muran 1996, 1998, 2000; Muran 2001, 2002; Safran et al. 2002). In reconceptualizing the alliance this way, Stevens et al. (2003) demonstrated how many traditional CBT interventions and assumptions work to promote change through the alliance, as well as how they can sometimes hinder treatment. Stevens et al. maintained that for therapy to be successful, both the therapist and the patient need to acknowledge their own needs and those of the other in order to negotiate a viable working relationship. When this endeavor goes well, much of the negotiating process occurs out of awareness. However, when there is a breakdown in the alliance and a rupture occurs, over-reliance by cognitive-behavioral therapists on cognitive rationales and techniques worsen ruptures (Castonguay et al. 1996; Stevens, Muran, & Safran 2003). Strict adherence to CBT principles and techniques without seeking to understand the nature of the rupture and how it reflects the patient's difficulties ignores important therapeutic issues and strains the alliance further (Stevens et al. 2003). Stevens et al. described decentering and disembedding techniques, such as mindfulness and metacommunication, to resolve ruptures.

Elsewhere, Muran and Safran (2002) conceptualized termination as "an ultimate alliance rupture, as a valuable opportunity to deal with critical issues surrounding acceptance, being alone, separation and loss" (Muran & Safran 2002, 3). They conceptualized the process of treatment, and by extension the process of termination, in a manner different from that in traditional CBT. The course of treatment is seen as aphasic and the usual content focus is replaced with a process focus on the therapeutic alliance. Metacommunication about the patient-therapist relationship and the development of mindfulness skills are emphasized rather than gaining insight into and mastering a core conflict (Muran & Safran 2002; Safran & Muran 2000).

Treatment begins with a collaborative discussion of the tasks of therapy. This dialogue establishes the treatment rationale and the formation of the alliance. Patients are informed of the focus on the therapeutic relationship, and on the explicit goal of improving awareness of one's thoughts, feelings, fantasies, and relational self. Modifications to tasks and goals are negotiated repeatedly as treatment ensues. The negotiation process changes with the therapeutic relationship, and it is this ongoing negotiation that lies at the heart of therapeutic change (Safran, Muran, & Rothman 2006). The implications of this model for termination within CBT are considered next.

We contend that in order to enhance generalization and maintenance of change in CBT, the therapist and patient need to engage in an ongoing meaningful dialogue about the nature of their work together (goals, progress, and expectations for the future) and their relationship during treatment and at its close. It is the premise of our chapter that the process of terminating treatment in CBT involves the disruption of the patient-therapist relationship and that these ruptures need to be actively addressed. "Because therapy is an interpersonal relationship of potential significance for the patient, it is likely that complex feelings and characteristic ways of handling separation will emerge" (Safran & Segal 1990, 214). We believe that it is important that CBT therapists approach the task of termination as an opportunity to explore patients' maladaptive way of responding to and managing separations, as well as to monitor patients' progress toward meeting other treatment goals. Termination as a process involves resolution of the ultimate alliance rupture, the letting go of the therapeutic relationship, and we believe that artful negotiation of this loss within a CBT paradigm is a key ingredient of optimal outcome, generalization and maintenance of treatment gains, and prevention of relapse.

Strategies for Ending Treatment

We believe that there are three main skills (decentering, becoming one's own therapist, and resolving ruptures within the therapeutic relationship) that enable patients to manage problems outside of therapy once therapy has ended. Each skill is developed by using a set of specific tools and is geared toward helping patients develop new ways of responding that free them from the constraints of rigid maladaptive schemas. This process in turn leads to enduring schema change, increased self-efficacy, and independence. A patient's proficiency in the techniques associated with these skills signals to the therapist that the patient is approaching readiness to end treatment and that generalization and maintenance of gains is possible.

Decentering

Decentering promotes schema change by teaching patients to step outside their immediate experience and observe themselves in the process of interpreting a situation negatively (Segal et al. 2002). Doing this allows the meaning of a thought to be reinterpreted. Decentering can also involve observation by patients of their role in an enactment that occurs within the patient-therapist relationship. Patients are asked to notice (cultivate an awareness of) their own adaptive and maladaptive relational schemas in the here and now, so that they can "disembed" from their entrenched beliefs about relationships (Muran & Safran 2002; Stevens et al. 2003).

Decentering requires practice. Safran and Segal (1990) commented that patients frequently are aware of their negative, self-critical thinking and question the value of monitoring thoughts. Therapists may also question the value of patients monitoring their thinking when they have already become aware of their thoughts. However, "knowing that one engages in negative self-critical thinking is very different from having the tangible experience of observing oneself in the process of interpreting a situation negatively. It is the stance of the dispassionate observer of one's own construction process that is the essential ingredient" (Safran & Segal 1990, 118).

We believe that decentering facilitates maintenance of treatment gains and can prevent relapse. For example, by using decentering techniques, such as mindfulness, patients become aware that aspects of experience are not within their direct control, but that they can have some influence over these aspects by how and whether they evaluate them. Through this awareness, responses to negative thoughts and feelings are de-escalated, and patients step back from the experience in the moment, refocus, and employ adaptive problem-solving skills. Decentering allows patients to be aware of alternative ways of responding rather than returning to maladaptive patterns, and in this way, facilitates the maintenance of the positive changes (Rotgers & Sharp 2005). For this reason, we suggest that the three techniques described next (mindfulness, questioning, and metaphors) be included in the armament of CBT tools, as they are particularly useful in helping patients learn to decenter.

Mindfulness. Mindfulness is a skill from which patients learn to step back from an experience and observe their own contributions to the exchange. Patients learn to direct their attention to aspects of their internal and external worlds as they are occurring "without preference, judgment or interpretation" (Muran & Safran 2002, 8). This heightened awareness to experience in the moment allows a patent to disengage from automatic responses and to experience themselves as active participants in constructing reality rather than passively living it, giving them a greater sense of agency (Muran & Safran 2002; Stevens, Muran, & Safran 2003). Questions such as, "What are you experiencing right now?"; "What are you aware of?"; and "You seem distant to me right now, what are you experiencing?" are useful in directing the patient's awareness to his or her experiences in the here and now. Therapists can also model this technique through judicious self-disclosure, that is, by revealing their own awareness and observations of experiences during the session. For example, a therapist might offer a comment such as, "I am feeling stuck right now. I am wondering what you are experiencing?"

Questioning. A technique that underlies the process of decentering is systematic questioning. Its aim is to disconfirm entrenched beliefs that contribute to the repetition of maladaptive schemas. Patients are taught to question the validity and viability of held beliefs, while also considering alternative explanations. Patients are taught to ask three questions: (1) "What is the evidence for and against the belief?" (validity), (2) "What are its true implications, if the belief is correct?" (viability), and (3) "What are alternative interpretations of the event or situation?" (alternatives). These questions help a patient analyze a core belief by identifying distorted or biased thinking. This strategy also opens up a patient's thinking so that he or she can consider additional experiences and information, thereby allowing the thoughts to be modified. What was previously held as a fact might be reformulated as a hypothesis, which then allows the patient to problem solve by generating alternative explanations (Beck et al. 1979).

Metaphors. Patients reinterpret thoughts through the use of metaphor. Metaphors communicate elements of "the big picture" in shorthand (Marlatt & Gordon 1985; Muran & DiGiuseppe 1990). Specifically, cognitions or behaviors that may not be identified easily by the patient become clear in the context of someone or something else. For example, one patient who believed that she "should be in charge all the time" was told, in addition to this being impossible, that she would have to be the Queen Bee in order to be in charge all the time. This metaphor served as a cue each time the patient began to operate under that belief system. "You're being the Queen Bee again today?" It is reasonable to expect that the patient will begin to apply this metaphor to routine daily experiences, opening up the possibility that the belief will be challenged. The decision to employ metaphors must be based on the characteristics of the patient since some patients will have difficulties with the abstraction involved in this strategy.

Patient-as-Therapist Strategies

A goal of CBT, which when met signals a patient's readiness to end treatment, is the patient functioning as his or her own therapist. This process takes place as patients learn to actively examine their thoughts and to generate new ways of responding to problems with decreasing reliance on the therapist for help. These techniques include: problem solving, activity scheduling, relaxation training and breathing retraining, diversion strategies, and of course, various homework exercises, all of which are instrumental in facilitating the transition from patient to "patient as therapist."

Each technique is practiced during the session with the aid of the therapist. When a patient becomes confident in his or her mastery of them, the use of strategies is generalized to negotiating daily life situations. Patients are at first asked to collaborate actively with the therapist in defining therapeutic tasks, including homework assignments. As therapy progresses toward termination, patients assume greater decision-making responsibility for specifying and completing the tasks of therapy (A. T. Beck et al. 1979; J. Beck 1995; Nelson & Politano 1993). Maintenance of gains is more likely to occur after treatment if patients believe in their competence to negotiate daily life experiences, and rely on their own decision-making skills.

In CBT, patients are also taught skills to manage recurrence of symptoms. In addition to the techniques we mentioned above, psychoeducation plays a big role. Identifying early warning signs that symptoms are emerging will allow patients to nip symptoms in the bud rather than relapse. Educating the patient that symptoms reemerge and fluctuate, particularly in stressful times, prepares the patient for this eventuality. Consideration of the circumstances under which symptoms might develop is also important. At these times, encourage use of the coping skills that the patient has learned in therapy, stressing the patient's mastery of them. It is also useful to anticipate future problems before the end of therapy, which prepares the patient with a plan for coping with a situation before facing it. Developing an action plan for the times when symptoms recur or a new problem is identified (i.e., what strategies have worked or failed in the past; what can be done differently next time to prevent repeat of the situation) is very helpful for patients in maintaining a sense of control. A patient's lifestyle, sleep patterns, diet, exercise routine, and schedule, which might contribute to relapse should also be discussed and modified before terminating treatment (A. T. Beck et al. 1979; J. Beck 1995; Ledley et al. 2005; Linehan 1993; Nelson & Politano 1993).

Interpersonal Strategies: Ending the Relationship

CBT traditionally assumes that when problems exist in the therapeutic relationship they have developed largely as a result of patient's cognitive distortions. In contrast, from a relational perspective, conflicts within the therapeutic relationship are understood to develop from the interaction between the therapist and patient, where each person unwittingly brings their unconscious ways of relating to create the problematic interaction. When ruptures occur, it is the therapist's task to engage the patient in a dialogue about the contribution each person brings to the difficulty and to challenge the enactments experientially. This task presumes a bond between the two individuals. Collaborative exploration of the therapeutic alliance as conflicts emerge within session allows the therapist and patient to "unhook" from an exchange, and opens up the opportunity to resolve conflicts by creating a new, productive relationship (Muran & Safran 2002).

The end of treatment naturally disrupts the therapeutic relationship and evokes certain themes, which we will address in this section (see Safran & Muran 2000, for more elaborate discussion and relevant literature). The resolution of ruptures during termination often poses challenges for the therapist that are not unlike those he or she faced in working through ruptures with a particular patient throughout the course of treatment (though perhaps more intense), which is why we have referred to the termination process as the resolution of the *ultimate alliance rupture* (Muran & Safran 2002).

Critical themes in termination. Termination obviously involves the theme of *separation and loss*, and thus can evoke sadness, as well as tension between the needs for individuation and relatedness. The process of individuating is inherently guilt producing and fraught with anxiety because it threatens relatedness. Paradoxically, however, the attainment of true individuation and relatedness is dependent upon one another. One cannot maintain a mature form of relatedness to others until one has developed a sense of oneself as an individual. This is a critical theme that therapist and patient must negotiate as treatment comes to an end.

Another critical theme concerns *acceptance*. The problem of faith lies at the heart of the human change process. At some fundamental level, one has to have some hope that one has the ability to change and that the healer has the ability to help one change. In the final analysis, however, therapists must have tolerance for their own impotence as helpers and their own inability to solve patient's problems for them or take their pain away. It is inevitable that patients will want the impossible from their therapists. They will want them to transform their lives and take their pain away. Therapists who have difficulty accepting their own limitations and being *good enough* as helpers will respond defensively in the face of patients' impossible demands. It is thus critical for therapists to come to terms with the fact that in the end there is a limited amount that one human being can do for another. No matter how deeply empathic the therapist is, when the session is over, the patient goes home and the therapist goes on with his life. The recognition of this limitation becomes particularly poignant when confronting treatment's end.

Finally, there is the theme that by the very nature of our existence we are paradoxically alone and yet in the world with others. We are alone at a fundamental level in that we are born alone and ultimately we must die alone. Although we are able to share many things with other people, many of our private experiences will never be shared with others. At the same time, we are inescapably tied to others. We are born in relationship to others and attain a sense of self only in relation to others. As human beings we thus spend our lives negotiating the paradox of our simultaneous aloneness and togetherness. This theme can also become salient as the patient faces the end of treatment and the therapeutic relationship. The critical task for the therapist is to help the patient work through this disappointment in a constructive way. This process involves coming to accept one's needs and desires as valid and legitimate, while at the same time living with the pain of recognizing that they will never be met in an absolute sense. We contend that development of metacommunication skills, associated with rupture repair, is crucial to the successful negotiation of these themes as the therapeutic relationship ends.

Metacommunication. Metacommunication allows both a patient and therapist to communicate about a communication that is taking place. This can be understood as a form of mindfulness in action (Safran & Muran 2000). It is an attempt to bring ongoing awareness to the interaction between therapist and patient as it unfolds in immediate experience. The process is usually initiated by the therapist who makes explicit his or her immediate experience of some aspect of the therapeutic relationship (either the therapist's own feelings or immediate perception of some aspect of the patient's actions). When metacommunication skills are applied to the process of terminating treatment, the patient's sadness over the loss of the therapeutic relationship can be explicitly addressed as a rupture to negotiate. For example, the therapist may say, "I feel like what I say could bring up feelings in you of being abandoned." Self-disclosure by the therapist plays an important role. The therapist's task is to identify his or her own feelings and use them as a starting point for collaborative exploration. For example, the therapist may say, "I experience you as sad right now as we talk about ending our work together." These statements by the therapist are aimed at articulating his or her implicit sense of what taking place in the therapeutic relationship in order to initiate an explicit exploration of what is being unwittingly enacted. It is also often useful for therapists to pinpoint specific instances of patients' eliciting actions. For example, "I feel closed out by you, and I think it may be related to the way in which you tend not to want to reflect on what I'm saying about our ending therapy." Both the therapist and patient have ambivalent feelings about ending their relationship and the wish on both parts for continued interaction must be explicitly negotiated in order to say good-bye.

The following is a list of some basic principles in the process of metacommunication. Elsewhere we have described these principles, as well as others, in much greater detail (Safran & Muran 2000).

1. *Start where you are.* Metacommunication should always emerge out of the inspiration of the moment. It should be based upon feelings and intuitions that are emerging for the therapist in that moment. What was true one session may not be true the next session, and what was true at the beginning of a session may not be true later in that same session. Furthermore, what is true for one therapist in relationship to a particular patient will not necessarily be true for another. Therapists must begin by accepting and working through their own feelings in the immediacy of the moment rather than trying to be somewhere they are not.

2. *Focus on the here and now.* The focus should be on the here and now of the therapeutic relationship and on the present moment, rather than on events that have taken place in the past (i.e., either in previous sessions or at different points in the same session). Commenting on what is happening in the moment facilitates the process of mindfulness for patients. To the extent therapists are able to comment on whatever is happening in the moment, it will become easier for patients to develop a grounded experiential awareness of both their actions and the internal experience associated with them.

3. *Focus on the concrete and specific.* The focus should be concrete and specific, rather than general. Whenever possible, questions, observations, and comments should focus on concrete instances. This promotes experiential awareness rather than abstract, intellectualized speculation. When patients' attention is directed to the concrete and specific, they can make their own discoveries rather than buying into the therapist's version of reality. This type of concreteness and specificity helps them to become observers of their own behavior. It thus promotes the type of mindfulness that fosters change.

4. *Explore with skillful tentativeness.* Always communicate observations in a tentative and exploratory fashion. The message

at both explicit and implicit levels should always be one of inviting the patient to engage in a collaborative attempt to understand what is taking place, rather than one of conveying information with an objective status. It is critical to remember that relational implications of a communication are as important as, if not more important than, its content. The tentative and exploratory nature of the therapist's intervention should be genuinely felt by the therapist and not simulated.

5. *Establish a sense of collaboration and we-ness.* The implicit message should always be one of inviting the patient to join the therapist in an attempt to understand their shared dilemma. During periods of therapeutic impasse, patients typically feel alone and demoralized. The therapist becomes one of an endless succession of figures who are unable to join with the patient in his or her struggle. He or she becomes another foe rather than an ally. By framing the impasse as a shared experience, the therapist begins the process of transforming the struggle by acknowledging that the therapist and patient are stuck together.

6. *Emphasize one's own subjectivity.* All metacommunication should emphasize the subjectivity of the therapist's perception. This plays a critical role in establishing a climate that emphasizes the subjectivity of all perceptions and the importance of engaging in an ongoing collaborative effort to clarify what is taking place. Emphasizing the subjectivity of the therapist's observations also helps to establish a more egalitarian role relationship. When the subjectivity of the therapist's observations is emphasized, patients are more likely to feel free to either make use of them or not, and are less likely to feel a need to cling to their own perspectives and defensively reject the therapist's stance.

7. *Gauge relatedness and responsiveness.* Therapists should monitor their sense of emotional closeness with or distance from patients on an ongoing basis. This continuous assessment provides an important source of diagnostic information because it provides information about the quality of relatedness with patients in a given moment. This quality of relatedness reflects an ongoing interplay between interpersonal and intrapersonal dimensions.

A sudden shift in the direction of decreased relatedness may signal that the therapist's intervention has been hindering, rather than facilitative, and indicate the need to explore the way in which the patient has construed or experienced the intervention. Conversely, a sudden shift in the direction of increased relatedness may signal that the therapist has developed a more attuned understanding of the patient's internal experience. In a similar vein, therapists should monitor the quality of patient's responsiveness to interventions on an ongoing basis.

8. *Recognize that the situation is constantly changing.* It is important to bear in mind that the situation is constantly changing. What was true about the therapeutic relationship a moment ago is not true now. It is thus critical for therapists to use whatever is emerging in the present as a point of departure for further metacommunication. All situations are workable provided that one fully acknowledges and accepts what the situation is. Even the position of "being stuck" is a position that is workable once one accepts it and ceases to fight against it.

9. *Accept responsibility.* Therapists should always accept responsibility for their contributions to the interaction. It is critical to bear in mind that as therapists we are always unwittingly contributing to the interaction with the patient. The task is thus one of working in an ongoing fashion to clarify the nature of this contribution. In many cases, the process of explicitly acknowledging one's contribution to the patient can be a particularly potent intervention that can help patients become aware of inchoate feelings that they are having difficulty articulating, that can validate patients' conscious and unconscious perceptions of what is taking place and help them trust their own judgment, and that can reduce patients' self-doubt, thereby decreasing the need for defensiveness and paving the way for the exploration and acknowledgment of the patient's contribution to the interaction.

10. *Judicious disclosure and exploration of one's own experience.* Therapists can begin the process of resolving a rupture by sharing their own experience (feelings, images, fantasies, or descriptions of their own actions) with their patients. During this process, it

is important to make it clear that their experience is not simply caused by the patient, and that there is no guarantee that it will help shed light on what is going on in the current interaction. The process of articulating one's feelings to patients can begin to free oneself to intervene more effectively. Therapists' feelings of being stuck or paralyzed often reflect difficulty in acknowledging and articulating to themselves what they are currently experiencing. Further, the process of acknowledging one's contributions to the patient can play a critical role in beginning to clarify the nature of the vicious cycle.

Other coping strategies for grief and separation. We have included several additional guidelines for negotiating the loss and grief that patients feel as treatment ends. Generalize reliance on the therapist to relationships with other people in the patient's life by encouraging the patient to rely on significant others for support. This can also be done by gradually decreasing the frequency of sessions so that patients are less reliant on the therapist for consistent feedback. Homework assignments can be designed to monitor the patient's progress toward being his or her own therapist. Establish the rules for contact between the therapist and patient once treatment ends, so that reasonable boundaries are maintained as the patient goes through the process of letting go. It is often useful to discuss the role of the therapist in a patient's life after therapy ends by clarifying what kind of relationship the patient can expect to have with the therapist (A. T. Beck et al. 1979; Beck 1995; Ledley et al. 2005; Linehan 1993; Nelson & Politano 1993).

General Considerations When Ending CBT

The end of therapy should not be treated differently than other components of treatment. Whatever emerges during termination should be understood systematically by exploring its significance for the patient and the therapeutic relationship.

Final Sessions

The structure of the last sessions is usually similar to that of earlier sessions. Maintenance of treatment gains becomes an explicit focus and can be promoted through active planning for termination. A review of problem-solving and other coping skills prepares the patient for managing future problems in adaptive ways independently. This can be done by highlighting the gains made in treatment, by specifying the techniques that were particularly helpful to the patient in changing beliefs and behaviors, and by anticipating future problems that might arise.

Relapse Prevention

Throughout the cognitive-behavioral literature, strategies to prevent relapse have been explicitly offered (Antony et al. 2005; J. Beck 1995; Segal et al. 2002). One strategy is to discuss with the patient when or if he or she should return to therapy. A dialogue with patients about how to manage new problems, about the likelihood that problems will develop as life progresses, and about the fact that thoughts and feelings will fluctuate, which does not necessarily signify relapse, can reassure patients that their experience is within the norm. It is also common to offer patients booster sessions after treatment so that the therapist can help the patient monitor progress and refresh coping skills. This can be very helpful in identifying ineffective coping strategies if symptoms reemerge before a full relapse occurs (A. T. Beck et al. 1979; J. Beck 1995; Ledley et al. 2005; Linehan 1993).

Obstacles to Successful Termination

One primary mistake that therapists often make is that they frequently wait until the end of therapy to discuss termination. The issue of termination is one that should be explicitly considered throughout the therapy. From the beginning of treatment, the therapist needs to stress to the patient that he or she will not be in treatment indefinitely and that one goal of treatment is that the patient will become his or her own therapist.

A common concern expressed by patients as termination progresses is a fear that they are not "completely cured." It is important to review with the patient that the goal of treatment is to help him or her learn to effectively problem solve and cope with stress as it emerges rather than to "cure" all of their life's difficulties. It is helpful to point out to the patient how much he or she has progressed during treatment and in what ways change has been successfully made.

Both therapists and patients experience anxiety as therapy comes to an end. Comments by therapists such as, "We only have four sessions left. We won't be done by then," reveal their concerns. A patient's anxiety about the end of therapy often exacerbates this: "I feel like we are just getting started. I don't feel very different than when I first came." Often this gets translated into the therapist feeling incompetent. It is important that the therapist and patient recognize that the termination of therapeutic contact does not signal the end of the patient's own work as therapist or the change process.

Conclusions

CBT ends when the goals of therapy identified at the beginning of treatment are met, and the patient has acquired the tools by which to function as his or her own therapist when future difficulties arise. In order to function as one's own therapist, the patient is taught specific techniques for problem solving, learns to generalize (apply) these skills to new situations, which in turn increases the likelihood that treatment gains will be maintained after treatment, all of which reduce the risk of relapse. Relapse prevention is, after all, the paramount therapeutic goal.

In CBT, the concepts of generalization and maintenance of treatment gains are usually considered to serve as the backbone of relapse prevention, by facilitating the patient's gradually taking on the role of therapist for himself or herself, thereby increasing self efficacy (Goldfried 2002). Nelson and Politano (1993) went so far as to suggest that generalization and maintenance are so central to CBT treatments that "relationship and termination issues are important only in so far as they influence generalization and maintenance of treatment effects" (253).

We too acknowledge the value of the generalization and maintenance of skills in facilitating relapse prevention, but we also value the importance of relational skills in promoting schema change, in facilitating the stability of treatment gains over time, and for providing the patient with an optimal therapeutic experience. We view the close of treatment as an important therapeutic process that is affected by the ongoing negotiation of the therapeutic relationship throughout the treatment. The process of termination involves not only laying the groundwork for the generalization and maintenance of skills, but also includes the act of ending a relationship with another person who provided therapeutic (curative, remedial, and supportive) and emotionally meaningful services. We believe that inclusion of relational principles and strategies within a traditional CBT model will allow for the explicit exploration of issues that arise in the therapeutic relationship as termination approaches. We advocate teaching patients not only the problem-solving techniques traditionally used in CBT, but also those skills that focus on resolving alliance ruptures (i.e., metacommunication and mindfulness). It is in the farewell that patients learn to confront issues of loss and separation, to resolve the ultimate alliance rupture (saying good-bye), and to find a balance between autonomy and relatedness.

References

Antony, M. M., Ledley, D. R., & Heimberg, R. G. (2005). *Improving outcomes and preventing relapse in cognitive behavioral therapy.* New York: Guilford Press.

Beck, A. T. (2005). The current state of cognitive therapy. *Archives of General Psychiatry, 62,* 953–959.

Beck, A. R., Rush, A. J., Shaw, B. F., & Emery, G. (1979). *Cognitive therapy of depression.* New York: Guilford Press.

Beck, J. S. (1995). *Cognitive therapy: Basics and beyond.* New York: Guilford Press.

Beck, J. S. (2005). *Cognitive therapy for challenging problems.* New York: Guilford Press.

Bornstein, P. H., & Rychtarik, R. G. (1983). Consumer satisfaction in adult behavior therapy: Procedures, problems and future perspectives. *Behavior Therapy, 14,* 191–208.

Castonguay, L. G., Goldfried, M. R., Wiser, S., Raue, P. J., & Hayes, A. M. (1996). Predicting the effect of cognitive therapy for depression: a study of unique and common factors. *Journal of Consulting & Clinical Psychology, 64,* 497–504.

Freud, S. (1953). Analysis terminable and interminable. In J. Strachey (Ed.), *Collected Papers* (Vol. 5; pp. 316–357). London: Hogarth Press.

Garfield, S. L. (1983). Some comments on consumer satisfaction in behavior therapy. *Behavior Therapy, 14,* 237–241.

Goldfried, M. R. (2002). A cognitive-behavioral perspective on termination. *Journal of Psychotherapy Integration, 12,* 364–372.

Goldfried, M. R., & Davila, J. (2005). The role of relationship and technique in therapeutic change. *Psychotherapy: Theory, Research, Practice, Training, 42,* 421–430.

Hollon, S. D., & Beck, A. T. (2005). Cognitive and cognitive behavioral therapies. In M. J. Lambert (Ed.), *Bergin and Garfield's handbook of psychotherapy and behavior change* (5th ed.; pp. 447–492). New York: John Wiley.

Klein, M. H., Dittman, A. T., Parloff, M. B., & Gill, M. M. (1969). Behavior therapy: Observations and reflections. *Journal of Consulting and Clinical Psychology, 13,* 259–266.

Ledley, D. R., Marx, B. P., & Heimberg, R. G. (2005). *Making cognitive-behavioral therapy work.* New York: Guilford Press.

Linehan, M. M. (1993). *Cognitive-behavioral treatment of borderline personality.* New York: Guilford Press.

Marlatt, G. A., & Gordon, J. R. (1985). *Relapse prevention.* New York: Guilford Press.

Muran, J. C. (2001). Meditations on both/and. In J. C. Muran (Ed.), *Self Relations in psychotherapy process* (pp. 3–35). Washington, DC: American Psychological Association.

Muran, J. C. (2002). A relational approach to understanding change: Plurality and contextualism in a psychotherapy research program. *Psychotherapy Research, 12,* 113–138.

Muran, J. C., & DiGiuseppe, R. (1990). Towards a cognitive formulation of metaphor use in psychotherapy. *Clinical Psychology Review, 10,* 69–85.

Muran, J. C., & Safran, J. D. (1993). Emotional and interpersonal considerations in cognitive therapy. In *Cognitive therapies in action: Evolving innovative practice* (pp. 185–212). San Francisco: Jossey-Bass.

Muran, J. C., & Safran, J. D. (2002). A relational approach to psychotherapy: Resolving ruptures in the therapeutic alliance. In F. W. Kaslow (Ed.), *Comprehensive handbook of psychotherapy* (pp. 253–281). New York: John Wiley.

Nelson, W. M., III, & Politano, P. M. (1993). The goal is to say "goodbye" and have the treatment effects generalize and maintain: A cognitive-behavioral view of termination. *Journal of Cognitive Psychotherapy: An International Quarterly, 7,* 251–261.

Persons, J. D. (1989). *Cognitive therapy in practice: A case formulation approach.* New York: W.W. Norton.

Rotgers, F., & Sharp, L. (2005). Substance use disorders. In M. M. Antony, D. R. Lefley, & R. G. Heimberg (Eds.), *Improving outcomes and preventing relapse in cognitive behavioral therapy* (pp. 204–245). New York: Guilford Press.

Rowa, K., Bieling, P. J., & Segal, Z. V. (2005). Depression. In M. M. Antony, D. R. Lefley, & R. G. Heimberg (Eds.), *Improving outcomes and preventing relapse in cognitive behavioral therapy* (pp. 204–245). New York: Guilford Press.

Safran, J. D. (1998). *Widening the scope of cognitive therapy.* Northvale, NJ: Jason Aronson.

Safran, J. D., & Muran, J. C. (1996). The resolution of ruptures in the therapeutic alliance. *Journal of Consulting & Clinical Psychology, 64,* 447–458.

Safran, J. D., & Muran, J. C. (1998). *The therapeutic alliance in brief psychotherapy.* Washington, DC: American Psychological Association.

Safran, J. D., & Muran, J. C. (2000). *Negotiating the therapeutic alliance: A relational treatment guide.* New York: Guilford Press.

Safran, J. D., Muran, J. C., & Rothman, M. C. (2006). The therapeutic alliance: Cultivating and negotiating the therapeutic relationship. In W. O'Donohue, N. A. Cummings, & J. L. Cummings (Eds.), *Clinical strategies for becoming a master psychotherapist* (pp. 37–55). New York: Academic Press.

Safran, J. D., Muran, J. C., Samstag, L. W., & Stevens, C. (2002). Repairing alliance ruptures. In J. C. Norcross (Ed.), *Psychotherapy relationships that work: Therapist contributions and responsiveness to patients* (pp. 235–254). New York: Oxford University Press.

Safran, J. D., & Segal, Z. V. (1990). *Interpersonal process in cognitive therapy.* New York: Basic Books. (2nd ed. Northvzle, NJ: Jason Asonson)

Segal, Z. V., Williams, J. M. G., & Teasdale, J. D. (2002). *Mindfulness-based cognitive therapy for depression.* New York: Guilford Press.

Stevens, C. L., Muran, J. C., & Safran, J. D. (2003). Obstacles or opportunities? A relational approach to negotiating alliance ruptures. In R. L. Leahy (Ed.), *Roadblocks in cognitive-behavioral therapy* (pp. 274–294). New York: Guilford Press.

10

Termination and Long-Term Treatments

Steven J. Ellman

Of necessity, this chapter will have its roots in other publications where I have considered the topics of termination and long-term analyses (Ellman 1991, 1997), or, to paraphrase Rose (1974) and Klauber (1977), the question of interminable analyses and interminable analysts. The criteria for termination in analysis have changed a good deal over the last twenty years and this change has paralleled the changes that have occurred in the practice of psychoanalysis. In this chapter I will first briefly state one view of termination and some definitions that have been put forth by Novick (1976, 1982). I will then go over some aspects of analytic treatment that I think are crucial for a successful termination to occur. A clinical example will be presented, and after discussion of this case illustration I will review some of the literature on termination. During this review I will try to reconcile divergent views of termination in terms of my own views of the analytic process.

Brief Illustration

When I was in training (in the 1970s) I analyzed a graduate student as one of my training cases. She was twenty-eight when she began analysis and she entered treatment with two distinct self-identified issues. What was most troubling to her was the fact that she had been engaged twice and both times she had severe panic attacks before her wedding date. On both occasions (with different men) she subsequently terminated her wedding plans. Although she considered this to be her primary concern, she was also quite anxious about her performance in graduate school. She reported that she was considered a bright promising student, but she despaired about ever being able to finish her doctoral thesis. While her attempts at finishing her thesis did not completely panic her, she had enough anxiety to keep her from making meaningfully progress in her writing. Whenever she would decide on a topic she would be plagued with doubts about the originality of the topic, the importance of the topic, and so forth. In the few instances where she was able to work for a period of time on a topic, she was then constantly concerned with the issue of plagiarism; that is, were her written attempts plagiarizing other writers? These concerns would then be associated with her losing interest in the topic and going to yet another topic. These two issues were her key concerns when she began treatment, and she felt that if she could successfully get married and finish her thesis her analysis would be a success.

After 4½ years in analysis, Ms. G had accomplished both of her goals, she had married a man with whom she shared a great deal and whom she seemed to deeply love. In addition she finished her thesis. She was now being offered jobs in her field and her thesis was being published as a book. My supervisor told me that we had reached the end of the analysis and that I should inform the patient that the analysis was over. His criteria were clear, she came into the analysis with certain symptoms (conflicts) and these conflicts had been resolved. He maintained that we had understood the reasons for her conflicts and had provided her with this insight. Because we had both helped her understand and resolve her conflicts, we had met his criteria for termination. It was his view (as is also true of Brenner 1976, 1982) that when the analyst considered these two conditions to be satisfied, the analysis should be considered complete. It is the analyst's decision, but, to paraphrase Brenner (1976), if the patient agrees with this determination so much the better. In some ways I was of course delighted to find out that I had completed an analysis, since in this training program it frequently took a long time to complete an analytic treatment. I inquired in supervision whether I should be looking for the termination phase of treatment; my supervisor informed me that I should create the termination phase by declaring that it had started.

This is one standard for termination—when the analyst sees that the patient has analyzed their core conflicts and reduced or eliminated the issues that precipitated the analysis. The analyst should make this declaration and set a time for the end of the treatment. This model is at least to some extent based on a medical model where the physician is the authority and the patient is the passive recipient of the treatment. In a definition that Novick put forth, Brenner's view of termination might at times be considered a *forced termination*, that is, one where the analyst decides to end the treatment while the patient wishes to continue the treatment. The patient in my example did not want to stop treatment, and if I had simply decided to terminate the treatment, it would have been an example of a forced termination. The opposite of a forced termination is a *unilateral termination*, where the patient decides to end the treatment while the analyst believes that the treatment should continue. *Mutual terminations* are where analyst and patient make a joint decision to end the treatment. We will discuss these different types of termination as well as the question of whether there is typically a termination phase of analytic treatment, but before I discuss these views of the termination process, let me briefly state some conditions that I view as essential in the psychoanalytic situation. Moreover, it is my view that unless the conditions I am positing are met, there is a low probability of achieving a mutual termination.

Beginnings and Analytic Trust

Although it is my view that what I am positing is important for all analytic patients, let me focus on two types of patients—narcissistic and borderline patients. Kohut (1968, 106) posited that if the analyst maintained an empathic stance and "did not interfere by premature transference interpretations," some form of either idealizing, mirroring, or in later parlance self-object transference would form. Kohut suggests that the analyst initially provide "forms of mirroring and echoing responses" (100), so that a form of the mirroring transference will firmly occur. Here, Kohut advocates the analyst meaningfully reflect the patient's responses, which is intended to demonstrate that the analyst can accurately feel what the patient is presenting. The mirroring, if done mechanically, can of course have an adverse effect, and so the analyst must be able to reflect in her/his own words and within his/her style.

In my interpretation, Kohut (1968, 1977, 1984) began to enable the analyst to enter the patient's world, and Bach (1994, 2006) describes this entry in a more subtle, nuanced, and utilizable paradigm. Both caution against early interpretations and state, "that for a long time it is a mistake to emphasize to a patient that his demands are unrealistic" (Kohut 1968, 100). Following this logic we are not trying to assist the patient in reality testing or provide support as a remedy, but rather we are trying to establish the conditions that allow the patient to develop what I will call a consistent and utilizable transference.*

Bach emphasizes the idea of narcissistic states, and in his concepts of anti-worlds explains the emptiness of the narcissist in terms of difficulties in agency. Anti-worlds are, in Bach's terms, ways that the narcissistic and borderline person has of warding off the environment and keeping it outside their psychological world (states). It is a way of reacting against the outside environment's having an impact on the person's internal states. Bach's writings have led me to state (Ellman 1991, 1998; Ellman & Moskowitz 1998) that what Grunes (1998) and I have called the *affective interpenetration* in the analytic dyad is a crucial aspect of a patient's being able to tolerate ruptures in the treatment situation. The analyst must be able to feel the anxiety, turmoil, and psychic pain the patient is experiencing, and be able to communicate this in a way that it becomes a shared analytic experience. In my view, this is the crucial aspect of the beginning of an analytic treatment—the ability of the analyst to facilitate affective interpenetration. This can be done in a number of ways (besides echoing and reflecting); a simple synthetic comment allows the patient to know that the analyst is able to feel that two experiences have a certain affective equivalence. Thus, for the analyst to comment, "this experience with your uncle seems to feel like what you have been describing with your

---

* Here when I use the term *transference* I am referring to the idea that the patient's conflicts can gradually be expressed in the treatment with respect to the analyst. This in my mind is the most convincing form of treatment since the patient can experience their conflicts with immediacy. This, of course, is not the only form of psychoanalytic treatment, or even a treatment that focuses on the transference, should transference be the only or at times even the most important issue.

fiancé," indicates that the analyst has felt the affect in both situations and recognizes the similarity in the two different situations. Synthetic comments also help the patient begin to integrate a more unified sense of self.

Early stages with some patients (narcissistic or otherwise) may require the analyst to tolerate a certain level of meaninglessness or non-symbolic communication (Freedman 1994; Steingart 1998) in which he is not perceived or related to as anything like a whole object. Such patients often have limited ability to self-reflect. This situation seems best described by terms such as *narcissistic* or *self-object* transference*, during which the analyst must often accept the patient's transference but not interpret it verbally. At this point in treatment the patient perceives and needs a one-person field in the analytic situation. By this I mean that it is only the patient's concerns that are center stage in the analytic situation. The analyst's theories or hypotheses are, at this stage, irrelevant to the progress of the treatment. Thus before a rupture in the treatment can be endured or be repaired, there must be a certain stability of structure so that the repair can be anchored and cohere in a stabilized configuration.

Borderline Beginnings

Affective interpenetration is often more difficult with patients who seem to need to destroy the analytic relationship. Each position that in some manner begins to develop a holding environment (Winnicott 1971) frequently needs to survive a (borderline) patient's sense of rage, betrayal, or, in a less dramatic but perhaps more continuous sense, a patient's sense of being misunderstood. Bion's (1983) ideas about containment are implicitly present in various forms of Winnicott's (1960) formulation about treating the patient who is "not well chosen for classical psychoanalysis" (586). Paraphrasing Winnicott, I would say that surviving rather than sidestepping or avoiding the destructive aspects of the analysand is a necessary condition for successful analysis to take

---

* The term *self-object* is used here to reflect the fact that some patients (people) cannot tolerate opposing views. Thus, if an analyst differs with patients' views of themselves, there is frequently a rupture in the treatment situation.

place. One has to survive the patient's negative affect, but in the course of survival it is crucial to be able to return the affect expressed in a manner that is *detoxified,* to use Bion's term. In more ordinary language, it is important to survive and talk, for example, about the patient's rage without moving away from it or being excessively retaliative. My assumption is that there is always some form of enactment (Ellman & Moskowitz 1998) that takes place around negative and destructive tendencies. With most narcissistic patients, this not a striking issue in the beginning phases of treatment. However, as vertical splitting* becomes more prominent in what many analysts would characterize as borderline experiences, there is a greater chance of containment being a central facet in the beginning phases of treatment. In the kind of treatments that I am alluding to, the ruptures are externalized and frequently enacted, and the first rupture that must be endured is one that threatens to disrupt or terminate the analytic couple.

More dramatic splitting presents at least two different issues that lead to difficulties in the analytic situation. Frequently affect is quickly eliminated during some form of action or in a rapid negation, projection (for me the correct term is *projective identification*), or rapid oscillation to another state or sense of self and other. Here the interpenetration of affect is even more important with the analyst not only being able to experience the affect, but gradually present it to a patient who has already left the affective state and clearly wants no part of the experience. Frequently this type of patient kills the affect with action, which at times involves substance abuse, and in such cases it is particularly important to reexperience with the patient the affect and experience that had to be destroyed. This must be done gradually and in successive approximations.

Although I have focused on the beginning of the treatment, trust is not established once and for all during this phase of analysis. It is my view that during an analysis there are transference shifts that occur as new understanding and experiences are processed in the treatment situation. Frequently new understanding occurs as a result of interpretative work that hopefully involves collaborations between analyst and

---

* By *vertical splitting* I mean a defense that divides conscious states as opposed to a defense, such as repression, which keeps certain ideas out of consciousness.

analysand. At times though, the analyst provides an interpretation that is disruptive.* Usually an interpretation creates some distance (rupture) between the analyst and patient. In other terms, analytic trust is disrupted, to some extent, after an interpretation. Frequently interpretations in analysis are more meaningful if the patient can experience the conflict or psychological disturbance in the transference, that is, in his/her relationship with the analyst. Given that interpretations are important they achieve importance for two quite different reasons. First, it provides intellectual and affective insight into an issue that previously was not well understood. Second, it allows for the two parties to have differing points of view and survive these differences. Usually these differences involve issues with a good deal of sensitivity in terms of the patient's psychological world, and so differing points of view are not academic but crucial to the patient's sense of well-being. It is an important step when the patient can utilize a depth interpretation. If this can happen, the trust in the relationship is strengthened. It signals that the patient can accept something from another that is not necessarily part of their present view of their psychological world. In a parallel way, the analyst's ability to modify his or her understanding and admit limitations is a crucial aspect of analytic trust, which I will not be able to discuss more fully in this chapter.

Dr. A

Dr. A was a surgical resident when a senior colleague first referred him to me. He came for a consultation because of an "embarrassing incident" that he did not want to relate to me in his first consultation session. He mentioned to me that he had discussed this event with a previous analyst he had seen (in consultation), but that the analyst had a "supercilious" attitude. Since Dr. A's first language was not English, I asked him to tell me a bit more about this attitude. He mentioned that the analyst began to question him and to take a type of history.

---

* Here I am referring to an intervention where the analyst provides an explanation of how processes outside the patient's awareness (unconscious processes) are affecting the patient's emotional state and actions. This is how I am defining the term *interpretation*; thus, this definition always refers to the analyst explaining something that is outside of the patient's conscious awareness.

In short, the first analyst began to treat Dr. A like a patient, and this was clearly a humiliating experience for him. During the first meeting he told me that he was having some difficulties with his fiancée and his chief resident. It was important for him to tell me that despite these difficulties he was probably going to be chief resident next year and that he already had several excellent job offers. At the end of our first meeting he thanked me for my time and told me that I had been of "good value" to him. He said that he would think about the treatment, but thought that he had cleared up his difficulties. I was surprised when a week later he called and asked if he could see me another time. When we met he wondered if I had any questions, and I asked what he wanted to talk about. After several moments of awkward silence he began to tell me about the "incident." He knew a famous actor from his homeland and he, the actor, and his fiancée went out together one night. For the rest of the session Dr. A. described some of his feelings about the fact that the three of them had sex together. His fiancée was very upset that he had forced (or suggested) this arrangement, and Dr. A was upset that he had been so influenced by this famous man. He began to tell me that famous people had always fascinated him, and that his father is considered a famous patriot in his country. At this point the session was almost over. I asked him whether he wanted to schedule another session, but he again rose and thanked me for my help and said that he thought that he was feeling better and he would not need my services. To make a long story short, after a number of starts and stops he began analytic treatment with four sessions per week. He needed no coaxing to use the couch since he preferred not to see my face but rather wanted to fill the room with his feelings, thoughts, fantasies, and projections. Whenever there was a break that was longer than our normal weekend break, Dr. A would at the beginning of the session thank me and tell me that he had decided to end the treatment. He always included the idea that I had been of help to him. Thus one might say that every longer-than-normal separation was experienced as a rupture for him, where trust in me was at the very least diminished. The reason for this was one of the central questions in our eight-year treatment episode.

As the treatment progressed Dr. A began an idealizing transference where he considered me not only a good analyst but also an outstanding neuroscientist. Most of our sessions had an intermingling of his pain in contemporary relationships and a description of his family life and why he felt that he had to leave his birthplace. Gradually he began to tell me about his alcoholism (his alcoholic blackouts) and a type of delusionary idea that he had developed syphilis at the age of seventeen (he was now twenty-nine).* At the same time that his idealizing transference was forming, he began to talk about the alteration of states that would at times overtake him; when he performed a successful operation he would fantasize for a period of time that he was or would be the greatest surgeon in the world. He felt that none of the faculty or attendings had anything to teach him and that soon he would be recognized for his unrivaled talent. If he felt that he made a mistake, he seriously worried for a period of time that he would be demoted to a scrub nurse. It took a while for him to talk about why his perceived failures were usually accompanied by the fantasy of becoming a scrub nurse. His mother had been a scrub nurse, and in his move to the United States, he at first worked as a scrub nurse because he felt he could not get a job as a physician until he was licensed. In my mind, clearly his move to the United States had some aspect of identification with his mother. He talked about how his mother had been independent and how both she and his father had affairs. He mentioned a number of things about his past, but none of them seemed to touch his extreme sensitivity to our separations.

I will try to make this long case fairly short and say that gradually, as the treatment progressed, he began to improve; he broke up with his fiancée but met a woman who eventually became his wife. His alcoholic bouts (and blackouts) were mostly a thing of the past, and his relationships with his peers and supervisors (now partners) had greatly improved. However he still quit analysis at each separation, and this was something that neither of us understood.

At the end of the fourth year of the analysis the patient decided to marry and was offered a post in Texas. Accepting the post meant that he would have to stop analysis, and it was not clear to him (or to me) that this opportunity was one that would be of benefit to him.

---

* Obviously, if this had been untreated for this amount of time, he would have severe symptoms, which he knew in a way.

Nevertheless, he seemed compelled to take this job with what seemed like diminished clinical and research possibilities as compared to the position he held in the New York area. I wondered about my reaction to the idea of what I considered to be his unilateral termination (or premature termination). He seemed determined to go forward on this path until one more long separation (a week of my vacation) occurred, and he had the following dream:

> You were giving a lecture and it seemed to me that you were doing well. I was in the audience and watching you. For some reason I was watching your face and your expressions seemed vacant (he said a version of vacuous). The audience was enthusiastic but you still seemed not to respond, and then suddenly I was in Bucharest and I thought this is the most beautiful city in the world.

Although by that time he worked well with dreams, he began to say how this dream was meaningless, and how this time he was serious, and "that analysis had gone as far as it could go." I told him that he talked about analysis as if it was a person; he belittled my remark and I could feel for one of the few times with Dr. A that I was getting angry. I said that he if wanted to leave it was certainly his right, and that there was nothing I could do about it. After this annoyed interchange things in the session shifted and Dr. A began to talk about an operation he had just performed. Suddenly he said that it seemed to him that I looked sick. He said that he wasn't sure why he thought that, but that when he came into the office he felt that I looked sick. In my view this remark brought us back into the dream, and I commented that in the dream even though things seemed to be going well for me I seemed sick, or at least nonresponsive. At that point he became quite sad and said that he really felt that I had helped him a great deal and that he wanted to know in reality, not in the dream, whether or not I was sick. I told him that the dream was very real to him and that it was beginning to feel real to both of us. Perhaps he thought that I was ill because he was leaving me? He was somewhat disoriented and the session ended with my feeling that something important had happened but I wasn't sure what it was.

In the next session he began by saying that he was disappointed that I did not answer his question, and that he never seemed to have my full attention. This seemed odd to me, and again I was reminded of the dream from the session the night before. I said that his reaction to the separation was one where he felt that I was unresponsive to him, but that he then excused me by saying that I must be sick. He said that he thought I was sick even though he knew (sort of) that perhaps I wasn't. I mentioned that he never talked about how he felt when these separations occurred, and he began to talk about another event in his life involving a dream about his mother wherein she was there but not really moving. After talking about his mother for a time, I began to picture an immobile mother not responding to her child. I said to him that I thought that at some point in his life his mother was sick or depressed, and that no matter how good an audience he was for her, he couldn't please her. Moreover, in the dream about me he was also the audience and perhaps if he could really please me I would never leave him. He reminded me that in the dream he didn't try to please me. I said that while this was true, I was telling him what it felt like to me. This led to a string of thoughts (some were memories), one of which concerned being told how precocious he was as a child. He also remembered how he was unable to tolerate criticism when he went to school. He would begin to cry if he made a mistake. We began to realize that with his (maternal) teachers he always needed to always please them, and if he was told that he was wrong or did not understand something, anxiety about, or a derivative of maternal separation, surfaced. Over a period of several sessions we put together a reconstruction where his mother was taken away ill (I thought depressed) and that he fantasized that he had not "been delightful enough" (his word from another language), and so she left to be with others (although she was in reality in a despondent state). Later that year his mother visited him (for the first time in several years) and he asked her about this. She told him that she had been depressed after the birth of his sister and was hospitalized the first time for one month, and when that was ineffective, for a several months more after being home for only two or three weeks between hospitalizations.

This transference-countertransference sequence, which led to a reconstruction, was a turning point in the treatment. A number of issues around sibling and oedipal rivalry gradually emerged, and as they emerged in different contexts they occurred in an increasingly object-related manner. His somatic delusion was gradually understood as a damaged penis unable to really delight his mother or any other woman in a continuous manner. It was also seen as a punishment for his desire to be delighted by or receive pleasure from a woman. His homosexual concerns were in part a wish to be willing to tolerate assistance from a man who would help him navigate the difficulties of keeping a woman happy. His idealizing transference had largely homosexual underpinnings, both in the sense of Freud's use of the term in normal narcissistic development (Freud 1911), as well as his various submissions to the powerful male. Repair of the maternal rupture that was continuously reproduced in the treatment situation was nevertheless key to allowing other issues to effloresce in the transference.

Termination of Dr. A and Termination Issues

Of necessity the case of Dr. A is presented in truncated form. I have not included the times before the fourth year when I attempted to interpret his reactions and was rebuffed in my attempts. His wish to leave for Texas was a wish to leave the treatment before he could experience the pain associated with his earlier trauma, which was continuously reexperienced during his life. When he entered treatment he was about to leave his residency, his friends, and so forth, and this had been a pattern throughout his life where he would abruptly change friends and situations. The fact that he could dream about his issues and talk about this dream in treatment indicated to me that he had built up enough trust in the analytic situation that he felt we could survive this encounter. I could attempt to describe this case in greater detail, but I would prefer to move to the termination phase of the treatment. In my view of analysis there is a termination phase of treatment where the patient, in milder form, repeats the core conflicts that had been the subject of analysis and seemingly had been worked through. Thus, toward the end of our treatment Dr. A began to repeat some of the separation themes that I have described. To be sure, he began to repeat these experiences with a different tone, and I began to trust that he could navigate the treatment without my interpretative efforts. In fact most of the time we began to see that he was able to self-reflect in a manner that indicated that he knew what he was experiencing better than I did. This new self-reflective capacity is what I would term the patient becoming his or her own analyst or developing a self-analytic capacity. The trust that he gradually placed in me was now returned to him in a full manner. I began to trust that he knew his internal world and that he could navigate his conflicts and adjust his behavior in a creative manner that did not depend on repetition.

The Cycle of Trust and Termination

I have tried to indicate that the beginning of treatment is meaningful if the analyst can affectively penetrate the patient's world. The patient can then begin to trust that the analyst can know (feel) the types of conflicts that the patient is experiencing. This is done in subtle and rarely in dramatic fashion. At some point toward the end of the beginning phase of treatment the analyst attempts to impart a perspective that is part of the patient's internal life, but has been outside of his or her awareness (usually, but not always, part of the patient's unconscious). This defended piece of the patient's reality* is rarely accepted by the patient without at least some disruption in the analytic process. Even if both parties see the analyst's interpretation as correct and helpful to some extent, it places the analyst in a different position than she/he had been in at the beginning of treatment. Frequently the interpretive analyst is seen as part of the defended material, and this puts the analyst in a position where, to some extent, trust is disrupted. If the interpretation is effective and leads to new material that is seen as useful therapeutically, then trust can be reestablished and strengthened. The analyst's nondefensive attitude when the patient makes mistakes or is not empathically attuned can also strengthen trust if the analytic pair can work through these difficult moments. Gradually, as trust is established and reestablished the analyst begins to gain a growing sense of confidence in the patient's self-analytic capacities. The termination phase is marked by a mutual trust where the analyst has gradually ceded the treatment over to the patient. This is not done in a complete or absolute fashion, but gradually the analyst becomes more and more unnecessary in the final part of this phase of the analytic process. Termination then consists of a completed mourning over the loss of this intimate relationship and the

---

* At least from the analyst's point of view.

beginning of a new relationship. This new relationship may exist only in the minds of the two parties, for they may not any longer have contact but it is a new relationship nevertheless.

Some Controversies and Further Commentary

I have presented one view of termination in the analytic situation. At this point let me review other approaches and then attempt to reconcile these views within the matrix that I have tried to construct. Although Freud wrote about endings (Freud 1936) in analysis, he was not primarily concerned with what modern analysts have called the termination phase of treatment. Rather Freud presented criteria for how to understand success in the analytic situation, as well as the limitations of analytic treatment (Ellman 1991). He does point out that in analyses there are not always mutual terminations, but his interest is in understanding the obstacles inherent in the analytic situation and some factors in individual differences in the analytic situation. Contemporary analysts have attempted more generally to study the way analyses end, and Novick (1982) relates that mutually agreed-upon terminations are the exception in modern analytic treatment. Novick, in a review of termination themes, brings up a number of issues that relate to termination.

1. Before one can fully talk about actual terminations, there must be categories for the different types of terminations that can occur.
2. If termination issues are discussed one naturally has to bring up the goals of treatment because it is assumed that successful terminations happen when the goals of analysis have been satisfactorily attained.
3. Because Novick (and others) consider there to be a terminal phase in analysis, he must state criteria that can allow us to identify this phase of treatment. Naturally he is also interested in the preconditions that allow one to enter the terminal phase and for this phase to be successfully traversed.
4. If one can specify all of the above, then it is possible to ask some practical questions about how the date for termination is brought up and by whom (analyst, or analysand, or both).

5. During the termination phase, various analysts have reported that the patient's original symptoms reappear as a normal aspect of the analytic process. Novick questions the normality of this phenomenon. It is also observed that analysands typically mourn the loss of the analyst in the termination phase of treatment. Understanding the nature of that mourning reaction is a question that Novick considers.

6. As a last point, Novick reviews some issues concerning the postanalytic phase. Various analysts have argued that major changes frequently occur after the treatment has been ended. They have come to regard this as a normal aspect of the treatment. Novick questions this interpretation of post-analytic change.

Some Definitions in the Terminal Phase

As previously mentioned, premature terminations are divided into two main categories: terminations initiated by the analyst and those initiated by the patient. Reasons for termination may vary, but terminations that are decided upon by the analyst are designated, forced terminations, while those initiated by the patient are labeled, unilateral terminations. Forced terminations can include the analyst relocating, contracting a prolonged illness, pregnancy, or even death. Grouped with these reasons are the more common analytic issues, "a premature decision made by the analyst for counter-transference reasons, such as dealing with entrenched preoedipal transference situations, especially those of the sadomasochistic kind, or dealing with seemingly interminable patients" (Novick 1982, 330). Similarly unilateral terminations include such divergent factors as "geographic moves or physical illness, to intensive resistances to the transference" (330). Although the problem of premature termination is certainly not limited to analytic treatment or to psychological treatments, there are obviously important reasons to understand the difficulties along the path of mutually agreed-upon terminations.

Part of the difficulty in understanding the reasons for premature termination may lie in the way analysts conceive of or at least label the issue. The word premature in this context has a negative implication that colors the whole issue of the validity or success of the treatment in question. If a patient terminated prematurely, is it possible to think of the treatment as anything but a failure? The implication of Novick's review of the literature is that the percentage of premature terminations is underestimated. In reviewing eight cases that Firestein (1978) presents in his book on termination, Novick relates that while Firestein refers to only one of the eight cases as a premature (forced) termination, "in reading through the summaries, it becomes evident that six others were prematurely forced by the analyst and one termination was based on a unilateral decision by the patient" (quoted in Novick 1982, 350). If I have correctly counted, Novick is stating that all eight cases ended prematurely (the one that Firestein reported and the others that Novick assessed as premature). It is not my intention to reconcile these two markedly different views of these cases, but only to comment on one possible reason for this marked discrepancy. In making his assertion, Novick wasn't saying that these were poorly conducted analyses, but without intending to, this is nevertheless the common inference that many readers would draw. It may be that these analyses were of considerable benefit to the patient, but for one reason or another, the patient or the analyst did not successfully complete the termination phase of treatment. Freud attempts in his last articles to say that the idea of successful mutual termination is perhaps a myth, yet his words are seen by many as a statement, by the founder of a field, who did not have the benefit of viewing modern developments in psychoanalysis. Perhaps we should say that mutual termination is an ideal (like any other analytic standard), and that it should not be considered a necessary precondition for success in the analytic situation. Put in my terminology, it may be that in some analyses it is so difficult to obtain trust in the earlier parts of the treatment that either or both participants are unwilling to give up their established trust for an independent view of each other. Successful termination necessarily implies a separation between analyst and patient that is frequently final. The finality of termination may not be endurable by many analytic pairs. Interestingly, a separation that is viewed by one or both parties as indicating an inadequate result will not allow the separation to be fully finalized, and the loss cannot be mourned.

Assessing Criteria for Success

Let us go back to Novick's statements and assume that he is warranted in his assumptions about Firestein's cases. Are we correct in proposing that a prematurely terminated case can be termed a successful analysis? Before one can entertain such a question, there would have to be some statement of the criteria for analytic success. Once this question is broached, we see that we have entered into one of the murkiest of analytic regions. Freud's early criteria were seemingly straightforward—if the patient's symptoms were removed or dissipated, then the treatment could be considered a success.* When Freud began to make pronouncements about making the unconscious conscious, or expanding the domain of the ego, (in the structural model) he implicitly stated goals for analytic treatment that are difficult to unravel. It is hard to specify operational criteria for these statements, although I would venture that most analysts can come up with their own versions of what Freud meant.

Novick reports that for many modern analysts, self-analysis is an important if not overriding criteria for the success of analytic treatment. Novick sees the roots of this idea in Sterba's discussion (1934) of the fate of the ego in analysis. In this article Sterba implicitly gave criteria for elucidating the concept of ego autonomy at the end of analysis. Hoffer (1950) is the first analyst cited as stressing the importance of identification with the functions of the analyst. Treatment can be terminated when the analysis can be turned over to the analysand. This idea, while meeting with a good deal of explicit and implicit acceptance, has not stood without some criticism. Brenner (1982) sees this goal as one that is more appropriate for analysts in training as opposed to patients who are undergoing a purely therapeutic analysis. A number of other analysts have seen this goal as overly ambitious and unrealistic. Novick (1982, 358) implies that it is not known to what extent the self-analytic function is retained after analysis or how important it is for the maintenance of the improvement. He also says, "We know from our work with children that many of them can achieve and maintain positive results without developing a self-analytic function"

---

* These criteria are similar to those of my supervisor and Brenner's criteria.

(1982, 358). This last statement is indicative (to me) of the difficulties of discussing this point as well as other related issues in psychoanalysis. We might ask Novick how he knows that children maintain positive results without developing a self-analytic function? We can ask the obvious question about whether he really has done a follow-up study to be able to make this type of empirical statement. More importantly we can ask how he is conceptualizing the self-analytic function in children. Is it seen as appearing in the same way we would expect it to be manifested in adults? Is it possible that in children this function takes a different form? Is it possible that the analytic results in children are not a good model in the discussion of psychoanalysis of adults? It is hard to discuss the autonomy of a young child, who is usually still living with his or her parents, in the same way we can discuss the autonomy of an adult, who one hopes can develop a life of his or her own with the assistance of analytic treatment. This brings up a more basic question: How are we conceiving of the self-analytic function in adults? Novick refers to Hoffer (1950), but Hoffer at best gives us a concept of this function. There has been nothing approaching a study of how patients fare who have more of this function as opposed to patients who have less. It may not even be entirely clear what one would look at in such a study. Perhaps before we could attempt such a study we would have to clearly understand what we mean by the self-analyzing function.

We might ask what different functions of the analyst the patient might come to internalize. Clearly in the literature most analysts, in one way or another, refer to the analysand's ability to self-interpret. This follows the premium that Freud and many modern analysts put on the role of insight in the analytic situation. There may be other functions of the analyst that are of equal importance. A possibility is that patients may internalize different analytic functions depending on what is important in a given analysis. The analyst's equanimity in the face of conflict may be an analytic attitude that is extremely important in the analysand's ability to face their postanalytic conflicts. The analysand may consciously be able to call on this function at times of conflict, but it is questionable whether many analysts would call this a self-analyzing function. When Freud tells us that in analysis we extend the ego's control (over the id), one can imagine that this can be accomplished in a variety of ways. Analysts traditionally have seen the ability to verbally formulate explanations as the primary avenue of analytic cure and postanalytic prophylaxis. Perhaps we can formulate the goals of analysis in terms of the analysand's ability to be able to internalize, and then voluntarily call upon those traits of the analysts that have been curative during the course of the analysis. Certainly one of the traits of the analyst will be the ability to formulate the patient's conflicts in verbal terms. This may be the prime trait that needs to be internalized, but other traits can also be considered quite important. The willingness to consider the patient's problems worthy of detailed consideration may be considered as a preliminary step to understanding the patient's conflicts or it might, with some patients, have considerable importance in its own right. A child who is brushed aside and considered only in the context of the parent's needs is introduced to a new world with an analyst who can listen to their associations.

Although Novick reports that there is an increasing emphasis on self-analysis as a goal of treatment, and it is clear that he as well as others have some reservations about this goal. The definition of the goal remains to be fully explicated. A full explication of the goal may provide links between adult self-analysis and self-analytic modes in treatment of children. As a preliminary step, if we define a goal of analysis as the internalization of those traits of the analyst that help patients to face and understand their conflicts, we may consider that children do develop some self-analytic abilities after analysis. To state the central point in a more concise form, the difficulties that Novick sees in the goal of self-analysis may be due to a restrictive definition of self-analysis. This restrictive definition may also be related to his notions of the curative aspects of analytic treatment.

Beginning the Terminal Phase

Novick conceives of the preconditions for the terminal phase as being related to what he calls an adolescent pattern of premature termination. The pattern of adolescent type resistance is in his view a "major resistance to a positive Oedipal transference and thus to the start of a terminal phase" (339). This resistance or pattern "must be interpreted before a true termination phase can begin" (339). The terminal phase is thus seen as a period when conflicts around positive Oedipal themes are manifested.

What is accomplished during the terminal phase of treatment? Most commentators agree that there is no prototypical pattern in this phase, although certain themes seem to be commonly expressed. There are, as Gitelson (1962) points out, "more 'good hours' and the therapeutic alliance is at its maximum efficiency" (198). The major tasks, as seen by most authors, are those of working through and synthesizing the insights gained (Ekstein 1965), turning insight into effective and lasting action (Greenson 1965), and, most important, doing the work of mourning—the final working through of a separation from the analyst as an object representative of drive derivatives from all levels of development, but especially the *oedipal level*. The major defense during this phase is an attempt to avoid the painful work of mourning, either by denying the importance of the analyst as a transference object (for example, by immediately displacing the transference wishes onto another object), or, as is more usual at this phase of treatment, by denying the irrevocability and inevitability of the loss.

The importance of the oedipal phase of development is, of course, a legacy of Freud's later theorizing. It is by no means my experience of the termination phase of treatment. What I have seen is that the phase of development that is important during the treatment situation (which may be expressed in only adult terms) is the phase of development that is the focus of termination. This aspect of the patient's life may start at any point and may or may not include oedipal themes.

Controversies

Analysts have often observed, during the terminal phase of analysis, that there is a revival of initial symptoms (Ellman 1991). Thus the patient repeats, in attenuated form, the symptoms or difficulties that originally brought them into analysis. While some analysts have viewed this revival as a normal part of the terminal phase, Novick sees this as a sign that the termination is premature.* There is also a question of

---

* This may be part of the criteria he uses in assessing Firestein's cases as premature terminations.

what the analysand relinquishes and works through during the terminal phase of treatment. Does the patient give up the analyst as a real as well as transference object, or is what is given up purely a function of the transference, even during the terminal phase of treatment? A third point of controversy relates to observations of a number of analysts that there are major changes in the patient after the analysis has ended. Analysts have related these changes to the continuation of analytic work that the patient carries on himself. They have also assumed that this is a natural aspect of the analytic process. Novick interprets these postanalytic changes as a result of treatments that are involved with unilateral premature terminations. Novick's interpretations of the terminal phase of treatment lead one to conclude that the work of analysis is by and large accomplished within the confines of the analytic situation and the transference relationship.

What are we to make of Novick's contention that the revival of symptoms during the terminal phase is related to premature terminations that are forced by the analyst? Novick's own clinical experience seems to yield evidence to support his view since he does not find that patients demonstrate revival during the terminal phase. It is his contention that "this may be due to my own technique of picking up and analytically addressing adolescent terminal phenomena before broaching and setting the date for the terminal phase" (Novick 1982, 263). I must admit that in my experience I have seen patients who did and did not demonstrate symptom revival. Interestingly, in two patients who did relive symptoms, there was a good deal of preparation and in Novick's terms it certainly seemed as if adolescent terminal phenomena were addressed. However these patients originally suffered from more intense conflicts and it was not surprising to see a revival of conflicts during the termination phase. It seems to me that Novick's review leaves out perhaps the most crucial issue—the individual differences in the way patients react to the analytic situation. These individual differences no doubt elicit different reactions (as well as different fantasies) on the part of the analyst, but it may be that these differences are a normal aspect of analytic experiences. It may be that we have to think of a range of normal experiences rather than prototypical analytic experiences, as Novick tends to relate. This range of experiences would have to take into account the different reactions that some types of patients both manifest and tend to elicit. Moreover, a truly sophisticated analytic discipline would take into account a range of responses that different styles of analysts tend to elicit in the terminal as well as in other phases of the treatment. Thus, differences in the analyst and in the severity of symptoms of the patient might lead to different types of terminations.

Loss of the Analyst

One aspect of the position that highlights analytic trust is that the analyst really listened to the patient in a manner that is different from the patient previously experienced. This difference is a real one and is not simply the patient's fantasy or transference reaction. Thus the mourning in the terminal phase is in part a recognition that a certain aspect of the patient's life is coming to an end. I suspect that many analysts would agree that a typical countertransference difficulty that is encountered in termination is one where the analyst has fantasies of being irreplaceable and necessary for the patient's continuing functioning. At the very least there may be a tendency to view most of what goes on in the analytic situation as totally unique instead of in the context of the transference. Thus while the terminal phase has aspects of transference experiences that recur, there is also, and perhaps more importantly, the mourning on the part of both analyst and analysand, which allows the relationship to end in a satisfactory manner.

Postanalytic Experience

We are now at the point of considering the postanalytic phase, and here again it seems to me that Novick is taking a position that is clear and strong, if indeed somewhat, overstated. His contention is that major changes that occur after the termination of treatment are a result of premature termination. This seems to be a reasonable hypothesis that would apply to many examples, but certainly would not apply universally. Moreover, there is a recent large-scale study (Sandell et al. 2000) indicating that patients continue to improve after they have ended their analytic treatment. Interestingly this is not true of other forms of treatment. Perhaps not all of these analysts (it was a large-scale study) have performed analysis in the way that Novick would require, but it may be that an important benefit of analytic treatment is that patients develop the ability to analyze aspects of themselves after treatment is over. It is my view that in a good analysis, an analyst trusts that patients can be their own analyst at the end of a good analysis.

References

Bach, S. (1994). *The language of perversion and the language of love.* Northvale, NJ: Jason Aronson.

Bach, S. (2006). *Getting from here to there.* Hillsdale, NJ: Analytic Press.

Bion, W. R. (1983). *Learning from experience.* New York: Jason Aronson.

Brenner, C. (1976). *Psychoanalytic technique and psychic conflict.* New York: International Universities Press.

Brenner, C. (1982). *The mind in conflict.* New York: International Universities Press.

Ekstein, R. (1965). Working through and termination of analysis. *Journal of the American Psychoanalytic Association, 13,* 57–78.

Ellman, S. J. (1991). *Freud's technique papers: A contemporary perspective.* Northvale, NJ: Jason Aronson.

Ellman, S. J. (1997). Criteria for termination. *Psychoanalytic Psychology, 14,* 197–210.

Ellman, S. J. (1998). The unique contribution of the contemporary freudian position. In C. S. Ellman, S. Grand, M. Silvan, & S. J. Ellman (Eds.), *The modern Freudians; Contemporary psychoanalytic technique* (pp. 237–268). Northvale, NJ: Jason Aronson.

Ellman, S. J., & Moskowitz, M. (1998). *Enactment: Toward a new approach to the therapeutic relationship.* Northvale, NJ: Jason Aronson.

Firestein, S. (1978). *Termination in psychoanalysis.* New York: International Universities Press.

Freedman, N. (1994). More on transformation: Enactments in psychoanalytic space. In A. Richards & A. Richards (Eds.), *The spectrum of psychoanalysis: Essays in honor of Martin Bergmann* (pp. 103–132). New York: International Universities Press.

Freud, S. (1911). Psycho-analytic notes on an autobiographical account of a case of paranoia (dementia paranoides). *The Standard Edition of the Complete Psychological Works of Sigmund Freud* (Vol. 12; pp. 9–82). New York: W.W. Norton.

Freud, S. (1937). Analysis terminable and interminable. In *Collected Papers* (Vol. 5; pp. 316–357). New York: Basic Books.

Gitelson, M. The curative factors in Psycho-analysis. *International Journal Of Psychoanalysis.* 43:194–205.

Greenson, R. (1965). The working alliance and the transference neurosis. *Psychoanalytic Quarterly, 34,* 135–145.

Gruness, M. (1998). The therapeutic object relationship-II. In C. S. Ellman, S. Grand, M. Silvan, & S. J. Ellman, *The modern Freudians; Contemporary psychoanalytic technique* (pp. 129–140). Northvale, NJ: Jason Aronson.

Hoffer, W. (1950). Three psychological criteria for the termination of treatment. *International Journal of Psychoanalysis, 31,* 194–195.

Klauber, J. (1977). Analyses that cannot be terminated. *International Journal of Psychoanalysis, 58,* 473–478.

Kohut, H. (1968). The psychoanalytic treatment of the narcissistic personality disorders: Outline of a systematic approach. *Psychoanalytic Study of the Child, 23,* 86–113.

Kohut, H. (1977). *The restoration of the self.* New York: International Universities Press.

Kohut, H. (1984). *How does analysis cure?* A. Goldberg (Ed.) with the collaboration of P. Stepansky. Chicago: University of Chicago Press.

Novick, J. (1976). Termination of treatment in adolescence. *Psychoanalytic Study of the Child, 31,* 389–414.

Novick, J. (1982). Termination: themes and issues. *Psychoanalytic Inquiry, 2,* 329–366.

Rose, G. J. (1974). Some misuses of analysis as a way of life: Analysis interminable and interminable 'analysts'. *International Review of Psychoanalysis, 1,* 509–515.

Sandell, R., Blomberg, J., Lazar, A., Carlsson, J., Broberg, J., & Schubert, J. (2000). Varieties of long-term outcome among patients in psychoanalysis and long-term psychotherapy. *International Journal of Psychoanalysis, 81,* 921–942.

Steingart, I. (1998). A contemporary-classical Freudian views the current conceptual scene. In C. S. Ellman, S. Grand, M. Silvan, & S. J. Ellman, *The modern Freudians; Contemporary psychoanalytic technique* (pp. 161–176). Northvale, NJ: Jason Aronson.

Sterba, R. F. (1934). The fate of the ego in analytic therapy. *International Journal of Psychoanalysis, 15,* 117–126.

Winnicott, D. W. (1960). The theory of the parent-infant relationship. *International Journal of Psychoanalysis, 41,* 585–595.

Winnicott, D. W. (1971). *Playing and reality.* New York: Basic Books.

11

BEHAVIOR THERAPY AND TERMINATION

GEOFFREY L. THORPE,
ELAINE MCMILLAN,
LINDSAY R. OWINGS, AND
RACHEL DAWSON

Although the topic of termination has been largely neglected by its formal professional literature, behavior therapy seems ideally suited to deal with the various matters attendant upon drawing treatment to a close (Goldfried 2002; Nelson & Politano 1993). Typical definitions of the field emphasize its specificity, in that behavior therapists and their clients focus on demarcated and, often, narrowly delineated problems (Erwin 1978). Treatment tends to be highly structured, and is focused on producing tangible results and helping clients reach specified goals. Empirically supported behavioral treatment regimens are usually time limited and can involve following detailed procedural manuals that have been tested experimentally. Examples of such applications include obsessive-compulsive disorder (Abramowitz 2006), attention-deficit/hyperactivity disorder (Barkley 1990), and panic disorder (Barlow & Craske 2000; Hecker et al. 2004). The practice of behavior therapy is normally guided by a treatment contract in which the targets, methods, modalities, and duration of therapy are designated. These characteristics of behavioral practice aid and facilitate termination because the processes and procedures of concluding the intervention are anticipated from the outset.

Behavioral assessment is integral to behavior therapy. Appropriately enough, clinicians usually think of assessment as a precursor to treatment interventions, but in the behavioral model, assessment typically continues throughout the course of treatment, providing a valid barometer of progress that can signal when the client's goals have been reached. Because behavior therapists focus on following specified procedures to produce particular outcomes, with realistic solutions acceptable to client and therapist agreed upon in advance, the treatment contract ends when assessment confirms that the problems have been resolved and predefined outcomes attained.

In participating in a therapeutic contract that specifies the expected nature and course of treatment, and that requires termination of services when treatment is ineffective or no longer necessary, behavior therapists are acting consistently with the ethical codes of the professions of psychology and social work (Bucky, Callan, & Stricker 2005). For example, Ethical Standard 10.01 of the ethics code for psychologists requires that "psychologists inform clients/patients as early as is feasible in the therapeutic relationship about the nature and anticipated course of therapy" (American Psychological Association 2002).

The Professional Relationship in Behavior Therapy

From its beginnings in the 1950s as a systematic approach to mental health work, behavior therapy was presented as an alternative to psychoanalysis. Joseph Wolpe claimed, on the basis of his clinical series of over 200 "neurotic" outpatients, that behavior therapy produced positive results and that these were attained in a relatively short period of time (Wolpe 1958). Termination itself received scant attention, for empirical and theoretical reasons. First, the goals of behavior therapy were specified and mutually agreed upon at the outset; therefore, attaining those goals meant concluding treatment. Second, treatment did not and does not revolve around analyzing the dynamics of the client's unconscious projections onto the therapist; hence, there was no need to address a transference neurosis, to work through the issues raised by the treatment relationship, or to establish treatment termination as a distinct activity that required its own place as an important and lengthy phase of a prolonged intervention. Behavior therapy pioneers rejected the internality and subjectivity of psychoanalytic treatment, focusing instead on external objective events and seeking to address presenting problems directly. Following resolution of the problem that brought the client to treatment, other issues may be pursued, but ethical practice requires that the manner of determining goals and selecting interventions is discussed and agreed upon by client and therapist at the outset (Goldfried 2002).

In typical outpatient settings, behavior therapy is an egalitarian enterprise in which clients' perspectives on problems and their solutions are accepted as valid starting points for treatment planning, itself a collaborative process. Accepting clients' perspectives as meaningful, as opposed to viewing them with suspicion as the product of irrational, unconscious forces, implies that behavior therapists can adopt straightforward relationships with their clients. There is no need to maintain an aloof and colorless persona because the therapist is not trying to present him or herself as a form of projective test stimulus. Thus, bringing treatment to a close does not require that extraordinary attention be paid to extricating the client from the professional relationship with the therapist.

As in the practice of medicine, the professional relationship itself is not the central vehicle of change in behavior therapy. To say that the client-therapist partnership is not the chief transformative mechanism of treatment is not to say that this relationship is insignificant or irrelevant, of course. It can be defined in many different ways and comprises several features. One familiar component of medical treatment is the physician's "bedside manner" (typically viewed as having a "you know it when you see it" quality, defying formal definition), which we assume to be a desirable characteristic of medical professionals. Without an engaging, respectful, and reassuring interpersonal style, physicians run the risk of failing to elicit their patients' active participation in treatment, or of failing to mobilize their constructive expectations of benefit, both of which may be necessary in ensuring optimal outcomes. The same goes for behavior therapists, who, like other mental health professionals, are expected to develop competence in relationship skills (Spruill et al. 2004).

A review of relationship variables in the behavioral treatment of panic disorder concluded that early client evaluations of therapists' empathy, warmth, and genuineness predicted positive behavioral outcomes. Clients who viewed their therapists as respectful and understanding made the greatest gains. In a study of junior therapists providing cognitive-behavioral interventions for panic disorder and agoraphobia, differential effects of distinct styles of interaction were seen at different stages in therapy. Directive statements predicted positive behavioral outcomes, but only when delivered during the later stages of treatment; in the first session of treatment, directive statements were detrimental. By contrast, therapist expressions of empathy and warmth also predicted positive behavioral outcomes, but only in the context of the first session; toward the end of treatment, such expressions were associated with a poorer client response (Key & Craske 2004).

Despite the documented importance of relationship factors as a necessary component of effective professional practice, physicians and behavior therapists would argue that unaided, even the most superlative display of empathy, concern, respect, warmth, and understanding would be unlikely to remedy (for example) the blood sugar regulation problems seen in diabetes or the experiential avoidance associated with anxiety disorders. Specific intervention techniques beyond those inherent in the relationship are usually required to correct diagnosed malfunctions in metabolic, behavioral, and cognitive processes.

A Coping Skill Model of Change

Ideally, behavior therapists subscribe to an educational model of change in which clients learn useful techniques and strategies that can be applied when and if problems arise in the future. The *coping skill model of change* (Goldfried 2002) is grounded in the view that in addition to alleviating clients' specific problems and enhancing their daily functioning, behavior therapists also seek to help clients gain general coping skills that they can utilize independently and autonomously following treatment termination. Examples of behavioral techniques that transcend narrow applications to current problems are problem-solving methods, relaxation training, cognitive restructuring, and communication skills training (Goldfried 1980). Within treatment, difficulties in clients' affective, cognitive, and behavioral functioning are addressed and alternative ways of feeling, thinking, and behaving in the extratherapeutic environment are identified and rehearsed. Once more adaptive functioning has been established, clients can acquire more general coping skills that equip them to serve as their own therapists in the future. A key element of this model is the development of clients' *self-efficacy*—the confidence that they have at their command the skills necessary to deal adequately with new problems as they arise.

When these skills are in place and the treatment goals have been met, behavior therapy moves into a maintenance phase. The therapist ensures, through monitoring, that the client can adequately utilize the coping strategies acquired during treatment. During this phase treatment sessions are phased out, the idea being that the client actually takes over as the therapist in dealing with the problems of everyday life, with the therapist on hand as a safety net if needed. Once the client has encountered a difficult problem and has demonstrated effective use of his or her coping skills, therapy can be terminated (Goldfried 2002).

Empirical Support for Behavioral Termination Programs

Because the therapeutic partnership tends to be egalitarian, collaborative, and straightforward, terminating a course of behavior therapy follows a different pattern from that seen in psychodynamic insight-oriented therapies. As treatment draws to a close, behavior therapists and their clients review the progress that has been made, discuss clients' attributions as to the reasons for their improvement, take steps to ensure that therapeutic gains will transfer to life in the community, and make contingency plans in the event that further interventions may be needed in the future (Nelson & Politano 1993).

There are several patterns for termination in behavior therapy. Treatment can end with the last of a brief series of regular outpatient sessions, often a fixed number of meetings that has been specified in advance. Consistent with learning principles and to facilitate generalization of treatment gains from the period of active therapy to the client's life after therapy, treatment sessions can be gradually tapered off, for example, moving from weekly outpatient visits to meeting once in two weeks, once per month, and so on. In residential settings dealing with severely incapacitating disorders, inpatients could be discharged immediately to the community with various forms of aftercare support from outside agencies, or preferably make a gradual transition through a series of intermediate "stepping stones," such as halfway houses, group homes, therapeutic communities, and so forth. In all settings, before termination, behavior therapists strive to promote the generalization or transfer of gains and assure the maintenance or durability of treatment effects (Nelson & Politano 1993).

Although they are tangential to termination issues as traditionally construed, empirical findings from several areas of behavioral practice are helpful in informing and directing termination procedures and processes. The behavioral literature on mood and anxiety disorders, behavioral medicine, disorders in children, and severe and persistent disorders such as schizophrenia includes evidence on the differential effectiveness of various termination regimens, and on the utility of particular measures of improvement that predict long-term outcomes. Selective findings from that literature illustrate the implications for treatment termination.

Mood and Anxiety Disorders

Improvement in scores on the Attributional Styles Questionnaire (ASQ) at treatment termination predicts depression level at longer-term follow-up assessment. Reduced ASQ scores could provide an empirically supported criterion for terminating treatment (Barber et al. 2005).

Unlike interpersonal psychotherapy, cognitive-behavior therapy tends to be followed by continued progress and a reduced risk of relapse after termination in depressive clients (Hollon et al. 2005), and similar results are seen for anxiety (Hollon, Stewart, & Strunk 2006). This implies that a complete resolution of all mood symptoms may not be necessary before client and therapist discontinue active treatment.

Research has indicated that generic treatment for panic disorder produces outcomes commensurate with those derived from individually tailored interventions. Clinicians' concerns about the uniqueness of an individual client's presentation may be unfounded when providing time-limited, effective treatment in this context (Brown et al. 1997). Other studies have shown that manual-based therapy is more effective than following an individualized treatment protocol (Barlow 1996; Wilson 1996). Such findings support the viability of delivering an empirically supported treatment package when careful assessment of the client has shown that the intervention is suitable.

Delivering a brief course of treatment within a fixed period is becoming more common and has been justified by research findings. No benefit was found in providing a twelve-session cognitive-behavioral intervention for social phobia over eighteen rather than twelve weeks; in fact, in the extended treatment condition people tended to terminate before goals had been reached (Herbert et al. 2004).

A case study illustrated the treatment of a client with a pattern of comorbid obsessive-compulsive disorder, posttraumatic stress disorder, and borderline personality disorder, showing that complex psychopathology can be treated successfully when the disorders are targeted concurrently, leading to clear criteria for termination (Becker 2002).

When the focus of behavior therapy is on skill acquisition rather than symptom elimination, the objective measurement of attainments guides the termination process. Pertinent measures may include the use of self-report questionnaires together with in vivo demonstrations of techniques learned in therapy. For example, a one-day workshop for individuals at risk for panic disorder used an assessment of information retained at the end of the workshop as its primary outcome measure (Key & Craske 2004). A treatment study on adolescent females who had been sexually abused employed a skills mastery test pre- and post-treatment; using a multiple-choice format, this test assessed participants' knowledge of techniques for coping with stress and anger (Key & Craske 2004).

In the treatment of anxiety disorders, behavioral approach tasks are useful not only in assessing clients' response to treatment, but also in evaluating the extent to which therapeutic gains have generalized beyond the specific stimuli used within treatment. This requires that clients demonstrate the ability to engage in previously avoided tasks (such as a person with a snake phobia who is going camping in the woods, or someone with agoraphobia entering a crowded shopping mall alone). In terminating a course of brief treatment, the therapist needs to ensure that clients understand the importance of stimulus generalization in the natural environment. Treatment gains such as reduced muscle tension and an ability to view graphic depictions of snakes on a computer screen may not automatically generalize to sudden, unexpected confrontations with real phobic stimuli. Additional self-exposure activities may be necessary, with post-termination follow-up and booster sessions to ensure the retention of long-term therapeutic gains (Key & Craske 2004).

Behavioral Medicine

Routine client self-monitoring of target behavior between sessions can provide an alternative to formal behavioral observations in assessing treatment outcome. However, client compliance is not always easily secured, and significant differences between objective and subjective reports of the frequency of target behavior have been observed. For example, a client with chronic fatigue syndrome self-reported significant gains in walk time during treatment, yet there was an actual decrease in objectively monitored mean weekly step counts. Using objective measures can help separate general enhancement of mood and morale from demonstrable improvement in specific, disorder-relevant behaviors (Friedberg 2002). This is reminiscent of early findings from anxiety research, in which lasting improvement in phobic clients was seen only in those who had shown within-treatment improvement in each of the three modalities of self-report, behavioral enactment, and psychophysiological monitoring, as opposed to self-report alone (Barlow, Mavissakalian, & Schofield 1980).

Approximately 30 percent of clients in treatment for eating disorders leave therapy before the conclusion of the planned program (Mahon 2000). Clinicians often speculate about clients' reasons for dropping out of treatment, but systematic data on this subject are available. One study examined this phenomenon by asking the clients why they dropped out of treatment, and by looking at objective measures of change between pre-treatment and follow-up assessments (Pekarik 1983). Clients were grouped according to their stated reason for leaving treatment; in all cases, therapists believed that further treatment was necessary. Results indicated that among these forty-three participants, "no need for services" was the most cited reason for dropping out of treatment. In fact, this group did show a significant decrease in symptomatology from pre-treatment to follow-up. The two other categories cited were "dislike of services" and "environmental constraints." The findings, that most clients who left treatment against the therapists' advice believed they no longer needed services and that they had significantly improved on objective measures, raise questions about the therapists' view that treatment had been incomplete.

It is important to be cognizant of clients' distance from specialized services and consequent treatment-related travel time, which can be substantial in some rural communities and could have an adverse impact on treatment completion. In a study of 209 adults in outpatient eating disorders treatment, travel distance had no bearing on client attrition; in fact, clients who dropped out early tended to live closer to the treatment site than treatment completers. However, clients who traveled further did attend fewer appointments. Employed clients were more likely to drop out than were unemployed clients (Swan-Kremeier et al. 2005). These results signal the need for therapists to attend to and evaluate the obstacles clients encounter in attending treatment sessions, as the reasons for client attrition may not be obvious. Addressing these issues could decrease premature termination.

Disorders in Children

Behavioral treatment of many childhood disorders is usually accomplished through training the parents or other caregivers in the consistent use of appropriate behavior management principles and procedures. As a result, the child's involvement in treatment and adherence to the intervention protocol depend almost entirely upon the cooperation of the parents. In a study of 207 children and their families, attrition from child treatment was associated with family adversity, socioeconomic disadvantage, parental stress, and life events, but not parents' psychopathology (Kazdin 1994).

When treatment addresses a focused problem that can feasibly be dealt with in a fixed number of sessions, it can be helpful to mark the termination formally by a mini-ceremony of some kind, awarding the child a certificate or a prize in recognition of his or her achievement. Parents are encouraged to continue to reinforce the child's use of coping strategies and other techniques learned in therapy (Nelson & Politano 1993).

The importance of the family's sustained involvement in treatment depends on the severity and typical clinical course of the disorder. A specific phobia is likely to require a briefer commitment than a pervasive developmental disorder, of course. In the latter case, it could be unrealistic to adopt as the criterion for a successful termination the complete absence of distress or impairment. More appropriate would be a progression from intensive behavior management within the home to a system of supports that extends to the community. For children who need indefinite treatment, some of the responsibilities for continued management are appropriately passed to special programs in the schools and other agencies.

Severe and Persistent Disorders

Inpatient treatment can be more intensive than what is available outside the hospital, of course, and may be necessary when a patient with a severe disorder such as schizophrenia shows a resurgence of florid psychopathology. Residential treatment in such cases can be intermittent and relatively brief. Behavior therapists have researched inpatient treatments based on social learning theory that focus on building skills necessary for successful functioning in the community. These include appropriate hygiene and self-care activities, social skills development, and problem-solving training (Bellack & Mueser 1994; Kendall 1987; Paul & Lentz 1977; Trower 1995). It would make no sense to a behavior therapist to discontinue such an intensive treatment program abruptly and immediately discharge the patient to a community setting without careful planning.

The successful rehabilitation of long-term psychiatric inpatients requires special aftercare programs involving a transition from the hospital to a structured halfway house setting, an extension of the hospital, before returning to the general community (Fairweather & Fergus 1993; Paul & Lentz 1977). Patients who had been initially discharged to a transitional community lodge, in which they received an intermediate level of therapeutic supervision, remained outside the hospital for longer periods and were more likely to have jobs in the community than people who had been discharged in the usual way (Fairweather et al. 1969).

Improving family interactions can help patients avoid rehospitalization when family members show high levels of *expressed emotion*, a set of communication styles marked by criticism, hostility, and emotional overinvolvement (Hooley 2004; McNally 1994; Suinn 1995). For example, overinvolved parents might have the attitude: "I hate to leave him home alone even for an hour or two; I worry about him constantly" (Hooley 2004). The particular attributions made by family members as to the patient's behavior can predict the likelihood of relapse. Overinvolved relatives tend to mobilize more benign attributions, predicting more favorable outcomes; critical and hostile relatives tend to blame the patient for his or her problems, predicting less favorable outcomes (Barrowclough, Johnston, & Tarrier 1994). Hooley (2004) notes that when expressed emotion is evident, the family's behavior is not especially pathological, but has a disproportionate impact because people with schizophrenia are especially sensitive to stress.

Specific Termination Techniques

An important goal of behavior therapy is to help clients learn the skills they need to deal more effectively and independently with problematic situations as and when they arise in the natural environment. Therapists therefore seek to aid clients in gaining a greater understanding of their problem behaviors, and to assist them in developing more effective problem-solving strategies and coping behaviors. The focus on increasing clients' independence outside therapy sessions makes explicit the need for therapists to establish the expectation that therapy will be short term and focused. Often the therapist is the first to propose treatment termination, with the hope that the client will agree (Nelson & Politano 1993). As treatment progresses successfully, clients who experience symptom alleviation may themselves initiate treatment termination. Other precipitants of therapy termination include changes in a client's life circumstances (e.g., moving out of the area, financial constraints) or dissatisfaction with services.

Preferably, treatment termination is a collaborative decision-making process between client and therapist, but even with clearly defined expectations, some clients may resist a therapist's suggestion that treatment draw to a close. Clients may doubt their readiness to go it alone, or fear that they will be unable to remember the skills learned. They may present a "new" problem, implicitly requiring extended treatment. This provides an ideal opportunity for therapists to encourage clients to apply their new skills to a different problem, and to redress such misconceptions as the idea that one must be perfectly prepared and competent before terminating treatment. Nelson and Politano (1993) suggest that from the beginning clients should be encouraged to view therapy as a training period during which they acquire the tools necessary for subsequent, appropriate problem solving, rather than as a vehicle for complete removal of problems before the treatment contract ends.

Nelson and Politano (1993) recommend that prior to fading out or terminating treatment, therapists should assess clients' self-efficacy and address any remaining doubts. In the latter stages of therapy, strategies to enhance clients' confidence in their ability to employ their newly learned skills should be introduced. Setbacks and lapses into problem behavior can be welcomed by therapists as an opportunity to help clients use *relapse prevention* techniques, which include recognizing new challenges as momentary problems that can be solved, rather than evidence of generalized client incompetence and across-the-board treatment failure. It is helpful for therapists to schedule follow-up or booster sessions to foster client self-efficacy and reinforce a continued focus on problem solving. Fading treatment out gradually allows clients to test their ability to apply newly learned strategies in vivo with the assurance of therapist assistance if necessary. Intermittent follow-up sessions or telephone check-ins over the course of several months post-treatment can help evaluate whether treatment gains have been retained and reinforce the role of the client as the primary agent of change. Whenever this is feasible in a client's treatment, involving more than one therapist and delivering treatment in more than one location helps with generalization and encourages the client to recognize that treatment gains can persist across people and settings.

Complications and Challenges

Termination does not always proceed smoothly and in accordance with professional ideals. We have noted the example of new problem presentation as a potential impediment to ending treatment in a timely manner. This and other examples will illustrate the complications and challenges that can arise.

New Problem Presentation

Example: A professional person sought help in dealing with a depressive episode sparked by a complaint to her licensing board and a subsequent malpractice suit. Treatment of her dysphoric mood, poor sleep pattern, self-criticism, and irritability progressed steadily and efficiently. Therapist and client were moving toward termination when the client brought up her concern about long-standing marital dissatisfaction.

In this case therapist and client could terminate as planned; they could start afresh with a new treatment plan to address the new issue, or the therapist could recommend a referral to a colleague. Terminating as planned could be the most helpful direction to take if it were established that the client could use what had been learned in the mood-disorder therapy to cope with the interpersonal problems. That may or may not be the case. The view that behavior therapy always teaches general coping skills for universal application has to be qualified when one recognizes that in several applications, such as the treatment of depression, only some interventions have received empirical support, and these interventions may be specific to the particular application. Determining when a new problem requires a new intervention requires professional judgment.

Alternatively, when the therapist becomes concerned that the client is seeking to prolong the professional relationship unnecessarily, he or she could point out that the client is apparently viewing therapy as "an activity in and of itself rather than as a means to develop independent problem-solving behaviors" (Nelson & Politano 1993, 257).

Example: A client was successfully treated for agoraphobia, but her consequent increased mobility led to new challenges, including the need to address her interpersonal assertiveness deficits.

In the early days, behavior therapists became accustomed to a peculiar set of reactions to such developments from psychodynamically oriented colleagues. Such reactions typically took the form, "Aha!

I could have told you that there were deeper issues underlying all this. It had to come out eventually!" accompanied by knowing looks and sagacious head nodding in deference to this apparently incontestable confirmation that the workings of a dynamic unconscious had operated behind the scenes all along to conceal the true state of affairs and to make a mockery of the misguided efforts of the hapless client and naïve therapist. But the presentation of previously undisclosed or unrecognized problems after the successful treatment of a focused concern hardly verifies psychodynamic theory.

A client may have a phobia of driving over bridges and a long-standing difficulty in making commitments to romantic relationships. One behavior therapist might treat these problems sequentially; another might focus on what could be seen as a broader pattern of unnecessary avoidance. The two treatment plans could look quite different. Which one is preferable could be an empirical matter to be settled by the results of systematic, objective monitoring of the client's progress toward the specified goals. But both treatment plans could be appropriate, theoretically and pragmatically. Recognizing that the client avoids things other than bridges does not necessarily mean that the therapist has missed the boat by treating the specific phobia. We would not consider a physician to be clueless or lacking in insight if he or she treated hypertension with medication, then prescribed physical therapy to help improve the patient's poor locomotion, even if both problems could be seen as related to sedentary habits. It is possible that treatments focused on one problem at a time could be more helpful empirically than an intervention that seeks to address both in a holistic manner, however attractive the latter option may look at face value (Lazarus 1976).

Research on the behavioral treatment of agoraphobia in the 1970s occasionally produced some unexpected offshoots. The successful treatment of agoraphobic avoidance in married individuals was sometimes followed by an upsurge of psychopathology in clients' spouses (Hafner 1977a). For example, a woman who had been housebound for years and had typically drawn from her husband's support in dealing with the outside world found herself free to travel without restriction. This left her husband with a different role in the household, one to which he apparently adjusted poorly, leading to the development of back pain and depression. Hafner found a possible explanation of this in the concept of *assortative mating*, in which couples find and select each other on the basis of similar general levels of perceived mental health. When one partner overcomes problems and improves in functioning, the argument goes, the spotlight now falls on the other's problems and deficiencies, creating further stress and psychopathology. This interesting phenomenon has not been extensively documented, and is acknowledged by its scholars to arise only rarely (Hafner 1977b).

As in the preceding examples, new problem presentation can sometimes be understood as a predictable consequence of successful treatment. Eliminating agoraphobic avoidance can make it possible for the client to enter the workplace for the first time, thus encountering new challenges. Or it can occasionally expose some of the spouse's long-standing problems, hitherto adumbrated by the pressing concerns of the client's disabling anxiety disorder. In this context it can be helpful to anticipate such problems by asking clients at the outset to consider the possible effect of successful treatment on their daily routines and family life. As far as we know, it would not betray learning principles if behavior therapists were to take a leaf from the Adlerians' book and make a practice of asking clients "The Question." To paraphrase, "If a miracle occurred during sleep and your presenting problem were suddenly and completely removed, what would be different, and how would you and others recognize that this had happened?" (Mosak 1995).

Difficult or Unproductive Client-Therapist Relationships

Clinical situations that present obvious challenges include the court-mandated treatment of sex offenders or substance abusers, and providing services to clients with personality disorders or who are at risk for suicide. However, any therapeutic relationship can become unsatisfactory or unproductive. A mismatch of expectations is a common feature of difficult client-therapist relationships.

Example: A client who had "fired" his previous therapist viewed each treatment session as a forum for reviewing at length the frustrations of the past week. These included the termination of his jobs by incompetent employers and the ending of his relationships by shallow and self-centered romantic partners. He began a session by saying: "At last I have found a therapist I'm comfortable with! Now, I have a lot to talk about today."

This client saw therapy as an obligatory ritual to be performed for its own sake, and viewed the therapist's role as simply that of a sympathetic listener. He deflected any attempt by the therapist to examine the client's contributions to his difficulties. As the last of the series of sessions approved by his insurance plan approached, the client reminded the therapist that he had had several psychiatric hospitalizations following suicide attempts.

The therapist drew from Marsha Linehan's *dialectical behavior therapy*, developed as a comprehensive treatment for borderline personality disorder, in seeking a constructive approach to helping this client (Robins, Schmidt, & Linehan 2004). Treatment emphasizes emotion regulation, interpersonal effectiveness, and distress tolerance. Therapists are careful to avoid reinforcing crisis and parasuicidal behaviors, and require clients to make an explicit commitment to behavior change (Huffmann et al. 2003).

Despite earnest efforts by the therapist to channel treatment in a more productive direction, the client was adamant in refusing to contemplate personal behavior change as a reasonable goal. The client persisted in assigning only the most passive of roles to the therapist, but was strongly averse to terminating treatment. After consultation with a colleague and some emotionally charged concluding sessions with the client, the therapist was able to obtain the client's cooperation in bringing the professional relationship to an acceptable, though disappointing, close.

Need for a Regimen of Maintenance Therapy

Example: A client with a severe and persistent mental disorder requires continuing therapy over a period of years in order to help her avoid re-hospitalization and maintain her community adjustment.

The challenge here is to recognize at the outset that it would be unrealistic to expect a satisfactory resolution of the client's psychopathology from a limited series of outpatient psychotherapy appointments. According to typical criteria, if termination were to occur only after all presenting problems had been resolved, then treatment might proceed interminably. However, even an indefinite course of treatment could be defended professionally if it can be shown that the intervention does indeed reduce the need for and use of expensive residential services. Practically, clients with the most debilitating and pervasive disorders are unlikely to be working full time and thus are probably ineligible for coverage through commercial third-party health insurance payers. In this context, outpatient care will probably be financed by government entitlement programs with their own utilization review and accountability procedures that must be satisfied.

> Example: Behavioral treatment of obesity is typically followed by eventual weight gain.

To address this, one author has proposed a "continuous-care" model of obesity management (Perri 1998). That does not mean that weekly individual treatment sessions have to continue indefinitely. A carefully designed treatment plan will make maximal use of each outpatient visit by focusing on daily behavioral self-management by the client, monitored by the therapist through frequent intersession correspondence and infrequent face-to-face meetings. Similar recommendations have been made with respect to depression (Hollon, Thase, & Markowitz 2002). After a period of intensive treatment addressing a particular mood episode, client and therapist move to a maintenance mode in which the client's progress is monitored systematically, yet infrequently.

Summary and Recommendations

Behavior therapy is typically structured, time limited, and focused. Manual-based, empirically supported treatment protocols are available for use in several applications. Using established, generic treatment packages like these usually produces results comparable with or better than those derived from individually tailored behavioral treatment. In some applications, delivering brief treatment within a fixed period of time has been shown to be more effective than drawing treatment out over a longer interval. These characteristics of behavior therapy provide a sound rationale for specific termination procedures, and suggest guidelines for drawing treatment to a close in an efficient and logical process. Further research on the immediate and long-term results of efficient, time-limited treatment protocols in specific applications is welcomed and encouraged by behavior therapists.

It is recommended that clinicians:

1. Plan for and anticipate termination from the very beginning of the treatment contract, and keep termination matters at the forefront throughout the course of therapy.
2. Establish the expectation at the outset that treatment will be short-term and focused.
3. Assess potential obstacles to successful treatment completion, and develop strategies to forestall unnecessary client attrition.
4. Decide with the client whether treatment will end after a fixed number of sessions or taper off gradually after initial progress has been demonstrated. Fading treatment out gradually can help promote generalization and maintenance of gains. The final phase of treatment can follow a relapse-prevention model.
5. Recognize that a client's reluctance to terminate treatment may spring from misconceptions that can be addressed therapeutically. Typical misconceptions include the ideas that the client is unable to deal with life and its problems without the constant availability of a therapist, and has to be perfectly competent before being able to go it alone. The implicit idea that it would be catastrophic if the client failed, made a mistake, or had to confront new challenges independently could be addressed by inviting him or her to view these ideas as hypotheses, not facts. The client could even consider engineering a deliberate setback so as to provide an opportunity to use his or her newly developed coping skills (Nelson & Politano 1993).
6. Consult other professionals for independent, objective advice when the termination process becomes unduly arduous. The appropriate use of colleagues as a resource in ensuring the delivery of competent clinical services is highly consistent with conscientious case management and ethical professional practice.

References

Abramowitz, J. S. (2006). *Obsessive-compulsive disorder.* Cambridge, MA: Hogrefe.

American Psychological Association. (2002). Ethical principles of psychologists and code of conduct. *American Psychologist, 57,* 1060–1073.

Barber, J. P., Abrams, M. J., Connolly-Gibbons, M. B., Crits-Christoph, P., Barrett, M. S., Rynn, M., & Siqueland, L. (2005). Explanatory style change in supportive-expressive dynamic therapy. *Journal of Clinical Psychology, 61,* 257–268.

Barkley, R. A. (1990). *Attention deficit hyperactivity disorder: A handbook for diagnosis and treatment.* New York: Guilford Press.

Barlow, D. H. (1996). The effectiveness of psychotherapy: Science and policy. *Clinical Psychology: Science and Practice, 3,* 236–240.

Barlow, D. H., & Craske, M. G. (2000). *Mastery of your anxiety and panic: Client workbook for anxiety and panic* (3rd ed.). Boulder, CO: Graywind.

Barlow, D. H., Mavissakalian, M. R., & Schofield, L. D. (1980). Patterns of desynchrony in agoraphobia: A preliminary report. *Behaviour Research and Therapy, 18,* 441–448.

Barrett, M. Rynn, &. Siqueland, L. (2005). Explanatory style change in supportive-expressive dynamic therapy. *Journal of Clinical Psychology 61:* 257–268.

Barrowclough, C., Johnston, M., & Tarrier, N. (1994). Attributions, expressed emotion, and patient relapse: An attributional model of relatives' response to schizophrenic illness. *Behavior Therapy, 25,* 67–88.

Becker, C. B. (2002). Integrated behavioral treatment of comorbid OCD, PTSD, and borderline personality disorder: A case report. *Cognitive and Behavioral Practice, 9,* 100–110.

Bellack, A. S., & Mueser, K. T. (1994). Schizophrenia. In L. W. Craighead, W. E. Craighead, A. E. Kazdin, & M. J. Mahoney (Eds.), *Cognitive and behavioral interventions: An empirical approach to mental health problems* (pp. 105–122). Boston: Allyn & Bacon.

Brown, G. K., Beck, A. T., Newman, C. F., Beck, J. S., & Tran, G. Q. (1997). A comparison of focused and standard cognitive therapy for panic disorder. *Journal of Anxiety Disorders, 11,* 329–345.

Bucky, S. F., Callan, J. E., & Stricker, G. (Eds.) (2005). *Ethical and legal issues for mental health professionals: A comprehensive handbook of principles and standards.* Binghamton, NY: Haworth.

Erwin, E. (1978). *Behavior therapy: Scientific, philosophical, and moral foundations.* Cambridge, UK: Cambridge University Press.

Fairweather, G. W., & Fergus, E. O. (1993). *Empowering the mentally ill.* Austin, TX: Fairweather.

Fairweather, G. W., Sanders, D. H., Cressler, D. L., & Maynard, H. (1969). *Community life for the mentally ill: An alternative to institutional care.* Chicago: Aldine.

Friedberg, F. (2002). Does graded activity increase activity? A case study of chronic fatigue syndrome. *Journal of Behavior Therapy and Experimental Psychiatry, 33,* 203–215.

Goldfried, M. R. (1980). Psychotherapy as coping skills training. In M. J. Mahoney (Ed.), *Psychotherapy process: Current issues and future directions* (pp. 89–119). New York: Plenum.

Goldfried, M. R. (2002). A cognitive-behavioral perspective on termination. *Journal of Psychotherapy Integration, 12,* 364–372.

Hafner, R. J. (1977a). The husbands of agoraphobic women and their influence on treatment outcome. *British Journal of Psychiatry, 131,* 289–294.

Hafner, R. J. (1977b). The husbands of agoraphobic women: Assortative mating or pathogenic interaction? *British Journal of Psychiatry, 130,* 233–239.

Hecker, J. E., Losee, M. C., Roberson-Nay, R., & Maki, K. (2004). Mastery of your anxiety and panic and brief therapist contact in the treatment of panic disorder. *Journal of Anxiety Disorders, 18,* 111–126.

Herbert, J. D., Rheingold, A. A., Gaudiano, B. A., & Myers, V. H. (2004). Standard versus extended cognitive behavior therapy for social anxiety disorder: A randomized-controlled trial. *Behavioural and Cognitive Psychotherapy, 32,* 131–147.

Hollon, S. D., Jarrett, R. B., Nierenberg, A. A., Thase, M. E., Trivedi, M., & Rush, A. J. (2005). Psychotherapy and medication in the treatment of adult and geriatric depression: Which monotherapy or combined treatment? *Journal of Clinical Psychiatry, 66,* 455–468.

Hollon, S. D., Stewart, M. O., & Strunk, D. (2006). Enduring effects for cognitive behavior therapy in the treatment of depression and anxiety. *Annual Review of Psychology, 57,* 285–315.

Hollon, S. D., Thase, M. E., & Markowitz, J. C. (2002). Treatment and prevention of depression. *Psychological Science in the Public Interest, 3,* 39–77.

Hooley, J. M. (2004). Do psychiatric patients do better clinically if they live with certain kinds of families? *Current Directions in Psychological Science, 13,* 202–205.

Huffmann, J. C., Stern, T. D., Harley, R. M., & Lundy, N. A. (2003). The use of DBT skills in the treatment of difficult patients in the general hospital. *Psychosomatics, 44,* 421–429.

Kazdin, A. E. (1994). Family adversity, socioeconomic disadvantage, and parental stress – Contextual variables related to premature termination from child-behavior therapy. *Psicologia Conductal, 2,* 5–21.

Kendall, P. C. (1987). Cognitive processes and procedures in behavior therapy. In G. T. Wilson, C. M. Franks, P. C. Kendall, & J. P. Foreyt (Eds.), *Review of behavior therapy: Theory and practice* (pp. 114–153). New York: Guilford Press.

Key, F. A., & Craske, M. G. (2004). Assessment issues in brief cognitive-behavioral therapy. In Bond, F. W. & Dryden, W. (Eds.), *Handbook of brief cognitive behaviour therapy.* Chichester, UK: Wiley.

Lazarus, A. A. (1976). *Multimodal behavior therapy.* New York: Springer.

Mahon, J. (2000). Dropping out from psychological treatment for eating disorders: What are the issues? *European Eating Disorders Review, 8,* 198–216.

McNally, R. J. (1994). Introduction to the special series: Innovations in cognitive-behavioral approaches to schizophrenia. *Behavior Therapy, 25,* 1–4.

Mosak, H. H. (1995). Adlerian psychotherapy. In R. J. Corsini & D. Wedding (Eds.), *Current psychotherapies* (5th ed.; pp. 51–94). Itasca, IL: F.E. Peacock.

Nelson, W. M., III, & Politano, P. M. (1993). The goal is to say "goodbye" and have the treatment effects generalize and maintain: A cognitive-behavioral view of termination. *Journal of Cognitive Psychotherapy: An International Quarterly, 7,* 251–263.

Paul, G. L., & Lentz, R. J. (1977). *Psychosocial treatment of chronic mental patients: Milieu versus social learning programs.* Cambridge, MA: Harvard University Press.

Pekarik, G. (1983). Improvement in clients who have given different reasons for dropping out of treatment. *Journal of Clinical Psychology, 39,* 909–913.

Perri, M. G. (1998). The maintenance of treatment effects in the long-term management of obesity. *Clinical Psychology – Science and Practice, 5,* 526–543.

Robins, C. J., Schmidt, H., & Linehan, M. M. (2004). Dialectical behavior therapy: Synthesizing radical acceptance with skillful means. In S. C. Hayes, V. M. Follette, & M. M. Linehan (Eds.), *Mindfulness and acceptance: Expanding the cognitive-behavioral tradition* (pp. 30–44). New York: Guilford Press.

Spruill, J., Rozensky, R. H., Stigall, T. T., Vasquez, M., Bingham, R. P., & Olvey, C. de V. (2004). Becoming a competent clinician: Basic competencies in intervention. *Journal of Clinical Psychology, 60,* 741–754.

Suinn, R. M. (1995). Schizophrenia and bipolar disorder: Origins and influences. *Behavior Therapy, 26,* 557–571.

Swan-Kremeier, L. A., Mitchell, J. E., Twardowski, T., Lancaster, K., & Crosby, R. D. (2005). Travel distance and attrition in outpatient eating disorders treatment. *International Journal of Eating Disorders, 38,* 367–370.

Tran, G. Q., & Smith, J. P. (2004). Behavioral assessment in the measurement of treatment outcome. In S. Haynes & E. Heiby (Eds.), *Comprehensive handbook of psychological assessment* (Vol. 3; pp. 269–290). New York: Wiley.

Trower, P. (1995). Adult social skills: State of the art and future directions. In W. O'Donohue & L. Krasner (Eds.), *Handbook of psychological skills training: Clinical techniques and applications* (pp. 54–80). Boston: Allyn & Bacon.

Wilson, G. T. (1996). Empirically validated treatments: Reality and resistance. *Clinical Psychology: Science and Practice, 3,* 241–244.

Wolpe, J. (1958). *Psychotherapy by reciprocal inhibition.* Stanford, CA: Stanford University Press.

12

Termination of Psychotherapy With Children

BRIE A. MOORE,
BRENDA BURSCH,
AND PATRICIA WALSHAW

As with adults, the termination stage of psychotherapy with children has clinically been known to trigger powerful feelings and can be an extremely productive component of treatment. While a small amount of research has been conducted predicting premature termination of psychotherapy with children, there are no research studies that specifically examine best practices for termination with children. This chapter will briefly review the literature of premature termination and then provide guidelines for termination of psychotherapy with children that are based on treatment manuals, clinical experience, and extrapolation from the adult literature on this topic.

Premature Termination

Ideally, termination of psychotherapy occurs when marked therapeutic gains have been made. However, practitioners and families terminate psychotherapy under a variety of conditions. Much of the empirical literature on psychotherapy termination with children examines those individual and family factors that predict premature termination. This literature has focused on the process of engaging and retaining families in treatment and of preventing premature termination. In addition to the further refinement of the definition of early termination and the careful delineation of subgroups, this research has led to a greater understanding of the process of engagement and termination in the treatment of children and families.

Kazdin and Mazurick (1994) examined child, parent, and family factors that predicted early termination from therapy. Children ages four to thirteen years who were referred for treatment of oppositional, aggressive, and antisocial behavior participated in the study. Treatment consisted of individual, weekly sessions consisting of child-directed cognitive problem-solving skills training and parent management training. Completion of treatment was defined as completion of the full seven- to eight-month treatment regimen. Premature termination was defined as dropping out on the basis of a unilateral decision on the part of the parent or family. Early dropouts were defined as those children and families who completed six or fewer treatment sessions. Late terminators were defined as families who dropped out of treatment after seven to fourteen weeks of treatment. These researchers hypothesized that factors predicting premature termination would vary as a function of whether families dropped out early or late in treatment. For families, socioeconomic disadvantage, parental stress, psychopathology, parent history of antisocial behavior, and adverse family child-rearing practices were evaluated. Child evaluations assessed antisocial behavior, emotional and behavioral problems, academic dysfunction, and social behavior.

Results indicated that early dropouts averaged two to three weeks of treatment, whereas late terminators averaged two to three months of treatment. Across assessment modalities and informants, several factors related to family, parent, and child functioning predicted premature termination from treatment and differentially predicted early and late termination. Early terminators were likely to have children with more severe and chronic antisocial behavior, greater academic dysfunction, problems with social behavior, and greater family stress. These families were typically headed by young, single parents from an ethnic minority group. Late terminators were less likely to be from an ethnic minority group, had higher family incomes, and better living accommodations. Late terminators also reported better adaptive functioning at school, less contact with antisocial peers, and fewer adverse child-rearing practices. When compared to completers, children who terminated late in treatment were more likely to have younger mothers, antisocial history, lower full-scale IQ scores, nonbiological heads of households, and poor adaptive functioning at school. These factors appear to predict early termination in play therapy as well (Campbell, Baker and Bratton 2000).

In another study, Kazdin, Holland and Crowley (1997) examined how the family's experience of barriers to treatment influenced premature termination. According to their model, families experience multiple barriers associated with participating in treatment. Barriers may include practical obstacles to accessing treatment, such as child care difficulties, perceptions that treatment is demanding and of little relevance to the child's problem, or a poor relationship with the therapist. An increased number of barriers was hypothesized to be associated with an increased risk for early termination. Additionally, these variables were expected to uniquely contribute to termination, beyond more well-studied family, parent, and child characteristics. To evaluate the role of perceived barriers, families of 242 children who were referred for treatment for oppositional, aggressive, and antisocial behavior participated in the study. In addition to other sociodemographic measures, parents completed the Barriers to Treatment Survey (Kazdin, Holland, & Breton 1991).

Analyses indicated that early terminators reported significantly higher levels of barriers than did completers. Perceived barriers to participation in treatment contributed significantly to early termination of treatment ($R^2 = .26$). Of 95 families who showed equal to or greater than 6 risk factors, 52.6% terminated prematurely. Only 34% of families with few barriers terminated before completing treatment. As the number of barriers increased, so did risk for premature termination. Among high-risk groups, perception of fewer barriers to treatment served to attenuate risk for premature termination. Barriers were not better accounted for by more well-established family, parent, and child factors that also contribute to dropping out of treatment. These findings were consistent across both parent and therapist ratings of perceived barriers to treatment.

Based on these findings, perceived barriers to treatment participation, including stressors and obstacles associated with coming to treatment, perceptions that treatment is not very relevant, and a poor relationship between the parent and therapist, are related to premature termination from treatment. Such barriers appear to be important to address in order to reduce the rates of premature termination in child therapy.

In a similar study, Kazdin and Wassell (1998) evaluated the relationship between therapeutic change and treatment completion. They examined the functioning of 304, three- to thirteen-year-old children referred for oppositional, aggressive, and antisocial behaviors. Five domains of functioning were examined as predictors of treatment completion and improvement: (1) socioeconomic disadvantage, (2) parent psychopathology and stress, (3) child dysfunction and impairment, (4) problems in treatment attendance, and (5) perceived barriers during the course of treatment. Families were provided twenty sessions of cognitive problem-solving skills training (PSST) and sixteen sessions of parent management training (PMT) alone or in combination.

Results indicated that 38 percent of the sample terminated prematurely, completing on average, fifteen weeks of treatment. Of treatment completers, 77 percent were rated by parents and therapists as definitely improved. However, parent and therapist ratings of improvement were only moderately correlated. There was a strong and reliable relation (0.61) between treatment completion and improvement. This relationship was not accounted for by differences in the types of cases that drop out and complete treatment.

Discrepancies in defining improvement may suggest that therapists and parents have different expectations of what treatment can do and ought to do. These differences might influence improvement and completion of treatment. Because children who drop out typically have more severe impairment, more parent dysfunction, and perceived barriers to treatment, improvement is often difficult to evaluate clinically. Due to a greater presence of psychosocial risk factors, outcomes for this population may not differ significantly whether or not they complete treatment. Based on these results, the authors conclude that it is important to focus on improvement and patient change over the course of treatment rather than on completion of a specific treatment regimen. Additionally, systematic evaluation of client progress should be used to inform the number of sessions, duration, and completion of a prescribed regimen, as some drop outs improve while some completers do not.

In summary, these findings illustrate that research has reliably identified specific family, parent, and child factors that predict early termination (Armbruster & Kazdin 1994; Gould, Shaffer, & Kaplan 1985). Most notably, families who are struggling with socioeconomic disadvantage, are members of a minority group, report high levels of stress and family dysfunction, and have difficult living circumstances (e.g., single-parent families, homes headed by a nonbiological parent) are at highest risk of premature termination from treatment. Specific barriers to treatment have also been implicated in premature termination. Perceived treatment demands, stressors, or obstacles to treatment, perceived low relevance of treatment, and poor relationship with the therapist increase the likelihood that a family will terminate treatment prematurely. However, no single characteristic appears to be necessary or sufficient for dropping out (Kazdin & Mazurick 1994). Rather, multiple influences accumulate as risk factors to increase the likelihood that families drop out of treatment. Therefore, these studies emphasize the importance of an individualized assessment of those factors that may increase the risk of early termination and promote the systematic evaluation of client progress over the course of treatment. Based on these findings, strategies for addressing barriers to treatment can be evaluated.

However, several limitations to this literature exist. The generality of these findings across populations and presenting concerns is unknown. To better understand those factors that predict early termination, researchers must explore the full range of participants who terminate from treatment prematurely. Future research may seek to systematically identify those families who terminate from treatment after one session, who refuse treatment after being on a waiting list, or terminate at other points in treatment. In addition to sociodemographic variables, future research is also needed to address the contribution of therapist variables, treatment approaches, and structural variables that may influence early termination. Lastly, these studies lack attention to proposed mechanisms of early termination. Sociodemographic variables act merely as proxies for specific behavioral factors that directly impact early termination or retention. Specification of proposed mechanisms is needed in order to refine existing treatment approaches with an eye toward maximizing retention and ultimately, outcomes.

Guidelines for Termination of Psychotherapy with Children

Attachment relationships, formed within the first year of life, are considered by many to form the cornerstone of healthy psychological functioning. With development, attachment bonds broaden from a primary focus on caregivers to include siblings, other family members, friends, teachers, and clinicians. Effective attachment relationships provide children with a sense of security, trust, and confidence. Disturbances of attachment relationships can lead to a variety of behavioral and emotional problems, which may cause a caregiver to seek mental healthcare for the child. As with adults, the termination of therapy with an emotionally healthy child may cause feelings of grief, loss, abandonment, anger, or rejection. These responses may be particularly strong for children (and children with parents) who have attachment difficulties. Despite the fact that children do not have the same abstract reasoning skills as many adults, it is equally important to be thoughtful about and attentive to the termination phase of treatment with this younger population.

Several aspects of termination with children can be seen as similar across diagnostic populations and modalities of treatment. Perhaps the primary thread across groups is that in the majority of cases, children are not self-referred for treatment. Parents and other caretakers are often the referral source for children in treatment. When a parent brings a child in, the child may or may not be a willing participant in treatment, which in turn affects not only the child's initial engagement in and commitment to therapy, but also his or her level of anxiety and emotional connection regarding termination.

Second, children always come with caretakers, usually parents. The level of direct involvement of the parents in therapy can vary by treatment modality, but parents are invariably involved at some level given they must consent for the child to receive treatment. It is important to consider the parents in termination with children as they have often formed a professional bond with the individual providing care to their child. Research indicates that parental expectancies and perception of treatment (Kazdin, Holland, & Crowley 1997; Nock & Kazdin 2001) are a good predictor of early termination of child treatment by parents. Thus, this connection cannot be neglected as these caretakers may often need to continue providing the child with assistance in areas of previous nonfunction, which referred them to treatment. While adolescents and adults may have an intrinsic motivation to sustain treatment gains and improve beyond treatment termination, children's behavior, adaptive or not, has a tendency to be more egosyntonic. In this case, children may need assistance from parents to maintain treatment gains. Thus, it is vital to ensure that the parents have ample opportunity to discuss termination issues with the therapist, such as anxieties regarding future management of the child's behavior and how to recognize the need for additional treatment in the future if it is warranted. Patients approach termination with a wide variety of emotional responses (Roe et al. 2006). Some families may experience termination as the natural progression of treatment. Others may approach termination with some trepidation. Regardless, the process of termination may present a significant change for all involved.

Finally, the age of the child must be considered a factor in termination. For example, a young child running out of the therapist's office on the day of the last session without saying good-bye should not be viewed as a reflection of the therapist's competence in terminating adequately with his or her clients. At an age where abstract thinking is limited, children may not fully grasp the concept of termination as an end to treatment, and may not understand the utility of treatment as an abstract concept. It can be important to ensure that the child understands why treatment is ending. Younger children have a tendency to view the external events as correlated with their good or bad behavior. Consequently, a younger child may think that therapy is ending because they did something wrong. The therapist should keep in mind the child's age and level of cognitive development when planning for termination and adjust accordingly.

As with adults, consideration of termination issues should occur before a patient is accepted into treatment. For example, it may be contraindicated for a child with significant attachment problems or loss history to be assigned to a student therapist who will be rotating (and therefore required to terminate care) before a full course of treatment is complete. Likewise, it is important to consider one's own attachment and termination capacities, such as in cases of therapy with a terminally ill child.

Treatment planning often includes markers for termination such as resolution of symptoms. Some structured CBT (cognitive-behavioral therapy) programs have a set number of sessions. Other treatment courses are based on length of stay in a hospital setting, length of a rotation for a student in a therapist training role, or number of therapy appointments approved by insurance carriers. Whenever feasible, it is recommended that children be made aware of the expected length of treatment from the beginning, or how such a decision is likely to be made. Reminders and/or progress reviews as the treatment progresses can be helpful. The number of sessions devoted to discussing treatment termination will depend on the nature of the child's therapy, the length of treatment, attachment to the therapist, reason for treatment, and history of previous losses. Regardless of the treatment plan, it is important to start termination at the beginning of therapy by instilling confidence in the child that he or she will be able to cope with thoughts and feelings on his or her own following the end of therapy (Beck 1995).

Termination sessions may include: exercises or discussions designed to review and consolidate progress, planning for ongoing self-management or other treatment, education about what to expect in the future (normal developmental course, continued improvements and setbacks, crises, etc.) and available resources, rewards or acknowledgments of positive connections and accomplishments, processing of loss/grief, and inclusion of parents. Table 12.1 provides a termination checklist for providers.

Table 12.1   Termination Checklist

- Review and consolidate progress
- Process feelings of separation, progress, loss/grief
- Plan for ongoing self-management or other treatment
- Educate about what to expect in the future
- Review available resources
- Provide rewards and/or acknowledgments
- Plan for inclusion of parents

Parents should be provided with ample information regarding the process of termination, including normal grief reactions. Practitioners may engage parents in a discussion regarding referrals to community resources, problem-solving strategies for future symptoms or crises, and how or when to return to treatment. Planning must be done for inevitable fluctuations in symptoms and possible setbacks following termination. Thus, disposition planning must be done with the parents to provide either tapering of sessions (e.g., from every week to every other week) or the opportunity for booster sessions in the future. This provides both a sense of continuity in care and a sense of confidence in the parents that the therapist is accessible for the child and that the parent is not alone if problems arise again. Overall, termination is a time to highlight the parent's as well as the child's new strengths and to encourage the family to continue working toward positive change.

The process of termination should provide structure and predictability. The child and parent should be given ample opportunity to prepare for and process the termination. The approaches used to address termination issues can vary and are normally consistent with the therapy approach. In the literature, the termination process in play therapy has been described with great variability, taking anywhere from one to eight sessions (Nemiroff & Annunziata 1990). Typically, two to three weeks notice often provides ample time for termination for shorter-term structured treatment. Encourage the child to collaborate in the preparation of termination. Solicit the parents' guidance in structuring a termination session that will meet the needs of all involved.

Children may need a more intensive review and may benefit from a cumulative review each week during the entire course of treatment. Children may be poor reporters of their change in symptom level or may not be able to conceptualize overall change over time due to a lack of abstract thinking. Thus, as with reviewing skills, concrete stimuli often assist the child in visualizing their progress in treatment. Graphs of decreases in symptoms and negative cognitions are excellent visual aides for children to track their progress within a CBT model. Like the skill lists, these graphs are also helpful for parents in tracking symptom progress following treatment termination.

Children may have a more difficult time in generalizing skills learned in session to situations outside of the therapy room. Thus, it is important for termination to begin this generalization process from the beginning of therapy by providing not only concrete examples of situations for the child, but also by having the child generate additional examples of situations where the skills can be applied. In doing this, the therapist can quickly assess how well the child understands the application of the skill and how well he or she is able to generalize it. This will serve to be useful not only in determining when termination should take place, but also the potential for relapse. Children often align well with the "therapist as a coach" analogy, as it is an age-appropriate concrete representation of the therapeutic alliance between child and therapist. This coach analogy can be used in termination in that a coach will help the player during practice, but will watch them use their skills from the sidelines during a game. Additionally, some children may think they should not use their new skills or that they will not work if they are not in treatment. This is another topic that must be assessed and directly addressed with some children.

A goal of the final session with children is to provide the child with a rewarding experience for his or her efforts in treatment, and to instill confidence in the child that the therapist has faith that the child is ready to take to the field with the skills and will do well in the future. There are many creative ways to promote consolidation and review of progress with children in a rewarding manner. One example is an exercise designed for older children undergoing a CBT approach for the treatment of anxiety (Evans et al. 2005; Kendall & Hedtke 2006). Starting with the session when there are three weeks left, the therapist and child begin to discuss the creation and production of a commercial about his/her treatment experiences. Children are encouraged to use their imagination to create a product (such as an audiotape, videotape, or a brochure) describing to other children their strategies for coping with anxiety. The product, which promotes consolidation and communication with others, can be made during the last session and also serve as a tangible memento of the therapy experience for the child to keep. For some anxious children, it may even be an exposure task if they demonstrate their skills in a video. Another example, sometimes used in medical and psychiatric hospital settings, is the creation of a good-bye book. In the book, the child might document important events and concepts in words, drawings, magazine pictures, photos, or other mementos. Various professionals involved in the care of the child might write words of encouragement or reminders of progress in the book, while peers might contribute their good-bye messages. Children may be interested in selecting a treat for a termination "party" or a special activity for that day.

Extending therapy beyond the time frame needed to reach established goals is sometimes called *post-mature termination*. This can occur for a variety of reasons, including a desire to prolong the relationship or avoid saying good-bye, feeling a need to complete the number of sessions that are available or that it initially seemed would be necessary, or the financial convenience of the therapist. While the extension of therapy may initially seem to be a benign practice, it may inadvertently undermine the independent functioning of the child and parent. Providing the child and parent an opportunity to practice their new skills "without a net" can signal the therapist's confidence in them and also result in increased self-efficacy for self-management.

When talking to parents about normal grief reactions in their children, it is important to communicate that the identification of grief in children can be different from identification of grief in adults. Preschoolers may express grief with bedwetting, thumb sucking, clinging to adults, exaggerated fears, excessive crying, temper tantrums, other regression, and stubbornness. School-age children may express grief with somatic symptoms (stomachaches), school and learning problems, a preoccupation with the loss and related worries, daydreaming, trouble paying attention, bedwetting, regression, developmental delays, overeating, refusing to eat, nightmares, sleepiness, fighting, and anger. Preteens may exhibit mood swings, increased risk taking and self-destructive behaviors, withdrawal from adults, oppositional behavior, somatic symptoms (stomachaches, headaches), lack of concentration, anger, or depression. Children of any age may need help labeling emotions and opportunities for the expression of painful emotions through play and creative outlets, as well as talk. They may have questions related to their sadness, anger, fears and worries that can be answered in simple and honest terms. Identifying areas of control and effective coping strategies can be helpful.

Specific Considerations

Premature Termination by the Child

If a child disengages from therapy and is unable to be redirected back to treatment, the therapist may wish to revisit who should be present during sessions (i.e., child versus parents) or early termination may be indicated. If premature termination occurs with a disengaged child, it is important for the therapist to be empathetic to the child's stance regarding therapy and to provide the child room to ask any final questions he or she might have. Depending on the age of the child, it may also be beneficial to discuss the reasons the child has difficulty engaging in therapy. In a survey study conducted with children who prematurely terminated therapy, results indicated that lack of professionalism and caring by the clinician and poor hospital atmosphere were most associated with early termination (Chung, Pardeck, & Murphy 1995).

Terminating With Psychiatric Inpatients

Termination factors for inpatient psychiatric hospitalization vary greatly depending on length of stay of the child. For brief hospitalizations where crisis management and brief psychotherapy are the primary modes of treatment, termination factors will primarily be related to disposition planning. For any child, inpatient hospitalization is a frightening and chaotic process. Often children are unaware of what is going on around them and may or may not have an awareness of why they are being hospitalized. In all cases of brief hospitalization it is important for termination to focus on supporting the child's fears and providing reassurance of the disposition plan.

When children are hospitalized for a longer period of time, termination will mimic that of outpatient psychotherapy and will be a lengthier process. Often times preparation for discharge should begin early to provide the child with an easier transition, although there are certain instances where it may be clinically indicated to inform the child of details of disposition plans closer to the discharge date. In all cases, preparation to leave the hospital should take place early on to impart to the child that the hospital is only a temporary location for care. Termination should focus on both disposition planning and on the child's anxiety relating to functioning in the world outside of the hospital. Children may become comfortable with the more structured environment of the hospital and may have fears of how to manage their behavior and anxiety in the outside world. It is important to reinforce continuity of care to these children by explaining that discharge does not mean discharge from care in general, but a transfer of care to another location and level of intensity.

In all cases, both children and parents have rights regarding the information that is to be provided at the termination of treatment (Brewer & Faitak 1989). Parents must be informed of the disposition plan, including detailed information regarding recommendations for follow-up care, diagnoses of the child at discharge, discharge medications, and reason for termination. Parents should also have access to information regarding the hospital course and treatment goals that were obtained. Children should be informed of why discharge is occurring and where they will be going for follow-up care.

Medical Settings

In some locations, mental health services are integrated into primary care clinics, specialty pediatric clinics, and hospital settings. In such medical settings, the traditional structure of outpatient child psychotherapy is replaced with a flexible repertoire that is sensitive to a myriad of dynamic variables, including the child's health status and parent involvement. Not surprisingly, termination in medical settings also requires unique considerations and a diverse set of skills.

Terminating with Pediatric Outpatients—Primary Care   Integrated primary care psychology has been the subject of a growing body of literature (Cummings, Cummings, & Johnson 1997; Cummings, O'Donohue, & Ferguson 2003; O'Donohue et al. 2004). Some estimates state that up to 40 percent of cases presenting in primary care involve some form of child psychopathology (Kramer & Garralda 1998). Despite this growing awareness, the specific techniques for the delivery of primary care pediatric psychology have received little attention in the literature. Anecdotal reports suggest that families often bring their child's emotional or behavioral concerns to the pediatrician's office because of the trust that has developed over a long-standing relationship. The mental health clinician in this setting has the unique opportunity to form a similar relationship with the family. As the provider addresses the child's concerns over time and across contexts (e.g., after a transition to a new school or after the separation of parents), a therapeutic structure more consistent with focused intermittent psychotherapy across the lifecycle (Cummings & Sayama 1995) may emerge. In the outpatient primary care clinic, the mental health clinician may never actually "terminate" per se. Instead, contact with the mental health clinician may more closely follow the model of the pediatrician. Future contact will be based on the particular needs of each unique family throughout the child's development. By explicating this philosophy, the mental health clinician sets the stage for the family to develop trust that his or her door will always be open in the future, should any additional concerns arise.

In contrast, mental health assessment and/or intervention may be delivered in a brief and often "one-shot" format in clinics with less continuity of care or in cases of premature termination of care. In the primary care treatment of depression, for example, over 50 percent of patients may not return for a follow-up session (Lin et al. 2000). Therefore, practitioners are challenged to provide children and families with those resources that have the greatest likelihood of improving outcomes. Empirically based approaches, particularly those focusing on skills training, are highly preferred. Whether the mental health clinician is acting as a consultant/liaison or delivers services in parallel with the medical team, treatment and termination in the primary care setting may occur in the same session. Practitioners are advised to listen carefully to the problems described by the family, restate the problem to enhance understanding, validate the child and family's struggle, reinforce strengths, deliver clear, concise, empirically supported behavioral prescriptions, augment verbal recommendations with written materials, and encourage the patient and family to return for ongoing monitoring and follow-up sessions.

Terminating With Pediatric Inpatients—Tertiary Care   Some mental health clinicians work in tertiary care settings as consultants to the medical team (Shaw et al. 2006). After an initial consultation, the practitioner, on average, conducts three follow-up visits for further assessment, treatment implementation, and/or monitoring of symptoms and response to treatment. When contacts are brief and solution focused in response to a question posed by the primary medical team, the consultant may not have the opportunity to develop a strong rapport with the child and family. In these cases, terminating may be a fluid process in which the consultant explicates to the family the nature and duration of the contact. Frequently, termination is the natural consequence of discharge from the hospital.

In other situations the consultant my have a long and intense relationship with a child and family. This is more likely when the child has a long hospitalization, has frequent hospitalizations, or is strongly attached to the consultant. Additionally, without the usual privacy boundaries and weekly one-hour appointment times that are more reliably present in traditional outpatient psychotherapy, termination with an inpatient can be an especially complex process.

Conclusions

Termination of psychotherapy with children is an important stage of the therapeutic process. A clear understanding of the process, timing, and goals of termination may influence the selection of the therapist, the duration of therapy, and the therapeutic process. Whereas certain guidelines for psychotherapy termination with children can be extrapolated from clinical experience, treatment manuals, and the adult literature, and were presented here, these guidelines must be adopted as part of a flexible therapeutic repertoire that is sensitive to population, presenting concern, treatment approach, and setting. In order to meet the unique therapeutic needs of the individual child, the termination approach will differ significantly with children who are grieving, anxious, terminally ill, developmentally disabled, or physically healthy. Similarly, termination will take on a different form in outpatient versus inpatient settings. With these factors in mind, the termination process can present a valuable opportunity to consolidate treatment gains and encourage the child and family toward future growth.

References

Armbruster, P., & Kazdin, A. E. (1994). Attrition in child psychotherapy. In T. H. Ollendick & R. J. Prinz (Eds.), *Advances in clinical child psychology* (Vol. 16; pp. 81–108). New York: Plenum.

Beck, J. S. (1995). *Cognitive therapy: Basics and beyond.* New York: Guilford Press.

Brewer, T., & Faitak, M. (1989). Ethical guidelines for the inpatient psychiatric care of children. *Professional Psychology: Research and Practice, 20,* 142–147.

Campbell, V. A., Baker, D. B., & Bratton, S. (2000). Why do children drop-out from play therapy? *Clinical Child Psychology and Psychiatry, 5,* 133–138.

Chung, W. S., Pardeck, J. T., & Murphy, J. W. (1995). Factors associated with premature termination of psychotherapy in children. *Adolescence, 30,* 717–721.

Cummings, N. A., Cummings, J. L., & Johnson, J. N. (1997). *Behavioral health in primary care: A guide for clinical integration.* Madison, CT: Psychosocial Press.

Cummings, N. A., O'Donohue, W. T., Ferguson, K. E. (2003). *Behavioral health as primary care: Beyond efficacy to effectiveness.* Reno, NV: Context Press.

Cummings, N. A., & Sayama, M. (1995). *Focused psychotherapy: A casebook of brief, intermittent psychotherapy throughout the life cycle.* Philadelphia: Taylor/Francis.

Evans, D. L., Foa, E. B., Gur, R. E., Hendin, H., O'Brien, C. P., et al. (Eds.). (2005). *Treating and preventing adolescent mental health disorders: What we know and what we don't know, a research agenda for improving the mental health of our youth.* New York: Oxford University Press.

Gould, M. S., Shaffer, D., & Kaplan, D. (1985). The characteristics of dropouts from a child psychiatry clinic. *Journal of the American Academy of Child Psychiatry, 24,* 316–328.

Kazdin, A. E., Holland, L., & Breton, S. (1991). *Barriers to participation in treatment scale – Parent and therapist versions.* New Haven, CT: Yale University.

Kazdin, A. E., Holland, L., & Crowley, M. (1997). Family experience of barriers to treatment and premature termination from child therapy. *Journal of Consulting and Clinical Psychology, 65,* 453–463.

Kazdin, A. E., & Mazurick, L. (1994). Dropping out of child psychotherapy: distinguishing early and late dropouts over the course of treatment. *Journal of Consulting and Clinical Psychology, 62,* 1069–1074.

Kazdin, A. E., & Wassell, G. (1998). Treatment completion and therapeutic change among children referred for outpatient therapy. *Professional Psychology: Research and Practice, 29,* 332–340.

Kendall, P. C., & Hedtke, K. (2006). Cognitive-behavioral therapy for anxious children: Therapist manual (3rd ed.). Ardmore, PA: Workbook Publishing.

Kramer, T., & Garralda, M. E. (1998). Psychiatric disorders in adolescents in primary care. *British Journal of Psychiatry, 173*, 508–513.

Lin, E. H., Katon, W. J., Simon, G. E., Von Korff, M., Bush, T. M, et al. (2000). Low-intensity treatment of depression in primary care: is it problematic? *General Hospital Psychiatry, 22*, 78–83.

Nemiroff, M. A., & Annunziata, J. (1990). *A child's first book about play therapy.* Washington, DC: American Psychological Association.

Nock, M. K., & Kazdin, A. E. (2001). Parent expectations for child therapy: Assessment and relation to participation in treatment. *Journal of Child and Family Studies, 10*, 155–180.

O'Donohue, W. T., Byrd, M., Cummings, N., & Henderson, D. (2004). *Behavioral integrative care: Treatments that work in the primary care setting.* New York: Brunner-Routledge.

Roe, D., Dekel, R., Harel, G., Fennig, S., & Fennig, S. (2006). Clients' feelings during termination of psychodynamically oriented psychotherapy. *Bulletin of the Menninger Clinic, 70*, 68–81.

Shaw R. J., Wamboldt, M., Bursch, B., & Stuber, M. (2006). Practice patterns in pediatric consultation-liaison psychiatry: a national survey. *Psychosomatics, 47*, 43–49.

13

Termination With Adolescents

JAMES X. BEMBRY

Termination as a Phase of Treatment

In 1969 Fox et al. wrote an article titled, "The Termination Process: A Neglected Dimension in Social Work." In the article the authors argue that termination, as part of the therapeutic process, had been virtually ignored in the social work literature. The reason termination was ignored, they concluded, was due to "the general sensitivity to loss and separation" (63). They suggested that the worker's emotions when it came to termination with clients were painful, and ignoring the topic in the literature was a defensive response to the feelings termination evoked in the worker.

In a 1980 article titled "Termination: A Neglected Concept in the Social Work Curriculum," Shapiro claimed that far more attention was paid to "beginnings" with clients while "endings" were a neglected part of the social work curriculum and literature. This absence she attributed to a "denial of its importance as an integral phase in the therapeutic process (14). She laments this absence while acknowledging that the functional school, which was an early theoretical approach to social work practice developed in the 1930s by faculty of the School of Social Work at the University of Pennsylvania, emphasized the worker's conscious use of time phases (beginnings, middles, and endings) in the helping process (Smalley 1972).

Weddington and Cavenar (1979) voiced similar sentiments regarding the training of psychotherapists. They stated, "not only are criteria and techniques for termination not taught and discussed, but termination as a valuable therapeutic opportunity is undoubtedly neglected" (1303). In 1979 Maholick and Turner noted that little had been written in the professional literature on the nature and clinical management of termination in either individual or group psychotherapy.

Since those views were expressed, the professional literature on termination has grown considerably. While there may not be an abundance of literature in any single scholarly discipline when multiple disciplines such as social work (Levinson 1977; Siebold 1989; Bembry & Ericson 1999), psychology (Hynan 1990; Berry & Sipps 1991), counseling (Ward 1984), and psychiatry/psychotherapy (Simon 1994; Liegner 2003) are examined, an adequate theoretical and practical knowledge base emerges. However, in the view of this author, there is much work left to be done regarding an empirical knowledge base.

Regardless of its presence in the literature, termination has historically been recognized as an important part of the helping process. Freud divided the span of psychoanalysis into phases in a 1913 article (Shapiro 1980; Liegner 2003). Sandor Ferenczi, an early disciple of Freud, introduced termination as a natural consequence of analysis in an article in 1927. As noted above, the functional school, which departed from Freud's "mechanistic" and "deterministic" view of individuals, maintained the idea of time phases as a core principle. In 1949 two major symposia were held on the subject of termination; one by the British Psychoanalytic Society, and the other a joint effort by the Los Angeles and San Francisco Psychoanalytic Societies (Liegner 2003). Brill (1973), in her influential text *Working with People: The Helping Process*, discussed the phases of a helping relationship. She labeled them: Phase I—the beginning, Phase II—the middle, and Phase III—the termination. Most of the popular texts in social work education since Brill discuss termination as a distinct phase of the helping process (Pincus & Minahan 1973; Compton & Galaway 1975; Hepworth & Larsen 1982; Shulman 1984; Gambrill 1997). These authors agree that termination is integral to effective counseling or therapy.

The ending of any meaningful relationship has emotional significance for the participants. This is true even for a therapeutic situation where both the client and the therapist know, from the beginning, that their time together is limited (Brill 1973). The therapist must be aware that termination is a process and not simply a "sudden cessation of activity" (Ward 1984, 21), and if this process is understood and managed by the therapist, many important changes can occur for the client.

Shulman (1984) asserts that termination "offers the greatest potential for powerful and important work" (105). He attributes this to the fact that as a helping relationship ends

> Clients feel a sense of urgency as they realize there is little time left and this can lead to the introduction of some of the more difficult and important themes of concern. The dynamics between worker and client are also heightened in this phase as each prepares to move away from the other. Termination of the relationship can evoke powerful feelings in both client and worker, and discussion of these can often be connected by the worker to the client's general concerns and tasks. (105)

The feelings provoked by endings can be difficult for the client as well as the therapist. This is the time when therapists can take themselves too seriously or not seriously enough. In the former, as the ending of the helping relationship approaches, the therapist feels responsible for the client and imagines that the client will not be able to sustain any gains without their presence in the client's life. This expresses a lack of faith in the client's accomplishments. The latter implies that the therapist refuses to accept any credit for gains made by the client. In this case, clients may attempt to express sincere gratitude for the help they have received, but the therapist rejects this gratitude with comments such as: "I didn't do anything" or "you accomplished this on your own" (Shulman 1984). Dolliver and Woodward (1974) assert that the "role of giver carries with it the implication that the giver possesses various highly desirable characteristics" (68). Clients in therapy take while the therapist gives. When the therapist denies the client the opportunity to give (express appreciation for the help given), this too implies a lack of respect for the client's growth.

Clients may react to the ending of the relationship in several ways. They may deny that the ending is approaching and will happen, or they may express anger at the therapist in indirect and direct ways. The client may mourn the end of the relationship and become apathetic and lethargic. Clients may also regress to earlier forms of negative behavior. None of these responses should come as a surprise to a therapist who understands the nature and meaning of termination.

Adolescents Are Different

Much of the literature on adolescence gives credit to G. Stanley Hall and his colleagues at Clark University for creating adolescence as a distinct stage of human development in the late 1890s (Bembry & Ericson 1999). Offer (1987) disputes this and states that historical evidence suggests that adolescence as a stage of development was known to the ancient Romans, Greeks, and Egyptians. He acknowledges the concept disappeared during the Dark Ages, although it was mentioned in medieval texts as "the third age." This third age was said to end in the twenty-first year, but could go on to thirty or thirty-five years of age.

Today it is generally agreed that adolescence extends over several years and can thus be subdivided into early, middle, and late substages. Early adolescence—ages ten to fourteen—typically encompasses the profound physical and social changes that occur with puberty. Middle adolescence—ages fifteen to seventeen—is a time of increasing independence, and for a significant number of American youth it also marks the end of adolescence. Late adolescence—age eighteen to the mid-twenties—occurs for those individuals who, because of educational goals or other social factors, delay their entry into adult roles (Elliot & Feldman 1990).

G. Stanley Hall, who was president and professor of psychology at Clark University, was the preeminent figure in American psychology during his time, and his conceptualization of adolescence has remained influential to this day (Esman 1993). Hall saw adolescence as an era of "storm and stress" analogous to mankind's tumultuous progression from primitiveness to higher civilization (Bembry & Ericson 1999).

> The normal adolescent was conceived as a tempest, torn by unmanageable passions, impulsive, rebellious, and given to torrid swings of mood. Adolescent relations with parents and adults in general were seen as antagonistic and conflict ridden—a pattern later to be designated as "the generation gap." (Esman 1993, 6)

Hall's depiction of normal adolescent turmoil was sustained for more than fifty years by Anna Freud, and others. Freud described adolescence as a "developmental disturbance," and went as far as to declare that it was often difficult to distinguish "normal adolescent behavior from severe psychopathology of the neurotic, borderline, or even psychotic type" (quoted in Esman 1993, 8). Esman notes that it was not until the 1960s that Hall's and Freud's view faced a serious challenge. This led to a major reassessment of the concept of "normal adolescent turmoil" and a more balanced view of adolescence emerged.

Research has shown that the majority of adolescents do not experience personality disequilibrium, nor do they necessarily undergo a severe breach in relationships with their parents (Bembry & Ericson 1999). These early theories explained certain aspects of the psychology of adolescence, but cannot explain the psychology of adolescence in general (Offer 1987). Offer suggests that adherence to these early theories can lead to circumstances where the mood swings of the truly disturbed adolescent are characterized as being predictable, his negative affect described as typical, or his extreme rebellion as understandable.

The title of the first chapter in Meeks's (1971) book *The Fragile Alliance: An Orientation to the Outpatient Psychotherapy of the Adolescent* is "Adolescents Are Different." Meeks states that his book was "written in hope that it will assist therapists and those in training to feel more comfortable with the adolescent patient so that they can effectively utilize their skills with this important group of patients " (3). Working effectively with this population begins with the premise that *adolescents are different.*

Adolescence is a stage of life distinct from either childhood or adulthood. This has been found to be true not just for human beings but other species as well.

> American society promotes adolescence as a distinct stage of life by means of a variety of mechanisms, among them compulsory schooling, child labor laws that prohibit early adolescents from entering the work force, and a separate juvenile justice system that metes out legal consequences of socially unacceptable acts partly on the basis of age. These and other social devices plainly define adolescents as "not adults"; and yet neither are they children. They are changing physically, maturing sexually, becoming increasingly able to engage in complex reasoning, and markedly expanding their knowledge of themselves and the world about them. (Elliott & Feldman 1990, 4)

Similarly, when adolescents enter into therapeutic treatment, a frame of reference is needed that is different from those that guide work with either children or adults. Most children are brought into therapy by their parents. In most instances they have not participated in the decision to seek help, and they have little sense of the professional identity and role of the therapist. Children are more typically engaged through games, storytelling, and other indirect or metaphorical activities than through direct discussion. Children may also not understand the purpose of coming in for regular sessions (Weiner 1992).

Adults, on the other hand, ordinarily come voluntarily for help and participate in the therapeutic process through talking about themselves and their concerns. Even involuntary clients whose treatment has been mandated by someone else have made their own decision to participate in treatment rather than suffer some sanction. Most adults also understand that the treatment situation is a cooperative endeavor, with the goal of discussing and addressing their concerns. (Weiner 1992).

Because adolescents are in a transitional stage where they are no longer children and not quite adults, they are too old to accept the therapist as a substitute parent in the manner that a child might, and may not be amenable to indirect techniques. Adolescents also understand that they are being seen because someone perceives them as having "problems," which may make them feel anxious, angry, or embarrassed. Treating adolescents as adults also may cause problems. They are often too young to have come into therapy voluntarily, and too immature to understand the true nature or extent of their problems. Therefore, it is necessary for therapists to alter their approach according to the developmental level of the adolescent. The less mature adolescent may be helped by methods utilized in child therapy, while the more mature adolescent may respond to approaches most effective with adults (Weiner 1992).

Termination: Timing and Reasons

Maholick and Turner (1979, 587–588) identified seven areas useful for evaluating client readiness to leave counseling, including:

1. Examining whether initial problems or symptoms have been reduced or eliminated.
2. Determining whether the stress that motivated the client to seek counseling has dissipated.

3. Assessing increased coping ability.
4. Assessing increased understanding and valuing of self and others.
5. Determining increased levels of relating to others and of loving and being loved.
6. Examining increased abilities to plan and work productively.
7. Evaluating increases in the capacity to play and enjoy life.

Liegner (2003) states that there is no absolute criteria for knowing when to terminate, and ideally the therapist and the client should be able to stay "together as long as they both want if life goals and treatment goals are still in the process of being met" (130). Novick (1977), in presenting a case study, described a "terminal phase" that lasted sixteen weeks.

Regarding adolescents, Weiner (1992) states that termination becomes appropriate when they have achieved the limited insights and adaptive character synthesis that involves the degree to which they have increased their understanding of self and personality reorganization or a stabilization and improved functioning without major personality change. Miller (1990) recommends that termination with adolescents should ideally occur when the family no longer defines their

child's behavior or attitudes as pathological, when the adolescent can deal with stress without inappropriate psychological and behavioral responses, and when personality development can proceed independently of the therapist's direct presence. (84)

Schneider has similar indicators for terminating with the adolescent. He states that the process for termination may begin when the adolescent is no longer withdrawn, can make appropriate contact with others, and no longer relies on others (the therapist) to tell him or her what to do.

The reasons common for termination with adolescents fall into several categories (Fox et al. 1969). The first category consists of reasons related to treatment. Under this category we have the "ideal" circumstances where the treatment has been deemed successful by all of the significant parties involved. A second category consists of family-related reasons. Under this category the family may request that treatment be ended. This request may be the result of the treatment's being deemed successful or unsuccessful. Termination may also occur under this category because the family is leaving the community. A third category is client related. In this instance the adolescent engages in an "unacknowledged termination" (Mirabito 2001). In this case there is neither an acknowledgment nor a discussion between the worker and the adolescent (and/or family) about the discontinuation of service. A fourth category involves reasons related to the worker. The worker may end treatment because he believes it is not possible to provide successful treatment. Another worker-related reason is the worker leaving because of a transfer, a job change, or other personal reasons. A final category is related to the pressures of managed care mandates and insurance companies (Mirabito 2001). This category has changed the nature of treatment. Extended treatment is slowly becoming a thing of the past. Those patients in long-term therapy, defined as more than twenty sessions, account for only 15 percent of those who seek treatment. Insurance companies claim that patients can do just as well on medication as they can with traditional talk therapy. And if talk therapy is necessary, it should be short term (Talan 2005).

Termination With the Adolescent

Considering the many circumstances under which termination can take place, and because the clinician has little or no control over many of these circumstances, preparing the adolescent for the "undeniable ending" must start in the beginning of the therapeutic relationship (Bembry & Ericson 1999). Clinicians should explain, prepare, and educate adolescents about the process for ending treatment at the start (Mirabito 2001). Throughout the "middle" of the relationship the clinician should help the adolescent become increasingly aware of and open to the symbols of ending (Maholick & Turner 1979). For instance, the ending of each session is a separation experience. A therapist's vacation is another separation that can be used to introduce the undeniable ending. A change in the appointment time can cause feelings of loss and rejection one might experience at termination and these feeling can be discussed (Bembry & Ericson 1999).

Mirabito (2001) notes that just as separation-individuation and dependence-independence are central themes of termination, they are also essential tasks of adolescent development. Termination with adolescents, as much as possible, should be cognizant of these developmental challenges and what they mean for the adolescent or what has been described as "inherent contradictions" (Schneider 1992).

These contradictions reflect the struggle the adolescent is experiencing during normal adolescent development. During this time they are learning to be psychologically independent of their parents, developing relationships outside of the home and family structure, and seeking their own identity. Adolescents face this process of separation-individuation with ambivalence. They "vacillate between the desire for independence and the security afforded by childhood" (Daniels 1990, 105). Termination with the therapist often represents a microcosm of this developmental dilemma. At one session the adolescent may want to test out new skills and reject any further need for the therapist, and at the next session (or even during the same session) fixate on the therapist and expect the clinician to tell them what to do. If the clinician encourages this sense of independence, the adolescent may become angry interpreting the encouragement as rejection (Shulman 1984; Schneider 1992). The therapist who understands the issues related to adolescent development and the goals of therapy with adolescents, which has been described by Meeks (1971) as "increase(ing) self-understanding and inner psychological strength and flexibility, not to suppress annoying behavior" (93), will not be surprised by these "inherent contradictions."

This chapter will conclude with a discussion of the tasks and strategies associated with terminating with the adolescent.

1. *Assessment of goal completion and learning.* This task involves evaluating progress and measuring changes made over the course of the counseling relationship. Shulman (1984) has suggested a strategy where one week before the final session, the therapist asks the adolescent to be prepared to review significant gains in the final session. Ward (1984) states that while this is a mutual process, the adolescent should assume primary responsibility because the therapist will not be present to remind him or her of these gains after counseling ends. Additionally, it can be helpful to recall early sessions and avoid what Shulman has termed the Farewell-Party Syndrome, where ending sessions focus only on the positive aspects of the relationship.

It can be easy for adolescents to "fail to recognize their original status realistically, and minimize their gains as they begin to think, feel and behave more effectively" (Ward 1984, 23).

2. *Closure of affective and relationship issues.* This task involves inviting exploration of the separation issue and the feelings that may be associated with the ending. The counselor can encourage the adolescent to share feelings that arise during termination. The counselor can raise issues that the adolescent may want to ignore or deny, such as loss, grief, abandonment, sadness, and anger. The therapist can also share his or her own feelings regarding the ending. Ward (1984) and Shulman (1984) both stress that therapists should not overlook their own feelings, while acknowledging this is often difficult for them to do. In many cases, however, it may be necessary for the therapist to risk their feelings first, before the adolescent is able to risk their own. Ward (1984) cautions, however, "the essential guideline in the counselor's resolution of affective and relationship factors during termination is that counselor disclosure during counseling never be detrimental to the client" (23). Therapeutic judgment must be used in making the decision to share these affective and relationship issues, and if the worker is uncertain of the impact on the client, he or she should probably refrain from sharing them.

3. *Identifying areas for continued work.* The adolescent will not leave therapy as a "finished" product, and this should be acknowledged. Shulman (1984) asserts that it is important to convey to the client that the work will continue after the ending. If the focus of therapy has been helping the adolescent problem solve, the therapist can emphasize that the client is much better equipped to cope with the challenges that lay ahead. It is important for the therapist to be specific in helping the adolescent identify these new skills. Rehearsing these new skills and behaviors can be an effective strategy at this time. Shulman also states that the counselor should resist the temptation to reassure adolescents who express doubts about their competency. The counselor should convey a belief in the adolescent's potential to handle future issues without minimizing that the tasks ahead will not be accomplished easily.

4. *Transitioning to new experiences and support systems.* While acknowledging that the journey ahead may have rough spots, the

therapist can also help the adolescent identify family, friends, and other professionals who may be able to assist them in the future. Ward (1984) has suggested that the use of imagery may be effective: projecting the future and potential issues while also imagining the experiences and potential support systems that might be available to help them cope with and manage these issues.

The tasks and strategies discussed above deal with somewhat ideal circumstances where the adolescent willingly cooperates with the therapist and engages in the termination process. Therapists also deal with clients who precipitously decide to terminate therapy before satisfactory resolution or diminution of the presenting symptoms (Blotcky & Friedman 1984). When the therapist has warning that the adolescent will stop treatment, he or she should request at least one more face-to-face session. Blotcky and Friedman (1984) suggest that in this session the therapist communicate that there is still unfinished business, without attacking the adolescent's character or imposing a sense of guilt. If the adolescent still persists in ending treatment, the therapist should attempt to discuss what has been accomplished to reduce as many negative reactions as possible before the client resumes life without counseling, and help the adolescent identify potential personal and professional support systems. In cases where the adolescent simply does not return for a scheduled appointment and does not make contact with the counselor to reschedule, efforts should be made to contact the client. With some clients, and adolescents in particular, this absence may be a test of the counselor's concern for them (Ward 1984).

A key principle in managing termination with adolescents is to treat the termination process as a stage that is prepared for throughout the counseling relationship, and not something that occurs in the last session or the last few sessions. The therapist must understand that adolescents are different, and the inherent contradiction of separation-individuation and dependence-independence that they face as part of their development process as adolescents will invariably play itself out in the counseling process, and may be heightened as termination approaches. With this in mind, and managed effectively by the counselor, "parting can be such productive sorrow" (Ward 1984, 25).

References

Bembry, J. X., & Ericson, C. (1999). Therapeutic termination with the early adolescent who has experienced multiple losses. *Child and Adolescent Social Work Journal, 16,* 177–189.

Berry, G. W., & Sipps, G. J. (1991). Interactive effects of counselor-client similarity and client self-esteem on termination type and number of sessions. *Journal of Counseling Psychology, 38,* 120–125.

Blotcky, A. D., & Friedman, S. (1984). Premature termination from psychotherapy by adolescents. *Journal of Clinical Child Psychology, 13,* 304–309.

Brill, N. I. (1973). *Working with people: The helping process.* Philadelphia: J.B. Lippincott.

Compton, B., & Galaway, B. (1975). *Social work processes.* Chicago: Dorsey Press.

Daniels, J. A. (1990). Adolescent separation-individuation and family transitions. *Adolescence, 25,* 105–117.

Dolliver, R. H., & Woodward, B. T. (1974). Giving and taking in psychotherapy. *Psychotherapy: Therapy, Research and Practice, 11,* 66–70.

Elliott, G. R., & Feldman, S. S. (1990). Capturing the adolescent experience. In S. S. Feldman & G. R. Elliott (Eds.), *At the threshold: The developing adolescent* (pp. 1–13). Cambridge, MA: Harvard University Press.

Esman, A. E. (1993). G. Stanley Hall and the invention of adolescence. In S. E. Feinstein & R. C. Marohn (Eds.), *Adolescent psychiatry developmental and clinical studies* (Vol. 1; pp. 6–20). Chicago: University of Chicago Press.

Fox, E. F., Nelson, M. A., & Bolman, W. M. (1969). The termination process: A neglected dimension in social work. *Social Work, 14,* 53–63.

Gambrill, E. (1997) *Social work practice: A critical thinker's guide.* New York: Oxford University Press.

Hepworth, D. H., & Larsen, J. A. (1982). *Direct social work practice: Theory and skills.* Chicago: Dorsey Press.

Hynan, D. I. (1990). Client reasons and experiences in treatment that influence termination of psychotherapy. *Journal of Clinical Psychology, 46,* 891–895.

Liegner, E. (2003). The question of termination in modern psychoanalysis. *Modern Psychoanalysis, 28,* 119–131.

Levinson, H. L. (1977). Termination of psychotherapy: Some salient issues. *Social Casework, 58,* 480–489.

Maholick, L. T., & Turner, D. W. (1979). Termination: That difficult farewell. *American Journal of Psychotherapy, 63,* 583–591.

Meeks, J. E. (1971). *The fragile alliance: An orientation to the outpatient psychotherapy of the adolescent.* Baltimore: Williams & Wilkins.

Mirabito, D. A. (2001). Mining treatment termination data in an adolescent mental health service: A quantitative study. *Social Work in Health Care, 33,* 71–90.

Miller, D. (1990). The termination of treatment in adolescents. In S. Feinstein (Ed.), *Adolescent Psychiatry* (Vol. 17; pp. 82–90). Chicago: University of Chicago Press.

Novick, J. (1977). Termination of treatment in adolescence. In S. Feinstein & P. Giovacchini (Eds.), *Adolescent Psychiatry* (Vol. V; pp. 391–412). New York: Jason Aronson.

Offer, D. (1987). The mystery of adolescence. In S. Feinstein (Ed.), *Adolescent Psychiatry* (Vol. 14; pp. 7–27). Chicago: University of Chicago Press.

Pincus, A., & Minahan, A. (1973). *Social work practice: Model and method.* Itasca, IL: F.E. Peacock.

Schneider, S. (1992). Separation and individuation issues in psychosocial rehabilitation. *Adolescence, 27,* 137–145.

Shapiro, C. H. (1980). Termination: A neglected concept in the social work curriculum. *Journal of Education for Social Work, 16,* 13–19.

Shulman, L. (1984). *The skills of helping: Individuals and groups.* Itasca, IL: F.E. Peacock.

Siebold, C. (1989). Termination: When the therapist leaves. *Clinical Social Work Journal, 19,* 191–203.

Simon, R. I. (1994). How to terminate a client? With great care and with proper notice. *Psychotherapy Letter, 6,* 3.

Smalley, R. E. (1972). The functional approach to casework practice. In R. Roberts & R. Nee (Eds.), *Theories of social casework* (pp. 77–128). Chicago: University of Chicago Press.

Talan, J. (2005). Upsetting psychotherapy. *Scientific American Mind, 16,* 12–13.

Ward, D. E. (1984). Termination of individual counseling: Concepts and strategies. *Journal of Counseling and Development, 63,* 21–25.

Weddington, W. W., & Cavenar, J. O. (1979). Termination initiated by the therapist: A countertransference storm. *American Journal of Psychiatry, 136,* 1302–1305.

Weiner, I. B. (1992). *Psychological disturbance in adolescence.* New York: John Wiley & Sons.

14

Termination of Psychotherapy with Older Adults

Jeffrey A. Buchanan, Anne Bonsall-Hoekstra, and John L. Rodman

The current chapter addresses termination issues unique to psychotherapy with older adults (defined as individuals over the age of sixty-five). We will begin by orienting the reader to changes in demographics occurring in the United States that will demand that psychotherapists increase their understanding of the unique characteristics of conducting (and thus, terminating) psychotherapy with this population. Since the process of termination can differ depending on the client's presenting concern(s), the reader will then be introduced to common mental health concerns of the elderly. Finally, specific issues related to terminating psychotherapy are reviewed, including specific termination techniques, common themes and ethical dilemmas.

Mental Health and the Elderly

According to the United States Census Bureau (2005), 36.3 million Americans were 65 years of age or older on July 1, 2004. This age group accounts for approximately 12% of the United States population, and it is projected that this number will increase by 147% between the year 2000 and the year 2050. If this projection is correct, by the year 2050, there will be nearly 86.7 million adults in the United States ages 65 and older. These demographic trends suggest that the sheer volume of older adults suffering from psychological problems will increase greatly in the coming years.

Older adults may suffer from a wide variety diagnosable clinical syndromes, but some disorders are more likely to affect them. For example, it has been estimated that 11% of all older adults meet the criterion for an anxiety disorder (United States Surgeon General 1999), while approximately 10% of all adults aged 65 or older suffer from clinical depression (Hayes 1997). Additionally, substance abuse among adults aged 60 and over has been identified as one of the fastest growing public health concerns in the country (U.S. Department of Health and Human Services 1998). Research has also consistently shown that an individual's chance of developing sexual dysfunction dramatically increases with age (Feldman et al. 1994). Finally, if one considers all causes of dementia, approximately 6% to 10% of individuals over the age of 65 suffer from dementia (Hendrie 1997).

Developmental issues faced by older adults, such as adjustment to retirement, medical illness that results in loss of independent functioning, moving from home to a long-term care facility, providing care to a family member with a chronic disease, bereavement, marital discord, and end-of-life issues can also cause significant distress. Such issues often lead older adults to seek assistance from medical and/or mental health professionals. When these issues are included, the number of older adults requiring mental health attention rises dramatically.

Despite the fact that the one-month prevalence rates of psychological disorders is 12.3% and the fact that they make up nearly 12% of the entire population (Myers et al. 1984; United States Census Bureau 2005), older adults account for only 6% to 8% of all individuals seen in mental health clinics and outpatient mental health settings (Smyer & Qualls 1999, 15). Older adults are more likely to seek mental healthcare from their primary care doctor than a mental health professional (Mickus, Colenda, & Hogan 2000). This is due to many factors, including the stigma of experiencing emotional problems (particularly strong for this cohort), lack of education about the effectiveness of the psychotherapy, misunderstandings about what psychotherapy entails, and the fact that many mental health problems involve physical symptoms. Other barriers that may contribute to the underutilization of mental health services by this population include a bias toward older adults among service providers, as well as an overall lack of appropriate training and supervised experience with this age group (Nordhus, Nielsen, & Kvale 1998). These barriers highlight the need for mental health providers (especially those in primary healthcare settings) to have some specialized training in providing psychotherapy services to older adults. Obviously, an important aspect of psychotherapy is the process of termination.

Termination Issues

Given the importance of termination of therapy, surprisingly little has been written about this topic as it relates to therapy with older adults. Even more disheartening is that to our knowledge, there are no empirical studies specifically addressing the issue of how to most effectively terminate therapy with this population. Instead, there is empirical evidence suggesting that certain modes of psychotherapy are effective for certain problems in the elderly. For example, cognitive-behavioral therapy (CBT) has been demonstrated to be effective for late-life depression and distress related to care giving (Gallagher-Thompson & Steffen 1994; Thompson et al. 2001). Also, Interpersonal Psychotherapy (IPT) has demonstrated effectiveness for distress related to bereavement (Miller et al. 1994). These treatment modalities have developed termination guidelines that will be discussed below. It should be made clear, however, that empirical support for a given therapy is not equivalent to empirical support for the efficacy of the specific termination process.

The following sections will summarize the clinical literature regarding specific skills for terminating therapy with this population, common themes encountered when terminating psychotherapy, and ethical dilemmas therapists might face during termination. It should be mentioned that the process of termination with older adults will vary depending on the type and severity of problem treated, characteristics of the client, and the mode of psychotherapy one utilizes. The sections below will attempt to provide information that can be utilized: (1) by clinicians from a variety of theoretical orientations and (2) with a wide variety of client presentations. In addition, termination issues are discussed in the context of short-term therapy because empirically supported therapies are generally short-term in nature, and therapists are increasingly required to provide time-limited therapy due to managed care.

Case example The following case represents a relatively common issue for which an older adult might present to therapy. This case will be referred to periodically throughout the remainder of the chapter to help illustrate the various skills and techniques to be discussed later.

Mrs. B was a seventy-four-year-old woman providing care for her husband who had been diagnosed with Alzheimer's disease approximately one year before. She presented for psychotherapy due to "stress" related to her care giving responsibilities. Specifically, she was experiencing feelings of hopelessness about the future, was feeling overwhelmed with care giving duties as well as other family commitments, and frequently became frustrated with her husband when he would engage in behaviors such as repeating questions. She reported having always been a very patient person and found her recent anger uncharacteristic. She identified reducing angry outbursts directed at her husband as her primary treatment target. Short-term CBT was deemed to be most appropriate for this individual and was implemented over a period of ten weeks. Treatment focused on learning relaxation skills, cognitive restructuring techniques, and assertiveness skills in order to obtain more assistance and reduce the number of demands placed on her by her adult children who lived in the area.

Specific Termination Skills and Techniques

As was mentioned above, different modes of psychotherapy, such as CBT and IPT, can approach termination differently based on theoretical differences. Despite these differences, a reading of these literatures reveals many similarities with regard to techniques for terminating therapy with older adult clients. Therefore, what will be presented below might be regarded as a set of generally agreed upon "best practices" for terminating therapy with this population. Table 14.1 provides a summary of these techniques.

Choosing a certain number of sessions (typically between twelve and twenty sessions) or a specific termination date early in the process of therapy, once a treatment plan has been reviewed with the client, is often recommended for several reasons. First, a defined endpoint can help keep both the therapist and client focused on therapy goals. Second, because older adults may be more likely to look to the therapist

Table 14.1 Summary of Termination Issues

KEY TERMINATION SKILLS

- Discuss termination early and periodically throughout treatment
- Review treatment goals and assess progress subjectively and objectively
- Emphasize client role in creating improvement to increase self-efficacy
- Create written maintenance guide to list key therapy skills
- Therapist and client should create list of key therapy skills separately and then discuss together
- Anticipate high-risk situations and create a written plan
- Create a list of "danger signals" that indicate possible relapse
- Create a written contingency plan should danger signals occur, including signs that the client should contact the therapist.
- Conduct booster sessions

THEMES AND ISSUES TO ANTICIPATE	POTENTIAL ACTION(S)
Client issues	
• Client has strong feelings about termination	• Discuss and validate feelings
• Increase in symptoms near termination	• Normalize the experience
Therapaist issues	
• Therapist avoids termination due to:	
– Feeling ineffective	• Examine expectations for improvement (too high or low?)
– Inaccurate beliefs	• Explore possible ageist attitudes
– Attachment to the client	• Carefully prepare for termination
	• Utilize supervision or consultation
– Therapist grief over deceased client	• Utilize supervision or consultation

to determine when treatment should end (Mosher-Ashley 1994), a specific end date or session limit can prevent therapy from persisting for an unnecessarily long time. Third, a well-defined ending might dispel any fears and misconceptions older adults have regarding psychotherapy as an open-ended, long-term process.

Once session limits or a termination date has been chosen, it is recommended that termination be discussed with the client early in therapy and periodically throughout treatment. It is important to explain to clients that periodic reminders about termination are to be expected, and are not signs that the therapist dislikes the client or is attempting to push him or her out of therapy.

Mrs. B was informed during the second session that treatment would be time limited (ten sessions) in order to keep sessions focused on achieving her specific goals. She was assured that many clients respond positively within this time frame. Also, every other session was started with some version of the following statement in order to gently remind her that treatment was time limited: "Good morning Mrs. B. Let's get started by taking a look at your homework assignment to see what kind of week it has been. Since we have only x number of sessions left, I want to make sure we see how well the skills you are learning are working for you." Mrs. B periodically expressed some concern about termination, feeling that it was rapidly approaching and that she still had much to learn. These concerns were validated and she was provided with an opportunity to review what she had learned thus far. This reassured Mrs. B that she was making progress and normalized her apprehension about termination.

Once the formal process of termination begins, several techniques are recommended to ensure the elderly client obtains maximal benefit from the termination process. First, a formal review of treatment should be conducted. This process involves reviewing progress made toward treatment goals. The written treatment plan should be examined in session as a concrete reminder of the client's desired goals. The client should be encouraged to provide a subjective report of how much progress they made toward each goal. In addition, the therapist should provide not only a subjective assessment of treatment progress, but also summarize the objective questionnaire or test data regarding symptom change. Older clients may find this objective data more convincing that progress was "really" made.

Mrs. B's goal was to feel less stressed, feel more in control of her anger, and reduce the number of demands placed on her. Each of these goals was reviewed and progress assessed. Mrs. B. reported that she felt she had made progress toward all of these goals. In addition, Mrs. B completed the Beck Depression Inventory Short Form (Beck & Beck 1972) and the Caregiver Annoyance Interview (Steffen & Berger 2000) during the second session and again near the end of treatment, with both showing evidence of improvement. These results were reviewed, and according to Mrs. B, provided reassurance that her subjective report of improvement was accurate.

The therapy review process should also involve preparing the client for life without regular contact with the therapist. These discussions have, as their overarching goal, to increase self-efficacy and a sense that one can function independently, as well as prevent relapse after termination occurs. The goal of increasing a sense of mastery and efficacy may be particularly important with older adults who have dependent personality traits or are experiencing a loss of independence due to factors such as medical problems or limited mobility. Older clients may also be more likely to underemphasize their own role in creating positive change during therapy. Thus, it is important that the therapist repeatedly emphasize the *client*'s role in symptom improvement and problem solving during termination sessions (Hinrichsen 2006, 177).

There are several strategies that can be used with older clients to prevent relapse and promote a sense of efficacy about one's ability to function independently. First, reviewing therapy should involve having clients specify skills they have learned. Recounting seminal events that the client viewed as critical in the success of treatment may aid this process. CBT models suggest the use of written "maintenance guides" to facilitate continued use of skills once therapy has been completed (Coon et al. 1999). One strategy used to enhance this process is to have both the client and therapist separately write down their impressions of what was most helpful in therapy, and then discuss similarities and differences in these two lists. The client is then left with a comprehensive written summary of what occurred in therapy and what was learned, which can be referred to in the future if needed. Written summaries can also help compensate for any cognitive deficits that may be present.

Secondly, termination should also involve discussing stressful situations that are anticipated once therapy has ended. The client is encouraged to write an action plan describing what he or she will do if this situation occurs based on what they learned in therapy. This exercise provides the therapist with an assessment of what was learned and the client's ability to generalize skill use to novel situations.

It is common for clients to worry about what to do if a relapse in symptoms occurs. For example, bereaved clients may experience an increase in symptoms around important anniversaries, or clients providing care to an ill loved one may encounter new stressors as their loved one's condition changes over time. It is important that clients realize that a return to psychotherapy is sometimes appropriate, and not a sign of failure on their part. Openly discussing the possibility of returning to therapy in the future can provide comfort that help is available if needed and prevent barriers such as shame, fears of becoming dependent on the therapist, or feelings of vulnerability from inhibiting the client from returning to therapy (Lazarus & Sadavoy 1996). During the termination process the therapist and client should compile a list of "danger signals" that may be signs of an impending relapse (Coon et al. 1999). Some examples include an increase in alcohol consumption, social withdrawal, or more frequent and intense negative affect. An explicit plan of action should be created so the client knows what to do should these danger signals occur. Returning to psychotherapy should be included in this plan, along with other options such as utilizing available social support or visiting their physician. Coon and colleagues (1999) also advise that the client be provided with options to implement should the client wish to return to therapy but the therapist is no longer available.

> Mrs. B's final two sessions focused exclusively on preparing her for termination. Feelings regarding termination were openly discussed, although by this time Mrs. B was feeling more confident in her ability to control her anger and assert her needs with her family. Both the therapist and Mrs. B made a list of skills that were perceived to be most beneficial. Mrs. B identified relaxation and engaging in pleasant events as most helpful, while the therapist identified assertiveness skills as most beneficial. The therapist provided examples of Mrs. B's successful use of assertiveness skills both in session (e.g., asking to reschedule a session), and with her family (e.g., saying no to her daughter's request to babysit her grandson) to highlight the usefulness of this skill. High-risk situations that were likely to occur after therapy ended were also anticipated, and written plans were prepared for coping with these situations. For example, it was planned that assertiveness skills would be used when her daughter made unreasonable requests.
>
> Although Mrs. B was functioning much better by the end of therapy, a list of symptoms that were potential signs of relapse was made.

For Mrs. B, these warning signs included frequent headaches, muscle tension, and hopeless thoughts. A list of specific skills to implement should these warning signs occur was written down. Examples of these skills included deep breathing, taking a walk, and reviewing the number of commitments she had made. These written contingency plans reassured Mrs. B that she did not have to remember everything that was discussed in therapy, and that she could refer to this list in the future. Mrs. B was also informed that she could contact the therapist if she was having difficulties that she was unable to solve on her own.

It is generally recommended that once the formal process of termination is completed, additional sessions should be conducted by spacing out final sessions over progressively longer periods of time. This represents a type of extended or faded termination. For example, CBT models recommend scheduling three-, six-, and twelve-month booster sessions after the last formal therapy session (Coon et al. 1999). The spacing of booster sessions can be flexible and clients should provide input about the intersession interval. These booster sessions can help clients disengage from therapy in a gradual fashion and provide reassurance that assistance remains available if needed. Graduated termination can also function to attain updates on client progress, further assist with the application of skills learned in therapy, and to assess whether additional therapy or referrals are necessary (Coon et al. 1999).

Two booster sessions were scheduled for Mrs. B after her final therapy session. Although she was doing quite well at the end of therapy, she felt very reassured that these sessions were available in the event that new stressors occurred. These boosters were conducted at one month and six months following the final formal treatment session, and allowed for an assessment of maintenance and generalization of treatments gains. Mrs. B continued to do well at both of these follow-ups as verified by self-report and questionnaire data. No further sessions were scheduled, but she was reminded to use her written contingency plan (which included contacting the therapist) should problems arise in the future.

Common Termination Themes/Issues

Certain issues or themes are more likely to arise during the process of termination with older adults. We feel it is important for therapists to be aware of these issues, so they can anticipate and prepare for them when working with older clients. See Table 14.1 for a summary of these issues, as well as suggestions for handling them.

The case of Mrs. B illustrates how clients may experience apprehension about their ability to function independently after termination. Clients can also experience sadness or disappointment that therapy is ending. Although this may be true for clients of any age, these feelings may be particularly powerful and poignant for older adults given that they may have few existing relationships due to death, relocation, or limited mobility. Furthermore, current cohorts of older adults are from a generation where openly discussing personal matters and emotions was likely discouraged, making the therapeutic relationship particularly unique and important. Overall, the therapist should be aware that termination can be experienced by the older adult as a significant loss, particularly if in the context of other losses (Miller et al. 1994). The importance of the therapeutic relationship should not be underestimated and clients should be encouraged to discuss feelings about termination. With clients who have difficulties labeling emotions, the therapist should assist them in labeling their feelings about termination and then validate these responses. Termination should be a time where both parties have the opportunity to say their good-byes.

Furthermore, the therapist may anticipate an increase in symptoms near the end of therapy (Miller et al. 1994). For example, a client seeking therapy for bereavement issues may experience an increase in grieflike symptoms as termination approaches. The client may interpret these symptoms as a sign of relapse or a worsening of one's condition. Again, in these instances the therapist should validate this experience as a relatively normal part of the termination process, indicating that the symptoms may simply be normal sadness or anxiety about the end of therapy. Unless the client's condition appears to be deteriorating markedly (e.g., suicidal ideation, significant weight loss) over an extended period of time, the termination process should continue as originally planned. With clients who are particularly uncomfortable with termination, some authors have suggested that clients wait four to eight weeks after termination before considering a return to therapy assuming the client is not a risk to him- or herself or others (Miller et al. 1994).

Therapists may find that discussing termination with elderly clients is more difficult than with younger clients. Mosher-Ashley (1994) found that about twice as many terminations with older adults were initiated by clients instead of therapists. The result can be avoiding the topic of termination even when termination is warranted. There may be several reasons for this reluctance for therapists to broach the subject of termination. First, variables associated with aging, such as losses of close loved ones, the existence of chronic medical problems, limitations in mobility, and financial constraints can impose limitations on the amount of progress that can be made in therapy or slow therapeutic progress (Knight 1986, 150; Sholomskas et al. 1983). Therefore, it can be very challenging for therapists to terminate therapy if they believe that termination is not occurring under ideal circumstances. In fact, Mosher-Ashley (1994) found that in only 10 percent of cases did therapists believe termination occurred when the client's problem had been solved or improved significantly. Therapists can be left feeling as if they are abandoning a client and wondering if they have really helped (Knight 1986, 149). Therapists working with older adults need to have a realistic view of what they can and cannot do for some clients. Importantly, older adults, more often than younger adults, will cycle back into therapy as life circumstances change. Being aware of this dynamic can facilitate making the "best" termination decision. Additionally, open discussions about termination, particularly concerning the client's readiness and willingness to terminate, and carefully planning for termination are ways to offset these potential challenges.

Second, termination may be avoided with older adults due to inaccurate beliefs of which therapists might not even be aware. Ageism is quite prevalent in the United States, and mental healthcare providers are not immune to these attitudes. Therapists working with older adults need to educate themselves about ageism (see Palmore 1999 for an overview of ageism in America) and explore their own beliefs about the elderly and how those beliefs could impact termination. For example, therapists may underestimate their elderly client's ability to function independently due to beliefs that the elderly are generally frail, helpless, and lonely.

Third, therapists might avoid the topic of termination with older clients simply because they have developed a strong attachment to the older client and wish for the relationship to continue (what dynamically oriented individuals might refer to as a "grandparent countertransference"). Both therapist and client may find it difficult to prevent the therapeutic relationship from crossing into the realm of friendship. Therapists need to be observant of their own reluctance to terminate and look for behaviors such as continually finding "new" issues to address in therapy even when the client's original goals have been met. Supervision or consultation with colleagues is a useful way for therapists to address this issue.

Mosher-Ashley (1994) found that 13 percent of clients died during therapy, with even higher rates (19 percent) for clients seen in nursing homes. Therapists must be prepared for this possibility and utilize available supports such as colleagues or supervisors when needed.

Ethical Issues Related to Termination

In this section, ethical issues regarding termination with elderly clients will be explored including gift giving, confidentiality, termination in the context of providing time-limited psychotherapy in a managed care environment, and circumstances unique to older adults that can complicate the termination process.

Some authors have suggested, based on their clinical and research experience, that the elderly may be particularly prone to give gifts as an expression of appreciation (Sholomakas et al. 1983). Although the American Psychological Association (APA) ethical guidelines do not explicitly prohibit gift giving (APA 2002), the therapist must exercise judgment as to what an appropriate gift is and ensure that the client does not feel obligated to provide gifts. Therapists must be aware of their own boundaries regarding gifts and be prepared to explain this policy to clients. The available literature suggests that therapists might consider relaxing boundaries regarding gifts when seeing older adults because gifts may simply reflect the client's long-standing means for expressing appreciation and not represent some hidden or unconscious motive (Nordhus, Nielsen, & Kvale 1998). Therapists can emphasize that the real gift received is observing positive change in the client. At times, however, gifts may be too expensive to accept and the therapist must validate the generosity of the gift and perhaps find alternative ways to express appreciation (e.g., verbal expressions or donating gifts to an organization).

The issue of confidentiality can pose ethical challenges for the clinician working with older adults. Knight (1992, 184) points out that the right to confidentiality is more often overlooked with the elderly compared with younger adults. Family members or other healthcare professionals who initially encouraged the client to seek therapy are often important partners during the therapeutic process, and may take a keen interest in what is occurring during therapy. Some feel entitled to know what is occurring during therapy because they are family or they referred the client for therapy. Unless a client is deemed cognitively incompetent, however, the client's consent must be obtained before sharing therapy-related information (such as why or when therapy was terminated) with others. Even if a client does have documented cognitive impairment, that client still has the right to confidentiality and information should only be shared with caregivers when it is likely to benefit the client (Welfel 2004). It is important, therefore, for the therapist to clearly communicate issues of confidentiality to elderly clients, involved family members, and even healthcare providers (Welfel 2004).

Because managed care imposes limitations on practitioners regarding the number of sessions one can provide, practitioners may frequently find themselves in situations where the prescribed number of sessions has been completed, but termination is considered unjustifiable by the therapist (Welfel 2004). For example, termination may not be appropriate in cases where the older client continues to experience significant clinical symptoms, poses a risk to themselves or others, is in a potentially abusive situation, has a long history of recurrent psychological problems, has a very limited social network, is expecting future losses due to death or medical problems, or has a terminal illness (Newton & Lazarus 1992; Nordhus, Nielsen, & Kvale 1998). In these cases continuing treatment can pose a financial burden on the client (i.e., additional sessions are not covered by insurance) and the therapist (i.e., the therapist is not reimbursed for additional sessions). Clearly therapists must consider the well-being of clients while also protecting their own self-interests.

If the therapist believes termination is unwarranted at the end of a prescribed number of sessions, there are several courses of action. First, the therapist can continue to see the client for free or at a reduced rate. In these situations, sessions may be conducted less frequently if appropriate. Second, the therapist may provide referrals to competent low-cost service providers if they are available. Third, the provider may appeal denials for additional sessions (Welfel 2004). The first option seems particularly warranted when clients are judged to be a risk to themselves or others, low-cost providers are not available or have waiting lists, or while appeal decisions are being made. It should be noted that low-cost and free services can be discontinued when clients are no longer judged to be a threat to themselves or others. Referral options and an explicit discussion regarding termination must be conducted to ensure that the client understands why therapy is ending and the options that are available (APA 2002).

There are some unique circumstances under which termination can occur with older adults that can pose ethical dilemmas and require careful consideration. First, therapists might be seeing an older client who is known to have a condition that causes progressive dementia. The therapist should not assume that a cognitively impaired individual cannot benefit from psychotherapy, yet ethically should not continue to see a client who clearly cannot benefit. It is important, therefore, to frequently assess the effectiveness of therapy (e.g., do they seem to recall information from session to session, are symptoms improving). Because the validity of the client's self-report may be diminished, involving family or other healthcare providers (with the client's consent) is critical. These outside parties can provide information concerning the client's symptoms outside of session, the client's ability to recall information from sessions, and progression of cognitive impairment. When termination is warranted, the therapist must carefully and clearly explain to the client why therapy is ending. Additionally, before considering termination the therapist should make certain that the client is being regularly followed by a medical provider and determine the need/availability of services such as in-home companions or adult day care.

Second, some clients who have suffered a significant loss such as the death of a spouse, may have no family or other sources of support available to them for reasons such as living in a rural area, lack of reliable transportation, and physical health problems that limit mobility. If a client appears to heavily rely on the therapist for support, and there seems to be little possibility of increasing social support, termination in the sense of permanently ending sessions may not be appropriate or ethical. Instead the interval between therapy sessions can gradually lengthen over time (assuming the client has made some improvement and is not a suicide risk) with sessions serving as a "check in" as well as an opportunity for social interaction and support. As mentioned previously, open discussion between client and therapist will help determine how best to proceed.

Third, termination can also occur in the context of known or suspected elder abuse. Of course if there are good reasons to suspect elder abuse, the therapist is mandated to file a report with the appropriate agency, such as local law enforcement or adult protective services (APS). It is important for the therapist to have contact with APS once a report has been made so as to be informed about what steps have been taken to protect the individual. Whether abuse is known or suspected, termination of psychotherapy in these situations must proceed carefully. Before making a decision about termination, the therapist needs to assess factors such as whether the abuser still lives with the client (if so, can the client find other living arrangements), how frequently the abuser and victim have contact, is the abuser receiving rehabilitation services, how closely is the case being followed by local agencies, and does the client know how to appropriately respond should further abuse or neglect occur (e.g., calling the police, contacting the APS caseworker, or finding a safe place to go). If it appears as if the client is at relatively low risk for future abuse, termination can proceed as usual assuming the client's symptoms have improved. If a client is considered to be at risk for continued abuse, this may represent another situation where permanent termination is not ethical and sessions should continue at least periodically until risk decreases or appropriate alternative services can be found.

Fourth, clients in nursing homes have been found to terminate their own therapy less frequently than clients being seen in the community (Mosher-Ashley 1994). The ethical question is "do nursing home clients feel able to terminate therapy?" Nursing home residents might learn to adopt a passive role in this environment and may feel less able to initiate termination (Mosher-Ashley 1994). Also, unlike clients in the community, nursing home residents cannot simply stop coming to therapy. Therapists must repeatedly assess the client's desire to remain in treatment and provide the client with considerable influence over the process of termination.

Fifth, mental health professionals working in hospitals or nursing homes often encounter a very different kind of therapy termination—patients with terminal illnesses who are anticipating their own death. Patients may be struggling with the issue of whether or not to discontinue life-sustaining interventions and hasten the dying process. This decision is complex, but can be further complicated when the client is aware of the opinions and beliefs of medical providers and family. Therapists in these situations must explore their own beliefs regarding the right to die, and must be careful not to further complicate the issue or overly influence the client's decision by revealing their own personal values (Knight 1992, 184). Therapists could find themselves in a volatile situation if family members learn that the patient's decision was heavily influenced by the therapist. The therapist should be prepared to act as a supportive listener and assist clients in making their own decision based on their own values, whatever that decision happens to be.

Recommendations for Future Research

The lack of empirical work on the process of termination with older adults leaves many unanswered questions. Some of these questions include:

1. Does termination need to be gradually faded over longer periods of time or can terminations be relatively brief and abrupt in nature? The current available literature suggests that termination with older clients should occur gradually over an extended period of time to ease the transition for the client (e.g., Coon et al. 1999). This guidance is, however, based on clinical wisdom and not empirical data.

2. How effective are written termination summaries and maintenance guides in promoting maintenance of therapeutic gains? These written summaries are a standard part of CBT designed

for older adults. It is unknown, however, whether clients use this information and what role these written records might play in preventing relapse.

3. Is it useful or necessary to interpret a client's reactions to termination as indicative of unconscious motives or as replaying conflicts from previous relationships as suggested by some dynamically oriented therapies? Should these interpretations be shared and discussed with the client? These are just a few of the unanswered questions regarding termination with this population; the reader can likely generate many more.

The first step in gathering data and generating further research questions concerning termination could be to collect survey data from clients participating in clinical trials. Clients could be asked about the amount of time devoted to termination (too much or too little); the utility and continued use of written materials generated during termination; whether they would have preferred a gradual, faded termination versus a more final or abrupt termination; whether the therapist prepared them for termination adequately; whether it be more helpful to discuss termination periodically throughout treatment or save these discussions for the last few sessions; and whether the therapist showed confidence in his or her ability to function independently after termination. Answers to these questions could begin to address the overarching question of how to tailor termination procedures so they are more acceptable and effective for older clients.

Although survey data would be a good first step in this area, more rigorous experimental work is necessary to help separate what is actually more effective versus what we think is most effective. This would involve treating termination procedures as an independent variable to be manipulated and its effects on treatment outcome and maintenance measured. To illustrate, it was mentioned earlier that CBT is an empirically supported intervention for late-life depression and involves a certain set of termination procedures based on cognitive-behavioral theory. Saying that CBT is an empirically supported treatment for late-life depression is not, however, equivalent to saying that the termination process used in CBT is the most effective way to improve outcomes such as improving self-efficacy, promoting maintenance, and preventing relapse.

The following are examples of experimental studies that could help answer some of the questions posed previously. One study could involve comparing two versions of CBT (or any other type of therapy) with each version having different termination procedures. For example, one version of treatment could involve periodic discussions about termination occurring throughout treatment (e.g., every fourth session), while the other version would involve almost no discussion of termination until the last three sessions. Another similar study could involve manipulating whether or not clients complete written termination summaries and determining if maintenance is improved by having these written materials. One could also compare conditions where the final sessions of treatment are extended over progressively longer periods of time (i.e., faded termination) versus having the final sessions occur on the same schedule as all previous therapy sessions (e.g., every week). Larger and more complex studies comparing conditions that involve different modes of therapy combined with different termination procedures are also possible. This would allow for comparisons of the effects of different treatments, the effects of different termination strategies, and the interaction of these two variables. Any research in this area would need to involve careful measurement of "termination integrity" or adherence to prescribed termination procedures in order to make more definitive conclusions about the effects of different termination procedures.

Summary and Conclusions

The elderly are a rapidly growing population that mental health professionals will encounter more frequently in their practices, particularly those working in medical settings. Although much has been written about how the process of psychotherapy might differ when seeing older adults, little has been written specifically about the termination of therapy with this population. Empirical work regarding termination appears to be almost nonexistent and the available literature, which was briefly summarized here, is based mostly on clinical experience or theory. Therapists must be prepared for a number of unique clinical and ethical issues related to terminating therapy with this population. Overall, it is clear that there are numerous opportunities for clinical researchers interested in how to improve the process of termination with older adults.

References

American Psychological Association. (2002). *Ethical principles of psychologists and code of conduct.* Washington, DC: Author. Retrieved August 1, 2006, from http://www.apa.org/ethics/

Beck, A. T., & Beck, R. W. (1972). Screening depressed patients in family practice: A rapid technique. *Postgraduate Medicine, 52,* 81–85.

Coon, D. W., Rider, K., Gallagher-Thompson, D., & Thompson, L. (1999). Cognitive-behavioral therapy with late-life distress. In M. Duffy (Ed.), *Handbook of counseling and psychotherapy with older adults* (pp. 487–510). New York: Wiley.

Feldman, H., Goldstein, I., Hatzichristou, D., Krame, R., & McKinlay, J. (1994). Impotence and its medical and psychosocial correlates: Results of the Massachusetts Male Aging Study. *Journal of Urology, 151,* 559–623.

Gallagher-Thompson, D., & Steffen, A. M. (1994). Comparative effects of cognitive-behavioral and brief psychodynamic psychotherapies for depressed family caregivers. *Journal of Consulting and Clinical Psychology, 62,* 543–549.

Hayes, L. (1997). Suicide rate among older Americans remains unchecked. *Counseling Today, 40,* 6.

Hendrie, H.C. (1997). Epidemiology of Alzheimer's disease. *Geriatrics, 52,* S4-S8.

Hinrichsen, G. (2006). *Interpersonal psychotherapy for depressed older adults.* Washington, DC: American Psychological Association.

Knight, B. G. (1986). *Psychotherapy with the older adult.* Newbury Park, CA: Sage.

Knight, B. G. (1992). *Older adults in psychotherapy: Case histories.* Newbury Park, CA: Sage.

Lazarus, L. W., & Sadavoy, J. (1996). Individual psychotherapy. In J. Sadavoy (Ed.), *Comprehensive review of geriatric psychiatry – II* (pp. 819–850). Washington, DC: American Psychological Association.

Mickus, M., Colenda, C. C., & Hogan, A. J. (2000). Knowledge of mental health benefits and preferences for type of mental health providers among the general public. *Psychiatric Services, 51,* 199–202.

Miller, M. D., Frank, E., Cones, C., Imber, S. D., Anderson, B., Ehrenpreis, L., et al. (1994). Applying interpersonal psychotherapy to bereavement-related depression following a loss of a spouse in late life. *Journal of Psychotherapy Practice and Research, 3,* 149–162.

Mosher-Ashley, P. M. (1994). Therapy termination and persistence patterns of elderly clients in a community health center. *Gerontologist, 34,* 180–189.

Myers, J., Weissman, M., Tischler, G., Holeer, C., 3rd, Leaf, P., Orvaschel, H., et al. (1984). Six-month prevalence of psychiatric disorders in three communities: 1980–1982. *Archives of General Psychiatry, 41,* 959–967.

Newton, N. A., & Lazarus, L. W. (1992). Behavioral and psychotherapeutic interventions. In J. E. Birren, R. B. Sloane, & G. D. Cohen (Eds.), *Handbook of mental health and aging* (pp. 699–719). San Diego, CA: Academic Press.

Nordhus, I. H., Nielsen, G. H., & Kvale, H. (1998). Psychotherapy with older adults. In I. H. Nordhus, G. R. VandenBos, S. Berg, & P. Fromholt (Eds.), *Clinical geropsychology* (pp. 289–311). Washington, DC: American Psychological Association.

Palmore, E. B. (1999). *Ageism: Negative and positive* (2nd ed.). New York: Springer.

Sholomskas, A. J., Chevron, E. S., Prusoff, B. A., & Berry, C. (1983). Short-term interpersonal therapy (IPT) with the depressed elderly: Case reports and discussion. *American Journal of Psychotherapy, 37,* 552–566.

Smyer, M. A., & Qualls, S. H. (1999). *Aging and mental health.* Malden, MA: Blackwell.

Steffen, A. M., & Berger, S. (2000). Relationship differences in anger intensity during caregiving-related situations. *Clinical Gerontologist, 21,* 3–19.

Surgeon General. (1999). *Mental health: A report of the Surgeon General.* Retrieved July 31, 2006, from http://www.surgeongeneral. gov/library/mentalhealth

Thompson, L. W., Coon, D. W., Gallagher-Thompson, D., Sommer, B. R., & Koin, D. (2001). Comparison of desipramine and cognitive-behavioral therapy in the treatment of elderly outpatients with mild-to-moderate depression. *American Journal of Geriatric Psychiatry, 9,* 225–240.

United States Census Bureau. (2005). Older Americans month celebrated in May. Retrieved July 30, 2006, from http://www.census.gov/Press-Release/ www/releases/archives/factsforfeaturesspecialeditions/004210.html

United States Department of Health and Human Services. (1998). Substance abuse among older adults treatment improvement protocol series 26. Retrieved July 31, 2006, from http://www.health.org/govpubs/ bkd250/ 26b.aspx

Welfel, E. R. (2004). The ethical challenges of brief therapy. In D. Chapman (Ed.), *Core processes in brief psychodynamic psychotherapy: Advancing effective practice* (pp. 343–359). Mahwah, NJ: Lawrence Erlbaum.

15

TERMINATION WITH PERSONS WITH DEPRESSIVE DISORDERS

KEITH S. DOBSON AND
LAUREN C. HAUBERT

Although everyone experiences transient feelings of depression and unhappiness, the experience may be characterized as a depressive disorder when these feelings begin to dominate everyday life and cause emotional and functional impairment. According to the *Diagnostic and Statistical Manual of Mental Disorders* (*Diagnostic and Statistical Manual* [*DSM-IV*]; American Psychiatric Association [APA] 2000), the two main categories of depressive disorders include major depressive disorder (MDD) and dysthymic disorder (DD). Both disorders are defined by a similar pattern of symptoms, which may include depressed mood, anhedonia, sleep and appetite disturbances, fatigue or low energy, feelings of worthlessness, guilt, and/or suicidal ideation. While MDD lasts at least two weeks and is usually associated with moderate to severe symptoms, DD represents a more persistent and low-grade depression that lasts two years or longer. Major depression and dysthymia frequently co-occur (known as *double depression*), and depressive disorders, in general, tend to exhibit high rates of comorbidity with other Axis I and Axis II conditions, particularly anxiety disorders (Brown et al. 2001; Mineka, Watson, & Clark 1998).

MDD is one of the most prevalent mental health problems in North America. Various large-scale studies, such as the National Comorbidity Survey (NCS; Kessler et al. 1994) and the National Institutes of Mental Health Epidemiologic Catchment Area study (ECA; Regier et al. 1984) estimate that nearly one-third of the population may experience significant impairment as a result of depression at some point in their lives (Beutler, Clarkin, & Bongar 2000). In addition to the significant personal, emotional, and social dysfunction experienced by individuals suffering from depression, considerable economic and societal costs (e.g., lost workdays, lost productivity, treatment costs) are also associated with the disorder (Üstün 2001). Given far-reaching negative consequences across a variety of domains, the importance of assessing and treating depressive disorders appropriately and effectively is highlighted.

Cognitive and cognitive-behavioral therapies (CBT* e.g., Beck, 1995; Dobson 2001) have been established as among the most efficacious treatments for depression (Chambless & Ollendick 2001). Other well-established psychosocial treatments include interpersonal therapy (IPT; Weissman, Markowitz, & Klerman 2000) and more purely behavioral strategies such as "behavioral activation" (BA; Martell, Addis, & Jacobson 2001). Briefly, all of these treatments are explicitly defined as structured, time limited, and goal directed. The frequency and duration of therapy are typically set out in an initial contract made between the therapist and the patient. CBT-oriented therapists assist patients to systematically collect information about the patient's activities and thoughts in order to examine their maladaptive cognitions and to conduct behavioral "experiments" to examine whether thoughts and beliefs are accurate and/or functional (Beck et al. 1979). Patients are also taught a variety of cognitive restructuring methods in order to modify maladaptive thinking processes.

Similar to CBT, the BA approach focuses on the functional connection between behaviors and real-life outcomes; however, BA does not particularly focus on the role of cognition in generating behavioral patterns, and BA devotes less attention to the content of cognitions than does CBT. In IPT, the focus of treatment is on interpersonal events (e.g., interpersonal disputes or conflicts, role transitions) that have been implicated in the onset and/or maintenance of depression. IPT incorporates discussion of the potentially maladaptive interpersonal patterns the patient is using in his or her life, and the practical consequences of these patterns are addressed through interpersonal

---

* Since behavioral, cognitive, and cognitive-behavioral therapies share many commonalities, these approaches will be encompassed under the term *cognitive-behavioral therapy* or CBT for the remainder of this chapter.

homework exercises. The current chapter will focus on the issues and strategies related to the termination phase of psychotherapy with depressed patients, irrespective of treatment model.

Depression often follows a chronic course and is often considered a highly recurrent disorder (Gotlib & Hammen 2002; Judd 1997). It has been estimated that over 75 percent of depressed individuals experience more than one depressive episode, and that depressive relapse is often within two years of recovery from an episode (Keller & Boland 1998). In addition, the time between subsequent episodes decreases with recurrent depression. Given such findings, there has been an increasing focus in recent years toward incorporating methods of relapse prevention into psychological treatments for depressive disorders. For example, mindfulness-based cognitive therapy (MBCT) integrates *acceptance*, or a focus on embracing and "being with" thoughts and feelings, and meditation. MBCT has been shown to reduce risk of relapse in formerly depressed patients (Segal, Williams, & Teasdale 2002).

Psychotherapists are well aware that the treatment of depression is both an art and a science (O'Donohue, Cummings, & Cummings 2006). The treatment outcome evidence will shape the specific therapeutic approach adopted by a therapist, but other factors such as the therapist's training, experience, and theoretical orientation also influence treatment choices. In selecting a particular intervention, other factors that are often considered include both patient preference and previous response to treatment(s). For example, psychodynamic and psychoanalytic therapies typically last for much longer than interpersonal or cognitive-behavioral therapies. As such, different clinicians may focus on different aspects of functioning during the termination phase of psychotherapy, depending on their orientation.

When Should Psychotherapy Be Terminated?

Patients are often able to determine for themselves when they are prepared to terminate the therapeutic relationship. The patient may have noticed a considerable decrease in depressive symptoms, the successful amelioration of problems, or an increase in his or her sense of psychological well-being and functioning. Ideally, patients will have experienced a reduction in symptoms and will have learned the basic cognitive, behavioral, and/or interpersonal skills that will help them cope with stressful situations. In such cases, the termination phase may be initiated with relative ease. Other factors to consider in the decision to terminate psychotherapy include the patient's residual symptoms, psychosocial difficulties, history of psychological functioning, and the therapist's judgment regarding the patient's need for further treatment.

Occasionally, patients may simply choose to terminate their own treatment by withdrawing from therapy, often without informing the therapist of the reasons for their decision. Studies by Hunsley, Aubry, Verstervelt, and Vito (1999) and Todd, Deane, and Bragdon (2003) found that patients cite a wide range of reasons for terminating psychotherapy, including dissatisfaction with the treatment and/or therapist, reaching all or many of their treatment goals, environmental constraints (e.g., patient moved, no longer had money or insurance coverage, therapist finished training and left), and personal reasons (e.g., no longer having time for or interest in therapy, wanted to "take a break" from therapy). In addition, some of the symptoms that typically occur with depressive disorders, such as low energy, helplessness, and hopelessness, may contribute to a patient's poor attendance to therapy sessions or even an unplanned termination. In such instances, the therapist may attempt to target these symptoms more directly through therapeutic intervention in an effort to improve attendance, or may inform the patient that treatment for his or her depression may be sought again at some point in the future. The therapist may choose to make efforts to reconnect with the patient (e.g., through a letter or phone call); however, the decision to return to therapy ultimately rests on the patient's own decision.

In other instances, however, the decision to end therapy may not be as clearly defined. For example, a dependent patient may have developed a tendency to rely heavily on the therapist over the course of therapy and may be apprehensive about reclaiming personal responsibility for his or her own well-being, and transferring the skills and strategies he or she has learned in therapy into the "real world." Some patients may hold a mistaken belief that the therapeutic relationship should not be terminated until they have reached a state of complete remission of symptoms.

In these less well-defined instances, the decision to terminate therapy should be made in a collaborative way with the patient. The therapist should have a discussion with the patient about the nature of his or her apprehension and help to address these concerns in an adaptive and constructive way (as described below).

While there are no strict rules regarding how and when a therapist should terminate a patient's course of treatment, researchers have developed assessment procedures that may assist in anticipating the course of treatment and in tracking changes in patients with depressive disorders. For example, Howard and colleagues (e.g., Howard et al. 1996; Sperry et al. 1996) have advocated an individualized approach (i.e., patient profiling) to determining when a patient has met his or her treatment goals. Based on relevant feedback about the patient's conditions, Howard et al. (1996) suggest that assessment should focus on progress throughout treatment and not simply be an assessment of outcome following termination of treatment. Specifically, Howard and colleagues propose a three-phase conception of the change process that includes remoralization (as assessed by subjective well-being), remediation (as assessed at the symptom level), and rehabilitation (as assessed by life functioning). As an overall treatment criterion (which they refer to as the Mental Health Index, or MHI), scores from these three domains are combined. Although this phase model of psychotherapy is broad in scope, it may assist clinicians in determining when termination is appropriate specifically with patients with depressive disorders.

Relatively few specific guidelines are available to assist the clinician in determining when termination is appropriate with the depressed patient. Beutler, Clarkin, and Bongar (2000), however, extracted a series of hypotheses from previous research in depression and then cross-validated these hypotheses through a series of empirical tests in order to develop a set of treatment guidelines for clinicians who treat individuals with depressive disorders. Beutler et al. (2000) propose that certain patient variables, including problem complexity, patient expectations, and subjective distress or severity, can help determine the probable value of short- versus long-term interventions. Therefore, certain patient variables may be helpful in determining the length of intervention, and thus the point at which termination should take place. In like manner, Persons has advocated a problem-oriented focus to patient conceptualization (Persons & Davidson 2001), which also implies that as patient problems are solved, the therapist and patient should mutually move toward a positive decision to terminate therapy.

Preparing the Patient for Termination

Within time-limited treatments, preparation for termination typically begins even from the first sessions of therapy. For example, therapists educate the patient about the technique they employ so that the patient can use these principles at the end of treatment. Therapists also often give homework assignments in order to help patients generalize strategies they have learned in therapy to their daily lives. In this way, patients learn and practice strategies for relapse prevention throughout the course of treatment. Over the course of therapy, a patient will have ideally experienced a reduction in symptoms of depression and will have learned and developed basic tools or strategies to enhance well-being.

A therapist who takes on and conveys a strong sense of responsibility for solving the patient's problems can unwittingly engender patient dependency, and may inadvertently deprive the patient of valuable opportunities to practice and strengthen newly acquired skills (Beck 1995). Because of these concerns, one of the goals of CBT for depression is to help the patient learn to enhance self-efficacy, and to solve problems independently. As such, therapies for depression function in a somewhat paradoxical manner, where temporary dependence on the therapist (during early sessions involving psychoeducation and the teaching of skills), work in the service of encouraging ultimate disengagement and independent problem-solving and coping.

Exploring Patient Expectations About Therapy and Termination

It is important for the therapist to assess the expectations of depressed patients at the outset of treatment, as these are critical to engaging the patient in the treatment process. Hopelessness about treatment or life in general is critical to predicting and intervening with possible suicide risk (Beutler et al. 2000). These expectations also come to bear during the termination stage of therapy. For example, patients bring preconceived notions regarding treatment approaches or duration of treatment into psychotherapy, and expectations that treatment will be effective in ameliorating symptoms (Clarkin & Levy 2004). An understanding of such expectations and motivations allows the clinician to modify treatment, thereby increasing patient-therapist compatibility. Assuring that patient expectations are addressed during the course of treatment also facilitates mutually supported termination.

The therapist can help prepare the patient for termination and the possibility of relapse through discussions about realistic expectations for maintenance of treatment gains and future progress. During treatment, the patient should be prepared to anticipate temporary fluctuations, plateaus, and setbacks, rather than a steady and progressive path of improvement with no interruptions. Further, given the chronic nature of depression and the considerable risk of symptom recurrence (e.g., Judd 1997; Keller & Boland 1998), the patient should be prepared to anticipate the possible return of depressive symptoms following termination. Patients may find it helpful to view a visual diagram of their own history of depression, or the typical course of progress in therapy, depicting typical patterns of fluctuation.

Patients ideally learn and practice a variety of relevant coping methods and skills over the course of treatment. The recurrence of symptoms can be conceptualized as an opportunity to practice these new skills, rather than as a negative event to be feared. Through exploring and modifying patient expectations as necessary, the patient will be better equipped to face setbacks after termination and less likely to view setbacks as personal "failures" if temporary interruptions to progress do, in fact, occur. Along the same lines, the therapist should ask the patient about how he or she would respond if a setback were encountered after experiencing noticeable improvements. In response to any negative thoughts (e.g., "this means that therapy didn't work" or "I guess I will just always feel depressed"), the therapist can help the patient develop counterstatements for handling negative thoughts around setbacks (e.g., "this is only a temporary setback," or "let me use what I learned in therapy") and even have the patient write these statements down as reminders. Such an exercise could be performed either during a therapy session or as homework before the end of treatment.

Attributing Treatment Gains to the Patient

Another important strategy that the therapist can use to assist the patient in preparing for termination is to attribute progress to the patient (Beck 1995). Throughout the course of therapy, the therapist should pay attention to opportunities when the patient may be congratulated for making important changes and/or progress. Whenever possible, the therapist should attribute changes in thoughts, moods, and behaviors to the patients' own efforts and assist them in recognizing how they have been able to bring about changes. Some patients may believe that the therapist or other external factors and situations are the main reasons underlying their improvement (e.g., "I'm happier because my friend took me to a movie"), and depressed patients in particular are prone to attribute success to external factors (while blaming themselves for perceived failures). Although the therapist should acknowledge these outside factors as potential sources of support that play a role in the patient's progress, the patient's own contributions to their treatment gains and maintenance of improvement must also be emphasized (Beck 1995). A treatment goal should be to help the patient recognize his or her strengths and competencies.

Learning and Developing Tools and Techniques

A central focus of CBT is the patient's acquisition of techniques and strategies designed to help them manage not only depressive symptoms, but also other situations in which the patient might react in a maladaptive manner. Common CBT techniques that patients learn and practice during therapy include:

- Monitoring and scheduling activities
- Using dysfunctional thought records to monitor negative automatic thoughts
- Identifying and testing automatic thoughts and beliefs
- Evaluating the evidence (i.e., refuting and supporting) related to dysfunctional thoughts and beliefs, and modifying them accordingly

- Generating and employing alternative strategies to address problems
- Breaking problems down into smaller steps

Patients should be encouraged to view these newly acquired tools both as strategies that can be used in the short term to cope with depression, and as strategies that can be applied to other problem situations they encounter following termination. The utility of these methods for improving functioning across domains (e.g., personal, social, emotional, occupational) should be emphasized by the therapist.

In addition, it is critical to review the patient's social support systems during the final stages of treatment. For individuals who have less of a supportive social environment to return to following therapy, terminating treatment from the clinic and the support that it entails to the relative impoverishment of the patient's "real world" may be more difficult. It is important for both the patient and therapist to be cognizant of the fact that the therapist-patient relationship is meant to enhance the patient's well-being and competence and is not designed to serve as a substitute for other relationships (Weissman et al. 2000). Therefore, it may be important to spend time focusing on identifying, developing, and nurturing support systems prior to the termination of treatment. Based on a comprehensive review of treatment literature, Beutler and colleagues (2000) suggest that high levels of experienced social support may improve outcomes in treatment and decrease the likelihood of relapse. Furthermore, low levels of social support appear to be an indicator for long-term treatment, whereas high social support seems to be a contraindication for more long-term treatment. Therefore, the expansion and enhancement of sources of social support will likely enhance the long-term maintenance of gains.

It is important for both the patient and the therapist to keep in mind that not all patients respond favorably to psychotherapy. If a patient makes a concerted effort to engage in treatment and acquire new skills but fails to respond, it is possible that the patient may experience some feelings of guilt, worthlessness, frustration, or regret. In such a situation, the therapist should attempt to counter these feelings by highlighting for the patient that he or she has put forth their best effort and it is not the patient who failed but rather a particular treatment has failed to work for him or her (Weissman et al. 2000). The therapist should continue to encourage the patient to try alternative treatments and instill hope by emphasizing that depression is a very treatable disorder, and although this particular treatment may have not have been effective for him or her, there are a number of effective alternative treatment strategies that the patient may be interested in exploring. The therapist can also remind the patient that although he or she did not experience significant improvement, this does not necessarily mean that they will be ending therapy without making *any* gains. In fact, the patient may have made an important change in some aspect of his or her life, and the therapist should attempt to build on the patient's sense of satisfaction and/or pride that they were able to make this change, despite being depressed. By recognizing the accomplishments patients have achieved, the therapist helps set the stage for future treatments that may be successful in helping them, and at the very least, assists patients in not blaming themselves or viewing themselves as a psychotherapy "failure."

The Final Sessions

Although the therapist has likely prepared the patient for termination since the first session (both indirectly and directly), the issue of termination should be explicitly addressed, at least two sessions before therapy ends. At this point, the therapist should discuss arrangements for tapering sessions, if this is desirable to the patient. Rather than simply ending therapy at a given point, patients may be prepared for termination by gradually tapering therapy sessions. For example, sessions may be held on an every-other-week basis, as is commonly done in both CBT and IPT. When the patient is functioning well with biweekly appointments, the therapist may suggest meeting on a monthly basis. The therapist should evaluate the patient's response to this suggestion, as it can provide a clue regarding the patient's comfort with moving toward termination. For some patients, this arrangement may be tolerated and even welcomed; however, other patients may experience some feelings of anxiety and apprehension about tapering sessions. If so, a therapist would be advised to help the patient explore both the advantages and disadvantages of this strategy. For example, if a patient identifies a potential disadvantage with which he or she may not be able to cope without the therapist's assistance, the therapist may be able to help the patient reframe tapering therapy as a chance to test his or her ability to be their own therapist and solve their own problems, which will ultimately be in their long-term best interests.

Another technique that can be employed with more psychoeducational therapies, as part of the movement toward termination, is self-sessions. Self-sessions are appointments that the patient makes with him/herself, just as he or she would with the therapist. During this appointment, the patient identifies one or two important current issues, and sets these for consideration. During the session, the patient then uses the techniques that have been learned over the course of therapy, and assigns him/herself appropriate homework. Thus, self-sessions can provide an explicit bridge from sessions with a therapist to more self-reliance and personal management of ongoing life issues.

Addressing Patient Reactions Regarding Termination

The termination phase of the psychotherapeutic process can evoke a wide variety of reactions, feelings, and dysfunctional automatic thoughts regarding termination. Some patients experience positive feelings about termination including feeling empowered by and proud of the gains they have made, feeling satisfied with their relationship with the therapist, or having a sense of relief that they have a newly gained independence and will no longer require regular sessions. Other patients, however, may feel angry toward themselves (e.g., for not making expected progress) or toward the therapist, may have fear of regression without the therapist's help, or may experience a variety of other mixed feelings about termination. At the time of termination, the patient faces several potentially difficult issues, such as giving up an important relationship with the therapist and establishing a sense of competence to deal with future problems without the assistance of the therapist.

It may be helpful for patients to be assured by the therapist that the appearance of negative feelings around termination does not portend a return of depression. Instead, such feelings may be used as an opportunity to help the patient distinguish between sadness that is appropriate to the situation and a depressed mood that may be more pathological. The therapist should be prepared to acknowledge and normalize patients' concerns, and to respond to any questions they may have about the termination process.

The therapist may also have some strong feelings about termination. If so, the therapist may choose to express his or her own reactions to termination, which may involve some sadness or disappointment about ending the therapeutic relationship, but also an optimistic view that the patient has made enough progress to fulfill the role of being his or her own therapist. If the therapist is able to confront termination with a sense of confidence, this stance may help the patient feel more comfortable with ending therapy. It may also be helpful to remind the apprehensive patient that the ultimate goal of treatment is to treat the depressive episode and assist the patient to become his or her own therapist and not to remain in therapy indefinitely. As with tapering sessions, the therapist may also find it useful to examine the advantages and disadvantages of termination with the patient.

During the final sessions, the therapist should also have a discussion and/or have patients make a written list of important changes they have made or tools that they have learned during therapy. Reviewing progress with patients may enable them to more clearly see the significance of their treatment gains, potentially motivating them to continue maintaining gains and building on the progress that they have made during treatment.

Maintaining Gains and Managing Setbacks

As termination approaches, the therapist can encourage the patient to construct a "coping card" on which the patient specifies how he or she will handle a setback if it occurs following termination. As a first course of action, the patient should be urged to resolve setbacks and difficult situations without the aid of the therapist. If the patient is unsuccessful at doing so, the therapist should remain open to have a phone consultation or set up an appointment. At that time, the therapist can assist the patient in the identification of possible obstacles that may have interfered with success, and the exploration of alternative ways of approaching a problem or issue if it happens again. The same cognitive and behavioral techniques (e.g., problem solving and working through maladaptive automatic thoughts and core beliefs) used to address depression-related difficulties can be used to approach issues related to termination.

Beck (1995) suggests that therapists may choose to have a discussion with patients about developing a self-therapy program. Essentially, patients take responsibility for periodically conducting their own therapy sessions (e.g., setting an agenda, reviewing homework, addressing current problems/issues, setting new homework, and scheduling their next self-therapy session). Patients may also be encouraged to consult with a depression self-help manual to help them refresh their cognitive and behavioral "toolbox" from time to time (e.g., Burns 1999; Greenberger & Padesky 1995; McQuaid & Carmona 2004). Although the patient is encouraged to rely on his or her own skills and strengths following termination, it is also important that the therapist assesses the patient's future ability to determine when further help should be sought. The patient and therapist should have a discussion about early warning signs of acute distress, and methods of coping that may be used in potentially stressful situations.

Follow-up and Booster Sessions

The empirical literature has demonstrated fairly consistently that treatment with CBT can have long-lasting beneficial and prophylactic effects, and reduce the risk of relapse in depression following psychotherapy termination (Hollon, Stewart, & Strunk 2006). For instance, Paykel and colleagues (2005) conducted a follow-up study of individuals who had been treated with CBT and found effects of CBT in reduction of relapse and recurrence persist for up to 4½ years following treatment. Despite considerable evidence that discontinuation of CBT does lead to relatively long-lasting benefits following treatment, a significant portion of patients choose to engage in booster sessions in order to further increase maintenance of therapeutic gains and keep their supportive relationship with the therapist.

In the treatment of depression, most clinicians typically view termination as a *stage* of treatment rather than a complete severing of ties between patient and clinician. In fact, many clinicians operate on a "revolving-door" basis by which psychotherapy may be reinstated, to some degree, even after a patient's initial treatment program has been completed. Among individuals with recurrent depression, follow-up psychotherapy sessions are often scheduled in order to provide maintenance or booster sessions. In particular, individuals who lack a supportive environment or whose depressive symptoms are severe and chronic may benefit the most from such follow-up appointments. In CBT, patients are encouraged to schedule booster sessions approximately three, six, and twelve months following termination (Beck 1995).

Booster sessions can serve a number of important functions. For instance, simply knowing that the therapist is available and willing to offer booster sessions can ease a patient's anxiety or apprehension about terminating therapy. Booster sessions can also provide an opportunity for the patient and therapist to discuss how the patient has fared in applying newly learned skills and techniques to problem situations, and to discuss alternative courses of action if the patient has had some difficulties. These sessions provide the therapist with a chance to assess whether dysfunctional thoughts and beliefs have been reactivated or if maladaptive behaviors have reemerged. Patients also have an opportunity to define new goals that they can aim to accomplish. Finally, the therapist can check on the patient's functioning and can offer encouragement for continued maintenance of gains and future progress.

Managing Medication Issues Upon Termination

Many patients suffering from depressive disorders may be taking an antidepressant medication both prior to and during the course of therapy. While psychologists themselves do not prescribe medications, they often consult with the patient's prescribing physician (with the patient's permission) regarding issues concerning side effects, dosage, alternative medications, and sometimes termination of antidepressants. In some instances, the patient's depressive symptoms may have lifted to a level at which antidepressant medication may no longer be necessary, and at this point the therapist and patient may discuss terminating medications and any concerns that the patient may have about doing so. According to detailed practice guidelines developed by the Agency for Health Care Policy and Research (AHCPR 1993), patients who respond well to acute-phase medication are typically advised to discontinue medication approximately four to nine months after they have returned to a clinically well state (i.e., continuation treatment). Although long-term use of antidepressant medications is generally safe, medications should be discontinued if they are not required. Some types of antidepressant medications, such as tricyclic antidepressants, should be discontinued with the use of a tapering schedule in order to decrease adverse side effects associated with terminating medication. Occasionally the patient's depressive episode may recur, in which case antidepressant medication may be reinstated at the same full therapeutic dosage as before.

Psychotherapy booster sessions may be used to augment continuation medication, following acute-phase response to a combined treatment program. The AHCPR (1993) guidelines suggest that patients who have a history of three or more depressive episodes are candidates for maintenance antidepressant treatment due to a high risk of episode recurrence in this population. In the management of medication issues, it is important that decisions regarding medication use are made collaboratively with the participation of the patient, his or her physician, and potentially other mental health professionals involved in the patient's care.

Common Pitfalls and Ethical Dilemmas

It is important to help the patient recognize not only the impact of treatment on the reduction of depressive symptomatology, but also evaluate its impact in terms of improved functioning and adaptive capacities. In cases where the patient has made significant progress, the termination phase can be an invaluable opportunity to highlight the gains a patient has made and to further set the stage for continued maintenance of gains and future progress. In some cases, however, termination may be more difficult, or may be postponed for individuals who remain significantly symptomatic, or who have shown little or no improvement during the course of therapy. In such cases, alternative treatment options, such as pharmacotherapy or referral to another therapist who subscribes to a different psychotherapy orientation, may be helpful.

Based on the American Psychological Association's *Ethical Principles and Code of Conduct* (APA 2002), psychologists are obligated to terminate therapy when it becomes clear that the patient no longer needs the service, is not likely to benefit from the service, or is being harmed in some way by continuing to be in therapy. In some cases, patients may simply not want to continue therapy, or therapists may find that they do not desire to continue working with the patient. For example, the therapist may feel endangered or threatened by the patient or may have private issues (e.g., grief) interfering with his or her ability to conduct effective therapy. In addition, there may be practical reasons why the therapist feels it is necessary to terminate therapy, such as the therapist's retirement or transferring to another job or career. Whenever possible, the patient and therapist should make an effort to collaboratively settle on an agreement to terminate therapy. In any case, however, where therapy termination occurs prematurely, ethical concerns may arise that need to be considered. For example, the APA guidelines specify that psychologists provide termination counseling and give the patient suggestions for alternative service providers or refer them back to the professional or agency that made the initial referral to them, as appropriate.

The issue of suicide in relation to termination of psychotherapy is outlined in considerable detail in another chapter (Chapter 20); however, we deemed it important to briefly touch on this issue in the context of depression. As outlined in the *DSM-IV*, the lifetime rates of suicide attempts for individuals suffering from major depressive disorder and bipolar disorder are considerably higher than rates for other Axis I disorders and the rate within the population as a whole (e.g., Chen & Dilsaver 1996). In addition, it has been estimated that up to 15 percent of individuals with severe MDD die by suicide (APA 2000), and that the co-occurrence of anxiety and depression increases the risk of suicide over the risk associated with depression alone (Bronisch & Wittchen 1994). Therefore, it is crucial for risk management that the therapist takes steps to intervene with a suicidal patient if they can reasonably anticipate the danger.

Given this risk of self-harm, clinicians need to conduct a thorough suicide risk assessment with all depressed patients, and this assessment should be ongoing for patients who exhibit chronic suicidal ideation or behaviors. At a minimum, suicide assessment should include questions about the nature and severity of past and current suicidal ideation, history of past attempts, evaluation of potential risk (e.g., hopelessness, impulsivity, substance abuse) and resilience factors (e.g., social support, family or religious affiliation), and more immediate suicide indicators (e.g., specific plan, intent, and lethality of means). If a patient is actively suicidal, it would be unethical to terminate psychotherapy at such a point, at least without an appropriate referral or other services first being put in place.

Future Research and Recommendations

As previously noted, very little research has been conducted to examine psychotherapy termination specifically with individuals who have depressive disorders. However, a number of treatment manuals based on cognitive and interpersonal theories of depression (e.g., Beck 1995; Weissman et al. 2000) do provide clinician-friendly discussions of the termination process along with useful suggestions for therapeutic techniques.

Because every patient will respond in unique ways to therapeutic interventions, it is essential that future investigations explore whether patient and therapist variables exist (e.g., interpersonal relatedness, attributional style, depression severity, motivation, satisfaction with treatment, therapeutic alliance) that influence patient reactions to psychotherapy, specifically with regard to the termination phase. For example, a recent study of unipolar depressed patients who received cognitive therapy suggested that patients with nonresponsive hopelessness had poorer outcomes at therapy termination (i.e., endorsement of more depressive symptoms) than individuals whose hopelessness was responsive to treatment in the first four sessions (Kuyken 2004). Therefore, effectively addressing hopelessness early in therapy may have important implications for patient functioning at the termination stage.

The majority of research on psychotherapy termination is conducted within populations of patients presenting with a variety of disorders (i.e., heterogeneous diagnoses) and with psychoanalytic/psychodynamic forms of therapy (e.g., Frank 1999; Quintar 2004; Roe et al. 2006). Few empirical articles have addressed the issue of psychotherapy termination specifically with individuals presenting with depressive disorders or those engaged in relatively short-term, goal-focused therapies such as CBT or IPT. Further research in these domains is warranted to extend our knowledge about specific issues that are relevant to treating and terminating therapy within these populations and treatments. Given that the treatments garnering the most empirical support in the treatment of depressive disorders tend to be time limited, some researchers and clinicians may feel that the termination phase has less of an impact on both patients and therapists than other treatment models. It is our hope that the preceding discussion demonstrates the critical role that termination plays in solidifying progress and maintaining patient gains following treatment.

Summary and Conclusions

Based on a review of extant psychotherapy termination literature and well-established treatments for depression, the following guidelines for termination with previously depressed patients are proposed:

1. Begin preparing the patient for termination from the first session of therapy.
2. Assign frequent homework assignments designed to help the patient develop and practice tools to become his or her own therapist.
3. Determine if the patient has successfully acquired the techniques taught during therapy.
4. Encourage the patient to view the strategies and techniques that he/she learns as lifelong tools that can be used to combat depression and other difficult and stressful situations.
5. Collaboratively evaluate whether the patient has experienced a reduction in symptoms and/or an increase in adaptive functioning.
6. Assess patient readiness for termination and expectations for maintenance of treatment gains and progress post-termination.
7. Acknowledge and validate the patient's reactions and feelings (both positive and negative) about terminating therapy and help him or her to respond to any cognitive distortions.

8. Take advantage of opportunities to reinforce the patient's progress and attribute treatment gains to the patient's efforts.

9. Encourage the patient to schedule personal or booster sessions following termination.

Each patient is unique. The therapist must carefully assess and evaluate each patient throughout therapy, in order to collaboratively work through the various stages of psychotherapy, including termination. It is particularly important that the therapist attends to patient change during the course of treatment, since the nature of such changes will assist in determining when to end therapy. In most clinical work with depressed patients, treatment continues until significant progress is made (e.g., a noticeable reduction in depressive symptoms, impairment, or attaining a state of remission). It is critical that the therapist monitors systematic information related to determining whether the patient has made progress or reached his or her goal. Ideally, the process of termination will be conducted with as much success and shared sense of accomplishment as the rest of the treatment process.

References

Agency for Health Care Policy and Research. (1993). *Depression in primary care: Volume 2. Treatment of major depression.* Rockville, Maryland: U.S. Department of Health and Human Services.

American Psychiatric Association. (2000). *Diagnostic and statistical manual* (4th ed. text rev.). Washington, DC: Author.

American Psychological Association. (2002). *Ethical principles of psychologists and code of conduct.* Retrieved April 28, 2006, from http://www.apa.org/ethics/code2002.pdf

Beck, A. T., Rush, A. J., Shaw, B. F., & Emery, G. (1979). *Cognitive therapy of depression.* New York: Guilford Press.

Beck, J. S. (1995). *Cognitive therapy: Basics and beyond.* New York: Guilford Press.

Beutler, L. E., Clarkin, J. E., & Bongar, B. (2000). *Guidelines for the systematic treatment of the depressed patient.* New York: Oxford University Press.

Bronisch, T., & Wittchen, H. U. (1994). Suicidal ideation and suicide attempts: Comorbidity with depression, anxiety disorders, and substance abuse disorder. *European Archives of Psychiatry and Clinical Neuroscience, 244,* 93–98.

Brown, T. A., Campbell, L. A., Lehman, C. L., Grisham, J. R., & Mancill, R. B. (2001). Current and lifetime comorbidity of the DSM-IV anxiety and mood disorders in a large clinical sample. *Journal of Abnormal Psychology, 110,* 585–599.

Burns, D. D. (1999). *The feeling good handbook*. New York: Plume.

Chambless, D. L., & Ollendick, T. H. (2001). Empirically supported psychological interventions: Controversies and evidence. *Annual Review of Psychology, 52*, 685–716.

Chen, Y. W., & Dilsaver, S. C. (1996). Lifetime rates of suicide attempts among subjects with bipolar and unipolar disorders relative to subjects with other axis I disorders. *Biological Psychiatry, 39*, 896–899.

Clarkin, J. F., & Levy, K. N. (2004). The influence of patient variables on psychotherapy. In M. Lambert (Ed.), *Bergin and Garfield's handbook of psychotherapy and behavior change* (5th ed.; pp. 194–226). New York: John Wiley.

Dobson, K. S. (Ed.). (2001). *Handbook of cognitive-behavioral therapies* (2nd ed.). New York: Guilford Press.

Frank, G. (1999). Termination revisited. *Psychoanalytic Psychology, 16*, 119–129.

Gotlib, I. H., & Hammen, C. L. (Eds.) (2002). *Handbook of depression*. New York: Guilford Press.

Greenberger, D., & Padesky, C. A. (1995). *Mind over mood: Change how you feel by changing the way you think*. New York: Guilford Press.

Hollon, S. D., Stewart, M. O., & Strunk, D. (2006). Enduring effects for cognitive behaviour therapy in the treatment of depression and anxiety. *Annual Review of Psychology, 57*, 285–315.

Howard, K. I., Moras, K., Brill, P. L., Zoran, M., & Lutz, W. (1996). Evaluation of psychotherapy: Efficacy, effectiveness, and patient progress. *American Psychologist, 51*, 1059–1064.

Hunsley, J., Aubry, T. D., Verstervelt, C. M., & Vito, D. (1999). Comparing therapist and patient perspectives on reasons for psychotherapy termination. *Psychotherapy, 36*, 380–388.

Judd, L. L. (1997). The clinical course of unipolar major depressive disorders. *Archives of General Psychiatry, 54*, 989–991.

Keller, M. B., & Boland, R. J. (1998). Implications of failing to achieve successful long-term maintenance treatment of recurrent unipolar major depression. *Biological Psychiatry, 44*, 348–360.

Kessler, R. C., McGonagle, K. A., Zhao, S., Nelson, C. B., Hughes, M., Eshleman, S., et al. (1994). Lifetime and 12-month prevalence of DSM-III-R psychiatric disorders in the United States: Results from the National Comorbidity Survey. *Archives of General Psychiatry, 51*, 8–19.

Kuyken, W. (2004). Cognitive therapy outcome: the effects of hopelessness in a naturalistic outcome study. *Behaviour Research and Therapy, 42*, 631–646.

Martell, C. R., Addis, M. E., & Jacobson, N. S. (2001). *Depression in context: Strategies for guided action*. New York: W.W. Norton.

McQuaid, J. R., & Carmona, P. E. (2004). *Peaceful mind: Using mindfulness and cognitive behavioral psychology to overcome depression*. Oakland, CA: New Harbinger Publications.

Mineka, S., Watson, D., & Clark, L. A. (1998). Comorbidity of anxiety and unipolar mood disorders. *Annual Review of Psychology, 49*, 377–412.

O'Donohue, W., Cummings, N., & Cummings, J. (2006). The art and science of psychotherapy. In W. O'Donohue, N. Cummings, & J. Cummings, *Clinical strategies for becoming a master psychotherapist* (pp. 1–11). Amsterdam: Academic Press.

Paykel, E. S., Scott, J., Cornwall, P. L., Abbot, R., Crane, C., Pope, M., & Johnson, A. L. (2005). Duration of relapse prevention after cognitive therapy in residual depression: Follow-up of controlled trial. *Psychological Medicine, 35,* 59–68.

Persons, J. B., & Davidson, J. (2001). Cognitive-behavioral case formulation. In K. S. Dobson (Ed.), *Handbook of cognitive-behavioral therapies* (pp. 86–110). New York: Guilford Press.

Quintar, B. (2004). Termination phase. *Journal of Psychotherapy in Independent Practice, 2,* 43–60.

Regier, D. A., Myers, J. K., Kramer, M., Robins, L. N., Blazer, D. G., Hough, R. L., et al. (1984). The NIMH Epidemiologic Catchment Area program. *Archives of General Psychiatry, 50,* 85–94.

Roe, D., Dekel, R., Harel, G., Fennig, S., & Fennig, S. (2006). Patients' feelings during termination of psychodynamically oriented psychotherapy. *Bulletin of the Menninger Clinic, 70,* 68–81.

Segal, Z. V., Williams, J. M. G., & Teasdale, J. D. (2002). *Mindfulness-based cognitive therapy for depression: A new approach to preventing relapse.* New York: Guilford Press.

Sperry, L., Brill, P. L., Howard, K. I., & Grissom, G. R. (1996). *Treatment outcomes in psychotherapy and psychiatric interventions.* New York: Brunner/Mazel.

Üstün, T. D. (2001). The worldwide burden of depression in the 21st century. In M. M. Weissman (Ed.), *Treatment of depression: Bridging the 21st century* (pp. 35–45). Washington, DC: American Psychiatric Association Press.

Todd, D. M., Deane, F. P., & Bragdon, R. A. (2003). Patient and therapist reasons for termination: A conceptualization and preliminary validation. *Journal of Clinical Psychology, 59,* 133–147.

Weissman, M. M., Markowitz, M. D., & Klerman, G. L. (2000). *Comprehensive guide to interpersonal psychotherapy.* New York: Basic Books.

16

TERMINATION WITH PATIENTS WITH ANXIETY DISORDERS

HOLLY HAZLETT-STEVENS

Many empirically supported psychological treatments have been developed for the anxiety disorders over the past few decades. Clinicians working in this area often enjoy successful treatment outcomes with a wide spectrum of anxiety patients. Most of these therapy protocols are behavioral or cognitive-behavioral in theoretical orientation. Although there is much variation, many follow a similar format. After initial assessment, treatment typically begins with psychoeducation contrasting normal anxiety and fear with the patient's presenting anxiety symptoms and an explanation of leading cognitive-behavioral models. Patients may then learn anxiety management techniques, such as progressive relaxation or breathing retraining, to develop necessary coping skills. Cognitive restructuring strategies are often presented to address patients' misperceptions of threat. Finally, an exposure component is introduced in which patients gradually confront feared stimuli, images, or situations according to a hierarchy. Exposure can be conducted in a self-directed format between sessions or guided by the therapist during session time.

These cognitive-behavioral therapies lend themselves to the managed care setting in a number of ways. Their structured and time-limited format allows clinicians to follow a set of procedures that will likely lead to symptom reduction within weeks. Although most protocols were originally delivered over twelve to sixteen sessions, many have been further abbreviated. Effective brief treatments for panic disorder require as few as four sessions, and single-session exposure treatment is often effective with specific phobias (see Hazlett-Stevens & Craske 2002 for a review).

Another common feature of cognitive-behavioral therapy (CBT) is the use of homework assignments to promote practice of new skills and therapeutic strategies between sessions. Over the course of therapy, patients become increasingly more independent with the eventual goal of acting as their own therapist.

The therapeutic relationship seen in successful cognitive-behavioral treatment of anxiety disorders is often quite collaborative in nature. Sessions largely focus on anxiety-related content rather than interpersonal problems or patient perceptions of the therapist. As a result, the primary task of termination involves relapse prevention strategies. Patients are prepared for eventual therapy termination with the development of an action plan to follow in the event of residual or returning anxiety symptoms. According to this approach, patients have learned effective responses to relevant anxiety-related cues and have adopted behavior changes that promote fear reduction. A relapse prevention plan specifies ahead of time how the client will maintain therapy gains, as continued practice of new behaviors and faithful implementation of therapeutic strategies as new situations arise are both crucial. Ideally, this plan is the product of a collaborative effort between therapist and patient in which the patient assumes an active role.

This chapter presents and discusses the main issues surrounding therapy termination with anxiety disorder patients, such as when to initiate the termination process and how to address common problems and pitfalls. In addition, the typical course of termination and specific strategies to maximize therapy outcomes will be described. Finally, empirical evidence supporting the use of these strategies is briefly reviewed and directions for future research are recommended.

When to Consider Termination

Therapists must decide when to initiate therapy termination under a variety of circumstances. In many cases, termination begins once CBT techniques have proven successful and the patient no longer needs continued services. However, premature termination might be required when practical constraints limit access to treatment sessions. Therapy should also be terminated when a patient is not benefiting from treatment and the therapist determines that the patient is not likely to benefit from further intervention.

Therapy Goals Achieved

Under ideal circumstances, the therapist proposes termination after the patient has demonstrated acquisition of newly learned therapy skills. Before termination is initiated, the patient has successfully applied coping skills across a number of anxiety-provoking situations and experienced significant fear reduction following self-directed exposure to many of their fear hierarchy items. As a result, the patient reports clinically significant symptom improvement and an absence of functional impairment. Therapy outcome research has shown that such therapy gains are often achieved by the end of twelve- to sixteen-session protocols (see Craske 1999 for a review). However, less severe patients may reach this point even earlier, whereas others may show slower rates of improvement and benefit from further treatment sessions. The vast majority of investigations establishing empirical support for these treatments provided a predetermined number of sessions to each participant regardless of individual treatment response. Therefore, it is unclear exactly when a therapist can expect to see sufficient improvement in a patient with a given diagnosis.

Some researchers have begun to address this question. Following their "hybrid efficacy-effectiveness" investigation of brief CBT for panic disorder, Craske and colleagues examined the effects of the number of CBT sessions, the number of follow-up booster phone calls, and the number of cognitive-behavioral coping and exposure components on outcome variables (Craske et al. 2006). As expected, primary care patients who completed more of the six CBT sessions and six follow-up booster phone calls offered to them had better outcomes. Analyses of session content revealed that the number of occasions coping strategies were incorporated was associated with greater anxiety sensitivity. The authors suggested that this unfavorable outcome may have resulted from reduced session time available for the exposure component introduced in the fourth session. While results from the original investigation suggested that termination might be appropriate as early as the sixth session in the treatment of panic disorder (Roy-Byrne et al. 2005), results from the Craske et al. follow-up study further suggested that such termination would optimally occur after exposure elements have been introduced. Termination after presentation of coping strategies only (i.e., breathing retraining, cognitive restructuring) might not be beneficial.

Practical Barriers to Treatment Access

In many cases, termination is necessary before significant clinical improvement can be realized. Financial concerns, health insurance plan limits, or time constraints may prohibit the optimal number of sessions for a given patient. When such practical barriers lead to premature termination, it becomes even more crucial for the therapist to prepare the patient for future setbacks. Providing patients with additional cost-effective resources may promote continued acquisition of needed skills and therapeutic progress after the final therapy session. Some empirical evidence for this alternative approach to treatment exists. Lindren et al. (1994) found an eight-week self-help bibliotherapy treatment for panic disorder to be as effective as a similar treatment consisting of eight group therapy sessions. This self-administered therapy was also comparable to an eight-week individual CBT package (Gould, Clum, & Shaprio 1993). Newer self-help treatments are becoming available on the Internet. For example, Carlbring et al. (2006) provided a nine-week, Internet-based self-help program for social phobia. Participants were assessed with a diagnostic interview over the phone, and a therapist provided weekly feedback via e-mail. Significant clinical improvements were found on a variety of measures, and these gains were maintained at six-month follow-up. While purely self-help treatments for panic may have limited clinical effectiveness (Febbraro et al. 1999), directing patients to such self-administered programs when therapy sessions end abruptly can be crucial for continued symptom improvement.

Maximizing remaining therapy time with the development of a concrete plan for self-directed exposure may also prove beneficial. Ghosh and Marks (1987) reduced their exposure treatment for agoraphobia to as few as three sessions. Exposure practice was conducted in a self-administered format outside of therapy sessions. Substantial improvements on measures of agoraphobic avoidance were found six months later. However, purely self-administered exposure treatments are not as effective as therapist-directed exposure treatment for the specific phobias (Öst, Salkovskis, & Hellström 1991; Hellström & Öst 1995). Fortunately, the therapist-directed exposure treatment developed by Öst and colleagues can be delivered within a three-hour single session.

Poor Treatment Response

Termination should be considered in one final scenario: when the patient is not benefiting from treatment. The American Psychological Association ethical standard for terminating therapy (APA 2002) states that:

> Psychologists terminate therapy when it becomes reasonably clear that the client/patient no longer needs the service, is not likely to benefit, or is being harmed by continued service. (Standard 10.10a)

When a patient does not appear to be progressing as hoped, the clinician often struggles with determining if the patient is unlikely to benefit (and therefore therapy should be terminated) or if continued therapy can overcome obstacles with additional intervention strategies.

Indeed, not all anxiety disorder patients respond to CBT. In one psychotherapy outcome trial with panic disordered participants, 87 percent were panic free by the end of treatment (Wade, Treat, & Stuart 1998). While impressive, this figure also reflects that 13 percent of patients did not respond to the authors' CBT protocol. An even greater number of patients might fail to reach more stringent markers of therapy success. Clark et al. (1994) found that 30 percent of their panic disordered patient sample did not meet criteria for high end-state functioning following treatment. Generalized anxiety disorder (GAD) appears to be the anxiety disorder least responsive to CBT. Psychotherapy outcome research has consistently shown that approximately 50 percent of GAD patients exhibit high end-state functioning following CBT (Borkovec & Whisman 1996), although a recent CBT trial found that 77 percent of GAD patients no longer met diagnostic criteria (DSM-IV; American Psychiatric Association, 1994) after treatment (Ladouceur et al. 2000).

Poor cognitive-behavioral treatment response sometimes reflects underlying personality disorder pathology. Although results from this empirical literature are somewhat mixed, most studies have found that comorbid personality disorder diagnosis is associated with slower treatment response and poorer therapy outcome (see Mennin & Heimberg 2000 for a review). Little is known about the impact of other serious comorbid conditions such as psychosis, mania, suicidality, dementia, and substance abuse, because patients with these clinical problems were typically excluded from anxiety disorder psychotherapy research trials. In many of these cases, the clinician determines that CBT for anxiety is not appropriate and refers the patient to services targeting the comorbid clinical condition(s).

On the other hand, some patients may benefit from additional intervention strategies before their therapist decides to terminate CBT targeting anxiety disorder symptoms. A number of specific approaches to improve therapy outcomes have been proposed when treating panic disorder (McCabe & Antony 2005), social anxiety disorder (Ledley & Heimberg 2005), generalized anxiety disorder (Waters & Craske 2005), obsessive-compulsive disorder (Franklin, Riggs, & Pai 2005), and posttraumatic stress disorder (Feeny & Foa 2005). Common strategies include ensuring that the patient understands and buys into the underlying treatment rationale, problem-solving homework compliance difficulties, and assessment of subtle safety behaviors that could undermine exposure exercises. According to McCabe and Antony, panic patients ambivalent about actively engaging in CBT procedures might benefit from motivational interviewing techniques (Miller & Rollnick 2002). Finally, including the patient's significant other in therapy might enhance patient motivation and participation in therapy procedures. Inclusion of the significant other may also prevent the interpersonal discord that sometimes results when a patient adopts newly learned therapeutic techniques and behavioral changes (Milton & Hafner 1979). Spouse-assisted approaches are widely used in the treatment of panic disorder (Brown & Barlow 1992) and may be beneficial to patients with other anxiety disorders as well (e.g., Grunes, Neziroglu, & McKay 2001; Ritter & Hazlett-Stevens in press).

In cases of poor treatment response, therapists are faced with the difficult decision of whether or not to terminate CBT for the patient's anxiety disorder. If the therapist determines that factors outside the scope of the current therapy are responsible, termination with referral to alternative appropriate clinical services might be the best choice. Examples include most cases of current substance abuse, psychosis, mania, dementia, suicidal ideation, and severe personality pathology. Other obstacles might be overcome within the context of CBT for anxiety disorders. Problems such as low patient motivation and poor homework compliance should be addressed directly before termination is initiated.

The Process of Termination

As stated above, the primary goal of therapy termination with anxiety disorder patients is the implementation of relapse prevention strategies. Explicit procedures first introduced by Öst (1989) were designed to ensure maintenance of treatment gains and promote further improvement after termination. In that seminal article, Öst argued that successful behavioral treatments were less impressive after considering high rates of relapse and further treatment at follow-up. Low rates of continued improvement after termination were also found. Öst described his maintenance program for phobia, which could be slightly modified for the treatment of panic disorder, generalized anxiety disorder, and obsessive-compulsive disorder. In the original program, the concept of relapse prevention was introduced in the last session of therapy. This termination session was devoted to reviewing the patient's progress in treatment as well as the original therapy rationale, identifying upcoming high-risk situations in which return of symptoms would be likely, and developing a written relapse prevention plan. Thus, therapy was terminated only after each patient agreed to a concrete plan of continued practice. In addition, all patients were given step-by-step instructions to follow in the event of returning or residual anxiety. Finally, brief telephone contacts spread over the next six months were included to help patients adhere to the relapse prevention plan. Many of the specific procedures outlined by Öst can be found in empirically supported therapy protocols today.

Newer cognitive-behavioral therapies for anxiety disorders have since integrated Öst's (1989) ideas and procedures into the final sessions of therapy. Rather than focus on termination issues only at the final session, relapse prevention concepts are raised and discussed throughout the final few sessions before termination occurs. Thus, termination is considered a process that unfolds near the end of treatment. The termination process typically begins with discussion of the patient's progress and a joint decision about exactly how many more sessions are needed. Next, a rationale for the relapse prevention plan is introduced. Patients are reminded that anxiety symptoms do not simply disappear forever and that temporary increases in anxiety are likely, particularly in times of stress. The patient and therapist then identify possible situations in which a return of symptoms will be likely. They also work together to create a list of such potential problem scenarios. Fourth, specific ways in which patients can practice and apply therapeutic skills in the event of a setback are outlined. This fourth step leads to the development of a written, concrete relapse prevention plan for the patient to follow after the final therapy session. Relapse prevention plans typically include ongoing practice of coping skills and exposure exercises to promote continued improvement, as well as specific steps to follow in the event of returning symptoms and setbacks. Often additional booster sessions or follow-up phone calls with the therapist are included in relapse prevention plans.

Variations of this termination procedure can be found in leading empirically supported cognitive-behavioral therapies for anxiety disorders. For example, Craske and Barlow (2001) incorporated several relapse prevention strategies into the final three sessions of their panic control treatment, a widely used, empirically supported CBT protocol for the treatment of panic disorder with or without agoraphobia. In one case, the final three sessions were scheduled biweekly to enhance generalization of therapy techniques to the patient's real-life anxiety situations. Discussion of temporary setbacks occurred when the patient reported difficulty with an in vivo exposure task. Interoceptive exposure exercises from previous sessions were incorporated into new in vivo exposure exercises with the instruction that the patient should induce feared bodily sensations any time concern about an uncomfortable sensation was noticed. These relapse prevention principles were systematically reviewed at the final session. The patient terminated therapy with a written plan detailing how to apply coping skills to high-risk situations in the future and which in vivo exposure exercises to continue over the next few months.

In a case description of their empirically supported cognitive-behavioral group therapy for social anxiety disorder, Turk, Heimberg, and Hope (2001) utilized monthly maintenance sessions after an acute treatment phase. These infrequent booster sessions guided the patient through additional self-directed exposure exercises and behavioral experiments to test automatic thoughts. These maintenance sessions effectively targeted residual symptoms that persisted after the acute phase of treatment. Similar relapse prevention procedures prior to termination can also be found in empirically supported CBT protocols for GAD (Borkovec et al. 2002), OCD (obsessive-compulsive disorder, Foa & Franklin 2001), PTSD (post-traumatic stress disorder, Feeny & Foa 2005), and specific phobia (Craske, Antony, & Barlow 1997).

Specific Termination Techniques

This section reviews the main components leading up to successful termination with anxiety disorder patients. Termination typically begins with a review of patient progress, discussion of a relapse prevention rationale, and cognitive restructuring of future anxiety situations. High-risk situations are then identified and incorporated into a concrete written relapse prevention plan for the patient to follow after termination. Follow-up booster sessions or phone contacts often facilitate this transition.

Psychoeducation About Relapse Prevention

Seasoned cognitive-behavioral therapists skillfully provide patients with information about the nature of fear and anxiety as well as theoretical models of anxiety disorders. At the outset of treatment, it is imperative that the patient understands how his or her symptoms have developed, how this experience differs from normal human anxiety, and how treatment will address the cognitive and behavioral factors maintaining the disorder. Psychoeducation is best delivered during an interactive conversation between the therapist and patient about the patient's own idiosyncratic situation and symptoms. This approach contrasts sharply with a didactic exchange in which the therapist "talks at" the patient, stopping only on occasion to check for questions.

This interactive exchange between therapist and patient is even more critical when the therapist presents a relapse prevention rationale for therapy termination. Patients should be encouraged to articulate the possible advantages of planning for future setbacks and continued practice instead of the therapist trying to "sell" his or her relapse prevention agenda. The more collaborative this effort, the more likely patients will commit to the final relapse prevention plan and follow through after termination occurs. An active patient contribution can also enhance self-efficacy, empowering the patient to generate thoughtful relapse prevention goals and flexibly adjust the plan as needed. Although scientific evidence on this point is lacking, many clinical experts in the anxiety disorder treatment literature emphasize this collaborative approach to psychoeducation (e.g., Öst 1989; McCabe & Antony 2005).

When presenting patients with the relapse prevention rationale, a few key points should be covered. First, the therapist and patient should conduct a careful review of the patient's progress. The patient can be asked to recall markers of severity, such as activities he or she was unable to perform at the beginning of treatment. The patient should also be encouraged to articulate specific cognitive and behavioral changes implemented over the course of treatment that led to observed reductions in fear and avoidance. Second, the therapist invites the patient to explain the original therapy rationale in his or her own words as the therapist adds and highlights key points. This review of the original psychoeducation material first presented at the beginning of treatment can be quite enlightening to the patient when revisited at termination. Third, the therapist presents a rationale for continued practice of acquired skills. Similar to any other skill, the patient's newly learned anxiety management skills will likely strengthen and become more automatic with practice. Conversely, these skills will also weaken and become more difficult to implement during times of high anxiety if practice is neglected. Öst (1989) described a useful analogy when making this point. His patients were reminded of the skill involved when learning to drive a car. Although a person is able to drive upon receiving a driver's license, he or she needs to drive frequently in a number of traffic situations to refine these skills and become a good driver. If the person instead rarely drives a car, the initial skill will gradually deteriorate over time and that person will most likely experience difficulty driving effectively in challenging driving situations thereafter.

Cognitive Restructuring of Future Setbacks

Many anxiety disorder patients are reluctant to feel anxiety, even in situations where an anxious response would be considered normal. Indeed, each anxiety disorder (except specific phobia) is associated with elevated *anxiety sensitivity*, a tendency to fear the bodily sensations associated with anxiety (Taylor, Koch, & McNally 1992). Therefore, it is important for the therapist to remind the patient that anxiety is often a part of normal human existence. This can prevent catastrophic interpretations of the mild anxiety symptoms that are likely to occur after therapy termination. The therapist and patient can identify how a "black-and-white" thinking approach would lead the patient to interpret future anxiety as evidence that all therapy gains have been lost. Alternative interpretations of future anxiety sensations can then be generated, and the patient can identify how he or she plans to incorporate a more balanced perspective when anxiety sensations are encountered in the future. In their relapse prevention program for OCD, Hiss, Foa, and Kozak (1994) taught patients to identify cognitive distortions using an A (antecedent) B (belief) C (consequences) mnemonic. Patients then learned to apply this approach to returning obsessive and compulsive symptoms with the goal of generating more realistic beliefs about future anxiety symptoms.

Identification of Vulnerability Factors and High-Risk Situations

Once patients understand and accept the relapse prevention rationale, it can be fruitful for them to brainstorm upcoming situations or possible scenarios in which a return of symptoms would be likely. Times of general stress, such as holidays, a busy time at work, or conflict with family members, might make patients vulnerable to a temporary setback (Öst 1989). McCabe and Antony (2005) also suggested that many lifestyle factors (e.g., poor diet, lack of exercise, poor sleep hygiene, overcommitment to work projects) can increase patients' vulnerability to setbacks and relapse. In addition to high-risk situations in which the patient would expect a strong anxiety response, Waters and Craske (2005) recommended that GAD patients identify early warning signs. Subtle changes, such as increased worry about a particular topic or mild somatic symptoms, can be viewed as opportunities to implement and practice coping strategies.

Creating a Written Relapse Prevention Plan

Before termination occurs, it is crucial that the patient have a clear action plan to follow after the final therapy session. This written plan should contain specific steps to maintain and improve upon therapy gains. The patient should write down exactly which therapy skills will be practiced and how often. If indicated, additional self-directed exposure exercises should be listed with a schedule outlining when each will occur. The patient is also encouraged to engage in other behaviors believed to protect against future setbacks, such as good sleep hygiene and regular exercise. In addition to these planned behaviors, the patient should be encouraged to create and take advantage of any unplanned opportunities to practice new behaviors. For example, socially anxious patients can be encouraged to seize upon opportunities that naturally present themselves in day-to-day life, such as inviting a coworker out to lunch or coffee (Ledley & Heimberg 2005). The final component of the relapse prevention plan includes specific instructions the patient can follow when a setback occurs or symptoms return. Öst (1989) provided patients with standardized written instructions including steps such as remembering that this is only a temporary difficulty and applying a coping skill. Ledley and Heimberg described how the therapist and patient can generate these instructions together using a "quiz" approach. For example, a socially anxious patient could be asked how they would handle a personally relevant hypothetical social situation. Of course, contacting the therapist for refresher or booster sessions is always an option when setbacks occur.

Booster Sessions and Follow-up Phone Calls

After regularly scheduled therapy sessions end, patients might benefit from less frequent follow-up contact. During these in-person or phone contacts, the therapist can help problem solve any issues adhering to the relapse prevention plan and help the patient adjust the plan as needed. Additional encouragement and support during times of stress or symptom setbacks can be provided. These contacts can be scheduled in advance as part of the relapse prevention plan or the patient can agree to contact the therapist as part of their planned response to a setback. As mentioned above, Craske et al. (2006) provided some preliminary evidence supporting the use of follow-up contacts. After providing panic patients with up to six CBT sessions over the first three months and up to six follow-up booster phone calls over the next nine months (Roy-Byrne et al. 2005), Craske et al. examined treatment-related predictors of outcome. As expected, the number of CBT sessions predicted lower anxiety sensitivity three and twelve months after treatment. In addition, the number of follow-up booster phone calls predicted not only lower anxiety sensitivity, but also less phobic avoidance and less depression at the twelve-month follow-up assessment.

Common Problems and Pitfalls

Often when a therapist proposes termination, the patient expresses fear of losing therapy gains. Patients might feel dependent upon the therapist or attribute their progress only to the therapist, overlooking the contribution of their own behavior change. Such patient concerns can be transformed into motivation for developing and adhering to a detailed relapse prevention plan. The therapist might suggest a booster session schedule in which the interval between sessions becomes longer and longer over time, allowing for a gradual withdrawal from regular therapy sessions. In addition, automatic thoughts suggesting that the patient is not capable of continued progress after termination can be subjected to cognitive restructuring.

As mentioned above, sometimes termination occurs prematurely due to practical constraints. In this case, the therapist should offer the patient as many cost-effective alternatives to therapy sessions as possible. For some patients, self-help and bibliotherapy materials might be enough for the patient to finish treatment in a self-administered fashion. Effectiveness research for anxiety self-help treatment is promising, although many studies lack rigorous methodology (Bower,

Richards, & Lovell 2001). If the therapist learns that termination will occur before the final session, the remaining therapy session(s) can be spent developing a concrete plan for self-directed exposure and continued practice of coping skills.

Empirical Evidence for This Termination Approach

Öst (1989) provided initial indirect empirical support for these relapse prevention strategies prior to termination. Follow-up results from three outcome investigations in which patients with agoraphobia, panic disorder, and blood phobia were administered a final relapse prevention session before termination were compared to follow-up data from other outcome investigations without such termination procedures. Öst found that treatments including a final relapse prevention session led to sustained or enhanced clinical improvement at follow-up more often than reported in previous studies. However, other differences between the two sets of research investigations prevented Öst from making direct comparisons.

Subsequent indirect empirical support for these termination procedures is found in the numerous psychotherapy outcome investigations of CBT for anxiety disorders (see Craske 1999 for a review). As mentioned above, variations on Öst's (1989) termination techniques have been incorporated into several therapy protocols with demonstrated effectiveness, many of which have exhibited long-term improvement at follow-up. However, only a few studies have examined whether such relapse prevention procedures at termination independently contributed to CBT effectiveness at follow-up. Researchers have just begun to evaluate the direct effects of such relapse prevention treatment components at termination.

A couple of studies have investigated the effectiveness of relapse management and prevention programs for OCD. In an uncontrolled preliminary trial, Espie (1986) provided a ten-week relapse management program to a group of five patients. All patients were successfully treated for OCD with behavior therapy but had subsequently relapsed. Initial relapse management group sessions included review of behavior therapy principles and skills. Later sessions introduced anti-relapse components, such as spouse involvement, generation of

fear hierarchies for exposure to new target situations, and identification of early signs of returning obsessive and compulsive habits. All
five patients reported reductions in obsessions and behavioral rituals,
and these gains were maintained at one-year follow-up. These results
suggested that relapse could have been prevented if this material had
been presented before the termination of original therapy. However,
this conclusion is speculative at best because the anti-relapse program
was administered only after each patient suffered a relapse. Another
methodological limitation of this investigation was the lack of a control group. Thus, it is possible that these five patients would have experienced another period of remission without any further intervention.

Hiss, Foa, and Kozak (1994) addressed these limitations in their
investigation of a relapse prevention treatment component for OCD.
After three weeks of intensive exposure with ritual prevention, patients
were randomly assigned to receive either four additional ninety-minute
relapse prevention sessions or four ninety-minute sessions of a control treatment that appeared credible to patients. During the relapse
prevention sessions, patients were provided a standard rationale for
relapse prevention strategies and asked to identify upcoming situations
and stressors that might precipitate a setback. Significant others were
included in one of the sessions to address potential maladaptive interpersonal interactions. Cognitive restructuring techniques were also
introduced to combat misguided beliefs about returning obsessions and
compulsions. Finally, patients received nine brief telephone follow-up
contacts over the subsequent twelve weeks. At the six-month follow-up
assessment, only patients in the control group had experienced some
return of symptoms. Thus, this investigation provided direct empirical
support for inclusion of relapse prevention procedures prior to therapy
termination with OCD patients. Unfortunately, no additional outcome
data were collected after the initial six-month follow-up period. Therefore, the effectiveness of this relapse prevention program at longer
intervals following termination is not known.

Specific relapse prevention termination procedures have proven
beneficial in the treatment of panic attacks as well. Following a brief
bibliotherapy intervention, Wright et al. (2000) randomly assigned
panic patients to a self-administered bibliotherapy relapse prevention
program or to a wait-list control condition. Patients assigned to the

relapse prevention program were given a detailed instruction manual and received brief phone calls from a therapist to boost compliance and offer assistance with problematic panic-related situations. At six-month follow-up, clinically significant improvements on a variety of measures were found for the relapse prevention group; these rates of improvement were greater than seen in the wait-list control group. Results not only supported the use of relapse prevention strategies for panic disorder, they also suggested that such relapse prevention interventions can be implemented without therapy sessions. Although Wright et al. emphasized the importance of the intermittent phone calls, each contact was limited to fifteen minutes in duration. Thus, providing patients with bibliotherapy prior to termination might be an effective option when therapists are faced with a limited number of therapy sessions. However, the effectiveness of this intervention was not measured after the six-month follow-up period, and not all participants met *DSM-IV* diagnostic criteria for panic disorder prior to treatment.

Future Research Directions

Controlled trials comparing CBT without termination procedures to current CBT protocols including these procedures are clearly needed. The clinical effectiveness of relapse prevention termination procedures can be determined only after such dismantling design research is conducted. However, data addressing a number of other empirical questions may inform the process of termination. For example, at what point in therapy can a therapist begin the termination process without compromising therapy success? Is a certain number of sessions or a certain amount of material clinically indicated for a given anxiety disorder before termination should be attempted? Should relapse prevention always occur before termination, or are some relapse prevention procedures best administered after the acute therapy phase has ended?

Summary and Conclusion

Effective CBT protocols are available to treat each of the anxiety disorders. As these treatments have developed, specific relapse prevention procedures have been incorporated at termination to maximize therapy gains. Termination may be necessary when practical barriers to treatment arise or when the patient has not responded to treatment. In many cases, the therapist proposes termination once the patient has made sufficient therapy progress. Specific relapse prevention procedures covered before the final therapy session include educating the patient about relapse prevention, restructuring catastrophic beliefs about future anxiety symptoms, identifying vulnerable and high-risk situations, and development of a written relapse prevention plan. Booster sessions or follow-up phone calls after termination have also proven beneficial. Although most of the empirical support for this termination approach is indirect, a couple of studies have shown that addition of these relapse prevention procedures augment therapy outcomes. Future investigations should examine the effectiveness of these procedures by isolating them in research designs. Research addressing other questions about the process of termination is sorely needed.

References

American Psychiatric Association. (1994). *Diagnostic and statistical manual of mental disorders* (4th ed.). Washington, DC.

American Psychological Association (2002). Ethical principles of psychologists and code of conduct. *American Psychologist, 57,* 1060–1073.

Borkovec, T. D., Newman, M. G., Pincus, A. L., & Lytle, R. (2002). A component analysis of cognitive-behavioral therapy for generalized anxiety disorder and the role of interpersonal problems. *Journal of Consulting and Clinical Psychology, 70,* 288–298.

Borkovec, T. D., & Whisman, M. A. (1996). Psychosocial treatment for generalized anxiety disorder. In M. R. Mavissakalian & R. F. Prien (Eds.), *Long-term treatments of anxiety disorders* (pp. 171–199). Washington, DC: American Psychiatric Association Press.

Bower, P., Richards, D., & Lovell, K. (2001). The clinical and cost-effectiveness of self-help treatments for anxiety and depressive disorders in primary care: A systematic review. *British Journal of General Practice, 51,* 838–845.

Brown, T. A., & Barlow, D. H. (1992). Panic disorder and panic disorder with agoraphobia. In P. H. Wilson (Ed.), *Principles and practice of relapse prevention* (pp. 191–212). New York: Guilford Press.

Carlbring, P., Furmark, T., Steczko, J., Ekselius, L., & Andersson, G. (2006). An open study of Internet-based bibliotherapy with minimal therapist contact via email for social phobia. *Clinical Psychologist, 10,* 30–38.

Clark, D. M., Salkovskis, P. M., Hackmann, A., Middleton, H., Anastasiades, P., & Gelder, M. (1994). A comparison of cognitive therapy, applied relaxation and imipramine in the treatment of panic disorder. *British Journal of Psychiatry, 164,* 759–769.

Craske, M. G. (1999). *Anxiety disorders: Psychological approaches to theory and treatment.* Boulder, CO: Westview Press.

Craske, M. G., Antony, M. M., & Barlow, D. H. (1997). *Mastery of your specific phobia: Therapist guide.* New York: Graywind.

Craske, M. G., & Barlow, D. H. (2001). Panic disorder and agoraphobia. In D. H. Barlow (Ed.), *Clinical handbook of psychological disorders* (3rd ed; pp. 1–59). New York: Guilford Press.

Craske, M. G., Roy-Byrne, P., Stein, M. B., Sullivan, G., Hazlett-Stevens, H., Bystritsky, A., & Sherbourne, C. (2006). CBT intensity and outcome for panic disorder in a primary care setting. *Behavior Therapy, 37,* 112–119.

Espie, C. A. (1986). The group treatment of obsessive-compulsive ritualisers: Behavioural management of identified patterns of relapse. *Behavioural Psychotherapy, 14,* 21–33.

Febbraro, G. A. R., Clum, G. A., Roodman, A. A., & Wright, J. H. (1999). The limits of bibliotherapy: A study of the differential effectiveness of self-administered interventions in individuals with panic attacks. *Behavior Therapy, 30,* 209–222.

Feeny, N. C., & Foa, E. B. (2005). Posttraumatic stress disorder. In M. M. Antony, D. R. Ledley, & R. G. Heimberg (Eds.), *Improving outcomes and preventing relapse in cognitive-behavioral therapy* (pp. 174–203). New York: Guilford Press.

Foa, E. B., & Franklin, M. E. (2001). Obsessive compulsive disorder. In D. H. Barlow (Ed.), *Clinical handbook of psychological disorders* (3rd ed.; pp. 209–263) New York: Guilford Press.

Franklin, M. E., Riggs, D. S., & Pai, A. (2005). Obsessive-compulsive disorder. In M. M. Antony, D. R. Ledley, & R. G. Heimberg (Eds.), *Improving outcomes and preventing relapse in cognitive-behavioral therapy* (pp. 128–173). New York: Guilford Press.

Ghosh, A., & Marks, I. M. (1987). Self-treatment of agoraphobia by exposure. *Behavior Therapy, 18,* 3–16.

Gould, R. A., Clum, G. A., & Shapiro, D. (1993). The use of bibliotherapy in the treatment of panic: A preliminary investigation. *Behavior Therapy, 24,* 241–252.

Grunes, M. S., Neziroglu, F., & McKay, D. (2001). Family involvement in the behavioral treatment of obsessive-compulsive disorder: A preliminary investigation. *Behavior Therapy, 32,* 803–820.

Hazlett-Stevens, H., & Craske, M. G. (2002). Brief cognitive-behavioral therapy: Definition and scientific foundations. In F. W. Bond & W. Dryden (Eds.), *Handbook of brief cognitive behaviour therapy.* New York: Wiley.

Hellström, K., & Öst, L-G. (1995). One-session therapist directed exposure vs two forms of manual directed self-exposure in the treatment of spider phobia. *Behaviour Research and Therapy, 33,* 959–965.

Hiss, H., Foa, E. B., & Kozak, M. J. (1994). Relapse prevention program for treatment of obsessive-compulsive disorder. *Journal of Consulting and Clinical Psychology, 62,* 801–808.

Ladouceur, R., Dugas, M. J., Freeston, M. H., Leger, E., Gagnon, F., & Thibodeau, N. (2000). Efficacy of a cognitive-behavioral treatment for generalized anxiety disorder: Evaluation in a controlled clinical trial. *Journal of Consulting and Clinical Psychology, 68*, 957–964.

Ledley, D. R., & Heimberg, R. G. (2005). Social anxiety disorder. In M. M. Antony, D. R. Ledley, & R. G. Heimberg (Eds.), *Improving outcomes and preventing relapse in cognitive-behavioral therapy*. New York: Guilford Press.

Lindren, D. M., Watkins, P. L., Gould, R. A., Clum, G. A., Asterino, M., & Tulloch, H. L. (1994). A comparison of bibliotherapy and group therapy in the treatment of panic disorder. *Journal of Consulting and Clinical Psychology, 62*, 865–869.

McCabe, R. E., & Antony, M. M. (2005). Panic disorder and agoraphobia. In M. M. Antony, D. R. Ledley, & R. G. Heimberg (Eds.), *Improving outcomes and preventing relapse in cognitive-behavioral therapy* (pp. 1–37). New York: Guilford Press.

Mennin, D. S., & Heimberg, R. G. (2000). The impact of comorbid mood and personality disorders in the cognitive-behavioral treatment of panic disorder. *Clinical Psychology Review, 20*, 339–357.

Miller, W. R., & Rollnick, S. (2002). *Motivational interviewing* (2nd ed.). New York: Guilford Press.

Milton, F., & Hafner, J. (1979). The outcome of behavior therapy for agoraphobia in relation to marital adjustment. *Archives of General Psychiatry, 36*, 807–811.

Öst, L-G. (1989). A maintenance program for behavioral treatment of anxiety disorders. *Behaviour Research and Therapy, 27*, 123–130.

Öst, L-G., Salkovskis, P. M., & Hellström, K. (1991). One-session therapist-directed exposure vs. self-exposure in the treatment of spider phobia. *Behavior Therapy, 22*, 407–422.

Ritter, M. R., & Hazlett-Stevens, H. (2006). The use of exposure and ritual prevention in the treatment of harm obsessions with covert compulsions. *Clinical Case Studies, 5*, 455–476.

Roy-Byrne, P. P., Craske, M. G., Stein, M. B., Sullivan, G., Bystritsky, A., Katon, W., et al. (2005). A randomized effectiveness trial of cognitive-behavioral therapy and medication for primary care panic disorder. *Archives of General Psychiatry, 62*, 290–298.

Taylor, S., Koch, W. J., & McNally, R. J. (1992). How does anxiety sensitivity vary across the anxiety disorders? *Journal of Anxiety Disorders, 6*, 249–259.

Turk, C. L., Heimberg, R. G., & Hope, D. A. (2001). Social anxiety disorder. In D. H. Barlow (Ed.; pp. 114–153), *Clinical handbook of psychological disorders: A step-by-step treatment manual* (3rd ed.). New York: Guilford Press.

Wade, W. A., Treat, T. A., & Stuart, G. L. (1998). Transporting an empirically supported treatment for panic disorder to a service clinic setting: A benchmarking strategy. *Journal of Consulting and Clinical Psychology, 66*, 231–239.

Waters, A. M., & Craske, M. G. (2005). Generalized anxiety disorder. In M. M. Antony, D. R. Ledley, & R. G. Heimberg (Eds.), *Improving outcomes and preventing relapse in cognitive-behavioral therapy* (pp. 77–127). New York: Guilford Press.

Wright, J., Clum, G. A., Roodman, A., & Febbraro, G. A. M. (2000). A bibliotherapy approach to relapse prevention in individuals with panic attacks. *Journal of Anxiety Disorders, 14,* 483–499.

17

TERMINATION WITH PATIENTS WITH PSYCHOTIC DISORDERS

ANDREEA L. SERITAN

They went into a sunny room and the Housekeeper-Famous-Doctor turned, saying, "Sit down. Make yourself comfortable." There came a great exhaustion and when the doctor said, "Is there anything you want to tell me?" a great gust of anger, so that Deborah said to her . . . , "All right—you'll ask me questions and I'll answer them—you'll clear up my 'symptoms' and send me home . . . *and what will I have then?*"

The doctor said quietly, "If you did not really want to give them up, you wouldn't tell me." A rope of fear pulled its noose around Deborah. "Come, sit down. You will not have to give up anything until you are ready, and then there will be something to take its place." (Greenberg 1964, p.23)

The initial encounter is a harbinger of things to come in psychotherapy, and clearly "the termination process starts with the beginning of the treatment" (Werbart 1997, 18). As therapist and patient meet and reach their first impressions, useful clues to the therapeutic processes of transference and countertransference surface. To illustrate this point, the opening paragraphs depicted the initial exchange between the legendary Dr. Frieda Fromm-Reichmann and one of her patients, a young woman presenting with psychotic symptoms. After fleeing Germany in 1935, Dr. Fromm-Reichmann settled at Chestnut Lodge in Maryland, at that time the only institution specialized in psychoanalytic treatment for psychotic patients. She lived and worked there until her death in 1957. Building on psychoanalytic principles modified through application of interpersonal theory aspects, Dr. Fromm-Reichmann developed individualized treatment strategies for severely ill patients.

Her *Principles of Intensive Psychotherapy* (1950) remains a fundamental textbook to this day, inspiring psychotherapists to approach psychotic patients with a psychodynamic understanding.

> Years later, as treatment approached successful termination, Fromm-Reichmann, as was her custom, reviewed with her patient what she herself had considered most helpful and significant for the recovery. When questioned the girl said, "You shouldn't ask, doctor. It was the WE experience . . . don't you remember, doctor, the first day, when I said, you will take away my gut pain, you will take away my trances and you will take away my food, *and what will I have then?* . . . Don't you remember what you said . . . you did *not* say 'I will not take it away' . . . You said, 'You come and tell me about all of this—that tells me that you do not want it. What I hear is that you want *us* to free you from them.' I tell you, doctor, that word *us* did the trick. Here was somebody who did not think she could cure me, or do it for me, but who said, 'We'll do it together.'" (Bruch 1974, p.17)

The empiric literature covering the termination of psychotherapy with psychotic patients is rather limited (Fromm-Reichmann 1939; Kestemberg 1958; Ekstein 1978; Kates & Rockland 1994; Werbart 1997; Aguera-Ortiz & Reneses-Priesto 2003; Kingdon & Turkington 2005). In the following pages we will describe the termination phenomenon as an integral component of the art of intensive psychotherapy. We will present diverse psychotherapeutic approaches by integrating insights from classical psychoanalytic masters with modern supportive and cognitive-behavioral therapies, modified to fit the needs and goals of psychotic patients. Although the literature reviewed generally focused on schizophrenia, other aspects of the psychotic spectrum were included, such as bipolar illness or major depression with psychotic features, schizoaffective disorder, brief psychotic episode, schizophreniform disorder, and borderline personality disorder patients undergoing psychotic decompensations. The patients' ages ranged from childhood (Kestemberg 1958) and adolescence (Ekstein 1978) to old age (Aguera-Ortiz & Reneses-Priesto 2003). The patients who were described in vignettes as well as in the case reports had comorbidities, such as obsessive-compulsive disorder, posttraumatic disorder, and polysubstance dependence. Furthermore, variability of the treatment setting (inpatient or outpatient) and the duration of the psychotherapy course also played a role. In some of the highlighted cases, termination was planned and mutually agreed upon, whereas in others, therapist changes or patients' discharge from the treatment facility caused a premature interruption of care. Overall, the studies discussed represented a wide range of designs, from single case reports (Ekstein 1978; Seritan 2005) to a lengthy case series of ten individuals (Werbart 1997). No controlled studies were found. Keeping in mind the aforementioned limitations, the present chapter will review the significant aspects of psychotherapy termination with persons with psychotic disorders.

Background and Theoretical Considerations

Psychotherapy with psychotic patients poses important challenges. According to the orthodox psychoanalytic theory, individuals suffering from psychotic disorders could not establish a working transference, making insight-oriented psychotherapy impossible. In Freud's words, "paranoia and dementia praecox, when fully developed, are not amenable to analysis" (Freud 1915–1917, 636). Early psychoanalysts believed that most of the patient's communications would not be understandable to the psychiatrist, and that the psychotic patient's tendency toward health and desire for change were not sufficient to work with. Frieda Fromm-Reichmann challenged these concepts in her "Remarks on the Philosophy of Mental Disorder" (Fromm-Reichmann 1946). She suggested that "Serious mental disturbance—psychosis—can be treated successfully by a collaborative effort between the mentally disturbed person and the psychiatrist as participant-observer, with modified psychoanalysis—dynamically oriented psychotherapy—even after many years duration" (Fromm-Reichmann 1943). The main modification to the psychodynamic approach referred to the balance between the interpretive and supportive work, with reduced emphasis on interpretation.

Dr. Fromm-Reichmann listed several technical recommendations for psychoanalysts:

a. establish rapport and empathically listen to patients,
b. communicate in the patient's own way and make this meaningful, for example by sharing art and poetry, and

c. do not attempt to make the patients adjust. "Adaptation shouldn't be a goal of psychotherapy in itself," she emphasized, whereas "the goal of psychotherapy is growth and maturation" (Fromm-Reichmann 1946).

Notwithstanding the great value of this classical teaching, nowadays, social skills training in addition to cognitive-behavioral techniques increase the focus on social adjustment (Tarrier et al. 1999; Heinssen, Liberman & Kopelowicz 2000). The American Psychiatric Association practice guidelines for treatment of patients with schizophrenia in the stable phase recommend the following psychosocial treatments: assertive community treatment, family intervention, supported employment, skills training, and cognitive-behavioral therapy (American Psychiatric Association 2004, 249–439). In a study of fully recovered patients with schizophrenia, eight of the ten subjects had been in psychotherapy and attached great importance to it (Rund 1990). Along with pharmacotherapy, psychotherapeutic approaches play a salient role in the treatment of psychotic disorders.

Establishing a Therapeutic Alliance

The overwhelming majority of researchers and clinicians working with psychotic patients recommend gradually building a therapeutic alliance, without aggressively pushing the patient to explore uncomfortable territory. In Fromm-Reichmann's words, "One should be cautious about delving too deeply into material which is fraught with intense anxiety. The release of too much anxiety is unwise, if not dangerous, until the therapist feels certain that through continuation of treatment he will be available to help the patient handle his anxiety" (Fromm-Reichmann 1950, 65).

According to Melanie Klein's developmental theory, "In the first six months of life, the infant is in a *paranoid-schizoid position*. By that, Klein means that from birth the infant relies heavily on mechanisms of introjection, projective identification, and splitting and sees the world in terms of what she calls *part objects*. Aggression is preeminent and uncontrollable and cannot be neutralized. If successful, the child then moves to the *depressive position* by age six months when the realization occurs that objects are not entirely split but that they are indeed whole and the realization of the imperfection of the world and of the power of aggression takes hold" (Marmer 2005, p.131). This period in early development partly overlaps with Freud's psychosexual oral phase, as well as Erikson's basic trust versus mistrust conflict. For persons developmentally arrested in this paranoid position, intense anxieties involving contact with others are apparent. Concerns about the integrity of one's ego boundaries and the fear of fusion with others represent an ongoing problem that is often resolved by isolation (Gabbard 2005, 181–212).

Based on this theoretical background, several authors (Drake & Sederer 1986; Kates & Rockland 1994) argue that all therapeutic relationships with psychotic individuals must respect the patient's need for distance, allowing healing processes to proceed naturally and centering on a trusting relationship as the crucial issue in treatment. Psychotherapy should focus on healthy, adaptive, and competent aspects of the patient, avoid regression, enhance self-esteem, and promote stabilization (Kates & Rockland 1994). The same rationale applies when deciding the pace of psychotherapeutic sessions for patients with psychotic disorders, as weekly meetings might be too difficult for them to tolerate. The frequency of sessions and the therapeutic approach will be dictated by the patients' active symptoms and clinical presentation.

To illustrate the difficulties that paranoid patients may have with closeness or active inquiry on the part of the therapist, we will use the case example of a twenty-five-year-old young man with a history of severe childhood trauma and extensive drug use. Among his presenting complaints were mood instability with physically violent outbursts, long-standing anxiety, and paranoid ideation at baseline, which became exacerbated under stress. The patient was enrolled in weekly therapy, which he failed to attend in a predictable pattern, effectively being seen about every two to three weeks. When confronted on his absences by his therapist, he displayed increased anxiety. He talked in the next session about nightmares in which a former girlfriend was attacking him, biting his abdomen. The therapist attempted to explore more of the early history, interpreting the patient's oral aggression dreams as illustrative of infantile trauma. In response, the patient described frequent derealization episodes. These were dissociative states during which he felt that the world around him had disappeared and intense anxiety set in. The therapist realized that she was getting too close to core issues before having had the chance to establish a solid therapeutic alliance. In the next session, the patient entered a brief episode lasting a few minutes, during which he appeared to dissociate and was not responsive to the therapist's voice. When he verbally reconnected, he shared his intense thoughts of hurting the therapist. Fortunately the situation did not escalate and both therapist and patient remained safe. This therapist learned the value of respecting the boundaries of individuals with psychotic structure and not attempting to advance the therapy at a faster pace than warranted. Eventually the patient fled the therapy after he became paranoid with the therapist.

Establishing a fruitful therapeutic relationship may take anywhere between six and twelve months, with most authors agreeing that the first six months are critical. Frank and Gunderson (1990) examined the correlation between therapeutic alliance, treatment course, and outcome in 143 patients with nonchronic schizophrenia involved in the Boston Psychotherapy Study. The patients who formed good alliances with their therapists within the first six months of treatment were significantly more likely to remain in psychotherapy, comply with their prescribed medication regimens, and achieve better outcomes after two years, needing less medication than patients who did not.

Additional studies support the finding that a diagnosis of chronic mental illness does not lead to unilateral termination of psychotherapy by the patient, suggesting that a strong therapeutic alliance prevents premature discontinuation of care (McFarland, Johnson & Hornbrook 1996; Self et al. 2005). In a survey of service utilization of 323 patients newly referred to three community mental health centers in Vienna, Austria, one-third had dropped out within four months, one-third had discontinued care because of referrals or mutual agreement on treatment termination, and one-third were still in treatment. Multivariate analyses yielded a negative association of treatment discontinuation with the diagnosis of schizophrenia, availability of home care, living alone, and a high quality of life in the domains of living situation and family/significant others. By contrast, a positive association was found with unemployment, previous psychiatric admissions, low patient satisfaction with staff competence, and high self-assessment of global functioning (Berghofer et al. 2002).

Working Through, Transference and Countertransference

A middle-aged man with chronic schizophrenia was transferred into the care of a new provider in an outpatient clinic. Since his early twenties, he had developed a delusional system consisting of beliefs that some parts of his body were implants, placed there by malignant beings whose voices he also heard frequently. The patient had failed multiple antipsychotic trials and was currently taking clozapine, requiring weekly blood draws. Despite the prescribed high dosage of antipsychotic, the patient continued to complain of auditory hallucinations instructing him to address the psychiatrist in a derogatory manner. In the second meeting he expressed concern that the psychiatrist was malevolent because she ordered blood draws and wondered if this was done in order to place things under his skin through needles. The psychiatrist explained the purpose of the blood draws and the importance of medication adherence. The patient's anxiety was decreased. At the next appointment he shared his difficulties with oversedation and increased salivation due to clozapine, admitting that he previously hadn't been taking the medication consistently. As a therapeutic alliance developed, positive transference ensued and the patient communicated that the voices now allowed him to address the psychiatrist as a friend.

It is important to recognize and work through transference feelings of psychotic persons. Dr. Fromm-Reichmann emphasizes, "Schizophrenics are capable of developing workable relationships and transference reactions, but successful psychotherapy … depends upon whether the psychoanalyst understands the significance of these transference phenomena and meets them appropriately" (Fromm-Reichmann 1939). Kates and Rockland (1994) recommend encouraging a mildly positive transference and undermining the negative, idealizing, and erotized transferences. Most likely, a negative transference that is not adequately and promptly addressed will lead to the therapist being incorporated into the patient's psychotic phenomena (frequently, paranoid delusions) and undermine the therapeutic alliance, like in the example of the twenty-five-year-old man above.

Ekstein (1978) analyzes the particularities of termination and its relationship to outcome in adolescents with psychotic disorders. He suggests that if close attention is paid to the particularities of transference and countertransference, a successful termination will follow. "The psychotic transference makes it necessary to revise our model of the treatment process. ... Ordinarily we can rely on a strong observing ego organization as an ally in therapy. With the psychotic patient, however, the ego is either nonexistent or fluctuating and operates only in the presence of the therapist. ... In these circumstances we have to ally ourselves with delusional creatures. We must recognize the danger inherent in such reactionary, regressive helpers though their strength is derived from being more real and valid than the superficial façade of imitative ego functioning" (Ekstein 1978, 456). He expands, "The peculiar nature of the psychotic transference is paralleled by its peculiar countertransference potential with both positive and negative aspects. ... The therapist's unconscious is drawn into the psychotic process, and he is threatened with immense anxiety against which his only defense is to struggle to avoid delusional material. ... This may lead to attempts to confront the patient with reality, to reeducate him, to seek adjustments, thus avoiding the resolution of the inner struggle" (Ekstein 1978, 457). The writer also cautions us: "The therapist must anticipate feelings of helplessness and hate in the countertransference as well as feelings of wanting to become a godlike rescuing helper" (Ekstein 1978, 458).

Remarkable insights come from the Swedish author A. Werbart (1997), who studied long-term consequences of working through intratherapeutic separations in combined individual psychotherapy and milieu therapy in a long-term treatment facility. He reported on the longitudinal outcome of ten severely disturbed patients between twenty and thirty years of age, with diagnoses of psychotic problems and/or severe personality disorders, who underwent psychoanalytically oriented psychotherapy. The average length of stay was forty-seven months (between twenty-two and sixty months). All cases were retrospectively classified according to their predominant patterns of dealing with separation due to therapist changes during the treatment period. Pattern A: New solutions to difficulties with separation, dependence, and hostility, was defined as new ways of handling separation, including the associated problems with dependence and hostile feelings, both in the patient's inner world and in the realm of interpersonal relationships, accompanied by some working through of current strains. Pattern B: Retraumatization in connection with separation, described unresolved separation crises, and persistent problems with dependence and hostility left outside the therapeutic work. The outcome was assessed by change in diagnosis from admission to discharge and follow-ups; change in the global assessment of functioning (GAF) scores; utilization of psychiatric care (number of inpatient days) and psychopharmacological agents (average of chlorpromazine equivalent per day) two years before the treatment, two years after discharge, and at five-year follow-up.

Emotional changes were assessed by consensus summaries of interviews focused on areas concerning repetition, enactment, inner world change, and persistence versus modification of internal images of primary objects. Of the five patients who found new solutions to intratherapeutic separations, four showed emotional and functional improvement, and one was found to have functional improvement without inner changes. Even in this positive outcome group, object loss in connection with therapist changes during the treatment period was not worked through. Additionally, therapeutic work addressed negative transference only to a limited extent. The five patients who behaved in a pattern consistent with retraumatization had the following outcomes: only one improved in both the emotional and functional areas, one functionally improved without inner changes, and three showed persistent emotional and functional difficulties. Termination was a catastrophic experience for all these patients. They reacted with repeated breakdowns, self-destructive behaviors, and durable psychoses (Werbart 1997). In conclusion, inability to mourn was connected with less emotional and functional improvement, and the patients' ways of dealing with the trauma of termination, as well as the therapist's interventions in the middle phase, were decisive in the long-term outcome.

Kates and Rockland (1994) introduce a novel style of psychotherapy, psychodynamically oriented supportive psychotherapy (POST), which is based on ego psychology principles. POST blends supportive and psychodynamic aspects with the goal of strengthening the patient's ego functions and consequently improving adaptation to both inner and outer worlds. An indirect approach to strengthen ego functions (i.e., reality testing) is by decreasing the stress on the ego from the other psychic agencies. The therapist assumes a more "real" stance and tends to be more verbally active and less frustrating of the patient's transference wishes. He also tends to be more self-revealing and may supply some of his own realities and values, but only to the extent required by the patient's ego defects (Kates & Rockland 1994). The therapist is particularly at risk for acting out countertransference reactions because the treatment structure is less rigid. In this type of therapy, termination is replaced by a gradual decrease in the frequency and length of sessions as the patient develops increased autonomy and independent functioning. The door is always left open for future contacts, and in some cases the therapist may continue to meet with the patient every six to twelve weeks for psychological "refueling," monitoring the patient's clinical state, and managing medications. The authors recommend that the term *termination* be replaced by *attenuation* in the treatment of the schizophrenic patient.

Termination as Inherent Loss

The interruption of a meaningful therapeutic relationship brings with it inherent feelings of loss. For some patients, this will activate pre-existing sadness about earlier losses, like in the case of a middle-aged woman with severe depression with psychotic features, who had tragically lost her mother when she was two years of age (Seritan 2005). The patient was transferred from a graduating resident into the care of another trainee in an outpatient clinic. Upon saying good-bye to the previous psychiatrist, the patient became intensely depressed and developed auditory hallucinations of music and paranoid ideation. The new provider understood that this severe reaction to loss was bound to be repeated upon her own graduation one year later. The therapist used the time available to help the patient work through some of her difficulties related to the early loss of her mother, while anticipating the loss of the therapeutic relationship. In this case, although termination occurred not by choice but instead by default, it was used to help process loss issues through the vehicle of transference. The patient developed a maternal transference and was able to articulate her fear of losing the therapist and to link this to the devastating effect that the early traumatic death of her mother had on her. In bringing forth her disappointment at having to part with the therapist, the patient was able to get in touch with the sadness and anger she had felt with her mother for dying and leaving her behind. She resolved the transference by realizing that she was losing her therapist not to death, but to a future career opportunity and to life. Mild psychotic symptoms recurred around termination and were dealt with (Seritan 2005).

Not uncommonly, some presenting symptoms may recur around termination, which is consistent with the patient's increased anxiety at that time. As with any type of psychic symptom, psychosis may serve an adaptive purpose and be associated with a secondary gain, maybe through an unconscious need to stay sick and to be taken care of. Thus, the recurrence of symptoms that had previously been resolved could have an unconscious meaning of proving to the therapist that the patient is still ill and needs continued help. During termination, the patient may mourn the loss of the secondary gain of psychosis, as the treatment has removed resources that were previously available through delusional experience (Ekstein 1978).

Forced terminations may occur in training settings, where therapists rotate off service before the patient has accomplished the therapeutic goals or in managed care settings, where treatment planning is influenced by external constraints. These terminations may be used in the service of working through issues of premature loss echoed in therapy. The therapist has to be gentle and carefully titrate her interventions in order to avoid retraumatizing the patient through added loss. By repetition, reenactment, and working through, patients with stronger ego structures will be able to master previous traumatic experiences, this being the ideal outcome in psychotherapy (Freud 1914). Even if the therapy has reached a natural end and there is a mutually agreed-on termination, some of the same themes appear as in forced terminations (Gabbard 2004). The fantasy of the ever-available therapist has to be mourned. Negative transference may surface for the first time when the patient realizes that the therapist will not be there forever. In supportive treatments, the therapist must stress continuing positive rapport and avoid the mobilization of unmanageable negative transferences (Gabbard 2005).

Timing of Termination

Termination must be collaboratively assessed according to whether or not the patient's goals for therapy have been achieved (Gabbard 2004). Indications for termination include stability in the patient's functioning, a reversal of any regressive processes, and an overall quiescence of symptoms. However, a subset of highly disturbed patients may require ongoing, infrequent therapy indefinitely (Gabbard 2005). For individuals with psychotic disorders, discharge may be to other areas of the mental healthcare system, depending on the clinician's role within it. The therapist's role frequently involves overall executive responsibility for the entire treatment, pharmacologic management, and clinically appropriate referrals for family work, social skills training, and vocational rehabilitation (Kates & Rockland 1994).

Kingdon and Turkington adapted the cognitive-behavioral therapy (CBT) techniques to clients suffering from severe psychotic illnesses (Turkington & Kingdon 2000; Turkington et al. 2004). Their view on termination is: "In an ideal world, clients themselves initiate the process of discharge in collaboration with their therapists. They themselves recognize that they now have the internal resources and external supports to move on. The internal resources are such that either: (1) their symptoms have ceased and they feel confident about detecting and handling any incipient relapse, or seeking support at an early stage and preventing it from progressing; or (2) their symptoms continue but have stabilized, and they feel that their coping strategies are sufficient for them to get on with their life (but that they can make contact if necessary)" (Kingdon & Turkington 2005, 162). Stability, support, and the person's desire to discontinue therapy are important determinants. "External supports are those particularly involving confiding relationships with friends, family members, and other health and social services, as well as meaningful activity (though not necessarily employment). A person who remains very isolated and guarded about his or her symptoms is probably not ready for discharge—although a few people who have never seemed to need close relationships, and who have built a lifestyle that is not dependent on others, may be able to survive effectively" (Kingdon & Turkington 2005, 162–163).

In CBT, as well as in psychodynamic psychotherapy, it is important to prepare the patient for unpredictable events, such as the therapist's departure, as soon as possible. If therapy is unfinished, transfer to another therapist is desirable, although it may not be possible. Another worker or even a family member might be available to offer support to the client (Kingdon & Turkington 2005). It is realistic to anticipate that therapist and patient will not always agree on the timing of termination. When patients discharge themselves, they may be prepared to consider contact at some later specified date and frequently return to care later. Overall, "for most people with schizophrenia and their therapists, discharge from therapy is a very positive experience in which it is possible to reflect on the work done and the positive changes seen. Further support may be necessary, but the improved understanding and ability to cope with difficult circumstances and symptoms will remain with them into a much more hopeful and optimistic future" (Kingdon & Turkington 2005, 164).

"Open Termination"

Aguera-Ortiz and Reneses-Priesto (2003) are in agreement with Kates and Rockland's notion of "attenuation," advising an "open discharge" based on their experience with elderly persons with psychosis. Even in cases of excellent resolution of symptoms, they argue, some kind of contact and follow-up should be kept. This can be assured by distancing the frequency of the appointments to one or two per year, or asking the patient and family to call from time to time, even in cases where everything is going right. This loose clinical relationship will help prevent relapses. For most individuals, a long-term commitment should be the rule. Psychoeducation with the family and the family's involvement in the treatment, when possible, will help support the patient through the loss of the therapeutic relationship and sustain the gains. Given the chronicity of schizophrenia and related illnesses, patients can be expected at best to be able to function independently and without therapeutic support for limited periods, although the expectation that they will be off medications is less realistic. Less frequent contacts for medication checks should still be in place. Ideally, if the psychotherapist is a different person than the pharmacotherapist (split treatment agreements), the two communicate closely and are usually members of the same treatment team.

"The reassurance that the therapist will continue to be available is of particular importance for schizophrenics. At times the expression of this availability may not amount to more than an exchange of Christmas greetings, with an occasional letter dealing with some difficulty" (Bruch 1974, 142).

Interdisciplinary Teams and Consultation

Most often in today's health systems, the care of seriously chronically ill patients is shared by a treatment team, at times prepared to reach out in the community in crisis or if the patient has adherence difficulties (Stein & Test 1980). In the event the therapist is part of an interdisciplinary team, collaboration among team members (psychiatrists, psychologists, psychiatric nurses, social workers, occupational and physical therapists, recreation therapists, and addiction counselors) can prove fruitful by providing different vantage points based on the treaters' diverse expertise. We cannot emphasize enough the role of supervision and consultation in psychotherapy, especially when treating severely ill patients like the ones described in this chapter. Because termination is a stage when intense feelings are aired in therapy, the therapist is vulnerable to countertransference enactments. In a psychodynamic approach, the boundaries, previously strictly maintained, may become a little more permeable. Patients may feel the right to ask the therapist personal questions. Both patients and therapists have difficulty with losing a significant relationship, and therapists who feel guilty may take a more personal approach and reveal more about themselves (Gabbard 2004). Requesting a colleague's formal supervision or consultation in cases where the therapist feels stuck or confused is helpful.

Summary

In conclusion, a variety of psychosocial approaches are currently used for persons with psychotic disorders: psychodynamic, supportive, cognitive-behavioral therapy, and social skills training, in conjunction with psychoeducation, vocational rehabilitation, assertive community treatment, and family interventions. The basic principles of psychoanalytic treatment, modified through the interpersonal theory perspective outlined by Dr. Frieda Fromm-Reichmann more than half a century ago, still stand. They encompass empathic listening, making the communication with the patient meaningful, emphasizing the "we" experience, developing a strong therapeutic alliance, and use of less interpretive work. Particularities of transference and countertransference may be challenging and need to be appropriately managed. Not uncommonly, psychotic symptoms may recur around termination. More severely ill patients require ongoing, infrequent therapy. Most authors recommend an "open termination," allowing the patient to reenter treatment as necessary and helping prevent relapses. The family's role in treatment planning is crucial, providing support to the suffering individual. In split treatment arrangements, close communication between the psychotherapist and the psychopharmacologist is imperative, as is team collaboration in long-term outpatient, partial hospital, or inpatient programs. Supervision or consultation in cases when a therapist feels stuck or in danger of acting out countertransference feelings can be helpful. Despite these wonderful insights, a great deal of additional research is needed to elucidate the process of termination of psychotherapy with psychotic patients. Specifically, empirical studies of larger numbers of patients with psychotic disorders undergoing planned termination would be necessary.

Although written before the advent of multiple neuroleptics, the words of Hilde Bruch, major figure in psychodynamic psychotherapy and Frieda Fromm-Reichmann's mentee, still ring true: "Therapeutic procedure with schizophrenics is far from simple and predictable, even now when psychotropic drugs may help in periods of panic and disorganization. It makes great demands on the innate capacity and resources of the patient, on the skill, patience, and tolerance of the nursing staff, and on the sensitivity, intuitiveness, and personal security of the physician. But there are few experiences more rewarding for a therapist than being a participant in the emergence from the bondage of panic and isolation of a trusting personality willing to take part in life" (Bruch 1974, 128–129).

Acknowledgments

I wish to acknowledge Lori Rogers, M.D., for her helpful editorial comments. I also wish to thank my husband Marius for the English translation of the Kestemberg (1958) reference and for his endless support.

References

Aguera-Ortiz, L., & Reneses-Priesto, B. (2003). Practical psychological management of old age psychosis. *Journal of Nutrition, Health and Aging,* 7 (6), 412–420.

American Psychiatric Association. (2004). *Practice guidelines for the treatment of psychiatric disorders* (p. 260). Arlington, VA: Author.

Berghofer, G., Schmidl, F., Rudas, S., Steiner, E., & Schmitz, M. (2002). Predictors of treatment discontinuity in outpatient mental health care. *Social Psychiatry and Psychiatric Epidemiology, 37,* 276–282.

Bruch, H. (1974). *Learning psychotherapy.* Cambridge, MA: Harvard University Press.

Drake, R. E., & Sederer L. I. (1986). Inpatient psychosocial treatment of chronic schizophrenia: negative effects and current guidelines. *Hospital and Community Psychiatry, 37,* 897–901.

Ekstein, R. (1978). The process of termination and its relation to outcome in the treatment of psychotic disorders in adolescence. *Adolescent Psychiatry, 6,* 448–460.

Frank, A. F., & Gunderson, J. G. (1990). The role of the therapeutic alliance in the treatment of schizophrenia. Relationship to course and outcome. *Archives of General Psychiatry, 47* (3), 228–236.

Freud, S. (1914). Remembering, repeating and working-through. In *The Standard Edition of the Complete Psychological Works of Sigmund Freud.* London: Hogarth Press.

Freud, S. (1915–1917). A general introduction to psycho-analysis. *The Major Works of Sigmund Freud* (p. 636). Chicago: Encyclopaedia Britannica, Inc.; 1952.

Fromm-Reichmann, F. (1939). Transference problems in schizophrenics. *Psychoanalytic Quarterly, 8,* 412–426.

Fromm-Reichmann, F. (1943). Psychoanalytic psychotherapy with psychotics. *Psychiatry, 6,* 277–279.

Fromm-Reichmann, F. (1946). Remarks on the philosophy of mental disorder. *Psychiatry, 9,* 293–308.

Fromm-Reichmann, F. (1950). *Principles of intensive psychotherapy* (p. 65). Chicago: University of Chicago Press.

Gabbard, G. O. (2004). *Long-term psychodynamic psychotherapy: A basic text* (pp. 153–171). Washington, DC: American Psychiatric Publishing.

Gabbard, G. O. (2005). *Psychodynamic psychiatry in clinical practice* (4th ed.; pp. 112–113, 181–196). Washington, DC: American Psychiatric Publishing.

Greenberg, J. (1964). *I never promised you a rose garden* (p. 23). New York: Penguin Putnam.

Heinssen, R. K., Liberman, R. P., & Kopelowicz, A. (2000). Psychosocial skills training for schizophrenia: Lessons from the laboratory. *Schizophrenia Bulletin, 26* (1), 21–46.

Kates, J., & Rockland, L. H. (1994). Supportive psychotherapy of the schizophrenic patient. *American Journal of Psychotherapy, 48* (4), 543–561.

Kestemberg, E. (1958). Quelques considérations à propos de la fin du traitement des malades à structure psychotique [Various findings on the termination of therapy of patients with psychotic structure]. *Revue française de psychanalyse, 22* (3), 297–333

Kingdon, D. G., & Turkington, D. (2005). *Cognitive therapy of schizophrenia* (pp. 162–164). New York: Guilford Press.

Marmer, S. (2005). Theories of the mind and psychopathology. In R. E. Hales & S. C. Yudofsky (Eds.), *Textbook of clinical psychiatry* (4th ed.; pp. 107–152). Washington, DC: American Psychiatric Publishing.

McFarland, B. H., Johnson, R. E., & Hornbrook, M. C. (1996). Enrollment duration, service use, and costs of care for severely mentally ill members of a health maintenance organization. *Archives of General Psychiatry, 53,* 938–944.

Rund, B. R. (1990). Fully recovered schizophrenics: a retrospective study of some premorbid and treatment factors. *Psychiatry, 53* (2), 127–139.

Self, R., Oates, P., Pinnock-Hamilton, T., & Leach, C. (2005). The relationship between social deprivation and unilateral termination (attrition) from psychotherapy at various stages of the health care pathway. *Psychology and Psychotherapy: Theory, Research and Practice, 78,* 95–111.

Seritan, A. L. (2005). Of rose gardens and forced terminations. *Academic Psychiatry, 29* (1), 29–32.

Stein, L. I., & Test, M. A. (1980): Alternative to mental hospital treatment. I. Conceptual model, treatment program, and clinical evaluation. *Archives of General Psychiatry, 37* (4), 392–397.

Tarrier, N., Wittkowski, A., Kinney, C., McCarthy, E., Morris, J., & Humphreys, L. (1999). Durability of the effects of cognitive-behavioral therapy in the treatment of chronic schizophrenia: 12-month follow-up. *British Journal of Psychiatry, 174,* 500–504.

Turkington, D., & Kingdon, D. (2000). Cognitive-behavioural techniques for general psychiatrists in the management of patients with psychoses. *British Journal of Psychiatry, 177,* 101–106.

Turkington, D., Dudley, R., Warman, D., & Beck, A. (2004). Cognitive-behavioral therapy for schizophrenia: A review. *Journal of Psychiatric Practice, 10* (1), 5–16.

Werbart, A. (1997). Separation, termination process and long-term outcome in psychotherapy with severely disturbed patients. *Bulletin of the Menninger Clinic, 61* (1), 16–43.

18

Helping Them "Get Their Act Together?" An Action Theory Approach on Treatment Termination With Patients Suffering From Personality Disorders

GOLAN SHAHAR, NETTA HORESH, AND GUINA COHEN

The treatment of personality disorders (PDs) has increasingly become a pivotal concern for healthcare providers. Recent studies have linked the effects of PDs to a broad spectrum of dysfunctions stretching across disturbances in concepts of self, impairments in cognitive, social, and occupational functioning, increases in violence/suicide risk, medical utilization, and substance abuse, as well as heightened prediction of poor treatment response (for a review, see Smith and Benjamin 2002). Furthermore, PDs are not only difficult to treat, but given their high comorbidity rate with Axis I disorders, they also complicate and some-times impede the successful treatment of other disorders (e.g., Shahar, Blatt, et al. 2003). Hence, the need for developing effective ways to treat PDs is becoming evident as a key prerequisite to resolving both the aforementioned dysfunctions and to facilitate the treatment of other pathologies, even when PDs do not seem to be the main concern.

One aspect of treatment especially sensitive to the effects PDs is the termination phase of therapy—specifically, an imposed or unex-pected termination that might engender feelings of anger, grief, guilt, abandonment, loss, and separation by reenacting earlier traumatic experiences and hostile relationships (Warnes 1984–1985). Personality disordered individuals, especially those with borderline personality disorder (BPD), are prone to terminate treatment prematurely (Chiesa, Drahorad, & Longo 2000). Nevertheless, studies demonstrate considerable variability across PDs in terms of both attendance and dropout rates. For instance, Hilsenroth, Holdwick, Castlebury, and Blais (1998) found that while individuals with BPD characteristics (e.g., frantic efforts to avoid real or imagined abandonment; inappropriate, intense anger or difficulty controlling anger) and histrionic personality disorder (HPD) characteristics (e.g., considers relationships to be more intimate than they really are) tend to drop out of treatment unexpectedly, they do so later in the course of the therapy (i.e., three, six, or even twelve months into therapy) when compared to individuals with antisocial personality disorder (ASPD) characteristics (e.g., lack of remorse, indifference to or rationalizing having hurt, mistreated, or stolen from another), and narcissistic personality disorder (NPD) characteristics (e.g., requires excessive admiration) who tend to terminate treatment much closer to the cutoff criteria commonly accepted for early treatment termination (usually defined at between zero and eight sessions). Hence, the problem clinicians face when treating PDs is twofold: On the one hand, there is a need to get individuals with PDs to attend therapy and keep them there long enough for it to be efficient. On the other, due to the growing pressures imposed by the managed care era to conduct as brief a treatment as possible, and taking into consideration the subtleties distinguishing the different types of PDs, it is essential to develop an effective strategy to identify and designate an appropriate approach to the issue of termination when dealing with PDs.

Unresolved anger appears to be one trait that is common to most, if not all PDs, and that plays a major role in treatment termination. According to Benjamin (1994), anger manifests itself differently amongst the differing PDs as a function of the situational context. For example, anger in BPD will manifest when the individual feels abandoned in contrast to anger in NPD, which manifests when the individual's sense of entitlement is compromised. Treatment termination that is imposed by the therapist might generate feelings of abandonment in patients with BPD and narcissistic injuries in patients with NPD.

The individual's interpretation of the situation, which when distorted, serves as a factor impeding the course of treatment in general and of termination specifically, has its roots in the development of the disorder and the learned associations between specific situations and symptoms (Benjamin 1994). The development of personality disorders is influenced by an array of factors, such as genetic predisposition, temperament, individual constellations of unconscious wishes and desires, as well as defenses and cognitive distortions, to name a few (Benjamin 1994; Benjamin & Wonderlich 1994; Johnson et al. 1999; Posner et al. 2003; Widom 1999). It has been suggested that personality disordered individuals, mainly those with BPD, perceive social relations and situations in a more hostile and noncohesive way, and have shown decreased levels of self-control and increased levels of self-attack. These findings have been attributed to the internalization of hostile abandoning, abusive and neglecting relationships in a way that leads to increasing levels of self-attack and self-abandonment (Benjamin & Wonderlich 1994). Thus, in the course of the person's life, individual factors come into contact with different social situations, some more traumatic than others, and depending on their interaction, may lead to the development of self-destructive symptoms—a characteristic common to PDs. Take for instance, Benjamin's description of the development of self-destructive symptoms of the borderline personality:

> [the self-destructive symptoms] begin with an assertive temperament subject to a specific type of abuse. His or her history taught the borderline personality that *being left alone is likely to involve trauma* ... Usually the borderline personality is not aware of the connection between self-destructive behaviors and a specific form of incestual abuse (or any interpersonally similar prototype). *The patient does not know that she severely distorts normal separation experiences* or that her self-destruction likely is linked to an unconscious wish to reunite with the original caregiver/abuser. (Benjamin 1994, 310, italics added)

Hence, understanding the unconscious connections underlying the disorder and the phenomenology that led to their development sheds light on the difficulties experienced by the BPD individual who, when facing therapy termination, may actually be experiencing the threat of abandonment and may, in an act of self-preservation, resign from therapy prematurely. Similarly, an individual with NPD, who believes in his or her undeniable entitlement, might resent the fact that from the onset of therapy, the limited number of sessions (and/or any other pre-imposed regulation) is externally mandated and could, in turn, decide to drop out in an attempt to reappropriate his or her control and self-respect.

An additional facet adding to the body of knowledge on PDs and treatment termination concerns the positioning of PD individual qualities along a relational continuum, with a relational-oriented style and a relation-rejecting style on opposing ends (Hilsenroth et al. 1998). Thus, the specific point in therapy at which the individual chooses to resign may be influenced by his or her position on the relational continuum. Accordingly, Hilsenroth et al. (1998) explained their findings pointing to the tendency of individuals with BPD and HPD personality characteristics to stay longer in therapy, or in other words, terminate therapy later in its course, by identifying these specific qualities (stated above), as reflecting high relational-oriented style, tapping into "interpersonal neediness, a need to be connected to 'another', and/or the inability to tolerate being alone" (172). Consequently, on the opposing end, pertaining to early termination of therapy, they identified a high relation-rejecting style with the ASPD and NPD personality characteristics (also mentioned above), which "highlight an egocentric, self-serving position," and a lack of "concern for an 'other'" (172).

Support for the relational-oriented style characteristic of BPD can be found in Chiesa et al.'s (2000) study of 134 personality disordered inpatients, which compared attrition rates between two types of psychodynamic psychotherapy; a one-stage treatment model (one-year hospital stay, with no out-patient follow-up) versus a two-stage treatment model (six months in hospital followed by eighteen months psychosocial outreach work). Their findings point to lower attrition rates in general for BPD patients as compared to those diagnosed with other PDs. Within the BPD patients, those assigned to the one-stage model were found to be 5.5 times more likely to terminate treatment prematurely than their two-stage counterparts. It is possible that the two-stage treatment model, despite its shorter-term intensive treatment, facilitated the termination phase by addressing the BPD patients' needs to maintain a relationship by means of promising a longer-term period of contact as an outpatient. Furthermore, qualitative data attained from these patients suggests the need for therapy treatments that take into account individual differences and promote a containing and understanding environment rather than programs based on uniform, rigid, and excessively confrontational approaches (see also Blatt & Zuroff 2005, for a similar argument pertaining to treatment for unipolar depression).

Action Theory and Its Relevance to the Understanding of PDs

Given that on many occasions treatment in PDs cannot be open ended, and a less-than-optimal termination has to be imposed, what can we offer by way of guidelines for such a termination? In the present chapter we propose action theory (henceforth AT) as an overarching theoretical umbrella that is conducive to guiding treatment termination in PDs. Below we present AT and derive from it some guidelines for the assessment and treatment of PDs with a focus on treatment termination.

Action theory can be broadly defined as a theoretical and empirical paradigm postulating that individuals actively partake in shaping their personal and interpersonal environment, as well as their development and well-being (Shahar 2004, 2006). An amalgam of multiple perspectives emerging from a broad spectrum of disciplines, action theory permeated the realm of psychology mainly as a result of research in the developmental, social, and personality domains.

Observations in the area of social development and interpersonal behavior, for instance, have pointed to children's and adolescents' active, if inadvertent, role in directing their developmental course by evoking and promoting differential responses in parents, teachers, and peers. These responses, which are in turn fed back, affect the individual's further development, thus creating a reciprocal, interactive cycle of individual-context exchange, which is highly consistent with Bandura's (1978) term *reciprocal determinism*. Furthermore, as argued by Buss (1987), individuals selectively seek or avoid interpersonal situations, as well as purposely interact with their environments in ways that promote, maintain, and affect their personal interests and well-being (for a review, see Shahar 2006).

Adding to this perspective, research in personality psychology has largely emphasized the intentional or goal-directed character of individuals' actions on their context. While multiple terms addressing the intentionality of individual action have been introduced in the course of the last forty years (e.g. *life tasks*, Cantor 1990; *personal goals*, Brunstein 1993; *personal strivings*, Emmons 1986; *life planning*, Smith 1999; *personal projects*, Little 1999, etc.), they all pertain to the common view of individual motivation as the driving force behind the pursuit of long-term personal goals.

Concurrently, clinical studies have pointed to individuals' active contribution to their own suffering. Depressed patients, for instance, have been found likely to promote the persistence of negative life conditions such as stress, hardship, deficient social support, and stressful interpersonal events, thus aggravating their emotional state and sustaining their psychopathology (Depue & Monroe 1986; Monroe & Simmons 1991; Monroe & Steiner 1986), a process later depicted as the stress-generation model (Hammen 1991). Similarly, reassurance-seeking behavior (i.e., engaging in excessive requests for self-worth reassurance from a significant other) and need for self-verification (i.e., the need to have one's self-views confirmed), both characteristic of depressed individuals, have been associated with negative social circumstances, such as eroding relationships, eliciting negative feedback, and rejection, leading to the onset and maintenance of unipolar depression (for a review, see Shahar 2006). Cognizant of the notable comorbidity of depression and PDs, Hammen and colleagues examined stress-generating effects of individuals with PD features. As compellingly demonstrated by Hammen and her group, individuals with Axis II symptoms, especially those pertaining to cluster B disorders, generate interpersonal stress, which in turn exacerbates their propensity to experience depression (Daley, Burge, & Hammen 2000; Daley et al. 1999; Daley et al. 1998; for review, see Hammen 2006).

Conspicuous in its absence in this program of research is an examination of the effect of personality pathology on *positive life events*. It is a case in point that, in general, research on positive life events is conspicuously scarce (Needles & Abramson 1990; Zautra & Reich 1983), particularly when compared to the extensively studied role of negative life events in physical illness and psychopathology.

Nevertheless, evidence accumulates to suggest that positive events do play an important role in adaptation, by directly ameliorating emotional and/or physical distress, or by "buffering" the adverse effects of negative events (see Shahar & Priel 2002). However, it is seldom acknowledged that positive life events, like negative ones, do not simply occur *to* people but are, in part, actively generated *by* them. To illustrate this, Shahar and colleagues (Shahar & Priel 2003, Shahar, Henrich, et al. 2003) launched a program of research focusing on the role of personality and the self-concept in the generation of positive events. In investigating Israeli and American adolescents, they found that adolescents with strong dependency needs generate both negative and positive events, contributing to the mixture of risk and resilience that is associated with this personality construct (Borenstein 1998; Shahar 2001; Shahar forthcoming). In contrast, adolescents with strong self-critical tendencies were shown to generate negative events (e.g., Priel & Shahar 2000; Shahar & Priel 2003), and to fail to generate positive events (Shahar & Priel 2003; Shahar, Henrich, et al., 2003). Because the lack of positive events and resulting negative affect have been identified as the defining feature of clinical depression, this failure to generate positive events on the part of self-critical adolescents may explain, at least in part, why these individuals are so vulnerable to depression and to a host of other clinical conditions Blatt, 1995; Shahar 2001, 2004).

Why would self-critical adolescents fail to generate positive events? To address this question, Shahar, Henrich, and colleagues (2003) found that this default has to do with the motivational structure implicated in self-criticism. Namely, among American adolescents, self-criticism was strongly associated with lower levels of "intrinsic motivation orientation," that is, the tendency to engage in activities because of the joy they inspire. In turn, and in quite a straightforward manner, lower levels of intrinsic motivation predicted lower levels of positive events, and this effect fully accounted for the previously demonstrated effect of self-criticism on positive events.

These findings on the role of personality pathology in the generation of both negative and positive life events join similar findings on the role of personality pathology in "degenerating" (i.e., failing to generate) social support, a well-known protective factor (Cohen 2004). Here again the comparison between dependency and self-criticism is telling: whereas the former trait was shown to predict elevated levels of social support (Mongrain 1998; Priel & Shahar 2000), self-criticism was shown to predict lower levels of this protective factor (Mongrain 1998; Priel & Shahar 2000). Indeed, self-criticism was shown to erode social relations in general (Mongrain et al. 1998; Zuroff & Duncan 1999), both within and outside psychological and pharmacological treatment (Shahar et al. 2004).

Taken together, this AT-based program of research on the role of personality pathology and PDs in the generation of negative and positive events and social support is extremely pertinent to the assessment and treatment of personality disorders, and to issues of treatment termination. Specifically, we would like to suggest that the generation of a particularly noxious environment, which includes multiple chronic difficulties and elevated levels of negative events, as well as reduced levels of social support and positive life events, is PD's chief modus operandi. Drawing from the work of Benjamin (e.g., 1994) and Westen and colleagues (1990), and from Blatt's seminal work on the role of mental representations of self and others in psychopathology (e.g., Blatt, Auerbach, & Levy 1997), we suggest that PD's adverse action stems from their maladaptive, predominantly malevolent mental representations (i.e., "object relations"), which often develop in the context of childhood trauma and/or maltreatment (Widom 1999). Once these mental representations are consolidated, they tend to get enacted in the social arena, both within and outside treatment (Benjamin 1994; Shahar 2004; Wachtel 1994).

It is this tightly constructed causal chain leading from childhood trauma to maladaptive mental representations to adverse action, and culminating with a noxious social environment, extreme distress, and further consolidation of maladaptive mental representations (e.g., BPD patients, constrained by interpersonal representations of rejection, actually beget rejection by their dramatic interpersonal behavior, with therapy contributing to the consolidation of the rejection representations), which renders the treatment of personality pathology in general, and of PD in particular, particularly challenging. We view this treatment necessarily integrative, in that it requires the utilization of psychodynamic techniques aimed at helping patients get acquainted with their maladaptive representations, cognitive-behavioral techniques that address patients' maladaptive coping skills and behavior patterns and help them short-circuit vicious interpersonal cycles and employ "virtuous," protective ones (Shahar 2004, 2006), and sometimes family-system techniques that are geared to change patients' ecology so as to facilitate adaptive action. Resultantly, we also view the treatment of PDs as optimally long, even under the best circumstances (for a recent research illustration using manualized schema therapy and transference focused therapy lasting for three years [!], albeit with good results, see Giesen-Bloo et al., 2006).

Nevertheless, we would be remiss if we lost sight of real constraints imposed by managed behavioral healthcare, which severely restrict the length of treatment of all psychiatric disorders, including—perhaps particularly—PDs. We therefore propose an AT-based, minimalist approach to the problem of treatment termination in PDs, as follows: Assuming that serious constraints exist to treatment continuation, then treatment termination should be considered when patients "get their (adverse) act together" in the sense that they cease, or at least decrease, their tendency to generate stress and erode relationships, and instead begin to generate positive life events and elicit social support. The following clinical case illustrates this approach.

Case Illustrations

Claire, a gorgeous forty-year-old woman, sought therapy with one of us (Netta Horesh) after a series of therapeutic failures, including multiple cognitive-behavioral trials, a classical psychoanalysis, and pharmacological therapy. In these previous therapeutic attempts, Claire was consistently diagnosed with a severe borderline personality disorder (BPD). The presenting problem in this putative treatment was threefold. First, catching her having an affair with a mutual friend, her husband presented her with an ultimatum: "either break up with your lover, or we are getting a divorce." While she had already decided to break off the affair, and eventually did so, she seriously deliberated about the fate of her marriage. Second, Claire used marijuana heavily (i.e., five times a day). This made her drowsy, dopey, unable to focus, and highly irritable and unpleasant. Third, a mother of an eleven-year-old daughter and an eight-year-old son, Claire was having great difficulties making decisions pertaining to her children's health. For instance, her daughter constantly complained about abdominal pain and the family physician suspected Crohn's disease. To confirm or rule out this diagnosis, a relatively intrusive gastro-ontological test was needed, but Claire vehemently refused to subject her daughter to such a test. Similarly, she refused to take her son to the doctor to get vaccinated fearing that any type of vaccine would inadvertently make him ill.

Furthermore, Claire's family home environment was extremely chaotic, lacking any sort of boundaries or sense of structure. Physically the house was dirty and messy, partly due to the fact that animals (including goats, hens, and parrots) roamed the house freely, and partly because both Claire and her husband were too high most of the time to bestow order. There were no assigned sleeping arrangements within the family, nor did the children follow any sort of fixed schedule.

Anamnesis revealed that Claire had grown up in a notably tumultuous, particularly boundaryless, family setting. The first born to a celebrity father and his relatively obscure wife, Claire was exposed from a very early age to a sexually, aggressively, and criminally saturated lifestyle, given her father's long list of infidelities as well as his ties with organized crime. Moreover, as the eldest of three children, Claire took on the role of confidant to both her parents; the father would share his conquests and illegitimate liaisons with her, while her depressed mother confided with Claire on her frustrations and feelings of helplessness. In school, while an intelligent and bright student, Claire never fit in socially and always felt estranged from her peers.

At age eighteen, with hopes of escaping her unfortunate environment, Claire ran away from home, relocating to a foreign country. Not surprisingly, in a matter of weeks, Claire had managed to reenact the very settings she longed to escape, thus reinforcing her distorted conceptualization of herself and interpersonal relationships. Having no money, work, or stable living arrangements, Claire led a life filled with drugs, sex, and crime. Feeling lost and unsafe, she contacted her parents for help, only to be confronted with her father's rejection, conveyed under the pretense that she was now an adult and had to learn to take care of herself, while her mother remained passive, explaining to her that although she was sorry and wanted to help, she was prohibited from doing so by her husband. Thus, rejected and lonely, Claire remained abroad and continued with her chaotic lifestyle. Five years later, she had developed a genuine interest in theories of reincarnation, and thanks to her strong sense of intuition, intelligence, and charisma, became a well-known and sought-after spiritual advisor. Nevertheless, she had severed all ties with her family and remained alone until meeting her husband, a charming yet reckless man, whom she married a couple of weeks thereafter. While the birth of their daughter was a positive experience, the pregnancy and birth of their son was permeated with complications, resulting in several birth defects, for which Claire blamed herself.

Retrospectively, it was not difficult to see that consequent to her chaotic and frantic environment, Claire had developed warped mental representations, not only of the world, but of others, relationships, and of herself as well. Men were seen as strong, careless, deceitful, and destructive, while women were seen as necessarily weak, pitiful, and worthless. As a result, she viewed any type of relationship as inevitably painful. Finally, she saw herself as essentially fragmented, containing contradicting and conflicting parts, simultaneously hopeless and helpless as well as destructive, deceitful, and downright utterly dangerous.

In the course of her life she had internalized an existential sense of fear and helplessness within an unsafe and threatening world. She tried to compensate for this by developing a grandiose, almost magical sense of cosmic control. Throughout her childhood, for instance, Claire had feared her home was filled with monsters, ghosts, and demons. In an attempt to regain some sense of control, she pretended to possess the ability to banish and expel evil by closing her eyes, as well as be able to access "alternate worlds" to which she could retire when reality was too unbearable. A similar reenactment of her childhood defenses was reflected in her belief in reincarnation, which served a double purpose as it provided her with both a viable "reason" for her current unbearable and chaotic suffering, as well as hope for a better future. Nevertheless, the belief that she had such direct access to the secrets of others' previous and future lives enabled her to feel omnipotent while making others, among them her therapist, seem meek and helpless, yet simultaneously exacerbated her fear of the potentially uncontrollable urge for destructiveness she felt she had within her. Realizing this, it was essential for her therapist to both prove her wrong, that is, remaining assertive and strong amidst her "omnipotence," as well contain her psychic chaos and destructive feelings.

As is evident from the aforementioned description, these object relations were consistently enacted by Claire in her interpersonal arena, which contributed to her physical and social chaos. It was this environmental chaos that was first addressed in therapy. Specifically, espousing an integrative, psychodynamic/cognitive-behavioral approach, the therapist labored to first understand, and then help Claire understand and reintegrate, the fragmented parts of her personality, working through her internal contrasts and contradictions. Concurrently, practical behavioral schedules and cognitive restructuring techniques were used to enable Claire to concretely reorganize her life and take control of her environment. Thus, Claire generated differentiated structures and schedules (i.e., separating the animals from the people at home, and having the animals live outside the house; assigning specific sleeping arrangements, giving each of the children a room and a schedule to adhere to). The fear of subjecting her children to their required medical procedures was understood and interpreted in terms of the fear of invasiveness she had developed as a result of her threatening experiences. As a result of the connection she made between her internalized fears and her externalized behavior, Claire eventually agreed to let her husband take the children to have the respective test and vaccination completed. In addition, based on Claire's input and cooperation, a framework aimed at gradually reducing her marihuana use was successfully employed.

After a year of therapy, noticeable improvement was evident. Claire reported a renewed sense of agency. Although she did not overcome her habit completely, she had been able to stay sober for significant periods of her day, enabling her to take control of her time and maintain her home in order. Her daughter had been successfully treated for her condition and both her children seemed to be happier and doing better, restoring Claire's sense of competence as a mother. Her marriage, which was still recuperating from her infidelity, was now much more stable. Fights with her husband had diminished and they had even started a new business together, and were now contemplating a move abroad to start anew. Furthermore, Claire had decided, for the first time in her life, to host a holiday dinner at her home, inviting all her relatives, including her mother and siblings (her father had passed away), thus reflecting her effort to come to peace with her past in preparation for a better future.

Because of the eventual decision of Claire and her husband to go abroad, therapy had to come to an end. Throughout the last few sessions, Claire deliberated whether to continue therapy abroad, but eventually decided that she did not need to for the time being. The therapist, while acknowledging that much therapeutic work was still needed, nevertheless supported Claire's decision, mainly because of the patient's evident capacity for a benevolent, rather than adverse, action. Almost a year after termination, this decision appears to have been reasonable, as Claire appears to lead a stable, responsible, and gratifying life.

Formalizing the Decision to Terminate Treatment of PDs: The Action Formulation

This clinical case illustrates a spontaneous application of our aforementioned approach to treatment termination in PDs, namely, that termination might be considered once adverse action decreases substantially. Nevertheless, in the present chapter we would like to go beyond conceptualizing and illustrating this principle to suggest that the issue of treatment termination in PDs could be formalized by a judicial application of the action formulation (TAF, Shahar & Porcerelli 2006), a recently proposed heuristic for clinical case formulation. The purpose of TAF is to identify ways in which patients, constrained by their personality and psychopathology, are getting actively involved in vicious and "virtuous" or protective interpersonal cycles. TAF is based on the following four guidelines:

(a) *Map the client's social environment, and the role it plays in the pertinent outcomes.* Relying on evidence pointing to the centrality of social and interpersonal factors in individual mental and physical health, this objective aims at identifying the particular set of social and interpersonal vectors that facilitate and/or attenuate the client's clinical outcomes.

(b) *Identify how clients, constrained by their personalities, psychopathologies, and strengths, actively influence their environment.* Focusing on maladaptive personality and clinical characteristics, as well as on personal strengths that facilitate and promote interpersonal risk and protective factors respectively, this step assists in understanding the client's role in his or her self-generated social environment.

(c) *Differentiate between vicious, risk-related, interpersonal cycles, and "virtuous," protective-based ones.* Acknowledging the simultaneous existence of both beneficial and malevolent cycles, TAF seeks to identify them and decipher the interplay and dynamic equilibrium within which the client's predicament thrives.

(d) *Tailor integrative techniques to short-circuit the vicious cycle and bolster the virtuous ones.* This can be accomplished by incorporating both psychodynamic/object relational and cognitive-behavioral strategies into the treatment program.

Whereas guideline (d) lies outside the scope of the present article, we would like to focus here on guidelines (a), (b) and (c). Regarding (a), *map the client's social environment, and the role it plays in the pertinent outcomes*, we would like to suggest that during intake with PD patients, as well as periodically in the course of treatment, clinicians employ a comprehensive assessment of stressful events, positive events, and social support. Instruments such as the Derogatis Stress Profile (DSP; Derogatis & Fleming 1997) and the Life Stressors and Social Resources Inventory (Moos & Moos 1997) might be particularly pertinent here, particularly in assessing levels of negative and positive events and extant social support. As well, social network analysis, a data analysis procedure originating in sociology, enables mapping of the structure of individuals' social environment, including this network's density, the centrality of the patient in relation to it, and other pertinent indicators of embeddedness in the social structure. With respect to guideline (b), *identify how clients, constrained by their personalities, psychopathologies, and strengths, actively influence their environment*, we underscore the need, during intake, to comprehensively assess the content and structure of patients' mental representations of self and others, preferably using established procedures such as the Structural Analysis of Social

Behavior (SAS-B, Benjamin 1994), the Social Cognition and Object Relations Scale (SCORS, Westen et al. 1991) and the Object Relations Inventory (ORI, Blatt et al. 1997). The principal challenge pertaining to this guideline would be to link the data derived from the assessment of mental representations to the data derived from assessing the patients' social context, thus identifying how PD patients, constrained by their object relations, create a maladaptive social environment.

Finally, guideline (c), *differentiate between vicious, risk-related, interpersonal cycles, and "virtuous," protective-based ones*, is particularly pertinent to work with people with PDs, because the tumultuous nature of these people's behavior and environment often impedes clinicians' appreciation of their strength and resilience. However, to paraphrase Sullivan (who initially referred to people with schizophrenia), people with PD are "more human than otherwise." And hence they, too, have strengths (Marsh et al. 1996). Indeed, it is often the case that patients' PD features are not disabling but are also protective. For instance, as reported above, individuals with elevated dependency generate both negative events and positive events and social support (Mongrain 1998; Shahar & Priel 2003), and it is quite likely that this complex pattern is applied to individuals with dependent personality disorder (DPD); these individuals' social context consists of both rejecting and supportive significant others, and sometimes the very same significant other engages in both (see Bornstein 1998, for a call to "depathologize" dependency). Similarly, narcissistic individuals actively generate both competition and admiration from others, and both types of "action" create a fragile and dynamic equilibrium in these individuals' environment. It is incumbent upon the clinician working with PD to identify these protective interpersonal cycles, in addition to the more readily identifiable "vicious" ones.

Next, a systematic application of guidelines (a) through (c) might be used to assess progress in therapy, as well as the possibility of termination. To illustrate, to the extent that a patient with BPD begins treatment by repeatedly eliciting rejections from others (as in the case described above), a TAF-oriented evaluation of treatment progress, predicated not only on the impressions of the clinician and patient, but also on change scores derived from the contextual instruments mentioned above, might reveal that he or she no longer does so, or at least does so with markedly diminished frequency. If this is the case, and constraints for treatment termination exist, then it would be reasonable to terminate even if the basic personality structure is unaltered and more psychotherapeutic work would be optimal.

References

Bandura, A. (1978). The self system in reciprocal determinism. *American Psychologist, 33*, 334–358.

Benjamin, L. S. (1994). SASB: A bridge between personality theory and clinical psychology. *Psychological Inquiry, 5* (4), 273–316.

Benjamin, L. S., & Wonderlich, S. A. (1994). Social perceptions and borderline personality disorder: The relation to mood disorders. *Journal of Abnormal Psychology, 103* (4), 610–624.

Blatt, S. J. (1995). The destructiveness of perfectionism. *American Psychologist, 50*, 1003–1020.

Blatt, S. J., Auerbach, J. S., & Levy, K. N. (1997). Mental representations in personality development, psychopathology, and the therapeutic process. *General Review of Psychology, 1*, 351–374.

Blatt, S. J., & Zuroff, D. C. (2005). Empirical evaluation of the assumptions in identifying evidence based treatment in mental health. *Clinical Psychology Review, 25*, 459–486.

Borenstein, R. F. (1998). Depathologizing dependency. *Journal of Nervous and Mental Diseases, 186*, 67–73.

Brunstein, J. C. (1993). Personal goals and subjective well-being: A longitudinal study. *Journal of Personality and Social Psychology, 65*, 1061–1070.

Buss, D. M. (1987). Selection, evocation, and manipulation. *Journal of Personality and Social Psychology, 53*, 1214–1221.

Cantor, N. (1990). From thought to behavior: "Having" and "doing" in the study of personality and cognition. *American Psychologist, 45*, 735–750.

Chiesa, M., Drahorad, C., & Longo, S. (2000). Early termination of treatment in personality disorder treated in a psychotherapy hospital. *British Journal of Psychiatry, 177*, 107–111.

Cohen, S. (2004). Social relations and health. *American Psychologist, 59*, 676–684.

Daley, S. E., Burge, D., & Hammen, C. (2000). Borderline personality disorder symptoms as predictors of 4-year romantic relationship dysfunction in young women: Addressing issues of specificity. *Journal of Abnormal Psychology, 109*, 451–460.

Daley, S. E., Hammen, C., Burge, D., Davila, J., Paley, B., Lindberg, N., & Herzberg, D. S. (1999). Depression and Axis II symptomatology in an adolescent community sample: Concurrent and longitudinal associations. *Journal of Personality Disorders, 13*, 47–59.

Daley, S. E., Hammen, C., Davila, J., & Burge, D. (1998). Axis II symptomatology, depression, and life stress during the transition from adolescence to adulthood. *Journal of Consulting and Clinical Psychology, 66,* 595–603.

Depue, R. A., & Monroe, S. M. (1986). Conceptualization and measurement of human disorder in life stress research: The problem of chronic disturbance. *Psychological Bulletin, 99,* 36–51.

Derogatis, L. R., & Fleming, M. P. (1997). The Derogatis Stress Profile: A theory driven approach to stress measurement. In C. R. Zalaquett & R. J. Wood (Eds.), *Evaluating stress: A book of resources* (pp. 113–140). Lanham, MD; London: Scarecrow Press.

Emmons. R. A. (1986). Personal striving: An approach to personality and subjective well-being. *Journal of Personality and Social Psychology, 51,* 1058–1068.

Hammen, C. (1991). The generation of stress in the course of unipolar depression. *Journal of Abnormal Psychology, 100,* 555–561.

Hammen, C. (2006). Stress generation in depression: Reflections on origins, research, and future directions. *Journal of Clinical Psychology, 62,* 1083–1096.

Harris, A. (1984). Action theory, language, and the unconscious. *Human Development, 27,* 196–204.

Hilsenroth, M. J., Holdwick, D. J., Jr., Castlebury, F. D., & Blais. M. A. (1998). The effects of DSM-IV cluster B personality disorder symptoms on the termination and continuation of psychotherapy. *Psychotherapy, 35,* 163–176.

Giesen-Bloo, J., Van Dyck, R., Spinhoven, P., Van Tilburg, W., Dirksen, C., Van Asselt, T., Kremers, I., Nadort, M., & Arntz, A. (2006). Outpatient psychotherapy for borderline personality disorder: Randomized trial of schema-focused therapy vs transference-focused psychotherapy. *Archives of General Psychiatry, 63,* 649–658.

Johnson, J. G., Cohen, P., Brown, J. Smalies, E. M., & Bernstein, D. P. (1999). Childhood maltreatment increases risk for personality disorders during early adulthood. *Archives of General Psychiatry, 56,* 600–606.

Little, B. R. (1999). Personal projects and social ecology: Themes and variations across the life span. In J. Brandster & R. M. Lerner (Eds.), *Action and self-development: Theory and research through the lifespan* (pp. 169–220). Thousand Oaks, CA: Sage.

Marsh, D. T., Lefley, H. P., Evans-Rhodes, D., Ansell, V. I., & Doerzbacher, B. M. (1996). The family experience of mental illness: Evidence for resilience. *Psychiatric Rehabilitation Journal, 20,* 3–12.

Mongrain, M. (1998). Parental representations and support-seeking behavior related to dependency and self-criticism. *Journal of Personality, 66,* 151–173.

Mongrain, M., Vettese, L. C., Shuster, B., & Kendal, N. (1998). Perceptual biases, affect, and behavior in relationships of dependents and self-critics. *Journal of Personality and Social Psychology, 75,* 230–241.

Monroe, S. M., & Simmons, A. D. (1991). Diathesis-stress theories in the context of life stress research: Implications for the depressive disorders. *Psychological Bulletin, 110,* 406–425.

Monroe, S., & Steiner, S.C. (1986). Social support and psychopathology: Interrelations with preexisting disorder, stress, and personality. *Journal of Abnormal Psychology, 95,* 29–39.

Moos, R. H., & Moos, B. S. (1997). Life stressors and social resources inventory: A measure of adults and youths' life context. In C. R. Zalaquett & R. J. Wood (Eds.), *Evaluating stress: A book of resources* (pp. 177–190). Lanham, MD; London: Scarecrow Press.

Needles, D., & Abramson, L. Y. (1990). Positive life events, attributional style, and hopelessness: Testing a model of recovery from depression. *Journal of Abnormal Psychology, 99,* 156–165.

Posner, M. I, Rothbart, K. M, Vizueta, N., Thomas, K. M., Levy, K. N., Fossella, J., et al. (2003). An approach to the psychobiology of personality disorders. *Development and Psychopathology, 15,* 1093–1106.

Priel, B., & Shahar, G. (2000). Dependency, self-criticism, social context and distress: Comparing moderating and mediating models. *Personality and Individual Differences, 28,* 515–525.

Shahar, G. (2001). Personality, shame, and the breakdown of social ties: The voice of quantitative depression research. *Psychiatry: Interpersonal and Biological Processes, 64,* 229–238.

Shahar, G. (2004). Transference-countertransference: Where the (political) action is. *Journal of Psychotherapy Integration, 14* (4), 371–396.

Shahar, G. (2006). Introduction to the special section on the action perspective in clinical psychology. *Journal of Clinical Psychology, 62,* 1053–1064.

Shahar, G. (In press). What measure of interpersonal dependency predicts social support? *Journal of Personality Assessment.*

Shahar, G., Blatt, S. J., Zuroff, D. C., & Pilkonis, P. A. (2003). Role of perfectionism and personality disorder features in patients' responses to brief treatment for depression. *Journal of Consulting and Clinical Psychology, 71,* 229–233.

Shahar, G., Cross, L. W., & Heinrich, C. C. (2005). Representations in action (Or: Psychoanalytic theories of mental representations meet action models of development). *Psychoanalytic Study of the Child, 59,* 261–293.

Shahar, G., Henrich, C. C., Blatt, S. J., Ryan, R., & Little, T. D. (2003). Interpersonal relatedness, self-definition, and their motivational orientation during adolescence: A theoretical and empirical integration. *Developmental Psychology, 39,* 470–483.

Shahar, G., & Porcerelli, J. H. (2006). The action formulation (TAF): A proposed heuristic for clinical case formulation. *Journal of Clinical Psychology, 62,* 1053–1064.

Shahar, G., Blatt, S. J., Zuroff, D. C., Krupnick, J., & Sotsky, S. M. (2004). Perfectionism impedes social relations and response to brief treatment for depression. *Journal of Social and Clinical Psychology, 23,* 140–154.

Shahar, G., & Priel, B. (2002). Positive life events and adolescent emotional distress: In search for protective-interactive processes. *Journal of Social and Clinical Psychology, 21,* 645–668.

Shahar, G., & Priel, B. (2003). Active vulnerability, adolescent distress, and the mediating/suppressing role of life events. *Personality and Individual Differences, 35,* 199–218.

Smith, J. (1999). Life planning: Anticipating future life goals and managing personal development. In J. Brandtstadter & R. M. Lerner (Eds.), *Action and self development: Theory and research through the lifespan* (pp. 223–255). Thousand Oaks, CA: Sage.

Smith, T. L., & Benjamin, L. S. (2002). The functional impairment associated with personality disorders. *Current Opinion in Psychiatry, 15,* 135–141.

Wachtel, P. L. (1994). Cyclical processes in personality and psychopathology. *Journal of Abnormal Psychology, 103,* 51–66.

Warnes, H. (1984–85). The termination phase of psychoanalysis in a narcissistic personality. *International Journal of Psychoanalytic Psychotherapy, 10,* 159–171.

Westen, D., Lohr, N., Silk, K. R., Gold, L., & Kerber, K. (1990). Object relations and social cognition in borderline, major depressives, and normals: A thematic apperception test analysis. *Psychological Assessment, 2,* 355–364.

Widom, C. S. (1999). Childhood victimization and the development of personality disorders: Unanswered questions remain (commentary). *Archives of General Psychiatry, 56* (7), 607–608.

Zatura, A. J., & Reich, J. W. (1983). Positive events and quality of life. *Evaluation and Program Planning, 4,* 355–361.

Zuroff, D. C., & Duncan, N. (1999). Self-criticism and conflict resolution in romantic couples. *Canadian Journal of Behavioral Science, 31,* 137–149.

19

TERMINATION OF SUBSTANCE ABUSE TREATMENT: AN ENDING OR A BEGINNING?

ANNE HELENE SKINSTAD, DANA MILLER, PETER E. NATHAN, AND CANDACE PETERS

It's good to have an end to journey toward; but it's the journey that matters, in the end.

Ursula K. LeGuin

Introduction

Termination is an integral aspect of the treatment of any mental disorder. Careful consideration of the termination process, whether it is initiated by the clinician or by the client, is especially important for clients who come to treatment for substance use disorders. In fact, initial plans for termination of treatment ought to be included in the process of assessment of the patient, right at the beginning of treatment (Novick & Novick 2006). Clinicians who have treated clients with substance use disorders often have their clients drop out of treatment, not show up to appointments, or skip appointments and come back after a period of time. Doing research with clients with substance use disorders is also challenging for similar reasons. With this knowledge in mind, it is especially important for clinicians to address this issue with the client early in treatment.

Termination of treatment of clients with substance use disorders has taken many forms through the years, and has been heavily influenced by the perception of substance use as a disease, where motivation for change may or may not be present (Miller & Rollnick 2002). Termination practices in substance abuse treatment have not been based on empirically supported research. Instead, substance abuse practitioners have tended to terminate treatment when they perceive that clients have successfully completed treatment and "graduated." Termination of treatment has also occurred after the therapist has concluded that treatment has been unsuccessful, as when the client drops out of treatment, ends treatment against professional advice, and/or continues abusing substances. In these instances, therapists point to a lack of motivation for treatment as the principal reason for treatment termination. When this happens, practitioners very often feel they have failed. In this regard, Roget and Storti (2006) concluded that one of the most important reasons that practitioners leave the field of substance abuse treatment is the high level of relapse by the clients they treat.

This chapter is designed to provide an overview of the range of treatment termination practices used with substance abusers. In so doing, we hope to relate these approaches to the current definition of substance use disorder as a chronic, relapsing disease with oscillations in the client's motivation to change. Considerations of treatment termination, beginning very early in treatment, should be based both on a thorough assessment of the client and his or her substance abuse problem, as well as on the nature of the planned treatment approach. The goal is to reduce the likelihood of premature termination.

Some treatment manuals describe treatment termination processes. Accordingly, this chapter will review a few of those treatment manuals. In this context, we will also consider some of the most important issues in termination of treatment of clients with substance use disorders.

Termination of treatment, as one aspect of the entire treatment process, needs to be carefully planned by the therapist and anticipated by the client. The American Psychological Association (APA 2002) has included guidelines for the termination of treatment in its ethical code. Thus, the APA's *Ethical Principles* (10.10: Termination of Therapy) states the following:

(a) Psychologists terminate therapy when it becomes clear that the client/patient no longer needs the services, is not likely to benefit, or is being harmed by continued service.

(b) Psychologists may terminate therapy when threatened or otherwise endangered by client/patient or another person with whom the client/patient has a relationship.

(c) Except where precluded by the actions of clients/client or third-party payers, prior to termination psychologists provide pre-termination counseling and suggest alternative service providers as appropriate. (16)

The American Counseling Association (ACA) also provides ethical guidelines for termination (ACA 1995).

Termination of treatment can be initiated by the client or the therapist. Clients can terminate treatment either by dropping out of contact with the therapist, by terminating against medical advice, or by prematurely initiating the termination of the treatment (Novick & Novick 2006). Dropping from treatment and prematurely terminating treatment may create concerns about the client's welfare, specifically how he or she will handle his/her substance use disorder.

Of course, there are also times when premature termination of treatment does not mean that the patient is not doing well. To this end, 66.7 percent of clients who recover from substance use disorders in Germany and 77 percent of those who do so in Canada apparently did so spontaneously (Rumpf et al. 2000; Sobell, Cunningham, & Sobell 1996). In a related investigation, Walters (2000) found few meaningful differences between clients who continued using substances, spontaneous remitters, and those who stopped using substances after treatment. In like fashion, Klingemann's (1991) study of natural recovery showed that clients who had successfully used unassisted pathways to recovery were a very heterogeneous group that called upon a variety of forms of motivation to stop their problematic use of substances. Another related study indicated that social resources and problem severity had an important impact on successful natural recovery from substance use (Blomquist 1999). These few studies confirm that dropping from treatment does not necessarily mean treatment failure; in some situations, clients need to recover in their own way and without assistance.

Since the group of natural remitters is very heterogeneous, with different strengths, social support networks, and different levels of problem severity (Bischof et al. 2003), even the most diligent assessment may not predict who may need more assistance and who may not need as much therapeutic support to succeed among clients who seek treatment. Therefore, termination of clients according to their own decision should be handled in such a way that if they do choose to return to treatment after a lapse or relapse, they will be able to do so without negative consequences or being made to feel shame and guilt.

Premature Terminations or Dropouts

Dropping out or premature termination from treatment is associated with a number of factors, both on the treatment/therapist side and the client side. Thus, a high percentage of the clients who dropped out of cocaine treatment early (before the tenth session) were found to be in "prosocial institutions": those in stable relationships, in regular employment or members of social organizations do better in treatment and stay in it longer (Sayre et al. 2002). Educational level also influences dropout rate: premature dropout is associated with lower educational levels (Means et al. 1989). In one sample, African American males were significantly more likely to drop out of treatment than other clients (King & Canada 2004). Changes in prosocial status, such as losing a job or going through a divorce, can also be a relapse trigger for women with substance use disorders (Wilsnack & Wilsnack 1995).

Clients in treatment for substance abuse often leave treatment prematurely. Many believe that lack of motivation for change in addictive behaviors is a key determinant of the decision to drop from treatment (Ball et al. 2006). As well, cognitive dysfunction (McKellar et al. 2006), a disability (Brecht, Greenwell, & Anglin 2005), more severe drug use and lower severity of alcohol dependence have all been reported to increase the risk that males will drop out of treatment for substance use disorders (McKellar et al. 2006). Methamphetamine (meth) abusers with legal supervision status at admission to treatment have been found to stay longer in treatment and more often complete treatment than those meth users who are not under legal supervision (Brecht, Greenwell, & Anglin 2005).

Premature termination of treatment by the client is also predicted by certain therapist variables, including conflicts among staff, concerns about privacy, and boundary issues (Ball et al. 2006). By contrast, a less controlling and more supportive treatment environment has been reported to reduce dropout rates and increase retention in substance abuse treatment (McKellar et al. 2006). Not surprisingly, the nature of the therapeutic alliance also seems to be influential in reducing rates of premature termination from treatment. Two Finnish studies, for example, reported that rates of premature dropout from treatment were significantly reduced when the therapist and client independently rated their interaction as positive and the client felt positively about the therapist's interpersonal skills (Saarnio 2002). It has also been found that clients who had a positive attitude toward Alcoholics Anonymous or Narcotics Anonymous were less likely to leave treatment prematurely (Saarnio & Knuuttila 2003).

Discharge Against Medical/Psychological Advice

Treatment approaches in earlier years were more confrontational and more often predicated on the assumption that the therapist always knew what was best for clients (Miller & Hester 2003). Newer approaches acknowledge the importance of client participation in their own treatment planning, as well as in decisions about how long treatment should last (Brown et al. 2000). As a result, discharge against medical advice is no longer common, although it can happen when the client also has a serious medical condition. Termination in such situations should still permit clients to return to treatment when they are in need of further support or assistance.

Completion of treatment for substance use disorders is a strong predictor of positive treatment outcomes, while premature termination is associated with negative outcomes. Furthermore, the chances that clients who complete treatment, participate in aftercare, and do not relapse during the first three months after treatment will stay sober for longer periods are greatly enhanced (Miller, Westerberg, & Waldron 2003). Furthermore, previous assumptions of the negative impact on the client when they left AMA (against medical advice) may not be correct. A retrospective review of cases defined as AMA indicate that clients left the treatment programs for personal reasons, such as illness in the family, reconciliation with family members or significant others, or financial and legal problems (Green, Watts, & Dhopesh 2004). Pages et al. (1998), which suggest several methods to reduce AMA frequency, such as assessing the client's motivation for change early, focusing on psychosocial issues as well as introducing interventions early in the treatment process, and focusing on reinforcing the clients' successful strategies for change of the substance use disorder. Clients who have previous AMA discharges need specific attention and should be connected to aftercare services early in the treatment process.

A number of treatment approaches have been shown to be effective for substance use disorders (Finney, Wilbourne, & Moos 2006), including cognitive-behavioral coping skills therapy (Monti et al. 1997; Monti & O'Leary 1999), the community reinforcement approach (Higgins et al. 2002), contingency management (Lussier et al. 2006), motivational enhancement and motivational interviewing (Hettema, Steele, & Miller 2005), and behaviorally oriented couples and family therapy (Stanton & Shadish 1997). Most of these approaches include explicit efforts to prevent relapse (Witkiewitz, Marlatt, & Walker 2005).

Relapse prevention is especially effective for clients with alcohol use disorders (Irvin et al. 1999), although it has also been used effectively in conjunction with treatments for a number of other psychological disorders (Witkiewitz & Marlatt 2004).

Adolescents with substance use disorders tend to have higher dropout rates (Winters 1999) and lower rates of abstinence following treatment (Miller 1996), which suggests that adolescents tend to terminate treatment more often or more quickly than adults (Chung & Maisto 2006). One reason may be that the prospect of lifelong abstinence, which is the norm for most adolescent treatment for substance abuse, is a difficult treatment goal for young people. Gender differences in relapse patterns, such as symptoms of internal distress and unresolved problems with their children are also observed (Walitzer & Dearing 2006). One can also hypothesize that older adults have different reasons and perspectives on relapse as well, often provoked by feelings of loneliness and loss of family members and friends (DiClemente 2006).

Treatment Manuals That Include Specific Guidelines for Termination

Although termination of treatment by clients with substance use disorders is an important aspect of treatment and clearly needs to be carefully planned, neither the impact of termination on treatment outcome nor the most effective elements of the termination process have been studied. However, a number of manuals for treatment of substance abuse discuss termination and include suggestions for the material to be included in the termination session (Miller et al. 1994; Najavits 2002; Nowinski, Baker, & Carroll 1992; Carroll 1997; Kadden et al. 1992).

Thus, treatment manuals, including those used in PROJECT MATCH (Miller et al. 1994; Nowinski, Baker, & Carroll 1992; Kadden et al. 1992; Carroll 1997) as well as individual treatment manuals like the *Seeking Safety Manual* (Najavits 2002), all recommend that some of the same issues ought to be addressed during termination. They suggest, for example, that preparation for termination may be as important as the specific techniques and procedures used during the termination session itself. To this end, for example, the manual for cognitive-behavioral coping skills treatment for substance abuse recommends that clients be prepared for the end of treatment at least four to five weeks before the actual termination session (Kadden et al. 1992). Clarifying the length and limitations of this treatment is said to be important to decrease client anxiety, clinical deterioration, and acting out behavior at the time of treatment termination (Carroll 1997).

Among the most frequent recommendations made by the treatment manuals of relevance to termination are to summarize the gains the client has achieved prior to termination (Miller et al. 1994), to support the client's continuing capacity to change (Velasquez et al. 2001), to anticipate emotional and social emergencies and rehearse methods of dealing with them (Kadden et al. 1992), to identify the unfinished business in treatment on which the client and therapist agree (Glidden-Tracey 2005), and to explore additional areas of change the client may want to achieve in the future (Miller et al. 1994). Reminding the client of the importance of participation in aftercare (Miller et al. 1994) and in mutual self-help groups (Nowinski, Baker, & Carroll

1992) are also generally suggested in treatment manuals. This is also the time for the therapist to ask for feedback, both positive and negative (Najavits 2002). However, in doing so, the therapist needs to be aware of his or her own possible countertransference issues related to ending the relationship and losing the client.

Some of the other suggestions related to termination in therapy manuals refer to the treatment that has preceded the termination session. To this end, Miller et al. (1994) suggest that termination at the end of motivational enhancement therapy should include a review of the most important factors motivating the client to change in order to again elicit important self-motivational statements, reaffirm the client's commitment to change, and reconsider strategies to maintain the change process. Nowinski, Baker, & Carroll (1992) suggest that the process of termination from twelve-step treatment should include efforts to contrast the client's views on alcoholism before treatment and at treatment termination, their views on Alcoholics Anonymous (AA) before and after treatment, and their plans for using AA during the crucial ninety days following treatment.

Treatment Changes

Approaches to treatment for substance abuse have changed a great deal over the past thirty years. Thirty years ago, twenty-eight days of inpatient treatment was popular, and alcoholism and drug dependence were treated in different facilities with different methods and procedures (White 1998). The treatment philosophy at the time was that clients who experienced a relapse into substance abuse or decided to leave treatment against "medical advice," were insufficiently motivated for treatment and should be discharged from treatment. In both instances, termination from treatment typically went unplanned and appropriate termination procedures were not conducted. By contrast, nowadays, with changes in the definition and perception of substance use disorders as chronic relapsing diseases, a relapse into substance use does not usually lead to premature termination. Rather, a relapse is used as a way to teach clients how to handle urges to use substances and how to deal with feelings and situations they feel unprepared to handle without their substance as a crutch.

In contrast with the view that clients who relapsed were not motivated for change and hence deserved to be discharged, the view currently is that clients may experience varying stages of change (DiClemente, Bellino, & Neavins 1999) at various times in the recovery process, so that the treatment strategies should be adjusted to the client's particular stage of change throughout treatment. In other words, termination from treatment is not necessarily the strategy of choice for clients who relapse.

In a slightly different conceptualization of the change process during therapy, White and Kurtz (2006) describe four stages of recovery. They include (1) recovery priming, during which the client may discover for the first time some of the positive aspects of staying away from the problem behavior; (2) recovery initiation, in which the client has discovered workable ways to problem solve their problems, not exclusively those related to substances, but those deriving from other aspects of their life as well; (3) recovery maintenance, and (4) recovery termination which coincides for the most part with the maintenance stage in the stages of change (Prochaska & DiClemente 1984; Prochaska, Norcross, & DiClementi 1994). Here, White and Kurtz (2006) refer to the client's achievement of recovery stability, as well as to the client's sustaining and refining their problem-solving abilities (third stage) and achieving global health and diminished pre-occupation with recovery itself (fourth stage). Even though this model has not been tested empirically in its entirety, its elements make sense from a clinical perspective. As clinicians, we have seen on numerous occasions that clients, whom we thought would never relapse, did exactly that after many years of sobriety. Not until recovery termination is reached do White and Kurtz (2006) talk of recovery termination, which they call the thirteenth step and describe in terms of global health and increased capacity for intimacy and serenity, self-acceptance (White & Kurtz 2006), and even public service (White 2006).

Planned Termination

Professionals and clients alike can find it difficult to accept that substance use disorders are often chronic and relapsing diseases (White 2006). However, it is important for clients to come to terms with this aspect of the disorder in order to prepare themselves for urges to use and lapses so that they do not lead to full-blown relapses (Marlatt & Witkiewitz 2005). Arming a client with these strategies can also prevent premature termination and dropping out of treatment by lessening the guilt and stigma of these challenges to recovery. Planned termination should include discussing with the client the importance of recontacting with the treatment center in the event of a relapse. The therapist should make sure the client understands that the door to the therapist's office is open, contact will be welcomed, and the client will be able to return to treatment without losing face in the event of a relapse (Zane 2006).

A number of treatment programs in the United States use graduation ceremonies to formally end treatment of the substance use disorder (Jones 1996). Using graduation signifies an end to a process, which sometimes is not finished by the time a client graduates from treatment. Termination rituals are often considered a rite of passage, which indicates that the client has achieved major goals for participation (Shapiro & Ginzberg 2002). Clinical experience has shown us that sometimes final graduation rituals make it difficult for the client to return with no shame if faced with difficulties at a later stage. Graduation rituals, without any planning for aftercare, may also not acknowledge the chronic nature of a substance use disorder.

Miller (1996) and Miller and Marlatt (1987) developed methods to use both before, after, and at follow-up from treatment, often referred to as the Brief Drinkers Check Up. The latter is intended to keep the door open to clients and their families whether or not they have relapsed, and to give them the opportunity to discuss possible lapses and further assist them in controlling such situations. These assessment tools are used to assess many aspects of a client's life, how the client is using alcohol, and consequences of the alcohol use. This proactive approach may prevent dropout from treatment or early and premature termination of treatment.

As clinicians, we have often seen the chronicity of substance use disorders, and the following case illustrates how a client, who verbally exhibits motivation to change, has a hard time changing if the planned discharge is not quite as detailed or planned as the therapist and the client think it is.

Monty, nineteen years of age, began residential treatment after being charged with driving while intoxicated. Following his assessment he was recommended for residential care. The clinician diagnosed alcohol dependence and marijuana abuse. While in treatment, Monty displayed numerous outbursts of anger that required multiple staff members to intervene.

I first met Monty on the morning of his second day on the residential unit. He was a soft-spoken man with a childlike manner. He was a little taller than I am, had big brown eyes, and had a softness to his voice that reached out to everyone. Monty was quick to speak and took every chance to do so, generally starting with "I just need a minute." Fellow clients and staff alike were easily frustrated with Monty's constant display of high emotional need. Although Monty was punctual to group and individual sessions, he did not complete homework assignments. When reviewing this with him, he identified a willingness to write songs instead of answering questions. His ability to compose was outstanding and he soon began sharing his new works with anyone who would listen. After a short two weeks in residential Monty had demonstrated an ability to utilize his plan to control his anger, and had developed an aftercare plan. With tears in his eyes he said good-bye in a song to everyone on the residential unit. His aftercare plan was to attend Alcoholics Anonymous, find employment, and live with his nonusing family. That is exactly what he did.

After three months he was back at the door of the residential unit begging to return. He had relapsed, working his way quickly up to six quarts of beer daily over the preceding two weeks. He told the staff that his relapse occurred when he was with friends, celebrating the birth of their son. Remembering the injunction, "If I start to party I need to call or walk," he put one foot in front of the other and found his way back to the treatment facility.

During this residential treatment stay he was less eager to write songs, the anger outbursts were more frequent, and the staff became less responsive and less patient. Monty and I continued to work together during these six weeks to develop methods he felt would help him stay sober. On Wednesday, Monty decided he was ready to give it a try again. He had met the programming requirements, developed an aftercare plan that included attending intensive outpatient programming three nights a week, his family was waiting for him to return home. and he told the client community he was going to make this aftercare plan work. That is exactly what he did.

Only three weeks into intensive outpatient programming, Monty again found something he could celebrate, drank until morning, was admitted into the hospital emergency room, and within the hour died. The softness of his voice, his kind heart, childlike manner, and big brown eyes were gone.

Stages of Change

Monty's case illustrates a person who really wanted to change, but was not completely at the action phase, even though he verbally and in his prose was ready to make changes. Clients come to treatment with a range of levels of understanding of their individual problems and widely varying motivation to change (Prochaska & DiClemente 1984; Prochaska & DiClemente 1998). Preparation for termination of treatment should be based on the client's stage of change so that he or she feels comfortable returning to treatment if needed.

According to Prochaska and DiClemente's stages of change model, the person who is in the *precontemplation stage* does not recognize that his or her substance use is problematic and, accordingly, is not willing to change that behavior (Velasquez et al. 2001). This person is unlikely to approach a professional with a request for assistance with a substance use problem, although he or she may be urged by a spouse, an employer, or the court system to be evaluated. This person does not see that the negative consequences of substance abuse affect many aspects of life. As a result, the person in the precontemplation stage will probably be more defensive and resistant about changing the substance use problems after a meeting at which they are discussed rather than before such a meeting. This person sometimes benefits from information, and especially an open-ended opportunity to come to treatment if he or she changes his or her mind and chooses to do something about his or her problematic substance use. Their pride may be a hindrance if the therapist was confrontational about substance abuse. This person would not benefit from a termination of contact. He or she does not perceive the interaction with the therapist as anything other than an opportunity for information exchange; it is not seen as a consultation with someone who thinks of him or her as in need of treatment.

The person in the *contemplation stage* recognizes his or her problem and is actively engaged in considering whether or not to act on it, but he or she may not know how to deal with it. Persons in this stage who suffer from substance abuse not only recognize the existence of that problem, they may also have experienced its negative consequences and realized that its negatives outweigh its positives. Despite this recognition of the problem, this person may be very far from an actual commitment to change his or her substance-using behaviors. The contemplation stage may last for an extended period of time before the person is ready to move to the next stage of change. One of the therapist's most important responsibilities during this stage is to try to sway the balance between positive and negative aspects of substance use so as to initiate a change in the patient's behavior. The therapist might attempt to heighten the client's awareness of the negative impact of substance use on family, friends, and job in order to bring on a self-reevaluation and decision to make a change. Although therapy that ends in termination of contact is quite unlikely in this stage, it can happen. If it does, the client should be invited to return if he or she so chooses; he or she should also be given information about other treatment opportunities.

The following case describes Agnes, a person somewhere between the contemplation and preparation stages of change.

Agnes self-referred to outpatient treatment after she and her husband had become concerned about her alcohol consumption. She was a thirty-five-year-old woman who worked as an administrative assistant to the CEO of an insurance company. Her husband was the CEO (chief executive officer) of a shipping firm, who traveled a great deal. They had one son. Although Agnes had been in contact with the outpatient treatment program five years before this treatment episode started, she came to treatment at this time because she had concluded that her drinking had gotten a bit out of hand. However, because she accompanied her husband or her boss to business-related social events, she did not want to stop drinking or smoking altogether. Instead, she wanted to learn how to drink in a controlled fashion. Her consumption when she was admitted to the outpatient program was about a fifth of spirits per day, all consumed after work, before she went to bed.

Agnes was in the contemplation stage, in that she was prepared to learn how to control her drinking, unrealistic as that was in the therapist's eyes. At the beginning of treatment the therapist asked Agnes to self-monitor her drinking during the ensuing week. At this point the therapist was faced with deciding either to reject Agnes's unrealistic treatment goal and terminate further contact with her, or work in therapy to help her move to the preparation phase, in hopes she could be helped eventually to deal more realistically with her serious drinking problem.

By going along with Agnes's treatment plan, the therapist enabled her to return to treatment. After a time, her self-assessment led her to move to the preparation phase, where she successfully managed to achieve sobriety. Ultimately, she planned termination of treatment with her therapist and went back into the world armed with problem-solving strategies for high-risk situations, which enabled her to represent her boss and her husband without having to drink.

Persons in the *preparation stage* have begun to make concrete plans to change what they recognize as their substance use problem. Although they might have sought professional assistance previously, and might even have tried to change their behavior, they had likely not been completely successful in their efforts. At the same time, they probably have gained experiences that would be valuable in this effort to recover from substance abuse. Although they might well have support for their plan for recovery from family and friends, many of these persons also need assistance from a therapist to reach a firm commitment to recover. The therapist's principal responsibility in working with a person in the preparation change phase is to facilitate the change process by enhancing the person's self-efficacy and sense of self-liberation, as well as by supporting his or her efforts to continue healthy relationships after recovery. During this stage of change, the person sometimes needs assistance in organizing a stimulus control system to enable him or her to decide which high-risk situations he or she can handle without relapsing and which should be avoided (Velasquez et al. 2001). Understandably, the person is highly vulnerable during this stage, in part because he or she might be too confident of success. Termination of treatment during this stage is obviously premature, even though the client may feel he or she can manage things on his or her own. Accordingly, maintaining an open door for the client to return to treatment in case there is a lapse or a full-blown relapse is very important for eventual stable recovery.

Research has shown that when a client considers a lapse an irreversible failure or sign of disease (the *abstinence violation effect*), the lapse is more likely to develop into a full-blown relapse (Miller et al. 1996). The abstinence violation effect has predicted relapse in alcoholics (Collins & Lapps 1991), smokers (Curry, Marlatt, & Gordon 1987), and marijuana smokers (Stephens, Curtin, & Roffman 1994). Accordingly, the therapist's role in working with a client in the preparation stage should focus on enhancing problem-solving skills in high-risk situations, as well as teaching the client the differences between a lapse and a relapse. By contrast, termination of therapy at this change stage may lead the client to believe that a lapse/relapse is a problem that cannot be solved by reconnecting with the therapist.

Persons in the *action stage* have begun to make changes in their substance use disorder problem. These persons are motivated to do what it takes to change their behaviors. The principal pitfall for both therapist and client in this phase of change is the possibility that the therapist will overlook the challenges the client faces in undertaking these changes, especially when they seem to be doing well. Thus, the client might become overly optimistic and self-assured, so that he or she overlooks the challenges he or she will surely face in the future. Accordingly, as the client moves forward in this process, the therapist needs to support the client's self-efficacy and his or her problem-solving efforts, and help him or her control the temptation to assume that the problem is solved when sobriety has been achieved (Velasquez et al. 2001). Another goal for this stage is to assist clients in understanding that if they experience a relapse situation, it will be considered a learning experience by the therapist rather than a reason for rejection or termination of treatment. The message to clients should be that the longer they can stay away from their substance use behaviors, the more likely they are to succeed in the long run.

Cindy's case (below) illustrates the plan of action that we would recommend when clients reach the action phase.

Cindy was thirty-six years old. She had spent sixteen of those years drinking and using various drugs. She had three healthy children who had never left her care. I met Cindy in the late afternoon on the residential unit after she had again brought her counselor to tears. We talked about her remaining choices and she decided to give residential treatment one more try. Over the next four weeks she struggled with "everything." Eventually, she said to me that the light bulb had come on. As we talked further, she told me that she had a dream—a drug-using dream. These dreams were not uncommon for Cindy. What made this dream different was the vivid drama of her injecting methamphetamine into herself and her kids. When the needles were empty the kids wanted to help as they unscrewed the light bulbs and found more drugs. She awoke crying and swinging her arms to fend off everyone around her. After gathering herself together as best she could, she began to write in her journal. Cindy shared her words with me aloud. At times there was no meaning or structure to the writing, but it meant everything to Cindy. She cried, wiped away the tears, and continued to read.

When she was finished, she handed me another piece of paper. Cindy had developed an aftercare plan, which was detailed down to every hour of every day. She said that groups were not for her and asked to meet five times a week with a counselor for the first two weeks after she left the treatment setting, which we granted. She also wanted to call the treatment facility three times a day just to check in during the first two weeks, which we also granted. After two weeks she wanted to meet three nights a week and call in twice daily, and when that time had passed, twice a week with no calls for three months. Cindy was certain that this plan would help her to stay sober. She apologized to every staff member she felt she had verbally hurt, read her plan to the client community, and politely left the building.

Cindy's plan worked very well for her. She felt supported and heard for the first time in her life. As time passed, she was able to be more and more independent from the therapist and the treatment facility. Cindy's story is a good example of the importance of working with the client on what she thinks will work for her, assisting in a gradual termination of contact, as well as being available to assist when she needed support. For women this is especially important according to Brown et al. (2000), who believe that the stages of change may be different for women than men.

Ken's case is included as that of a client who was in an action phase and moved into a maintenance stage shortly after the first treatment episode.

Ken was a forty-five-year-old man who had spent his life working in construction. He was single and lived with his mother. Ken and his mother attended their family church of many generations weekly. After the service he and his mother would enjoy eating at the same local restaurant.

While in high school Ken and his friends began to drink beer after sporting events. As a young adult he continued to drink with friends after work at the area sports bar. This was a time for Ken to wind down from work, enjoy talking about recent events, and stay in touch with his community.

On a Thursday morning on the job, Ken's foreman came to him with the news that his mother had fallen and was being rushed to the hospital. Ken immediately responded and went to her side. His mother had twisted her knee and would need to stay in the hospital through the night. Of course Ken stayed at her side. As the sun began to set, he found himself becoming very agitated. He was unable to stop thinking about his friends at the bar after work. He wanted desperately to leave the hospital, "just for a little while," and join his friends. Despite this very strong urge, Ken did not leave his mother's side.

In part as a result of this experience, Ken called the treatment facility requesting assistance, received an assessment, and was placed in intensive outpatient treatment. When he entered my office, he had written a long list of names of people, places, and things that he had identified as related to his drinking. He talked about the difficulty he had at the hospital, and that he still wanted to join his friends each afternoon at the local bar. While he had resisted doing so, he understood that he needed assistance in building the skills that would ensure that he never picked up another drink. Ken talked about the importance of his mother and church in his life. He said he had not realized until she was harmed that there was anything wrong with the way he lived. Ken had an action plan that he intended to put into place and he followed it without exception. Over four treatment sessions, he talked about feeling physically and emotionally stronger as a result of his follow-through. We developed a plan for him to handle an urge to drink, how he should handle a lapse, and how he could contact the outpatient clinic if he felt a need for more extensive contact.

Approximately one year after I had last seen Ken, I was walking down the street. I heard a voice saying my name and, as I turned, I saw it was Ken. He said with pride that he had not had a drink and had been promoted to supplies buyer for his company.

Ken's case is an example of a client who really was in an action phase when he was admitted to treatment, and moved into a maintenance stage quickly. He was very concerned about his alcohol use disorder. He used the tools discussed in the sessions to stay sober. The "termination" of contact was made with Ken with the understanding that if he needed more contact and support to handle his alcohol use disorder, he should contact the treatment facility and his therapist.

A person in the *maintenance stage* has successfully traversed the action stage, changed the problem behavior, and now works to maintain the change. However, to do so is difficult. Clients struggle to prevent relapse into problem behaviors for a long time after the behavior has been confronted and sobriety has been achieved; the maintenance stage can last from 6 months to a lifetime. To this end, the difficulty of maintaining these changes in substance use can be best understood in accordance with the chronic, relapsing character of the substance use disorders. For some clients this may mean that as professionals we would try to provide long-term recovery management (White & Kurtz 2006).

The Most Effective, Research-Based Techniques for Discontinuing Treatment

The chronic disease model for understanding chronic substance abuse should also include a careful plan for aftercare once the intensive part of the treatment plan has been completed. A plan for aftercare can prevent premature relapse and premature termination; for these reasons, it is clearly associated with positive outcomes (Carroll 1996; Donovan 1996). The aftercare plan should be based on a careful assessment of the strengths, weaknesses, and interests of the client, as well as the resources of the community to which the client is discharged (Brown et al. 2002). Participating in mutual self-help group meetings and other kinds of substance-free programs enhance the probability of abstinence at six-months follow-up and better long-term aftercare attendance compared to clients in standardized aftercare treatment (Lash et al. 2004).

Aftercare should include focus on leisure activities and social connections such as involvement in religious activities and observances (Brown et al. 2004). It should also engage clients with community volunteers and networking activities (Hawkins et al. 1989) and focus on activities other than just substance use; it should directly address general family and marital problems (O'Farrell, Choquette & Cutter 1998). Although a thorough review of the aftercare literature is mixed, it does suggest that the more specific the interventions, the more likely the aftercare program will result in positive outcomes for the clients (McKay 2001).

Planned Termination

According to Novick and Novick (2006), termination from treatment is dependent on the phase of treatment in which it occurs: early treatment, the middle phase of treatment, or toward the end of treatment. As indicated earlier, different issues should be addressed as a function of when in treatment termination occurs; throughout the treatment process, plans for termination need to be a matter of concern for both therapist and client. Although there are many pitfalls in therapy with substance abusing clients, some can be mitigated by programming a thorough assessment of the client at the beginning of treatment. Every treatment episode should start with a question about how many other treatment episodes the client has had, and what led him/her to terminate treatment and later to return to treatment. Knowledge about the number of treatment episodes a client has had and the reasons reported for termination can prepare the therapist for the kind of relationship that can be developed and the kinds of reasons the client will use to end a therapeutic relationship (Wormnes 1985).

Summary of Principles of Successful Termination of Treatment of Substance Use Disorders

First of all, it is important to plan for termination in collaboration with the client early in the therapeutic relationship, and to dedicate one session to the discussion of the implications of termination for the client. Cindy's case really shows the importance of accepting the client's need for dependence and gradual development into independence from you as a therapist.

It is important to summarize the accomplishments of the client through treatment, and relate it back to the goals and objectives the client presented at the beginning of treatment. In addition, it is important to summarize the identified challenges to managing the substances, and the problems related to the use of the substances. The outlined aftercare plan is also important to review as well as reinforcing the importance of following up on the aftercare plan, attend mutual self-help group meetings, and not feel ashamed to contact treatment facilities or other people identified in the aftercare plan if need be. If the client and the therapist have identified "unfinished business," this should also be discussed and possible solutions should be offered. At last, the therapist can model openness and ask for feedback from the client, both positive and negative, and be prepared for the transfer and countertransference issues related to ending a relationship and losing a client (Najavits 2002).

References

American Counseling Association. (2005). ACA Code of Ethics, 2005. Retrived July 10, 2007, from www.aca.org

American Psychological Association. (2002). *Ethical principles of psychologists and code of conduct.* Washington DC: Author.

Ball, S. A., Carroll, K. M., Canning-Ball, M., & Rounsaville, B. (2006). Reasons for dropout from drug abuse treatment: Symptoms, personality, and motivation. *Addictive Behaviors, 31,* 320–330.

Bischof, G., Rumpf, H. J., Hapke, U., Meyer, C., & John, U. (2003). Types of natural recovery from alcohol dependence: a cluster analytic approach. *Addiction, 98,* 1737–1746.

Blomquist, J. (1999). Treated and untreated recovery from alcohol misuse: environmental influences and perceived reasons for change. *Substance Use and Misuse, 34,* 1371–1406.

Brecht, M. L., Greenwell, L., & Anglin, M. D. (2005). Methamphetamine treatment: Trends and predictors of retention and completion in a large state treatment system (1992–2002). *Journal of Substance Abuse Treatment, 29,* 295–306.

Brown, B. S., O'Grady, K., Battjes, R. J., & Farrell, E. V. (2004). Factors associated with treatment outcome in an aftercare population (2004). *American Journal on Addictions, 13,* 447–460.

Brown, T. G., Seraganian, P., Tremblay, J., & Annis, H. (2002). Matching substance abuse aftercare treatment to client characteristics. *Addictive Behaviors, 27,* 585–604.

Brown, V. B., Melchior, L. A., Panter, A. T., Slaughter, R., & Huba, G. J. (2000). Women's steps of change and entry into drug abuse treatment: A multidimensional stages of change model. *Journal of Substance Abuse Treatment, 18,* 231–240.

Carroll, K. M. (1996). Relapse prevention as a psychosocial treatment: A review of controlled clinical trials. *Experimental and Clinical Psychopharmacology, 4,* 46–54.

Carroll, K. M. (1997). *Improving compliance with alcoholism treatment.* Project MATCH monograph series, No. 6. Bethesda, MD: National Institute on Alcohol Abuse and Alcoholism.

Chung, T., & Maisto, S. A. (2006). Relapse to alcohol and other drug use in treatment of adolescents: Review and reconsideration of relapse as a change point in clinical course. *Clinical Psychology Review, 26,* 149–161.

Collins, L. R., & Lapp, W. M. (1991). Restraint and attributions: Evidence of the abstinence violation effect in alcohol consumption. *Cognitive Therapy in Research, 15,* 69–84.

Curry, S., Marlatt, G. A, & Gordon, J. R. (1987). Abstinence violation effect: Validation of an attributional construct with smoking cessation. *Journal of Consulting and Clinical Psychology, 55,* 145–149.

DiClemente, C. C. (2006). Natural change and the troublesome use of substances: A life-course perspective. In W. R. Miller & K. M. Carroll (Eds.), *Rethinking substance abuse: What the science shows, and what we should do about it* (pp. 18–96). New York: Guilford Press.

DiClemente, C. C., & Prochaska, J. O. (1998). Toward a comprehensive, trans-theoretical model of change. In W. R. Miller & N. Heather (Eds.), *Treating addictive behaviors* (pp. 3–24). New York: Plenum Press.

DiClemente, C. C., Bellino, L. E., & Neavins, E. M. (1999). Motivation for change and alcoholism treatment. *Alcohol Research and Health, 23,* 86–92.

Donovan, D. M. (1996). Marlatt's classification of relapse precipitants: Is the Emperor still wearing clothes? *Addiction, 91* (Suppl. 2), 131–137.

Finney, J. W., Wilbourne, P. L., & Moos, R. H. (2006). Psychosocial treatments for substance use disorders. In P. E. Nathan & J. Gorman (Eds.), *A Guide to treatment that works* (3rd ed. pp. 179–202). New York: Oxford University Press.

Glidden-Tracey, C. (2005). Terminating therapy with substance abuse clients. In C. Glidden-Tracey, *Counseling and therapy with clients who abuse alcohol or other drugs: An integrative approach* (pp. 248–272). Mahwah, NJ: Lawrence Erlbaum.

Green, P., Watts, D., Poole, S., & Dhopesh, V. (2004). Why clients sign out against medical advice (AMA): Factors motivating clients to sign out AMA. *American Journal of Drug and Alcohol Abuse, 30,* 489–493.

Hawkins, J. D., Catalano, R., Gillmore, M. R., & Wells, E. (1989). Skills training for drug abusers: generalization, maintenance and effects on drug use. *Journal of Consulting and Clinical Psychology, 57,* 559–563.

Hester, R. (1994). *Cognitive-behavioral coping skills therapy manual: A clinical research guide for therapists treating individuals with alcohol abuse and dependence.* National Institute on Alcohol Abuse and Alcoholism: Project Match Monograph Series: Volume 3. NIH Publication No. 94–3724.

Hettema, J., Steele, J., & Miller, W. R. (2005). Motivational interviewing. *Annual Review of Clinical Psychology, 1,* 91–111.

Higgins, S. T., Alessi, S. M., & Dantona, R. L. (2002). Voucher-based incentives: A substance abuse treatment innovation. *Addictive Behaviors, 27,* 887–910.

Irvin, J. E., Bowers, C. A., Dunn, M. E., & Wang, M. C. (1999). Efficacy of relapse prevention: A meta-analytic review. *Journal of Consulting and Clinical Psychology, 67,* 563–570.

Jones, D. M. (1996). Termination from drug treatment: Dangers and opportunities for clients of graduation ceremony. *Social Work with Clients, 19,* 105–115.

Kadden, R., Carroll, K., Donovan, D., Cooney, N., Monti, P., Abrams, D., et al. (1992). *Cognitive-behavioral coping skills therapy manual: A clinical research guide for therapists treating individuals with alcohol abuse and dependence.* Rockville, MD: National Institute on Alcohol Abuse and Alcoholism.

King, A. C., & Canada, S. A. (2004). Client-related predictors of early treatment drop-out in a substance abuse clinic exclusively employing individual treatment. *Journal of Substance Abuse Treatment, 26,* 189–195.

Klingemann, H. K. (1991). The motivation for change from problem alcohol and heroin use. *British Journal of Addiction, 86,* 727–744.

Lash, S. J., Burden, J. L., Monteleone, B. R., & Lehman, L. P. (2004). Social reinforcement of substance abuse treatment aftercare participation: Impact on outcome. *Addictive Behaviors, 29,* 337–342.

Lussier, J. P., Heil, S. H., Mongeon, J. A., Badger, G. J., & Higgins, S. T. (2006). A meta-analysis of voucher-based reinforcement therapy for substance use disorders. *Addiction, 101,* 192–203.

Marlatt, G. A., & Witkiewitz, K. (2005). Relapse prevention for alcohol and drug problems. In G. A. Marlatt & D. M. Donovan (Eds.), *Relapse prevention: Maintenance strategies in the treatment of addictive behaviors* (2nd ed.; pp. 1–44). New York: Guilford Press.

McKay, J. R. (2001). Effectiveness of continuing care interventions for substance abusers: Implications for the study of long-term effect. *Evaluations Review, 25,* 211–232.

McKellar, J., Kelley, J., Harris, A., & Moos, R. (2006). Pretreatment and during treatment risk factors for dropout among clients with substance use disorders. *Addictive Behaviors, 31,* 450–460.

Means, L. B., Small, M., Capone, D. M., Capone, T. J. Condon, R., Peterson, M., & Hayward, B. (1989). Client demographics and outcome in outpatient cocaine treatment. *International Journal of Addiction, 24,* 765–783.

Miller, W. R. (1996). What is a relapse? Fifty ways to leave the wagon. *Addiction, 91,* 1099–1108.

Miller, W.R. (1996). *Manual for Form-90: A structured assessment interview for drinking and related behaviors.* Project MATCH Monograph series: Volume 5. Rockville, MD: National Institute on Alcohol Abuse and Alcoholism.

Miller, W. R., & Hester, R. K. (2003). Treating alcohol problems: Toward an informed eclecticism. In R. K. Hester & W. R. Miller (Eds.), *Handbook of alcoholism treatment approaches: Effective alternatives* (3rd ed.; pp. 1–12). Boston: Allyn & Bacon.

Miller, W. R., & Marlatt, G. A. (1987). *Manual supplement for the Brief Drinker Profile, Follow-up Drinker Profile, and Collateral Interview form.* Odessa, FL: Psychological Assessment Resources.

Miller, W. R., Westerberg, V. S., Harris, R. J., & Tonigan, J. S. (1996). What predicts relapse? Prospective testing of antecedent models. *Addiction, 91* (Suppl.), 155–171.

Miller, W. R., Westerberg, V. S., Waldron, H. B. (2003). Evaluating alcohol problems in adults and adolescents. In R. K. Hester & W. R. Miller (Eds.), *Handbook of alcoholism treatment approaches: Effective alternatives* (3rd ed.; pp. 78–112). Boston: Allyn & Bacon

Miller, W. R., & Rollnick, S. (2002). *Motivational interviewing: Preparing people for change* (2nd ed.). New York: Guilford Press.

Miller, W. R., Zweben, A., Diclemente, C. C., & Rychtarik, R. G. (1994). *Motivational enhancement therapy manual: A clinical research guide for therapists treating individuals with alcohol abuse and dependence.* Project MATCH monograph series, No. 2. Rockville, MD: National Institute on Alcohol abuse and Alcoholism.

Monti, P. M., & O'Leary, T. A. (1999). Coping and social skills training for alcohol and cocaine dependence. *Psychiatric Clinics of North America, 22,* 447–470.

Monti, P. M., Rohsenow, D. J., Michalec, E., Martin, R. A., & Abrams, D. B. (1997). Brief coping skills treatment for cocaine abuse: Substance use outcomes at three months. *Addiction, 92,* 1717–1728.

Najavits, L. M. (2002). *Seeking safety: A treatment manual for PTSD and substance abuse.* New York: Guilford Press.

Novick, J., & Novick, K. K. (2006). *Good goodbyes: Knowing how to end in psychotherapy and psychoanalysis.* Lanham, MD: Jason Aronson.

Nowinski, J., Baker, S., & Carroll. K. M. (1992). *Twelve step facilitation therapy manual: A clinical research guide for therapists treating individuals with alcohol abuse and dependence.* Project MATCH monograph series, No. 1. Rockville, MD: National Institute on Alcohol Abuse and Alcoholism.

O'Farrell, T. J., Choquette, K. A., & Cutter, H. S. G. (1998). Couples relapse prevention sessions after behavioral marital therapy for male alcoholics: Outcomes during the three years after starting treatment. *Journal of Studies on Alcohol, 59,* 357–370.

Pages, K. P., Russo, J. E., Wingerson, D. K., Ries, R. K., Roy-Byrne, P. P., & Cowley, D. (1998). Predictors and outcome of discharge against medical advice from the pshyciatric units of a general hospital. *Psychiatric Services, 49,* 1187–1192.

Prochaska, J. O., & DiClemente, C. C. (1984). *The transtheoretical approach: Crossing traditional boundaries of treatment.* Homewood, IL: Dow Jones-Irwin.

Prochaska, J. O., & DiClemente, C. C. (1998). Comments, criteria and creating better models. In W. R. Miller & N. Heather (Eds.), *Treating addictive behaviors* (2nd ed.; pp. 39–45). New York: Plenum.

Prochaska, J. O., Norcross, J. C., & DiClemente, C. C. (1994). *Changing for good.* New York: Avon Books.

Roget, N. A., & Storti, S. A. (2006). Gender and substance abuse treatment workforce. *How can we better nurture the substance abuse treatment workforce.* Presented at the College on Problems of Drug Dependence Annual Scientific Meeting; June 22; Scottsdale, Arizona.

Rumpf, H. J., Bichof, G., Hapke, U., Meyer, C., & John, U. (2000). Studies on natural recovery from alcohol dependence: sample selection bias by media solicitation. *Addiction, 95,* 765–775.

Saarnio, P. (2002). Factors associated with dropping out from outpatient treatment of alcohol-other drug abuse. *Alcoholism Treatment Quarterly, 20,* 17–33.

Saarnio, P., & Knuuttila, V. (2003). A study of risk factors in dropping out from inpatient treatment of substance abuse. *Journal of Substance Use, 8,* 33–38.

Sayre., S. L., Schmitz, J. M., Stotts, A. L., Averill, P. M., Rhoades, H. M., & Grabowiski, J. J. (2002). Determining predictors of attrition in an outpatient substance abuse program. *American Journal of Alcohol Abuse, 28,* 55–72.

Shapiro, E. L., & Ginzberg, R. (2002). Parting gifts: Termination rituals in group therapy. *International Journal of Group Psychotherapy, 52,* 319–336.

Sobell, L. C., Cunningham, J. A., Sobell, M. M. (1996). Recovery from alcohol problems with and without treatment: prevalence in two population surveys. *American Journal of Public Health, 7,* 966–972.

Stanton, M. D., & Shadish, W. R. (1997). Outcome, attrition, and family-couples treatment for drug abuse: A meta-analysis and review of the controlled, comparative studies. *Psychological Bulletin, 122,* 170–191.

Stephens, R. S., Curtin, L., & Roffman, R. A. (1994). Testing the abstinence violation effect construct with marijuana cessation. *Addictive Behaviors, 19,* 23–32.

Velasquez, M. M., Maurer, G. G., Crouch, C., & DiClemente, C. D. (2001). *Group treatment for substance abuse: A stages-of-change therapy manual.* New York: Guilford Press.

Walitzer, K. S., & Dearing, R. L. (2006). Gender differences in alcohol and substance use relapse. *Clinical Psychology Review, 26,* 128–148.

Walters, G. D. (2000). Spontaneous remission from alcohol, tobacco, and other drug abuse: seeking qualitative answers to quantitative questions. *American Journal of Drug and Alcohol Abuse, 26,* 443–460.

White, W. L. (1998). *Slaying the dragon: A history of addiction treatment and recovery in america.* Bloomington, IL: Chestnut Health Systems, Lighthouse Institute.

White, W. L. (2006). Recovery: The next frontier. In W. L. White, E. Kurtz, & M. Sanders (Eds.), *Recovery management* (pp. 1–6). University of Illinois at Chicago: Great Lakes Addiction Technology Transfer Center.

White, W. L., & Kurtz, E. (2006). The varieties of recovery experiences: A primer for addiction treatment professionals and recovery advocates. *Recovery management* (pp. 7–43). University of Illinois at Chicago: Great Lakes Addiction Technology Transfer Center.

Wilsnack, S. C., & Wilsnack, R. W. (1995). Drinking and problem drinking in US women: Patterns and recent trends. In M. Galanter (Ed.), *Recent developments in alcoholism: Volume 12, Alcoholism and women* (pp. 30–60). New York: Plenum Press.

Winters, K. C. (1999). Treating adolescents with substance use disorders: An overview of practice issues and treatment outcome. *Substance Abuse, 20,* 203–225.

Witkiewitz, K., & Marlett, G. A. (2004). Relapse prevention for alcohol and drug problems: That was Zen. This is Tao. *American Psychologist, 59,* 224–235.

Witkiewitz, K., Marlett, G. A., & Walker, D. (2005). Mindfulness-based relapse prevention for alcohol and substance use disorders. *Journal of Cognitive Psychotherapy: An International Quarterly, 19,* 211–228.

Wormnes, B. (1985). Personal communication. Department of Clinical Psychology, University of Bergen, Norway.

Zane, N. (2006). Speaking the language: Cross-cultural issues in treatment of pathological gambling and related disorder. *Lost in translation? The challenge of turning good research into best practices.* Presentation at the 7th Annual NCRG Conference on Gambling and Addiction; November 12–14; Reno, Las Vegas.

20

CLINICAL CONSIDERATIONS IN THE TERMINATION OF PSYCHOTHERAPY WITH SUICIDAL PATIENTS

KIRK STROSAHL AND JOHN CHILES

Introduction

One of the more fascinating paradoxes in the field of psychotherapy is the role that therapy termination plays in defining the process of therapy itself. On the one hand, the main goal of therapy is to help the client obtain a level of effective functioning that eliminates the need for therapy. On the other hand, the process of therapy itself, if handled inappropriately, can effectively seal the client into a state of dependence on both therapy and the therapist, making it difficult if not impossible for any type of therapy termination to occur. For all the importance attached to termination and the clinical issues that it can stimulate, there is strikingly little evidence available to support the vast amounts of clinical lore in this area. A disproportionate amount of theory in this area originates in the psychodynamic camp where addressing transference and countertransference and helping the client appreciate and transcend both conscious and unconscious dynamics define the treatment approach. Termination is seen as another example of addressing conflicts that arise around making attachments and ending them in a healthy way.

The problem is that core psychodynamic concepts have not been substantiated in clinical research, leaving one to wonder whether these therapy processes are intrinsically generated by clients or by the therapists who systematically reinforce certain behaviors in the service of staying true to their therapy paradigm. Another difficulty is that the literature on better-researched, clinically effective therapy models, such as behavior therapy and cognitive behavior therapy, do not place much emphasis on termination as a clinically problematic event. Although a good therapeutic alliance is just as important for successful cognitive-behavioral treatment outcomes, the role of the therapist is defined as being more detached, less preoccupied with interpersonal processes in therapy, and modeling a personal scientist approach to understanding and changing problematic behavior. This allows the therapist to function as a consultant to the client and perhaps leads to less concern about the relationship itself being a factor in the successful ending of therapy.

Nonetheless, it is obvious that any form of therapy has a beginning and an end, and the downside of the cognitive and behavioral models is that very little is written specifically about factors that would allow for clinical studies of termination strategies. This chapter will focus specifically on clinical considerations in the termination of therapy with suicidal patients. The reader must understand that the most effective, research-based treatment for suicidality is cognitive behavior therapy. Cognitive and behavioral treatments have been shown to decrease suicidal ideation (Jobes et al. 1997; Lerner & Clum 1990; Patsiokas & Clum 1985; Rudd et al. 1996) as well as decrease the frequency and lethality of suicide attempts (Liberman & Eckman 1981; Salkovskis, Atha, & Storer 1990; Linehan et al. 1991; Rudd et al. 1996). Thus, we would strongly recommend that the evidence-based therapist delve into the principles and strategies that define these treatment approaches (cf. Chiles & Strosahl 2005 for a systematic review).

This chapter introduces the reader to a clinical model for understanding suicidality, and describes some attributes of suicidal patients that are both research based and likely to play a role in therapy termination. We will then address a very fundamental question: When do you terminate therapy with a suicidal patient? This will lead to some counterintuitive principles that will suggest several specific clinical strategies for addressing termination.

Understanding Suicidality

One of the factors likely to interfere with the process of termination is the therapist's lack of understanding of the core processes that produce suicidal behavior. Because suicidality by its very definition involves life-threatening behavior, the temptation is to view suicidal behavior as highly abnormal and indicative of significant psychiatric pathology. The high-risk nature of suicidal behavior leads many therapists to believe that it is their job to protect the client from self-destructive impulses. This may lead the therapist to take an overly conservative stance with respect to termination of therapy and inadvertently create a dependent relationship with the client in the name of rescuing the client from a potential death. Ultimately, the therapist will be in the best position clinically when suicidal behavior can be approached from a clinical, as opposed to a moral and paternalistic orientation.

Suicidal behavior is extremely common in the general population. Research suggests that as many as 20 percent of all members of the general population report at least one serious episode of suicidal ideation sometime in their life time. Between 10 and 12 percent of the general population indicate that they have made at least one suicide attempt (Strosahl, Linehan, & Chiles 1984). Suicidal patients account for 10 to 20 percent of outpatient mental health populations, and suicidality seems to span multiple diagnostic groups including the mood and anxiety disorder, personality disorders, substance abuse, and psychotic disorders. The conclusion we draw from this pattern of data is that suicidal behavior is ubiquitous, both in the general population and in clients seen in mental health and substance abuse treatment settings. Completed suicide itself, even in the highest risk groups, is very rare when compared to the vast number of nonfatal self-destructive acts. Suicidal behavior refers to multiple forms of behavior and there is even a growing consensus among suicidologists that there may be multiple populations of suicidal patients. This means that a therapist should not assume that the main goal of working with a suicidal patient is to prevent death, because the vast majority of suicidal patients will never die because of a suicide attempt. This ubiquity needs to be explained in a way that removes a variety of therapist fears that will get in the way of successful termination.

In other writings (Chiles & Strosahl 2005, 1995), we have provided a clinical model of suicidality that emphasizes learning and reinforcement principles. We describe suicidal behavior in all forms (i.e., ideation, verbalization, attempt, and completed suicide) as a learned problem-solving behavior that is reinforced by the internal and external consequences of the behavior. The internal reinforcements often include a need for immediate emotional relief from anxiety, impulses to hurt oneself, a pervasive sense of hopelessness and/or anger/victimization. Once the client has acted, many of these dark private experiences seem to dissipate. This has a powerful impact on the likelihood that suicidal behavior will be used again if these private experiences resurface (which they often do). External consequences can involve escaping an otherwise negative, conflict-ridden environment, recovering lost relationships, and quick emotional relief. Ours is certainly not the only cognitive-behavioral account of suicidality, but it is representative of the general stance taken in the cognitive and behavioral community. Suicidal behavior is a form of problem-solving behavior and the "problem" that is being solved is negative private states that are viewed as intolerable, interminable, and inescapable (the Three I's).

Attributes of Suicidal Patients

In addition to understanding this simple model of suicidality, the therapist must appreciate the core personality and environmental attributes of suicidal patients. For well over three decades there has been extensive research conducted to identify the attributes that predispose people to suicidal behavior (cf. Chiles & Strosahl 2005 for a comprehensive review). Not surprisingly, some of these same factors can potentially complicate the process of psychotherapy termination if they not managed properly.

Experiential and Emotional Avoidance

Experiential avoidance is the unwillingness to make direct contact with unpleasant thoughts, feelings, memories, or bodily sensations. Experientially avoidant clients use any number of psychological strategies to avoid unpleasant private experiences. These include "numbing" behaviors such as drug/alcohol use, thought and emotion suppression, and situational avoidance. In a recent review of the experiential avoidance literature, Hayes et al. (1996) found that experiential avoidance is a reliable predictor of suicidal behavior, but is also linked to a variety of mental and substance use disorders. Put simply, clients who are unwilling to experience unpleasant private events are going to use avoidance as a primary coping mechanism. In the context of psychotherapy termination, a suicidal patient might revert back to suicidal behavior as a way of distracting him- or herself from uncomfortable thoughts, feelings, or memories that are triggered by talk of termination. Obviously, it is important to directly elicit these reactions in session and have the client "get present" with them without having to defend against them. This will help the client experientially understand that feelings of sadness, vulnerability, loss, or loneliness can be "accepted" for what they are. There is no need to run from them into self-destructive coping strategies. It is human to react in these ways to the end of an important relationship.

Poor Problem-Solving Skills

Numerous studies have found that suicidal patients are poor at personal problem solving. They tend to use passive problem-solving strategies that rely on behavior change by others, wait for complex problems to change without intervention, or use strategies that have a very low probability of success. Suicidal patients tend to generate fewer solutions to personal problems and do not implement solutions within a positive feedback cycle. Their desired problem-solving outcomes and time frames for achieving those outcomes tend to be unrealistic and are focused on regulation of emotion. This leads to a failure to pursue even effective solutions for the time necessary to truly observe whether the solution(s) worked. Finally, suicidal patients do not seem to profit from direct experience. They will tend to use the same solution for a problem over and over again, despite the fact that the solution historically has not been effective. There is some emerging evidence that suicidal patients may have inherent biases in memory that prevent them from learning from past mistakes (cf. Chiles & Strosahl 2005 for a more comprehensive discussion). In the process of therapy termination, this problem-solving style will show itself in a passive, less expressive approach to the "problem" of emancipating from therapy. The patient will tend to let the therapist figure out how to make termination happen and how to deal with the emotional and practical issues associated with it. It may be hard to get the patient to practice out-of-session strategies that would breed a greater sense of independence. Getting the patient "activated" to build a lifestyle that doesn't involve therapy is likely to be a challenge. Obviously, one goal of therapy itself is to help the client acquire effective and approach-oriented personal problem-solving skills. Our clinical impression is that many aspects of passive personal problem solving are fueled by experiential and emotional avoidance. If therapy is effective in teaching the client to accept unpleasant, evocative private content, it will also help the client take a more active approach to solving life problems.

Rigid Cognitive Style

Numerous research studies have shown that suicidal patients tend to be cognitively inflexible. They tend to view the world in black-and-white terms. There is no gray area. They tend to evaluate interpersonal situations, emotion states, and other similar events in highly charged terms. There is often a moral and judgmental tone applied to self and others. In other words, suicidal patients often see the world in a way that is fused with their evaluations of events (Strosahl 2005). They tend not to see their evaluations as thoughts that are separate from the events that are being evaluated. These evaluations are very often negative and tinged with such themes as right and wrong, friend or foe, fair or unfair, victim or aggressor. Obviously, clients with this type of cognitive style are likely to struggle with the murky waters of psychotherapy termination. On the one hand, the fact that therapy is ending is a good thing, but it brings with it a variety of reactions that are not well processed using a black-or-white approach. The way this style may be manifest during discussion of termination is a precipitous change in the client's emotional tone, accompanied by withdrawal or accusatory statements. The client is trying to put this event into either the "good" or "bad" camp, and it just won't fit that neatly in either. Successful therapy will focus on helping the client hold apparently competing evaluations "lightly," to see evaluation as an action that is separate from the events that trigger evaluation (see Strosahl 2005).

When to Terminate?

An obvious first question when discussing issues concerning psycho-therapy termination with suicidal patients is when to terminate. Many therapists believe that termination should occur when the client is no longer engaging in any form of suicidality. With some patients, this standard may be viable, such as when working with a highly functional client with an acute suicidal crisis triggered by an overwhelming life event. If the client has no previous history of suicidal behavior, it might be possible for therapy to completely eliminate all vestiges of suicidality. However, many clients come to therapy with prior histories of suicidality and at its most extreme; clients may report chronic suicidality going back to childhood. The standard of complete elimination of suicidal thoughts, impulses, or actions would virtually guarantee that the client would be in therapy in perpetuity. This could inadvertently create a situation in which the client is completely dependent upon the therapist and therapy for the management of suicidality. Withdrawing therapy in such a case is likely to stimulate an upsurge in suicidality, as the client has failed to internalize basic skills for self-management and will tend to see therapy as the antidote for any crisis.

Just as suicidality is a complex, multidimensional phenomenon, so to should be the standards employed to decide when to terminate therapy. With chronically suicidal patients, our stance has been to terminate therapy when the client begins to exhibit some degree of self-management ability. With chronically suicidal patients, the literature suggests that the best outcome is a significant reduction in the number and lethality of suicidal attempts, as well as a reduction in chronic suicidal ideation. Therefore, we apply the standard of reduction, rather than elimination, of suicidal events. We do not expect that all suicidal ideation, impulses, or mild self-destructive behavior will have been eliminated. Also, it will be evident in a later section that our approach to reframing termination makes it unlikely that the client will see termination as a single moment in time, but rather a process of reducing the frequency of sessions and increasing the time between sessions.

Our major goal in this regard is to avoid creating a reinforcement link between therapy and suicidal crisis in which the client learns that the best way to keep therapy ongoing is to continue to be suicidal. The failure to cut this link will have obvious negative repercussions when therapy termination is attempted.

Strategies for Successful Termination

In our view, troubles with psychotherapy termination start at the beginning of the therapy process and then build a negative momentum over time. To avoid these troubles, we stress a variety of specific messages that the client needs to hear about the purpose of therapy, what therapy can and can't do, and the likely course of therapy. We also emphasize reframing certain aspects of the termination process to emphasize the client's ability to continue the therapeutic process independent of the psychotherapist. Finally, many of our guidelines involve helping the client assume agency over the termination process.

Termination Starts Five Seconds Into Therapy

"Begin with the end in mind" nicely summarizes our basic approach to termination. The most important moment in therapy is the first five minutes of the first session. This is when the therapist describes the purpose of therapy, the likely course of treatment, and the goals of treatment. We will often say something like, "You know, the real goal of treatment is to help you become your own therapist so you won't need to keep coming in here. Coming to therapy is a real inconvenience for most people and my goal is to make every session count so you can stop coming here as soon as possible. I'm kind of like the family dentist. The less you see of me, the better you will like it."

Put Therapy in a Broader, Normal Life Context

This part of the discussion is designed to set the stage for understanding what therapy can and can't do for the client. The discussion helps define what the client and therapist will see that will tell them that it is time to begin to change the trajectory of therapy. Often, clients will indicate that it will be time to leave therapy when they feel completely free of emotional distress and no longer have any thoughts of suicide. As mentioned before, this might be an achievable goal for some clients. However, even functional clients that pursue the "complete freedom from personal pain" agenda might be headed for trouble. Life has a way of not cooperating to that degree. We might emphasize the following: "You know, being alive means that you have signed up to deal with problems, including negative emotions, personal setbacks, and so forth. The goal of therapy is not for you to feel good all of the time, but for you to learn to manage whatever feelings come your way. Therapy cannot immunize you against all of the stresses you will face. It can provide strategies that will help you grow as a human in the face of these everyday challenges." Ask your client: "This being the case, what would you see in terms of your actions that would tell you that you needed less therapy?"

How Will We Know We Are Done?

Another aspect of this discussion is to come to a joint agreement about what an acceptable endpoint will look like. This is where the therapist can suggest that in most cases, clients begin to notice that they are not as reliant on therapy as before. This does not mean that there are not any problems around, but rather that clients feel more confident in the steps they take to address problems. These steps or strategies don't always work, but the client is *acting more confidently.* Here, we often suggest that life isn't about doing things perfectly, free from personal pain and anguish. Rather, it is about taking steps to approach and solve problems and do so in a way that is consistent with one's personal values. The pain of living is *not* toxic. What is toxic is avoiding pain that is a natural consequence of being alive. We point out that suicidality is not a categorically bad thing. It seems to touch the lives of a large percentage of the general population. What makes suicidality toxic is running from it (which paradoxically increases the power of suicidal urges) or engaging in secondary coping strategies that are equally destructive (getting drunk to quell suicidal feelings). When the client is willing and able to look at suicidal urges for what they are, ineffective coping behaviors, this is a sign that the client has learned what therapy has to teach. Getting back into life will help the client learn the rest.

Shift From an Acute Care to a Chronic Condition Approach

Most therapists practice in an acute care model in which the intent is to deliver a single episode of treatment, followed by termination of the professional relationship. This approach to therapy can create more anxiety for the patient, who can be left to wonder when the therapist is going to "pull the plug." Our approach emphasizes brief therapeutic episodes spread across the life span. The purpose of a therapy episode is to pinpoint a specific clinical problem and to help the client develop the skills necessary to resolve it. The basic model of suicidal behavior does not view suicidality as the problem, but rather sees suicidal behavior as symptomatic of emotional avoidance, poor personal problem solving, and maladaptive, provocative cognitions. When clients present with suicidality, it gives the therapist an opportunity to build more effective skills in each of these areas. Then the patient is asked to go out and practice these skills in real life, so that they can be integrated into life outside of a therapy framework. The saying we often use is, "Practice doesn't make it perfect, but it does make it permanent." Experience suggests that shorter episodes of targeted care spread across a longer time span leads to less dependence upon therapy. The client is spending proportionately more time out of treatment than in treatment, and the clinical message is that the client can expect to return for "tune ups" at any time.

Grammatical Conventions That Make the Point

Therapy is an enterprise that is conducted using words, and the skilled therapist chooses words very carefully. This is also true in the process of decreasing the client's reliance upon therapy and increasing self-reliance over time. One word set we target is the difference between *needing* and *wanting* therapy. The etymologic root of the word *need* literally means, "for the lack of which the organism will perish." The root of the word *want* has to do with a state of desire or an approach to something that is deemed desirable. We encourage suicidal clients to make this distinction when determining their present and future plans for seeking treatment. Is this something that is actually needed, or is it a desire that might alternatively be fulfilled via skillful use of other social support resources? There are many word sets like this that subtly influence the client's perception of the necessity of being in therapy. Some of our favorites include being clear about the distinction between *deciding* and *choosing*, being willing to have troublesome private events versus wanting those events, using the word *and* instead of *but* during therapy and so forth.

Frame Out-of-Session Time as a Field Experiment

Research supports the importance of practicing new skills outside of the therapy session. Clients who complete various types of home-based practice between sessions consistently respond better to treatment than clients who do not practice. This seems intuitively obvious to most therapists, but it is surprising how often therapists fail to emphasize the importance of home-based practice. In our model of care, the time out of therapy is called a "field experiment." The client is building the field experiment in session with the aid of the therapist, or the client is engaging in a field experiment. The purpose of the field experiment is to see what would happen if the client emitted response "X" instead of the usual response "Y" in a situation where response "Y" has consistently failed to produce acceptable results. This approach to the workings of the therapy session inherently reframes the intended purpose of a therapy session. The therapist can only aid the client in developing a field experiment that will test the workability of a particular response. The client's job is to go out into life and run the experiment.

One Special Field Experiment: Increasing the Time Between Sessions

The main idea behind session tapering is to increase the client's experience with being out of session. This is a special type of field experiment that can be described exactly as the other field experiments. There is no need to change the language to reference termination, because in a chronic care approach, there is really no ending point. The client simply picks whether to return for another episode of targeted care. If the client never chooses to return, the client is still considered to be in care but is not actively seeking care. When introducing the idea of increasing the time between sessions, it is important to ask the client to specify the time frames. This might mean that the client is willing to experiment with going a month without a therapy session, if therapy sessions are currently occurring every two weeks. The goal, of course, is to increase the time span between sessions, but only at a rate that is palatable to the client. This puts the client in command of the tapering process and tends to undercut the unhealthy dynamics that can surface when termination is driven by the therapist.

Keep the Door Open

It is particularly important when initiating session tapering to have an open-door policy, even in the midst of a field experiment. The open door means that if the client feels things are really going backward, the client can come in for a session immediately to troubleshoot. We will typically reiterate this during the formation of a field experiment. This is not about forcing the client to stay out in the field, but rather to create a safe haven in which the client is interested in trying to function more independently. It is not a clinical failure to come back early for a troubleshooting session. Instead, we portray it as an example of excellent self-care. Knowing when to seek guidance and support is an especially important skill for suicidal clients, particularly those with a history of repetitious suicidality. Similarly, the therapist should respond in a positive way to whatever the client has tried during the out-of-therapy interlude. We will usually start with "what went right" before getting to "what went wrong." The goal is to shape positive coping responses instead of focusing on maladaptive coping responses.

Build in the Option of Booster Sessions

In keeping with the fluid framework described for session tapering, our practice has been to offer booster sessions on a prescribed schedule with the client who is about to discontinue treatment. Normally, the client will have gone through some type of tapering experiment and seems to be functioning reasonably well in the face of life challenges. Booster sessions are usually scheduled at fairly long time intervals, say six months or even a year. Once again, the goal is to defuse anxiety about termination by not really terminating in the conventional sense. Our experience suggests that most clients will attend one or two booster sessions and then state that they probably do not really need to be seen again. In response, we will always point out that the client seems to be choosing life without the aid of therapy and that the door is always open for a quick reentry should problems arise.

Special Clinical Circumstances

There are two specific issues that can complicate the course of termination with the suicidal client, again particularly those with chronic histories. One is the suicidal client with a history of trauma, abuse, and victimization. The other is the reemergence of suicidality near the end of an active treatment episode.

Being Right Versus Being Real

Chronically suicidal clients often present to treatment with a history of serious childhood trauma, abuse, and neglect, and they are heavily fused with a sense of victimization. One of us (Kirk Strosahl) worked with a client who openly stated that the only reason she had stayed alive was to punish her physically abusive mother. This is not only an example of the cognitive rigidity described previously, but it also represents a formidable clinical challenge at the point of therapy termination. The client is invested in remaining "broken" because this is the only way the world will know that the client has been abused. If the transgressor is made acutely aware of the "damage" done to the victim (as evidenced by blatant behavioral dysfunction), then the client is right and the transgressor is wrong. Of course, the problem with this response set is that in order for the client to remain right, the client must remain broken. Remaining broken requires the client to engage in self-destructive behaviors, often in a highly public way.

One clinical response is to help the client focus on the choice at hand and the essential dilemma it represents. To get healthy, the client might need to let go of the urge to seek vengeance and vindication. The transgressor might even conclude that no abuse occurred because the client is functioning just fine. The abuse might even be justified as helping the client achieve such a high level of functioning. While these responses can be seen by the client as irritants, working through them can lead to the prospect of a healthy, valued life. Which will the client choose—to be right in making the claim of abuse or to be real and move on into a healthy life? Sometimes it is useful to play with the word *forgiveness*, whose etymological root is "grace" or "gift." So the term forgiveness actually means to give oneself the gift of grace, which was there before the transgression occurred. Thus, forgiveness does not mean the transgressor is being forgiven but rather it is an act toward the self (cf. Hayes, Strosahl, & Wilson 1999 for more of this approach, and Strosahl 2005 for application to suicidal clients).

Reemergence of Suicidality

Therapists are often surprised to discover that clients who are apparently responding to treatment suddenly revert to suicidal behavior when discussions about therapy termination are initiated. In our experience, this type of reversion is very rare when the therapist understands the function of suicidality and has followed the various guidelines for termination described above. This is usually a form of emotional avoidance and passive personal problem solving. While it seems odd to think of something as risky as self-inflicted injury as a passive act, it is in fact a way of avoiding difficult feelings and not dealing directly with the therapist about any perceived slights. Faced with this type of situation, the therapist should have the client "get present" with his or her reactions to the prospect of ending the treatment episode, and to stay with these feelings in the therapy session. If suicidal behavior seems to be stimulated by talk of termination, then it is likely that the termination is "therapist driven" and the client is responding to feelings of loss, loneliness, and abandonment. It is very risky to intellectually approach these primary feeling states.

The better course is to simply evoke them in the session, deconstruct the feelings through various exposure exercises, and help the client experientially understand that these feelings are not toxic. It is also wise to point out (in the case of a chronically suicidal client) that the very occurrence of suicidality is proof that these responses may reappear in the client's life outside of active therapy. This is just one more opportunity to practice strategies that might help the client cope with suicidal impulses in the future.

References

Chiles, J. & Strosahl, K. (1995). *The suicidal patient: Principles of assessment, treatment and case management.* Washington DC: American Psychiatric Press.

Chiles, J., & Strosahl, K. (2005). Clinical manual for assessment and treatment of suicidal patients. Washington, DC: American Psychiatric Publishing.

Hayes, S., Strosahl, K., & Wilson, K. (1999). *Acceptance and commitment therapy: An experiential approach to behavior change.* New York: Guilford Press.

Hayes, S., Wilson, K., Gifford, E., Follette, V., & Strosahl, K. (1996). Emotional avoidance and behavioral disorders: A functional dimensional approach to diagnosis and treatment. *Journal of Consulting and Clinical Psychology, 64,* 1152–1168.

Jobes, D., Jacoby, A., Cimbolic, P., & Hustead, L. (1997). Assessment and treatment of suicidal clients in a university counseling center. *Journal of Counseling Psychology, 44,* 368–377.

Lerner, M., & Clum, G. (1990). Treatment of suicide ideators: A problem solving approach. *Behavior Therapy, 21,* 403–411.

Liberman, R., & Eckman, T. (1981). Behavior therapy vs. insight therapy for repeated suicide attempters. *Archives of General Psychiatry, 38,* 1126–1130.

Linehan, M., Armstrong, H., Suarez, A., Allman, D., & Heard, H. (1991). Cognitive-behavioral treatment of chronically parasuicidal borderline patients. *Archives of General Psychiatry, 48,* 1060–1064.

Patsiokas, A., & Clum, G. (1985). Effects of psychotherapeutic strategies in the treatment of suicide attempters. *Psychotherapy, 22,* 281–290.

Rudd, M., Rajab, H., Stulman, D., Joiner, T., & Dixon, W. (1996). Effectiveness of an out-patient intervention targeting suicidal young adults: Preliminary results. *Journal of Consulting and Clinical Psychology, 64,* 179–190.

Salkovskis, P., Atha, C., & Storer, D. (1990). Cognitive-behavioral problem-solving in the treatment of patients who repeatedly attempt suicide. *British Journal of Psychiatry, 157,* 871–876.

Strosahl, K. (2005). ACT with the chronically suicidal patient. In S. Hayes & K. Strosahl (Eds.), *A practical guide to acceptance and commitment therapy.* New York: Springer Publishing Science & Media.

Strosahl, K., Linehan, M., & Chiles, J. (1984). Will the real social desirability please stand up? Hopelessness, depression, social desirability and the prediction of suicidal behavior. *Journal of Consulting and Clinical Psychology, 52,* 449–457.

21

TERMINATION IN INPATIENT AND RESIDENTIAL SETTINGS

KEITH W. HARRIS AND
JENNIFER PIEN-WONG

Introduction

Among the chapters in this collection, our focus on termination in inpatient and residential settings is unique for several reasons. First and foremost, ours is likely the only context in which a single client terminates with a collection of providers. Unlike the typical 1:1 nature of individual psychotherapy, patients in inpatient and residential settings form many relationships during their treatment course, with both providers and fellow patients, and subsequently experience multiple terminations upon discharge.

A second unique characteristic of termination in inpatient and residential settings is the fact that discharge rarely signals completion of the treatment course. In individual therapy, termination typically represents the culmination of treatment (with perhaps periodic check-ins over time). In inpatient and residential settings, there is a tremendous focus on aftercare and *step-up treatment* (transfer to a greater intensity of care) or *step-down treatment* (transfer to a lower intensity of care). Thus, termination in inpatient and residential settings represents a transition point in treatment rather than an ending.

The absence of a single, primary therapeutic relationship in inpatient and residential settings has perhaps contributed to a relative lack of focus on termination in these settings. In fact, one rarely hears the term *termination* on an inpatient ward or in a residential facility. Instead, there is a great focus on discharge, with the connotation that one is leaving a site rather than ending a relationship. The deinstitutionalization movement of the past fifty years serves as an extreme example of how inpatient and residential settings sometimes fail to consider all of the complexities involved in termination. Begun as a worthy attempt to free the severely mentally ill (SMI) from a life locked in an asylum, the deinstitutionaliza- tion movement had the unfortunate side effect of discharging thousands of patients who were not prepared to terminate inpatient treatment. Due to factors including debilitating mental illness, poor physical health, and lack of family and/or community mental health resources, many of these discharged patients went from the ranks of the institutionalized SMI to the homeless and substance-dependent SMI—a debatable change in fortune to be sure. Later in the chapter we will discuss steps that inpa- tient and residential settings can take to approach termination in a safe and healthy manner while still promoting patient independence.

In this chapter, we will first review both empirical literature and clinical lore bearing on the process of termination in inpatient and resi- dential settings. We will then describe both research-based and practi- cal, clinically based techniques for terminating in these settings. We will conclude with suggestions for future research that could fill some of the many gaps in this area. Unless otherwise stated, subsequent references to inpatient settings will refer to both residential and inpatient treatment settings.

Research Findings Related to Termination in Inpatient Settings

Prior to beginning our own literature search, we consulted with two notable experts in the field (Peter Rosenbaum and Irving Yalom), and asked for promising references regarding termination in inpatient settings; both were stymied by the request. Our own literature review identified a number of useful articles but a surprising absence of exper- imental research. Therefore, our literature review will pull from the available literature, including review articles and quasi-experimental studies. This literature illuminates to some degree the processes, chal- lenges, and idiosyncrasies of termination in inpatient settings.

It has been suggested that termination in inpatient settings is best understood through a consideration of three factors: (1) the context in which the treatment takes place, (2) countertransference reactions, and (3) the unique needs of inpatients relative to outpatients (Brabender

& Fallon 1996; Halperin 1986). Contextual elements that influence the termination process in inpatient settings include, but are not limited to, institutional mission and structure, financial or length-of-stay constraints, relationships among caregivers within the facility, and legal considerations (Brabender & Fallon 1996, Chiesa, Drahorad, & Longo 2000). Brabender and Fallon (1996) will first be reviewed in some detail as it outlines a useful structure for understanding termination in inpatient settings; a wider variety of scientific evidence will be introduced subsequently.

Brabender and Fallon (1996) describe provider countertransference as a second important factor in considering termination in inpatient settings. These authors outline three kinds of countertransference that can affect termination processes and decisions in inpatient settings: (1) disappointment over patient progress, (2) concerns over frequent patient turnover within the unit, and (3) lack of control over the discharge process. In inpatient settings, patients and providers alike are frequently disappointed with treatment progress at the time of discharge, as the decision to discharge is rarely a function of completing all treatment goals (Halperin 1986). The authors caution that to counter the disappointment over lack of progress, providers will frequently overaccentuate positive statements from patients and limit the expression of negative ones. In so doing, the provider denies the patient the opportunity to process negative affect in a health environment and runs the risk of teaching an ineffective coping style.

Frequent patient turnover creates a second source of countertransference in that providers are continually mourning the loss of one patient while trying to establish a relationship with a new one (Brabender & Fallon 1996). The authors suggest that the never-ending development and termination of therapeutic attachments can leave providers detached and paralyzed, minimizing the strength of whatever relationship was formed.

Countertransference manifests itself in a third fashion when providers find themselves feeling angry and powerless over their lack of control in the discharge process (Brabender & Fallon 1996). When outside pressures influence a patient's decision to terminate prematurely, providers are often inclined to blame the system and subsequently approach inpatient treatment with an element of disillusion that can impact future termination processes.

The third factor suggested by Brabender and Fallon (1996) in understanding termination in inpatient settings involves the special needs of inpatients relative to outpatients. Although termination provokes anxiety in all forms of therapy, terminating inpatient treatment can be especially nerve-wracking due to the drastic change in environment. When inpatients are discharged to home, they transition abruptly from a controlled, safe environment in which they have gained a certain degree of mastery and comfort to an often chaotic and stressful environment that has proven itself threatening in the past. Suggestions will be made below regarding how to best therapeutically manage the anxiety associated with terminating inpatient treatment.

Much of the focus on inpatient termination falls on premature termination and discharge planning. Discharge planning is governed by the following principles: (1) patients should be placed in the least restrictive environment necessary for appropriate care, (2) the length of the treatment course should be restricted to the minimum amount of time necessary for maximum benefit, and (3) a high priority should be placed on ensuring a successful transition to the next treatment setting (step up or step down in intensity) (Sadock & Sadock 2005).

A vital facet of successful termination of inpatient treatment is the comprehensive arrangement of aftercare services. Compton et al. (2006) reviewed the attendance at aftercare appointments for 234 consecutively discharged patients from two inpatient units. Four factors were related to missed appointments: leaving against medical advice (AMA), appointment scheduled with an unfamiliar outpatient clinician, problems with the patient's support group, and increased length of time between discharge and the first aftercare appointment.

The termination process in inpatient facilities that treat children is in some ways akin to the traditional outpatient termination process. Children form intense therapeutic relationships with their providers in inpatient settings, necessitating a sensitive and careful approach to termination (Brewer & Faitak 1989). Several authors attribute children's formation of intense therapeutic relationships to transference and unresolved dependency needs (Halperin 1986; Leichtman & Leichtman 2004).

Interestingly, there are significant differences between adult hospitals and children's units regarding termination and discharge trends. Children's units are 44 percent more likely than adult units to discharge adolescents who have attempted suicide to a stepped-down inpatient setting (Levine et al. 2005). In this particular study, adult hospitals discharged the majority of adolescents to home. This difference is consistent with the notion that greater care is taken in terminating treatment with youth, and that the focus of termination is on the transition to the next level of care, rather than the completion of care (Leichtman & Leichtman 2004).

In a study of older adults (age seventy-seven and up), a shorter length of stay in inpatient treatment was associated with increased readmission rates (Dobrzanska & Newell 2006). Although it is impossible to address all of the factors associated with length of stay on an inpatient unit, it is clear that shorter stays leave less time for attention to termination processes and are likely associated with less attention to discharge planning. Although length of stay is frequently limited as a cost-savings maneuver, the increased readmission rate likely eliminates the benefit (Dobrzanska & Newell 2006). Patients benefit more from a careful termination process and complete discharge plan.

The facet of termination in inpatient settings that has received the most research attention is the area of treatment dropout or premature termination (e.g., Chiesa, Drahorad, & Longo 2000; Thunnissen, Remans, & Trijsburg 2004). Premature termination in inpatient settings is related to a number of factors, including excessive anxiety, occupational status, Axis II factors such as borderline personality disorder, lower restraint scores, and characteristics of the treatment setting itself (Brabender & Fallon 1996; Chiesa, Drahorad, & Longo 2000; Woodside, Carter, & Blackmore 2004). One study of premature dropouts found that 50 percent terminated treatment in the first two weeks and cited excessive anxiety as the primary reason for leaving (Thunnissen, Remans, & Trijsburg 2004).

Interestingly, Chiesa et al. (2000) found that borderline personality disorder was actually associated with fewer instances of premature termination. They reasoned that their two-phase program with a short inpatient stay followed by a long-term outpatient course made tolerable the intense emotional reactions to inpatient treatment. In contrast, borderline personality disordered patients typically exhibit high premature termination rates in traditional inpatient settings (e.g., Kelly et al. 1992).

Chiesa et al. (2000) conducted a qualitative analysis of reasons for premature termination and cited the following primary contributing categories: institutional culture and structure, organization of treatment, and relationship with other patients. Within the institutional culture, reasons for premature termination included staff misunderstanding of the vulnerabilities behind patient acting-out behavior, lack of patient involvement in staff decisions, and excessively high expectations of rapid patient improvement. Within the treatment organization, contributors to premature termination included lack of privacy and individual time, rote participation in unit activities, "attack therapy" in group meetings, lack of individualized treatment, and lack of a treatment rationale. Regarding relationships with other patients, contributing factors to premature termination included feeling pressured to support acting-out patients to the neglect of one's own issues, and subgroups of patients who intimidate and bully others in an untherapeutic fashion (Chiesa, Drahorad, & Longo 2000).

The Art of Termination in Inpatient Settings

"Termination is the phase of the psychotherapeutic process during which patient and therapist consider when and how to conclude their collaboration and then effect this conclusion" (Tyson 1996, 501). Because inpatient and residential settings offer a unique frame for psychotherapy, the termination process is accordingly affected. What follows is a discussion and review of the art of termination in inpatient settings as presented in previous literature, clinical lore, and case studies.

There are a number of treatment factors unique to inpatient settings, some of which were discussed in the previous section, including the following:

1. These environments frequently deal with involuntary treatment and complex legal issues.

2. Inpatient treatment is usually intensive with involvement of several levels of delivery of care—through a multidisciplinary staff of varying training and educational backgrounds, and also through other patients as peers through groups that synthesize into the treatment milieu as a whole.

3. Rather than a traditional single therapeutic relationship focus, treatment and thus termination occurs along several dimensions from individual providers, staff, and individual peers, as well as the milieu and not uncommonly the institution itself.

4. Individual, group, and system dynamics need to be addressed.

5. Third-party payer issues also influence termination in a more time intensive manner than outpatient settings.

6. Patients in inpatient settings commonly present in a crisis context affecting numerous psychosocial domains that need to be attended to for effective termination.

7. The isolation from the patient's usual life context and relationships can positively or negatively influence treatment and termination.

8. Inpatient settings are usually of a brief time duration leading to consideration of termination issues from the onset of treatment.

9. Treatment collaboration is sometimes influenced by conflicting interests of the institution or third-party payer.

Inpatient settings create unique patient populations that are at risk for difficult termination due to the increased psychopathology. Increased rates of characterological problems, impulsivity, severe psychopathology, substance abuse, medical comorbidities, poor social and community supports, failure of outpatient treatment, and increased suicidal or homicidal behaviors are a part of this population and present a challenge to termination (Bloom 1997). Inpatients often have difficult childhoods with trauma and abandonment histories resulting in developmental issues that impact both treatment and termination as discussed below.

Problems such as dependency related to separation-individuation, decompensation or regression themes, abandonment, or developmental issues can be intensified in inpatient settings. Awareness of these concerns and assisting the patient toward addressing these issues from the outset are crucial to successful termination. The patient must be prepared from the start for a goal of treatment termination. Fostering a balanced realistic view of treatment that is neither idealization nor denigration is optimal. One of the unique contributions of inpatient treatment settings is the creation of a structured environment in which the patient can safely learn and practice behaviors for dealing with stressors and conflicts and hopefully gain skills including how to successfully terminate their treatment. At the heart of this successful termination is the offering of hope for recovery and enhanced living in the outside world.

In traditional psychodynamic therapies, resolution of transference with the shift toward establishing a clear and realistic therapeutic relationship is essential (Weiner 1998). Inpatient settings rarely encourage a transference relationship; however, providers should be aware of this development and continue to ground the patient in a reality-based, present-centered working alliance.

Thoughtful inquiry of patients' emotional responses to termination can be important and therapeutic. Reactions can include denial, feelings of abandonment, disappointment, anger, grief, and depression. When termination responses are not dealt with, the therapeutic work is jeopardized, and this may impact the patient's ability to terminate effectively. However, care must be taken to balance against activating negative emotional responses, which the setting does not have adequate resources to address (Gabbard 2005).

Providers must deal with their countertransference issues or transitioning the patient to outpatient care can become problematic. Transference not only occurs with the individual providers and staff, but at an institutional level as well. Openly addressing these issues is crucial. One factor that complicates termination is the concern of whether that particular inpatient setting actively supports the process of encouraging patients to view the unit as a supportive aftercare environment (usually residential settings). Carefully balancing encouragement of independence along with the offer of aftercare without creating institutional dependency is a challenging process as illustrated in the following case examples.

Case study 1: Exploring themes of negative transference and countertransference and the impact of severe psychopathology and dependency issues on termination in an inpatient setting.

Mr. G. W. (not the patient's real initials) is a forty-five-year old Caucasian, homeless, unemployed patient with major depressive disorder and recent losses, including the destruction of his home from a natural disaster, and separation from his wife with subsequent geographic relocation to an area where he is without any social support. The patient suffered a work-related traumatic brain injury five years ago resulting in cognitive and memory impairment, subtle personality changes with increased impulsivity, and affective and irritability symptoms. He was admitted to a twenty-eight-day residential substance abuse treatment program where characterological traits of unexpressed resentment and hostility toward his life circumstance were channeled into persistent complaints about program mechanics and fellow peers in the program.

During the course of his admission, Mr. G. W. provided information that led to a peer's discharge from the program. That person discharged to a shelter on the same grounds as this program, and Mr. G. W. notified staff that the peer was physically threatening and intimidating. When the program did not respond in the manner in which Mr. G. W. wished, he left the unit, checked into a hotel, and binged on substances. He then returned to the unit requesting readmission. The patient was assessed for suicidality and was psychiatrically hospitalized for endorsing those symptoms. Mr. G. W. activated considerably intense negative countertransference and anger through creation of projective identification in his providers, frustration due to the intense level of management he required, as well as frustration over his persistent complaints and anger toward the program along with refusal to directly address his intense negativism and resentment toward his own life circumstances. He perceived life as unjust and destructive despite his own best efforts. Mr. G. W had no insight into his own contributions to creating his current circumstances, or his unresolved grief and anger over his losses, and channeled his remaining energy into problematic psychosomatic complaints.

Despite his anger toward the residential program, Mr. G. W. continued to request readmission. This is an example of a complex patient with multiple psychosocial domains of needs, and traits as described above, who was highly defended and unresponsive to the brief and time-limited exploration of his symptomatology. This treatment setting did not have the resources and long-term treatment time frame to adequately explore this patient's character-ological issues, which impacted his unsuccessful termination. The inpatient setting in this case must tolerate the patient's aggression (Tyson 1996). Careful awareness of negative countertransference and preventing it from affecting Mr. G. W.'s treatment was impor-tant to maintaining a therapeutic stance as this patient terminated his treatment.

Case study 2: Example of institutional dependency and patient refusal of recommended continuity of care planning leading to ineffective termination.

Mr. T. P., a fifty-year-old Caucasian veteran, unemployed and home-less, who carries psychiatric diagnoses of amphetamine and alcohol dependence, depressive disorder not otherwise specified, and psychotic disorder not otherwise specified, had a history of multiple inpatient psychiatric hospitalizations prior to being referred to a twenty-eight-day residential treatment facility. Mr. T. P. did exceedingly well in the program, becoming a leader of the community and demonstrating program skills adeptly. He discharged to outpatient substance abuse, medical, and psychiatric aftercare treatment. He refused program recommendations for continued residential treatment, and instead insisted on returning to essentially the same outside environment that precipitated his recent crisis and subsequent psychiatric hospitaliza-tion, in a state of overconfidence with his success in this program. Within days of his discharge, the patient called the program in dis-tress stating that he had returned to a difficult home situation and was not connecting with his outpatient providers. He called to request readmission to the program. Mr. T. P. was encouraged to work on establishing a therapeutic alliance with his outpatient providers and to follow his discharge plan.

Mr. T. P. subsequently relapsed and reentered psychiatric hospi-talization. He was assessed and readmitted to the same 28-day pro-gram, contingent upon his agreement that this time around he would apply for and if accepted, would transition to a more intensive 180-day psychosocial rehabilitation program for homeless veterans, with the goal of returning to independent, sober living and employment. He agreed, and again thrived in the 28-day program. He was then accepted into the next program; however, on the second day of his admission requested psychiatric hospitalization for suicidal ideation. The veteran's fear of failure, intimidation by the program, and impulsivity coalesced into his request for discharge. He was encouraged to give the program a chance but refused. Mr. T. P. requested either readmission to the 28-day program or back to the inpatient providers that were familiar with his case. Mr. T. P.'s providers explained his institutional dependency to him, along with the goal toward outpatient management and advised him that his case would be managed along those lines. This highlights the challenges of institutional dependency and lack of commitment to an aftercare plan. This case also clearly demonstrates that Mr. T. P.'s apparent successful navigation of a treatment program could not be truly considered a success until he had successfully and completely terminated and committed to the next level of treatment.

Ideally, the termination process can coincide with the point at which the provider and patient both agree that the goals of treatment have been accomplished (Tyson 1996). However, because patients may not necessarily enter inpatient treatment of their own internal motivation but as a result of other external factors such as court mandated or involuntary treatment or family/friend coercion, it is therefore crucial to the termination process that an engagement with the patient regarding the major goals of inpatient treatment be agreed upon from the outset.

A crucial element of treatment goals unique to inpatient settings is discharge planning. Providers should encourage both patients and inpatient settings to frame discharge planning instead as continuity-of-care planning to transition the patient to the next phase of treatment. For effective psychotherapeutic termination, practical issues regarding finances, discharge plans, aftercare, outpatient treatment, family issues, coping skills, and relapse prevention must be addressed in a timely fashion. These issues are especially relevant in inpatient settings as patients *and* providers can easily postpone or sabotage treatment goals due to dependency needs or transference/countertransference issues. Inpatient settings should encourage autonomy and self-assertion in these areas.

Research-Based Techniques for Termination in Inpatient Settings

There is a paucity of empirical studies regarding termination in inpatient settings and, consequently, limited information regarding research-based techniques for terminating treatment in these settings. In the next two sections, we will briefly outline a number of techniques gleaned from the literature and from our own clinical training.

Brabender and Fallon (1996) outline a number of approaches to dealing with termination in the inpatient context, including the following: (1) highlight the importance of the termination process throughout all levels of the system, (2) ensure that all members of the treatment team appreciate the importance of the termination process, and (3) incorporate a discharge-issues group into treatment. Brabender and Fallon (1996) distinguish between this type of group, in which patients discuss their fears and expectations regarding discharge, and a discharge-planning group, which focuses on concrete resources and plans. Depending on the setting, both are useful and can be implemented, either as separate groups or as one integrated group that includes processing in both areas.

Brabender and Fallon (1996) continue their list with the following: (4) ensure that all providers have input in planning the treatment course, (5) plan the discharge date in advance and plan for attendance at a group session on the day of discharge, and (6) recognize that avoidance of groups prior to discharge can indicate resistance to dealing with termination. With respect to item 5, in some settings there are significant barriers to this, such as required discharge times prior to groups starting. Furthermore, this recommendation is primarily relevant when the patient is attending a closed-ended group, with the benefit being that if patients know they are attending the group's final meeting, they are more likely to attend and can benefit from the group process regarding their termination. More typically, inpatient settings utilize open-ended groups run on most wards.

Data from Compton et al. (2006) suggest that in order to maximize attendance at aftercare appointments, the following steps should be followed at termination: (1) extra care must be taken with patients who terminate AMA (although this is frequently challenging, given that they are already uncooperative when leaving AMA), (2) the appointment should be made with an established clinician whenever possible, (3) problems with the primary support group should be addressed prior to termination when possible, and (4) the appointment be scheduled as close as possible to the discharge date.

Specific to terminating inpatient treatment with children, it is recommended that the final session with the child prior to discharge involve a review of the course of treatment and discharge plans, and processing of the child's reactions to termination (Brewer & Faitak 1989). As stated previously, the child patient is also reminded that discharge from the facility does not signal the end of treatment but rather a transition to the next step toward achieving his/her treatment goals.

With regard to terminating inpatient geriatric care, one important suggestion in the literature is to conduct home visits prior to discharge allowing assessment of the home environment and ordering of necessary equipment before the patient returns home (Nygard et al. 2004).

Accrediting organizations govern much of inpatient treatment, and one requirement that greatly influences termination decisions is the individualized treatment plan. Treatment plans must be specific and problem oriented. The treatment plan is tied directly to the termination process because it outlines the symptoms, behaviors, emotions, and various dysfunctions that must improve before the patient can be discharged to a stepped-down level of treatment (Sadock & Sadock 2005).

Practical Skills to Aid in the Termination Process in Inpatient Settings

Establishing clear treatment boundaries, treatment goals, specific aftercare referrals, and a consistent therapeutic methodology creates a strong foundation for an effective termination. Dealing with the patient's resistance toward engagement with step-down treatment through normalization of this approach to care and addressing termination-related affective reactions are crucial clinical elements in a successful termination.

The underlying therapeutic modality and philosophy of care of an inpatient setting informs the termination process. Inpatient settings utilize behavioral, supportive, and expressive psychodynamic processes to varying degrees. Principles of brief, time-limited psychotherapy inform inpatient settings through active acknowledgment of termination at the initiation of therapy. Utilizing successful strategies and techniques that are consistent with the institution's basic model of therapy for addressing termination is the underlying determinant of successful engagement in the termination process (Tyson 1996).

Literature in the area of forced termination has specific relevance to inpatient settings where there is ongoing pressure for reduced inpatient admission lengths, and/or pressure from third-party payers to limit care or terminate treatment prematurely. Clinicians may take both preventive and reactive steps in addressing forced termination due to third-party payer issues. Preventive steps include tailoring care to the time-limited nature of the setting, such as setting realistic expectations early on and communicating to patients that the goal is not to completely resolve all issues and symptomatology. Objectives and treatment goals that are reasonable in an inpatient, time-limited context include the following (Wolberg 1980): (1) reduction or removal of symptoms and relief of suffering, (2) restoration to prior level of functioning (3) psychoeducation about life-interfering actions and behaviors and alternative healthier substitutes, (4) initiating the learning process with respect to recognizing self-defeating patterns and exploration of their consequences, and (5) learning relapse prevention skills and constructive coping skills. Another obvious preventive step is to maintain open lines of communication with third-party payers so that all sides understand the conditions under which treatment is being provided and will continue to be provided.

There are also helpful steps a clinician can take in response to forced termination due to third-party payer issues. Forced termination can generate strong emotions, including abandonment, anger, and loss, which have a real and not purely transferential component. As such, the experience can trigger old emotions from previous abandonment experiences and risk retraumatizing the patient. Processing the patient's emotional reactions to the forced termination is vital to gaining closure, and gives the patient a semblance of control. Great care must also be taken in aftercare planning, as patients will be especially vulnerable to slips and setbacks, due in part to their disillusionment with a system that forces them out of treatment prematurely.

In our previous discussion, we highlighted the careful balance of institutional encouragement of independence versus being an aftercare resource. On the individual provider level, therapists must be clear with the patient about referral to new providers to prevent treatment splitting or engagement in complex clinical situations where the provider is no longer an active participant (Weiner 1998). It is recommended that the clinician assist the patient with the transition to outpatient care with frank, concrete discussions, advising him/her that subsequent and ongoing goals of treatment will be arranged with their future provider. Patients should be given specific referrals and resources, ideally with specific appointments made prior to the time of discharge with good patient notification. Along with the provider conveying appreciations of this current treatment relationship, the provider should also simultaneously give the patient firm instructions to contact and follow through with the new provider, emphasizing that the strength of their continued recovery and treatment rests on building a new therapeutic alliance.

The basic clinical skills of helpful clarification and interpretation of the patient's affective responses and working through those reactions are helpful. Reinforcing self-observational abilities is beneficial, as is avoidance of deep trauma issues and maintenance of clear boundaries (Weiner 1998). Managing negative termination reactions is a challenge. What follows is a list of clinical skills to assist with the management of difficult termination responses (Wolberg 1980):

1. As the provider, examine your own reactions to the patient's termination.
2. Allow patients to express their feelings of disappointment, sadness, and/or anger.
3. Be alert to previous experiences of termination that will inform the patient's current reaction.
4. As the provider, avoid guilt or defensiveness at termination. Provide clear explanations regarding termination and the need to avoid dependency.
5. Provide outside support for the transition.
6. Provide relapse prevention/coping skills. For example, anticipate and play out future stressors; discuss coping with setbacks.

Common Pitfalls, Ethical Dilemmas, and the Practical Skills for Avoiding Them When Terminating Inpatient Treatment

Common pitfalls in terminating inpatient treatment include the following: (1) unrealistic goals, (2) mismatched goals, (3) not anticipating termination issues from the start, (4) not allowing patient to effectively express negative emotions (i.e., not dealing with abandonment), or conversely allowing a flood of negative emotions without adequate treatment capability, (5) not dealing with countertransference issues, (6) poor aftercare setup, (7) poor coping skills and relapse prevention education, (8) lack of encouragement of hope and belief in the aftercare system, and (9) failure to address acute crisis factors or external factors that led to the current inpatient stay.

Ethical dilemmas relevant to termination in the inpatient setting represent a combination of inpatient clinical ethical issues and more general psychotherapeutic relationship ethical situations, and are beyond the scope of this chapter to discuss thoroughly. Briefly, these issues include establishing a treatment contract versus the patient's right to refuse treatment, and along those same lines, the provider's responsibility in providing continuity of care versus the patient's right to refuse treatment. Other issues include patient confidentiality versus patient protection in the event of poor termination, patient autonomy versus asserting beneficence, treatment termination versus open-ended treatment (themes of institutional dependency), and cost versus benefit of care.

Recommendations for Future Research

The most obvious gap in the literature involving termination in inpatient settings is the absence of randomly controlled trials (RCTs) or even group comparisons in which group membership was based on random assignment. The literature reviewed in this chapter is at best quasi-experimental in nature, and as such leaves the reader little opportunity to draw any firm conclusions regarding causative factors in the termination process. There are, of course, many reasons for the absence of experimental literature on inpatient termination. With so many external factors impinging on treatment decisions, inpatient settings do not lend themselves to RCTs in general, and especially not those focusing on termination. There are potential areas for termination research in inpatient settings, however, including understanding and reducing premature termination, and methods to enhance the termination process.

The area most amenable to an RCT is premature termination. In our own setting, a residential rehabilitation program treating homeless veterans, we recently completed a study in which patients screening for the program were randomly assigned to either a standard interview or a one-hour motivational interview (manuscript in preparation). Length-of-stay data revealed that those in the motivational interviewing group stayed significantly longer in the program than those in the standard group. Motivational interviewing (MI) has proven to be a powerful factor in decisions to admit and remain in treatment (e.g., Bien, Miller, & Tonigan 1993), but it has largely been studied in mildly to moderately distressed populations (Moyer, Finney, Swearingen, & Vergun 2002). We suggest randomly assigning patients screening for an inpatient or residential program to MI or standard interviews, and then assessing the percentage of premature terminations in each group. Furthermore, we suggest collecting data on psychiatric diagnoses and symptom severity, as we would predict that any group differences might be mediated through psychiatric symptom severity.

Research designed to enhance the termination process in inpatient settings could provide many benefits to patients and patient care. As stated previously, the termination process is undervalued in inpatient settings, and one method to change this undervaluation is by making it a focal point for research. The first step in such a research program would be conducting qualitative analyses of patients' termination experiences after discharge (similar to the study conducted by Thunnissen et al. 2004, but focusing specifically on the termination experience rather than the treatment experience). We predict that a number of salient factors related to quality of termination could be identified through such research, including attention from providers, sufficient time to discuss emotional reactions to termination, formal opportunities to say good-bye to peers and staff, and so on. The second step in such a research program would be to incorporate the salient factors into treatment and conduct basic program evaluation research comparing patient satisfaction with treatment and termination to previous scores. If a significant difference arises, the final step would be randomly assigning patients to a standard versus enhanced termination experience, either by having two tracks within the same program (very difficult and often unethical to do), or by identifying a relatively equivalent program without the enhanced termination piece. Through this research program, one could bring much-needed attention to termination processes in inpatient settings, as well as inform these settings of improved methods for handling such an important issue as termination.

Summary and Conclusion

In this chapter we have attempted to describe termination in inpatient settings through a summary of selected literature, as well as a collection of clinical lore and our own experiences working in a residential setting. Two things are abundantly clear: (1) termination in inpatient settings is a unique phenomenon with many characteristics distinguishing it from outpatient termination, and (2) there is a notable absence of clinical and research focus on termination processes in inpatient settings.

We have aimed in this chapter to highlight many of the termination characteristics that are unique to inpatient settings. Included in this list is the fact that patients form many relationships with peers and providers during inpatient treatment and therefore face multiple terminations upon leaving the facility. Patients also face complex legal issues far more frequently in inpatient settings than they do as outpatients, including involuntary holds and court-mandated treatment. Given the nature of inpatient treatment and the context in which patients arrive there, inpatients typically suffer from greater acuity and severity of psychiatric symptomatology than outpatients. Thus, the always-challenging termination process is rendered more difficult due to the array of emotional and behavioral complications present in this type of treatment population. And finally, a multitude of external pressures often forces termination from the inpatient unit prior to reaching optimal treatment benefit. As such, the traditional termination process involving opportunities to discuss and explore emotional reactions to loss is subverted. To account for these challenges, inpatient providers are encouraged to incorporate, wherever possible, opportunities for patients to formally and informally process their reactions to the termination of their treatment course in a safe and therapeutic fashion.

We hope that this chapter, and this volume as a whole, will contribute to an increase in attention paid to termination processes in inpatient settings. Patient needs in this area are too frequently ignored by providers, administrators, researchers, and even by the patients themselves. Patients often experience incredible growth and recovery during inpatient or residential treatment. It is a shame that a proper farewell, with its attendant opportunity to process the emotional responses to it, is frequently not afforded to them. With an increased clinical focus, and a growing research agenda, it is our sincere hope that we can begin to provide the proper farewell these patients deserve as they complete inpatient treatment.

References

Bien, T. H., Miller W. R., and Tonigan, J. S. (1993). Motivational interviewing with alcohol outpatients. *Behavioral and Cognitive Psychotherapy, 21,* 347–356.

Bloom, B. (1997). Planned short-term psychotherapy: A clinical handbook (2nd ed.). Boston: Allyn & Bacon.

Brabender, V., & Fallon, A. (1996). Termination in inpatient groups. *International Journal of Group Psychotherapy, 46* (1), 81–98.

Brewer, T., & Faitak, M. T. (1989). Ethical guidelines for the inpatient psychiatric care of children. *Professional Psychology: Research and Practice, 20,* 142–147.

Chiesa, M., Drahorad, C., Longo, S. (2000). Early termination of treatment in personality disorder treated in a psychotherapy hospital: Quantitative and qualitative study. *British Journal of Psychiatry, 177,* 107–111.

Compton, M., Rudisch, B., Craw, J., Thompson, T., & Owens, D. (2006). Predictors of missed first appointments at community mental health centers after psychiatric hospitalization. *Psychiatric Services, 57* (4), 531–537.

Dobrzanska, L., & Newell, R. (2006). Readmissions: a primary care examination of reasons for readmission of older people and possible readmission risk factors. *Journal of Clinical Nursing, 15* (5), 599–606.

Gabbard, G. (2005). Psychodynamic psychotherapy in clinical practice (4th ed.). Arlington, VA: American Psychiatric Publishing.

Halperin, D. (1986). Termination: Its therapeutic and legal dimensions in the long-term residential treatment center. *Residential Group Care & Treatment, 3* (3), 3–15.

Kelly, T., Soloff, P. H., Cornelius, J., et al. (1992). Can we study (treat) borderline patients? Attrition from research and open treatment. *Journal of Personality Disorders, 6,* 417–433.

Leichtman, M., & Leichtman, M. (2004). The integration of psychotherapy and intensive short-term residential care: The termination phase. *Residential Treatment for Children & Youth, 21* (3), 19–44.

Levine, L., Schwarz, D., Argon, J., Mandell, D., Feudtner, C. (2005). Discharge disposition of adolescents admitted to medical hospitals after attempting suicide. *Archives of Pediatrics & Adolescent Medicine, 159* (9), 860–866.

Moyer, A., Finney, J. W., Swearingen, C. E., and Vergun, P. (2002). Brief interventions for alcohol problems: A meta-analytic review of controlled investigations in treatment-seeking and non-treatment-seeking populations, *Addiction, 97,* 279–292.

Nygard, L., Grahn, U., Rudenhammar, A., & Hydling, S. (2004). Reflecting on practice: are home visits prior to discharge worthwhile in geriatric inpatient care? Clients' and occupational therapists' perceptions. *Scandinavian Journal of Caring Sciences, 18* (2), 193–203.

Sadock, B., & Sadock, V. (2005). *Kaplan & Sadock's comprehensive textbook of psychiatry.* Philadelphia: Lippincott Williams & Wilkins.

Thunnissen, M., Remans, Y., & Trijsburg, R. (2004). Premature termination of short-term inpatient psychotherapy. *Journal of Psychiatry (Dutch), 46* (11), 739–743.

Tyson, P. (1996). Termination of psychoanalysis and psychotherapy. In E. Nersessian & R. Kopff (Eds.), *Textbook of psychoanalysis* (pp. 501–524). Washington, DC: American Psychiatric Press.

Weiner, I. (1998). *Principles of psychotherapy.* New York: John Wiley & Sons.

Wolberg, L. (1980). *Handbook of short-term psychotherapy.* New York: Thieme-Stratton.

Woodside, D., Carter, J., & Blackmore, E. (2004). Predictors of premature termination of inpatient treatment for anorexia nervosa. *American Journal of Psychiatry, 161* (12), 2277–2281.

22

THERAPEUTIC ISSUES RELATED TO TERMINATION WITH MEDICATION

WILLIAM C. FOLLETTE AND DEBORAH DAVIS

Little research has addressed the issues that arise near the termination of therapy where the therapist and client are aware that one, if not the only, putative active components of any therapeutic improvement is attributed to the effect of a psychotropic medication. How the therapy process unfolds and how termination is handled can be complex. Because there is considerable variability in how medications are integrated into treatment, it is difficult to predict what issues will emerge. The goal of therapy, whether psychotherapy or pharmacotherapy, is to maximize patient functioning, control, and adaptability. In optimal outcomes, maximizing patient function may result in a return to normal functioning plus learning new skills to enhance responses to new challenges. In other cases, the best realistic outcome may be helping patients learn to recognize when it is time to seek more help during recurrent episodes of a clinical problem. In any event, it is important that the treating professional and the client share similar understandings of the role of medication in the therapy process.

Termination issues have been most intensively discussed in the psychodynamic literature. However, across psychotherapy treatment modalities, some commonalities exist (e.g., Curtis 2002; Goldfried 2002; Greenberg 2002; Wachtel 2002). Whenever the patient and therapist mutually agree to terminate therapy, most therapists will address common themes. It is preferable that patient and therapist agree on the timing of termination. In the end, it is the (competent) patient who makes the choice. Together, the therapist and patient determine the frequency and pattern of the last sessions. This may vary from an abrupt halt, to a tapering of sessions, or to planned, intermittent booster sessions. During termination, the therapist and patient will review previous stressors and highlight changes that have occurred during therapy that have been useful in learning new ways of behaving and adapting. The therapist may walk through how what seem like new stressors that might be encountered are, in fact, variations on issues that have already been addressed during treatment. In contemporary behavior therapies such as dialectical behavior therapy (Linehan 1984) or functional analytic psychotherapy (Kohlenberg & Tsai 1991), there is considerable emphasis on therapy teaching patients to recognize how many troubling and seemingly disparate behaviors are actually members of the same functional class. Therapy should be placed in context for the patient.

Patients and therapists might not always agree on the exact timing of the end of therapy, but the patient's decision can generally be supported. In the case where there is agreement between the therapist and patient, the above review will make up the bulk of the termination sessions. If the patient seeks to end therapy before the therapist might otherwise choose, it is important to frame termination positively. The important goal is to make therapy a place to which the patient can return without feeling like he or she would be admitting failure. Thus, the therapist can support the patient's leaving "early" in order to test how well what he has learned works and where some, if any, limitation may be encountered. The therapist will review conditions under which the patient may choose to reinitiate therapy. Sometimes patients have worked very hard to achieve a significant improvement. Though perhaps both the therapist and patient can see that more work can be done, it may be time for the patient to consolidate the changes without therapy and return when there is a clearer picture of what additional work remains.

It is important that the patient take credit for improvements that have occurred. This does not mean the therapist does not acknowledge a mutual commitment and effort to facilitate change, but it is the patient who makes the changes, and who must take those changes into the larger environment. In many instances, lapses or relapses can be discussed and even predicted. If therapy has addressed how to deal with lapses, it is useful to have the patient predict high-risk situations and discuss adaptive behavioral strategies. If this has not been an integral part of treatment, the therapist and patient can review indicators for returning to therapy before problems become overwhelming.

Relationship issues are frequently precipitants for seeking therapy. Similar issues may occur during therapy and can be a contributing reason for termination. Even in successful outcomes, in many therapist-patient dyads, difficulties can arise and should be discussed during treatment and certainly during termination.

Recognizing Termination

Part of the difficulty in researching and discussing termination involves the ways in which it is conceptualized, or rather *not* conceptualized, in many instances. What we have said above would certainly address what many would consider termination in therapy. However, the issues seem more complex than that. In many empirically supported treatments, the course of treatment is often, though not always, relatively structured.

Common elements of more standardized treatments generally include an assessment phase, a skills acquisition stage often including homework, a generalization phase, and some consideration of maintenance. Assessment often occurs throughout treatment with the therapist and patient examining what elements of treatment seem to contribute to improvement. If an assessment of symptoms near the end of treatment indicates a significant improvement, a summary session often ends treatment. A skillful therapist will still cover the above termination issues. However, the end of treatment is rarely an unanticipated, unscripted event if the treatment program is fully implemented.

If therapy has not produced the desired outcome, the therapist is ethically obligated to discuss treatment options including implementing other treatment approaches or making a referral to another provider. In either case, much of a final session or two is task oriented with an emphasis on having the patient and therapist assess progress and the work remaining.

In actual clinical practice settings or community agencies, therapies are often less structured in terms of what occurs during an intervention. In other ways, therapies may be more structured because of institutional or financial policies that limit the number of sessions or amount of services that can be utilized. In some of these cases, the termination issues are less of the therapist's and patient's making than of some outside agent.

However, let us consider the more generic version of termination when termination is not due to a specified time limit imposed by policy or protocol. The termination issues seem to reduce to a clearer set of issues. How do the therapist and patient recognize when it is time to terminate? What is the goal of the end of the portion of pharmacotherapy where frequent, regular visits occur and visits either end altogether or change to primarily medication monitoring? How is that process placed in an overall context that makes sense to both patient and therapist? How is it made positive rather than negative for the patient?

When Treatment Terminates as Planned

Most of this chapter will address the case where therapist and patient agree that it is time to end treatment. Ending treatment when psychoactive medications have or will continue to be used has different implications, depending on whether pharmacotherapy continues into the future or may be expected to resume at some indefinite time.

Recognizing When It Is Time to Terminate

By the time termination approaches in treatment, it is important that the therapist and patient share a similar understanding of the role pharmacotherapy played in any clinical changes that occurred during treatment. Consider the instance where a patient exhibits a high level of premorbid functioning prior to the onset of a stressor that precipitates seeking services for relatively uncomplicated anxiety. In such a case, anxiolytic medication may be used by itself or combined with psychotherapy for a brief intervention. Presumably, the rationale for using medication was presented as lowering the level of arousal and distracting symptoms so that the patient can utilize preexisting skills or those acquired during the psychotherapy portion of the treatment. The termination of medication is planned to precede the termination of therapy.

As the end of therapy approaches, the therapist has two goals. The first is to help the patient interpret any physiological responses to the tapering and discontinuation of medication so that changes to interoceptive cues are not interpreted as the reemergence of primary symptoms. Rebound anxiety or sleep alterations need to be anticipated and support provided while the patient adjusts to a drug-free environment. Since many therapies for this type of problem would include some version of distress tolerance training, this is an in vivo opportunity to utilize those skills. This, combined with a thoughtful tapering schedule, can allow medications to be terminated successfully. The second goal of the ending sessions is to make sure the patient recognizes what skills have been acquired or strengthened, and how to implement and maintain the skills as he or she faces new situations.

The problem the therapist must circumvent during the termination sessions is the patient's attributing improvement to medication rather than to his or her improved repertoire for anticipating and handling problematic situations more usefully than prior to treatment. For treatment gains to be robust, the patient needs to accurately assess those situations that can now be mastered, where they may previously have caused difficulty. Bandura describes the affective, cognitive, and motivational state that could arise from having accomplished significant change in therapy as enhancing the patient's sense of self-efficacy (Bandura 1977, 1997).

It is not clear exactly how one changes the patient's perceptions of how he or she will deal with new situations directly. Biglan (1987) has argued that self-efficacy can be understood as resulting from a reinforcement history for correctly predicting outcomes involving one's own behavior. The heuristic value of Bandura's idea of self-efficacy is very appealing. We point out Biglan's interpretation because it is more directly applicable to therapy termination. An important part of the termination process is having the patient make predictions about upcoming stressors and opportunities, and then assess the accuracy of how those predictions turned out as well as how adequate the patient's improved behaviors were in dealing with those challenges. This process is fundamental in demonstrating to the patient that his efforts, rather

than those of the drugs or the therapist, are what accounts for successful behavior change. That is not to say that the therapist cannot share
credit for helping create an opportunity where new adaptive learning
occurred. However, by the end of treatment the patient should be recognizing opportunities, assessing options, and behaving in ways that
maximize outcomes. In fact, there is probably no harm in the patient
acknowledging the role of medication in making the process easier
to tolerate in the beginning, but termination is about placing credit
where credit is due.

The research on the role of medications enhancing the ability of
the client to successfully engage in therapy is, in fact, unclear. That is,
medications may contribute to improved outcomes, but not necessarily
because the patient engages putative mechanisms of the psychotherapy
more successfully (e.g., Manber et al. 2003; Teusch et al. 2003). Thus, it
remains important that the end of the therapeutic process place as much
credit as possible on the actions of the patient now and in the future.

*The Role of Termination When Therapy and Pharmacotherapy End but
Reinitiating Treatment Is a Possibility*

The above scenario addresses the simple case where medication is used
early in treatment and is then withdrawn while the patient continues
to make progress. Even for the more biologically oriented therapist,
conducting the termination stated above should be relatively simple.
However, that instance had particular properties. There was a high
level of premorbid functioning and the stress or anxiety response was
generally appropriate, so that medications were appropriate to reduce
symptoms so that learning during therapy could occur more easily.
Therapy could have occurred without medication.

Let us now consider a case where more care is needed to ensure that
the patient is credited with having made substantial changes where
medication has been more central to the course of treatment. Whether
the patient undergoes split therapy, where therapy is provided by a
psychotherapist and pharmacotherapy is provided by a psychiatrist or
primary care physician, or integrated therapy, where both medication
and therapy are provided by a psychiatrist (Sperry 2006), the function
of medication needs to be explained to the patient.

While there is still significant debate about the effectiveness and mechanisms of medications and psychotherapy for the treatment of some anxiety and depressive disorders (cf., American Psychiatric Association 1993; Canadian Journal of Psychiatry 2006; Kirsch et al. 2002; Persons et al. 1996), there is no doubt that psychotherapy and pharmacotherapy are often presented as a combined treatment. To make it to a mutually agreed upon termination, it is important to provide an initial treatment rationale acceptable to the patient. The recent increase in advertising has promoted the use of pharmacotherapy for some disorders that may make medication a preferred choice for some individuals independent of supporting effectiveness data (for critiques of advertising practices, see Lacrasse 2005; Nikelly 1995).

In the case of pharmacotherapy, it is still important for the therapist to be able to provide an explanation of how the patient is to continue to maintain gains after treatment is terminated. Except for the die-hard dualist, most interventions can be presented in a biopsychosocial model. For the pharmacotherapist (or the patient for that matter) whose ontological position is that all mental illnesses are diseases and should be managed medically, there are thoughtful writings that address how both psychotherapy and pharmacotherapy affect the brain and even gene expression (Beitman et al. 2003; Kandel 1998). As mentioned, advertising biases consumers to favor certain practices even if data do not support those choices. It is useful to be able to frame one's therapeutic strategy in a language that makes sense to patients.

Let us return to an example of a more complicated instance where pharmacotherapy is more integral to the therapy. In this example, we will assume someone with a first presentation of major depressive disorder who is nearing the end of combined treatment. While all the issues discussed initially are important, two issues are central to termination. The first is the degree to which the patient attributes change to medication versus his or her own change with regard to how interpersonal difficulties are anticipated and handled more effectively. In an instance where this is the first presentation of depression, there is no clear indication for continuing pharmacotherapy if symptoms have remitted and interpersonal function appears normally adaptive. The termination should focus on changes the patient has made that can now be sustained when medication is appropriately withdrawn.

The patient may attribute improved functioning in part, to the effects of medication. The changes that are likely to sustain enhanced functioning derive from the changes in cognitive, behavioral, and affective processes, which were learned during treatment.

In the case where only minimal therapy was provided, termination still has to address how improvement is to be sustained when the medication is withdrawn. Pharmacotherapy alone can be justified if there were acute changes in the environment leading to disruption of access to a rich and successful social environment, which was followed by depression. If conditions have returned to a more normal state and mood has returned to normal, then a discussion of the return to a more predictable pattern in life may be sufficient. However, it is useful to lead the patient through an assessment of the degree to which he or she has contributed to the restoration of a more familiar environment.

What is not clear in this case is whether the patient has "recovered" normal functioning forevermore, or is in remission. Since epidemiological data suggests substantial rates of recurrence of major depressive episodes (e.g., Kessler & Walters 1998), termination issues have to include teaching the client to be tolerant of minor changes in mood so that attending to small changes is not itself a precipitant to further depression (Ma & Teasdale 2004; Teasdale et al. 2000). The difficult balance is strengthening the patient's repertoire for actively intervening in his or her environment using skills acquired or reacquired during therapy, and supporting the patient deciding to return to treatment early in a possible relapse.

Since patients decide when treatment ends, it is possible the therapist can help predict circumstances when the patient can successfully apply skills, as well as predict situations when the patient can anticipate difficulties. If we were to convey a difference between recovery and remission, it is that relapse entails there being probable circumstances when the patient lacks essential strengths to deal with certain types of challenges. Termination does not have to shy away from these kinds of discussions. Having deficits remaining is not a sufficient reason to struggle to get a patient to remain in therapy or on medications, and undermine the otherwise positive therapeutic experience the patient has had. It is possible that the person will not run into those circumstances either by good fortune or because he or she learns to guide his or her life around such circumstances. The essential point in terminating therapy is that the therapist and client review these vulnerabilities and position a return to treatment as a positive way of coping with predictable or exceptionally stressful circumstances.

Termination as a Change in Intensity of Contact Rather Than an End of Treatment

In some instances, the notion of termination may not even be appropriate. The nature of therapeutic interaction changes, but may not end at all. There are significant numbers of patients who have a clearly recurrent problem where, based on history or prognosis, one can predict that there will be multiple contacts with therapy and perhaps recurrent or chronic use of pharmacotherapy. There are patients with recurrent episodes of depressive disorder (Keller & Boland 1998) or more long-lasting or subclinical depression (Judd et al. 2000) and, of course, patients with schizophrenia or bipolar disorder who are clear examples of this class of healthcare utilizers. In these instances, as high levels of contact change to monitoring or more intermittent contact, the therapeutic process is better understood as one of *transition* rather than termination. The goal of therapy making use of medications is successfully moving from a more intense therapy to a change in roles where the therapist and patient are more like collaborators in monitoring, understanding, and predicting changes in patient status.

Though the issue of compliance or adherence with medication is briefly discussed later, any thorough review is well beyond the scope of this chapter. However, one of the guiding principles of working through this transition from frequent therapy/pharmacotherapy to monitoring and maintenance is to produce a relationship with the patient where information is comfortably exchanged, mutually evaluated, and respectful decisions are made. In the adherence literature, one view that seems clinically useful is that patients continually make their own cost-effectiveness analysis of whether the difficulty of adhering is worth the effects or benefits given the patients' competing short- and long-term values (Horne & Weinman 1999).

Lingam and Scott (2002) provide a review of factors influencing nonadherence in unipolar and bipolar disorders. One can reason backward from some of these factors to deduce some of the important issues that should be addressed by the time a healthcare professional and patient transition into a maintenance phase of their relationship. These issues will need to be addressed repeatedly during maintenance.

Certainly one issue that has to be addressed in any chronic or recurrent condition is the meaning the medication adherence has for the patient. Patients will frequently believe that they can pull themselves together and simply overcome their problem by the force of their will. This can be hard to distinguish from patients denying the seriousness of their problem, which also interferes with adherence (Greenhouse, Meyer, & Johnson 2000). The point is that patient's can interpret continually taking medication as admitting they have an unrelenting mental illness. This is likely to have an adverse impact on their self-perceptions. If that is the case, it is likely that patients will take it upon themselves to alter their medication regimen, reducing their medication as they feel better or as a way of managing side effects. The transition issue is to be sure to heavily reinforce patient efforts to self-monitor factors that enhance his or her adherence or factors that make it more difficult. Therapist-patient meetings can then focus on building on strengths and framing difficulties as challenges for both to solve collaboratively. The addition of family therapy may be a useful adjunct if family members do not support the importance of adherence.

Amazing as it may seem, patients often still do not understand or are not adequately informed about likely side effects of psychotropic medications. There may be a tendency for the pharmacotherapist to underplay side effects. This would be a mistake for at least two reasons. First, not fully informing patients about all aspects of their condition and its management is likely to harm therapeutic alliance, itself an important part of adherence (Barber et al. 2001; Bultman & Svarstad 2000; Frank et al. 1991). The second is that patients are then left to imagine or fear consequences that may not be attributable to the medication, which apparently they will do (Jamison & Akiskal 1983; Lingam & Scott 2002). The therapeutic alliance can be strengthened by reasonably informing the patient of what side effects are more or less likely with medications. The repertoire the therapist is trying to strengthen is having the patient become a good observer of things (including their medications) that affect the course of their symptoms, as well as the repertoire for sharing that information with the therapist. It may be surprising and comforting that some side effects do not occur or that they are mild and can disappear altogether. Side effects are significant problems with most psychotropic medications, and changing scheduling, dosages, or the medication itself is so common that the therapist should work diligently to establish a relationship were collaborative problem solving about adherence is welcome and extensively supported. Patients who have a choice in their treatment regimens are more likely to be adherent, as are those who feel they were better educated about their condition (Myers & Branthwaite 1992).

The transition period should not be limited to only discussing the status of the condition for which the patient originally sought treatment. Care should be taken to identify patient attempts to self-medicate because for some problems drug and alcohol abuse are associated with nonadherence (Keck et al. 1997). Likewise, communication can be strengthened if there is focus on positive activities in the patient's life. It is a difficult balancing act for the patient and the therapist not to focus excessively on negative events that occur during the course of more chronic problems. Noting positive events can be crucial to adapting to a life that requires vigilance. Neverthless, the dyad must guard against minimizing difficulties during discussions of positive events.

A technical analysis of how exactly to optimize this transition period from a behavioral or a social influence perspective is beyond the scope of this chapter. The goal during treatment and into the more permanent, less frequent contact is to create an environment where the patient assesses that it is in his or her best interests to communicate effectively with the physician/therapist, adhere with negotiated protocols, and structure life to optimize role functioning. One useful heuristic for guidance on this issue can be found in the health beliefs literature that has been evolving for over thirty years (Rosenstock 1974).

A relatively recent description of the interplay among health beliefs, quality of life, and the physician-patient relationship can be found in a description of how these issues relate to treatment intentions in patients with a chronic disease (Goldring et al. 2002). The elements that influenced patients' stated intentions to take medications seem to be sensible issues in this transitional stage where the transition is into a state of sustained attention to one's well-being. Several factors were modeled to predict medication intentions. As we mentioned earlier, patients behave as if they are constantly performing a cost-benefit analysis. Among the factors that are assessed in this analysis are patients' general quality of life and how it affects their specific problem. This analysis is an ongoing, dynamic process that takes into consideration the severity of the threat of a recurrence of the problem (e.g., an attack of inflammatory bowel disease, a major depressive episode, a recurrence of a manic episode, etc.), along with a concurrent appraisal of their susceptibility to that recurrence. Those assessments are moderated by the strength of the recommendations of the treating physician or therapist. The strength of the physician/therapist recommendation is strengthened by the patients' view that they share in the decision-making process and attenuated by any sense that they are excluded from that process.

The health belief model we briefly described is simply a conceptual scheme for considering how to structure long-term interactions between a patient and the treatment community. The best way to frame this kind of information is not a simple issue, and it is not easy to predict exactly how patients will react (e.g., Rothman et al. 2006; Rothman et al. 2003; Rothman & Salovey 1997). However, these elements seem useful to consider in constructing an ongoing, functional relationship that begins when intensive contact with a therapist transitions into a long-term relationship.

When Treatment Termination Is Unplanned

Ideally treatment proceeds to a mutually agreed-upon end or transition into an ongoing relationship. Unfortunately, that is not always the case. The data on how often mutually planned termination actually happens is extremely variable. In the psychotherapy literature, methodological variance as a result of the manner in which one measures premature termination yields estimates that vary from nearly 18 percent to 53 percent (Hatchett & Park 2003). Considerable differences in premature termination occur depending on whether patients are seen in public or private settings (DeBerry & Baskin 1989). An oft-cited figure resulting from a large meta-analysis places the estimated dropout rate near 47 percent or nearly half of those in therapy leave before the mutually planned end of treatment (Wierzbicki & Pekarik 1993). These data are quite similar to the general medication adherence estimates for chronic illness (c.f., Haynes et al. 2002, 2005) and in schizophrenia medication adherence (Lacro et al. 2002), and are consistent with the median estimate of 40 percent non-adherence for depression and bipolar disorders (Lingam & Scott 2002). In pharmacotherapy, the incidence of patients changing or discontinuing their medication without informing the physician is also high. Thus, for psychotherapy and pharmacotherapy, treatment usually does not proceed as originally planned.

Placing Treatment and Termination in Context

Clearly one object of therapy, whether or not it involves drug treatment, is to avoid or reduce the likelihood of an unplanned termination. Volumes have been written about the therapeutic principles (Castonguay & Beutler 2006; Lambert 2003) and relationship factors (Norcross 2002) that are associated with better outcomes. Though little empirical research has been done on the termination process, some have tried to summarize risk factors for unplanned termination. Ogrodniczuk, Joyce, and Piper (2005) reviewed the psychotherapy literature on premature termination and recommended strategies to reduce these events. Their suggestions include pretherapy preparation, patient selection, time-limited therapy, negotiated treatment, case management relating to life circumstances, appointment reminders, motivation enhancement, facilitation of therapeutic alliance, and facilitation of affect expression (60). Since, by definition, an unplanned termination can occur at any time, the pharmacotherapist must be vigilant for signs that all the positive aspects of the therapy and the therapeutic relationship are apparent to the patient. If the patient leaves therapy early, one wants to maximize the chance that he or she will return. Similarly, it is poor practice to avoid discussing apparent negative signs about how well the patient is receiving and responding to the therapeutic approach and the medications. In any session, the therapist should consider whether there are signs that it may be the last session.

There is strong evidence that the nature of the therapeutic relationship is an important factor in outcome and compliance. Whether by a primary care physician or a psychiatrist, medication and case management that lasts as little as fifteen to twenty minutes can indeed affect therapeutic alliance (Fawcett et al. 1987). Indeed, such findings were noted in the National Institutes of Mental Health (NIMH) Treatment of Depression Collaborative Research Program where initial patient alliance accounted for significant improvement even in the placebo pharmacotherapy condition (Krupnick et al. 1996). The main elements in the patient alliance factor of the scale used in the TDCRP (Treatment of Depression Collaborative Research Program; a modified version of the Vanderbilt Therapeutic Alliance Scale, Hartley and Strupp 1983) loaded on the degree to which the patient identified with the therapist's method of working, the patient's acknowledgment of having problems with which the therapist could help, and the patient and therapist sharing a common viewpoint. Thus, it is initially important to be sure that the patient and therapist share a common, or at least overlapping, view of the nature of the problem and intervention.

It is a mistake to assume that the patient has the same ontological view as the therapist, that the problem can be conceived of as medical in origin or at least appropriately treated by medication. Iselin and Addis (2003) have demonstrated that patient and therapist sharing similar views of etiology and treatment rationales can affect the perceived helpfulness of a particular intervention. General differences for treatment preferences also seem to vary across types of clinical problems (Mojtabai, Olfson, & Mechanic 2002).

It should not be assumed that initial agreement about etiology and treatment will persist if clinical response is inadequate, side effects are too onerous, or relapse occurs. The therapist needs to maintain an open dialog about treatment credibility. This can be harder than one might expect. Fontana and colleagues (2006) have shown that patients can be satisfied with how services are delivered, but make a distinction between that and satisfaction with treatment outcome. It would be easy for the therapist to mistake an affable interaction for satisfaction with outcome, and hence fail to predict that an unplanned termination might occur. If these issues were not difficult enough to track, keep in mind that for many patients, comorbidity is the norm and not the exception. Therefore, as focus on the patient's clinical presentation shifts, his or her willingness to accept medication may also shift.

In a healthcare delivery system where resources are stretched thinly, primary use of medication is common, yet the pharmacotherapist needs to be aware that there are many factors associated with differences in receptivity to medication as a form of treatment. Wagner and colleagues found few differences in receptivity to treatment options as a function of type of anxiety disorder, but noted several differences relating to demographic characteristics and patient attitudes toward treatment (Roy-Byrne, Wagner, & Schraufnagel 2005; Schraufhagel et al. 2006; Wagner et al. 2005). Ethnic and cultural factors have been found to influence adherence to medication by others as well (Diaz, Woods, & Rosenheck 2005). Our point, again, is that assessing and trying to bring congruence between therapist and patient may reduce unplanned terminations. There is evidence that relatively small changes in how primary care providers manage psychotropic medications can increase medication alliance and therefore increase and maintain patient compliance (Byrne et al. 2004).

Concluding Remarks

Termination can have special significance to both the therapist and patient. It is important that each understand the meaning of termination. For patients with acute problems that are self-limiting or within the patient's repertoire to respond when life circumstance return to normal, adjunctive medication can be useful. The patient and therapist need to share an understanding of the function of medication, the etiology of the difficulty, and the likelihood that there may be occasion to reinitiate therapy. Ideally, therapy ends when the patient and therapist concur that reasonable goals have been met.

In many instances, termination is not a discrete event. Several high-prevalence clinical problems have substantial recurrence rates. If both therapy and pharmacotherapy end, there may still be the need to review the kinds of progress the patient has made. These include skills at managing his or her interpersonal relationships and stressors. The skills may also include recognizing when it may be time to reinitiate therapy.

Several clinical problems will require long-term diligence by the patient. The termination process is better understood as a transitional period when the patient takes primary responsibility for self-management. Self-management includes monitoring of one's own well-being, keeping scheduled appointments, and, where agreed, behaving in line with the medication regimen prescribed. This transition period can extend into a maintenance phase where clinical management is built into the patient's environment by mobilizing social support wherever it is available.

Minimizing unplanned terminations is complicated. If there is one principle to which one must attend, it is making sure there is agreement on the part of the patient that the treatment approach makes sense and is producing the desired results. Failure to identify initial or evolving differences about treatment approaches vastly increases the likelihood that a mutually agreeable termination will not occur.

Therapy should be a positive experience. The patient should see the intervention as in their interests and worth the effort. Whatever obstacles arise, the patient should be placed in a position where successfully negotiating those obstacles enhances the likelihood he or she can take appropriate credit for a positive outcome. The therapist, even a primary care medication prescriber, can and should learn to watch for opportunities to engage the patient in the treatment, provide relevant information, and be willing to accurately assess patient satisfaction with outcomes.

Termination is a phase of treatment that can and should be integrated into the treatment plan from the beginning. One of the first questions one learns to ask in biopsychosocial interventions is, "How will we know when we're done?" This requires that we know where we started, how we are progressing, what is working, and how we understand our current status. A successful termination or transition is based on knowing the status of these issues.

References

American Psychiatric Association. (1993). Practice guidelines for major depressive disorder in adults. *American Journal of Psychiatry, 150* (4 Suppl.), 1–26.

Bandura, A. (1977). *Social learning theory.* Englewood Cliffs, NJ: Prentice Hall.

Bandura, A. (1997). *Self-efficacy: The exercise of control*. New York: Freeman.

Barber, J. P., Luborsky, L., Gallop, R., Crits-Christoph, P., Frank, A., Weiss, R. D., et al. (2001). Therapeutic alliance as a predictor of outcome and retention in the National Institute on Drug Abuse Collaborative Cocaine Treatment Study. *Journal of Consulting and Clinical Psychology, 69,* 119–124.

Beitman, B. D., Blinder, B. J., Thase, M. E., Riba, M., & Safer, D. L. (2003). *Integrating psychotherapy and pharmacotherapy: Dissolving the mind-brain barrier*. New York: W.W. Norton.

Biglan, A. (1987). A behavior-analytic critique of Bandura's self-efficacy theory. *Behavior Analyst, 10,* 1–15.

Bultman, D. C., & Svarstad, B. L. (2000). Effects of physician communication style on client medication beliefs and adherence with antidepressant treatment. *Patient Education and Counseling, 40,* 173–185.

Byrne, M. K., Deane, F. P., Lambert, G., & Coombs, T. (2004). Enhancing medication adherence: clinician outcomes from the Medication Alliance training program. *Australian and New Zealand Journal of Psychiatry, 38,* 246–253.

Canadian Journal of Psychiatry. (2006). Principles of diagnosis and management of anxiety disorders. *51,* 9S–21S.

Castonguay, L. G., & Beutler, L. (Eds.). (2006). *Principles of therapeutic change that work*. New York: Oxford University Press.

Curtis, R. (2002). Termination from a psychoanalytic perspective. *Journal of Psychotherapy Integration, 12,* 350–357.

DeBerry, S., & Baskin, D. (1989). Termination criteria in psychotherapy: A comparison of private and public practice. *American Journal of Psychotherapy, 43,* 1989.

Diaz, E., Woods, S. W., & Rosenheck, R. A. (2005). Effects of ethnicity on psychotropic medications adherence. *Community Mental Health Journal, 41,* 521–537.

Fawcett, J., Epstein, P., Fiester, S. J., Elkin, I., & Autry, J. H. (1987). Clinical management – imipramine/placebo administration manual: NIMH Treatment of Depression Collaborative Research Program. *Psychopharmacology Bulletin, 23,* 309–324.

Fontana, A., Rosenheck, R., Ruzek, J., & McFall, M. (2006). Specificity of patients' satisfaction with the delivery and outcome of treatment. *Journal of Nervous and Mental Disease, 194,* 780–784.

Frank, E., Prien, R. F., Jarrett, R. B., & Keller, M. B., et al. (1991). Conceptualization and rationale for consensus definitions of terms in major depressive disorder: Remission, recovery, relapse, and recurrence. *Archives of General Psychiatry, 48,* 851–855.

Goldfried, M. R. (2002). A cognitive-behavioral perspective on termination. *Journal of Psychotherapy Integration, 12,* 364–372.

Goldring, A. B., Taylor, S. E., Kemeny, M. E., & Anton, P. A. (2002). Impact of health beliefs, quality of life, and the physician-patient relationship on the treatment intentions of inflammatory bowel disease patients. *Health Psychology, 21,* 219–228.

Greenberg, L. S. (2002). Termination of experiential therapy. *Journal of Psychotherapy Integration, 12,* 358–363.

Greenhouse, W. J., Meyer, B., & Johnson, S. L. (2000). Coping and medication adherence in bipolar disorder. *Journal of Affective Disorders, 59,* 237–241.

Hartley, D. E., & Strupp, H. H. (1983). The therapeutic alliance: Its relationship to outcome in brief psychotherapy. In J. Masling (Ed.), *Empirical studies of psychoanalytical theories* (Vol. 1; pp. 1–38). Hillsdale, NJ: Lawrence Erlbaum.

Hatchett, G. T., & Park, H. L. (2003). Comparison of four operational definitions of premature termination. *Psychotherapy: Theory, Research, Practice, Training, 40,* 226–231.

Haynes, R. B., McDonald, H., Garg, A. X., & Montague, P. (2002). Interventions for helping patients to follow prescriptions for medications. Cochrane Database Systematic Review, CD000011.

Haynes, R. B., Yao, X., Degani, A., Kripalani, S., Garg, A., & McDonald, H. P. (2005). Interventions to enhance medication adherence. Cochrane Database Systematic Review, CD000011.

Horne, R., & Weinman, J. (1999). Patients' beliefs about prescribed medicines and their role in adherence to treatment in chronic physical illness. *Journal of Psychosomatic Research, 47,* 555–567.

Iselin, M.-G. v., & Addis, M. E. (2003). Effects of etiology on perceived helpfulness of treatments for depression. *Cognitive Therapy and Research, 27,* 205–222.

Jamison, K. R., & Akiskal, H. S. (1983). Medication compliance in patients with bipolar disorder. *Psychiatric Clinics of North America, 6,* 175–192.

Judd, L. L., Paulus, M. J., Schettler, P. J., Akiskal, H. S., Endicott, J., Leon, A. C., et al. (2000). Does incomplete recovery from first lifetime major depressive episode herald a chronic course of illness? *American Journal of Psychiatry, 157,* 1501–1504.

Kandel, E. (1998). A new intellectual framework for psychiatry. *American Journal of Psychiatry, 155,* 457–469.

Keck, P. E., Jr., McElroy, S. L., Strakowski, S. M., & Bourne, M. L. (1997). Compliance with maintenance treatment in bipolar disorder. *Psychopharmacology Bulletin, 33,* 87–91.

Keller, M. B., & Boland, R. J. (1998). Implications of failing to achieve successful long-term maintenance treatment of recurrent unipolar major depression. *Biological Psychiatry, 44,* 348–360.

Kessler, R. C., & Walters, E. E. (1998). Epidemiology of DSM-III-R major depression and minor depression among adolescents and young adults in the National Comorbidity Survey. *Depression and Anxiety, 7,* 3–14.

Kirsch, I., Moore, T. J., Scoboria, A., & Nicholls, S. S. (2002). The emperor's new drugs: An analysis of antidepressant medication data submitted to the U.S. Food and Drug Administration [electronic version]. *Prevention & Treatment, 5,* Article 23. Retrieved February 18, 2007, from http://journals.apa.org/prevention/volume5/toc-jul15-02.html

Kohlenberg, R. J., & Tsai, M. (1991). *Functional analytic psychotherapy*. New York: Plenum Press.

Krupnick, J. L., Sotsky, S. M., Simmens, S., Moyer, J., Elkin, I., Watkins, J., et al. (1996). The role of the therapeutic alliance in psychotherapy and pharmacotherapy outcome: Findings in the National Institute of Mental Health Treatment of Depression Collaborative Research Program. *Journal of Consulting & Clinical Psychology, 64*, 532–539.

Lacrasse, J. R. (2005). Consumer advertising of psychiatric medications biases the public against nonpharmacological treatment. *Ethical Human Psychology and Psychiatry, 7*, 175–179.

Lacro, J. P., Dunn, L. B., Dolder, C. R., Leckband, S. G., & Jeste, D. V. (2002). Prevalence of and risk factors for medication nonadherence in patients with schizophrenia: A comprehensive review of recent literature. *Journal of Clinical Psychiatry, 63*, 892–909.

Lambert, M. J. (Ed.). (2003). *Handbook of psychotherapy and behavior change* (5th ed.). New York: John Wiley & Sons.

Linehan, M. M. (1984). *Dialectical behavior therapy: A treatment manual*. Seattle, WA: University of Washington.

Lingam, R., & Scott, J. (2002). Treatment non-adherence in affective disorders. *Acta Psychiatrica Scandinavica, 105*, 164–172.

Ma, S. H., & Teasdale, J. D. (2004). Mindfulness-based cognitive therapy for depression: Replication and exploration of differential relapse prevention effects. *Journal of Consulting & Clinical Psychology, 72*, 31–40.

Manber, R., Arnow, B., Blasey, C., Vivian, D., McCullough, J. P., Blalock, J. A., et al. (2003). Patient's therapeutic skill acquisition and response to psychotherapy, alone or in combination with medication. *Psychological Medicine, 33*, 693–702.

Mojtabai, R., Olfson, M., & Mechanic, D. (2002). Perceived need and help-seeking in adults with mood, anxiety, or substance use disorders. *Archives of General Psychiatry, 59*, 77–84.

Myers, E. D., & Branthwaite, A. (1992). Out-patient compliance with antidepressant medication. *British Journal of Psychiatry, 160*, 83–86.

Nikelly, A. G. (1995). Drug advertisements and the medicalization of unipolar depression in women. *Health Care Women International, 16*, 229–242.

Norcross, J. C. (Ed.). (2002). *Psychotherapy relationships that work*. New York: Oxford University Press.

Ogrodniczuk, J. S., Joyce, A. S., & Piper, W. E. (2005). Strategies for reducing patient-initiated premature termination of psychotherapy. *Harvard Review of Psychiatry, 13*, 57–70.

Persons, J. B., Thase, M. E., & Crits-Christoph, P. (1996). The role of psychotherapy in the treatment of depression: Review of two practice guidelines. *Archives of General Psychiatry, 53*, 283–290.

Rosenstock, I. M. (1974). Historical origins of the health belief model. *Health Education Monograph, 2*, 328–335.

Rothman, A. J., Bartels, R. D., Wlaschin, J., & Salovey, P. (2006). The strategic use of gain- and loss-framed messages to promote healthy behavior: How theory can inform practice. *Journal of Communication, 56,* S202–S220.

Rothman, A. J., Kelly, K. M., Hertel, A. W., Salovey, P., Cameron, L. D., & Leventhal, H. (2003). Message frames and illness representations: Implications for interventions to promote and sustain healthy behavior. In L. D. Cameron & H. Leventhal (Eds.), *The self-regulation of health and illness behaviour* (pp. 278–296). New York: Routledge.

Rothman, A. J., & Salovey, P. (1997). Shaping perceptions to motivate healthy behavior: The role of message framing. *Psychological Bulletin, 121,* 3–19.

Roy-Byrne, P. P., Wagner, A. W., & Schraufnagel, T. J. (2005). Understanding and treating panic disorder in the primary care setting. *Journal of Clinical Psychiatry, 66,* 16–22.

Schraufhagel, T. J., Wagner, A. W., Miranda, J., & Roy-Byrne, P. P. (2006). Treating minority patients with depression and anxiety: What does the evidence tell us? *General Hospital Psychiatry, 28,* 27–36.

Sperry, L. (2006). Psychotherapy and medication: Mind-brain strategies for optimizing treatment with difficult clients. *Journal of Individual Psychology, 62,* 70–79.

Teasdale, J. D., Segal, Z. V., Williams, J. M. G., Ridgeway, V. A., Soulsby, J. M., & Lau, M. A. (2000). Prevention of relapse/recurrence in major depression by mindfulness-based cognitive therapy. *Journal of Consulting and Clinical Psychology, 68,* 615–623.

Teusch, L., Böhme, H., Finke, J., Gastpar, M., & Skerra, B. (2003). Antidepressant medication and the assimilation of problematic experiences in psychotherapy. *Psychotherapy Research, 13,* 307–322.

Wachtel, P. L. (2002). Termination of therapy: An effort at integration. *Journal of Psychotherapy Integration, 12,* 373–383.

Wagner, A. W., Bystritsky, A., Russo, J. E., Craske, M. G., Sherbourne, C. D., Stein, M. B., et al. (2005). Beliefs about psychotropic medication and psychotherapy among primary care patients with anxiety disorders. *Depression and Anxiety, 21,* 99–105.

Wierzbicki, M., & Pekarik, G. (1993). A meta-analysis of psychotherapy dropout. *Professional Psychology: Research and Practice, 24,* 190–195.

23

TERMINATION WITH JAPANESE CLIENTS

HIROAKI HARAI AND MIYO OKAJIMA

Introduction

This chapter describes healthcare practices in Japan. Japan began developing a unique healthcare system in 1961 when the government enacted the universal healthcare law. Now Japan has been able to achieve the seemingly impossible combination of cost containment, universal coverage, and no overt rationing of healthcare (Ikegami 1994). Ratings of nineteen OECD (Organisation for Economic Co-operation and Development) countries based on disability-adjusted life expectancy places Japan in third place and the United States in sixteenth place (Nolte & McKee 2003). Healthcare expenditure per capita in the United States is almost triple that of Japan (Deber & Swan 1999).

As termination of services is considered a major contributor in achieving cost containment, I believe that readers would be interested in how the Japanese healthcare system achieves this efficiency. To help readers understand how psychotherapy terminates in Japan, I will sketch the economical aspects of healthcare, chiefly the insurance system. Later in the chapter, I will describe the reality of termination for a mental healthcare provider.

The Focus of This Chapter

This chapter has several premises. First, the DSM-IV-TR (*Diagnostic and Statistical Manual of Mental Disorders*) (American Psychiatric Association 2000) classification system and empirically supported therapies are applied in Japan without special reservation; culture-bound issues are negligible. The main targets are adult ambulatory clients suffering from anxiety or depression, who are generally the major consumers of so-called talk therapy. Severe mental disorders like chronic schizophrenia, Alzheimer's disease, or drug abuse are not mentioned.

However, drug abuse merits further discussion with respect to the differences and similarities between Japan and the United States (Harai & Haning 2006). The prevalence of substance abuse is quite different between the two. Ozaki et al. (2000) surveyed five thousand members of the general population in Japan between October 3 and 31, 1995, and reported that illicit drug use was below 1 percent of the general population. On the other hand, in the United States, SAMHSA (Substance Abuse and Mental Health Services Administration) reported that 6.3 percent of the general population over the age of twelve had used illicit drugs during the last month (SAMHSA 2000). This means that fewer people in Japan are using related healthcare resources, especially self-help groups and drug rehabilitation facilities, which results in a smaller expenditure on mental healthcare.

Overview of the Japanese Healthcare System

In the Japanese healthcare system, payment for personal medical services is offered through a universal healthcare insurance system with fees set by a government committee. Figure 23.1 explains the flow of money within the Japanese healthcare system. Employees and their dependents participate in either corporate health insurance societies, government-administered employee health insurance, or fraternal health insurance societies. In 2005 there were 1,622 corporate health insurance societies covering 35.5 million people. Government-administered employee health insurance covers 30.1 million people. There are seventy-six fraternal health insurance societies covering 9.7 million people. Those who are not employed, for example, farmers, the self-employed, physicians in independent practices, and retirees, must participate in the national health insurance program, and its membership is 51.2 million.

In 2003 there were 1,073 mental hospitals, 1,451 psychiatric services offered in general hospitals, and an estimated 3,000 office-based

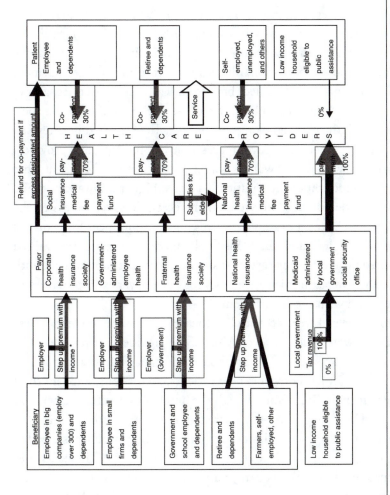

Figure 23.1   Money flow in Japanese healthcare. The premiums are split in half between the beneficiary and the employer. Premium slides with annual income. There is no discount for the beneficiary's individual health status, that is, there is no discount for nonsmokers.

psychiatric clinics in Japan. (Japanese Ministry of Health, Labor and Welfare 2003). These facilities provided various services, including psychiatric emergency, compulsory admissions, rehabilitation services, psychotherapy, and long-term residential treatment. Virtually all of the services are covered by health insurance. Most physicians and hospitals sold medicine directly to patients, but there were 36,000 pharmacies where patients could purchase synthetic or herbal medications. Patients are free to select any healthcare provider. Healthcare providers send their claims to either the social insurance medical fee payment fund or the national health insurance medical fee payment fund. Payments are scheduled, but are basically fee-for-service; allowances are the same for all plans, regardless of the kind insurance society to which the patient belongs or the area. The fee schedule is revised annually at a meeting of payer representatives, patients, and providers and the decisions on allowances is a matter of politics. Treatments that are considered important politically receive higher allowances, while those considered abused or redundant receive less, regardless of the actual cost. A recent example involves higher allowances for pediatric emergency as it is now the focus public media attention. The unified fee schedule and fee-for-service system enables cost containment with relatively lower administrative costs for both payers and providers in comparison with the U.S. system.

This universal free access to healthcare and the fee-for-service system has its downside, however. Most of the providers are private enterprises, and they are free to set their own management and policies. The number of patient visits, new patients, admissions, and length of stay are at their discretion. Though the number of psychiatric beds are regulated by local governments based on the local healthcare plan, the number of office-based clinics are not, and their number is steadily increasing (an estimated 1,000 in 1985, 3,000 in 2003). These facilities are encouraged to take as many patients as possible without selecting specific populations or targets. In general, office-based psychiatric clinics accept 300 to 500 new patients per year, and a single psychiatrist treats 50 to 100 patients per day. Few facilities make appointments and services are offered on a first-come, first-served basis. Patients have to wait long hours in the waiting room and the care provided is like assembly-line care. Under these circumstances, there is no reason for providers to offer specific and complicated treatment programs for specific targets or disorders. Overuse of medication (Ito, Koyama, & Higuchi 2005) is epidemic.

What Is Termination in Japan?

Any such service has a start and an end. Starting and terminating are decision-making processes that involve service recipients, providers, payers, and social contexts. With respect to an individual practitioner, the factors that affect his or her decisions are: (1) the practitioner's choice; treatment is successfully completed, that is, the practitioner is satisfied with what has been done; (2) the client's choice, that is, the client is satisfied and does not want more treatment, or is dissatisfied and chooses to seek help elsewhere. The best type of termination is where both parties are satisfied that no more treatment is necessary, and these decisions are rational and based on scientific evidence. However, this best-case scenario should be considered rather exceptional. Clients have many problems and goals, which often contradict each other, and achieving one goal comes with a trade-off. Clients are actually suffering from the ambivalence derived from these contradictions.

External factors exert decisive power over practitioners' and clients' choices. Many health insurance plans have certain limits with respect to coverage for healthcare services. Managed care in the United States has upper limits for the number of days of inpatient hospital care, and for the number of visits to outpatient clinics for individual diagnostic services. The 2006 fee schedule for health insurance in Japan does not impose these types of limits explicitly. The only effort toward cost containment from the payer's perspective was the introduction of a step-down fee schedule in 2004. For inpatient care, the allowance for the hospital facility charge and the physician's fee for one day of hospital care is around US$200 for the first three months, and US$100 thereafter. For outpatient care, the allowance is US$70 for the first visit, US$50 for the second visit, and US$30 for visits that occur after six months from the first visit. In summary, there is no explicit external limit for the length of stay in a psychiatric hospital or the duration of psychotherapy in an office-based practice. The duration of a hospital stay for a chronic mental disorder and termination of psychiatric services are considered as problems and discussed extensively (Asai 1993). The median length of stay is around 100 days in Japan, which is much longer than the average in developed countries (Senba et al. 1994).

From the patient's viewpoint, mental healthcare services are accessible and affordable. Although patients are expected to wait at the waiting room, it does not mean they must wait for days or weeks to be seen by psychiatrist. Inpatient care is readily available and affordable. Being a homeless alcoholic is a good reason to be hospitalized. It is easy for patients to change facilities, and there are no monetary penalties.

From the viewpoint of mental health professionals other than psychiatrists, this is not an acceptable condition. Services such as counseling, offered by clinical psychologists in independent practice, are not covered by insurance and they are sought by patients for economic reasons.

Information about treatments in the past two decades has radically restructured medicine. One issue involves the need for containment of healthcare costs. Another issue is the sense that the information revolution has changed expectancies concerning mental healthcare. A third concern involves increasing public awareness of variations in medical practice and the public's responses to that knowledge (Healy 1997). Japanese mental health is relatively isolated from these changes due to the language barrier. Most Japanese people cannot obtain healthcare information from English-language sources. Japan is notorious for not accepting immigrants, and all healthcare professionals are native Japanese. Yet information is increasing in Japan. This affects clients' help-seeking behaviors, and pharmaceutical industries know that Japan is the second largest market for prescription drugs, and their marketing efforts are universal.

In summary, Japanese healthcare delivery is characterized as (1) low in cost, (2) with universal access and freedom of choice for clients, and (3) of low quality and intensity, especially with respect to providers. The third characteristic greatly affects the provision of psychotherapy.

The types of psychotherapy services that are provided to clients, researched by academics, and taught to students is largely unique to Japan. One of the reasons is the isolation of Japan's practitioners. However, big pharmaceutical companies operate equally in Japan, and clients have been changing more rapidly than practitioners and academics, which is a cause of frustration for clients.

The Reality of Termination in Japan

Even if there is no external reason to terminate psychotherapy, it will be ended eventually by either the patient or physician. Physicians might stop practicing, and patients might move or change clinics. I have reviewed two sources on termination: (1) literature and (2) health insurance claim records in one mental hospital.

Review of Japanese Literature on Termination

A database from Japana Centra Revuo Medicina, a Japanese literature database, was searched beginning with the year 1981 to find literature written in Japanese with the keywords *termination* and *psychotherapy*; 163 articles were located. Among them, 93 were single case reports, 6 mentioned "control condition," 9 mentioned "cognitive therapy," and 8 mentioned "behavior therapy." No article mentioned "health insurance" or "economics." Most of the case reports are anecdotal with respect to psychotherapy. Sixty-two were case reports of psychodynamic or insight-oriented psychotherapies. It is impossible to draw specific guidelines or consensus from these Japanese academic publications.

Review of Health Insurance Claim Records

I am a psychiatrist and a behavior therapist working at Kikuchi National Mental Hospital. The hospital was established in 1977 to offer specialized care for demented patients; it has 150 psychiatric beds in total, 100 for general psychiatric disorders, and 50 for senile dementia. Kikuchi accepts 633 new outpatients and 354 new admissions per year (fiscal year [FY] 2003). It employs 13 physicians, 94 nurses, 3 occupational therapists, 2 psychiatric social workers, and 1 clinical psychologist. Table 23.1 shows the diagnoses of new outpatients in FY 2003.

I manage a specialized treatment program for anxiety and mood disorders. Of the approximately 100 new referrals per year, one-half are for obsessive-compulsive disorder, and one-half are for depression and other anxiety disorders. Patients need prior appointments to be seen, and the waiting list is now over two months. Patients come from across the whole country of Japan.

Table 23.1 New patient diagnoses in Kikuchi National Hospital, FY 2003.

DIAGNOSTIC CATEGORY[a]	NUMBER OF PATIENTS
F0 Organic, including symptomatic, mental disorders	204
F1 Mental and behavioral disorders due to psychoactive substance use	19
F2 Schizophrenia, schizotypal and delusional disorders	39
F3 Mood [affective] disorders	144
F4 Neurotic, stress-related and somatoform disorders	92
F5 Behavioral syndromes associated with physiological disturbances and physical factors	7
F6 Disorders of adult personality and behavior	5
F7 Mental retardation	13
F8 Disorders of psychological development	15
F9 Behavioral and emotional disorders with onset usually occurring in childhood and adolescence	9
G00-99 Diseases of the nervous system (Epilepsy)	30
Other	56
Total	633

[a] The diagnostic category is based on the International Classification of Diseases, 10th edition. (World Health Organization 2005)

The treatment program is typically two to three intensive CBT (cognitive-behavioral therapy) sessions for conditions like specific phobia and agoraphobia. For OCD (obsessive-compulsive disorder), the intensity varies from four sessions to over twenty-four per year. In some OCD cases, I make home visits or a nurse does them. Treatment outcomes for obsessive-compulsive disorders are fairly comparable to published data (Harai et al. 2005).

Table 23.2 shows the course of new patients who visited the outpatient clinic in Kikuchi National Hospital during FY 2003, with a primary diagnosis of depression, anxiety disorder, or somatization disorders; the age range of these patients was between eighteen and sixty-four years. Patients with missing data were excluded. I saw twenty-eight of these patients, while seventy-five were seen by other psychiatrists. Patients who were treated in the specialized program remained in treatment longer than those who were treated by other psychiatrists.

Table 23.2   Length of Treatment[a]

		PATIENTS SEEN IN SPECIALIZED PROGRAM BY THE AUTHOR	PATIENTS SEEN BY GENERAL PSYCHIATRISTS	SUM
Outpatient only	Number	23	59	82
	Remained after 30 days	61%	53%	55%
	Remained after 6 months	50%	42%	39%
	Remained after 12 months	43%	25%	30%
Involved inpatient treatment	Number	5	16	21
	Remained after 30 days	100%	94%	95%
	Remained after 6 months	100%	56%	67%
	Remained after 12 months	80%	38%	48%

[a] The percentage of patients who continued treatment is calculated. Those surveyed are new patients who visited the outpatient clinic in Kikuchi National Hospital during FY 2003, whose primary diagnosis was depression, anxiety disorder, or somatization disorder, and whose age range was between 18 and 64 years.

Among the twenty-eight patients I treated, those with anxiety disorders, who were also on medications, tend to stay longer on maintenance treatment, in some cases as long as eight years. Patients with chronic or recurrent conditions, primary obsessive slowness, somatoform disorder), recurrent major depressive disorders, and bipolar disorders usually need maintenance treatment to sustain therapeutic gains, which may be a lifetime proposition. Over 70 percent of these remained in the specialized program over one year. On the other hand, patients with these problems who are treated by general psychiatrists terminate treatment on their own. Less than 30 percent remained over one year.

In summary, specialized care for anxiety disorder and comorbid conditions require longer treatment episodes. If termination is the goal, holding back specialized care and offering nonspecialized care is the less expensive answer, and this is exactly what Japanese health-care as a whole is doing.

Summary

This chapter described characteristics of healthcare provision, help-seeking behaviors of patients, and the policy-making process in Japan. The uniqueness of Japanese healthcare economics involves (1) universal cover-age for healthcare by national health insurance, (2) a fee-for-service-based fee schedule, (3) universal pricing for all patients, payers, and providers, (4) successful containment of costs and good overall health outcomes, (5) virtually no coverage for other services provided by nonphysicians, that is, no coverage for clinical psychologists in independent practice, and (4) good access and freedom for patients to choose and change providers.

These benefits come with a negative side. Quality management efforts are scarce. Only three SSRIs (selective serotonin reuptake inhibitors) are available by prescription, therapists trained in CBT are rare, and outpatient clinics are packed with patients. There is a large variance in practice style among psychiatrists. And yet if these problems were properly addressed and improved, the changes would result in higher healthcare costs.

The chapter describes one year's outcome data of several physicians at an ambulatory setting in Japan. Two-thirds of the patients involved terminated treatment within one year on their own, and the attrition rate differed largely from physician to physician. The difference in outcomes was larger for anxiety disorder than for depressive disorder.

Conclusion and Future Direction

Every developed country has experienced this expansion of supply and demand in mental health services; Japan is not unusual. The number of attendees at seminars for psychotherapies and in programs or courses for clinical psychology in universities are increasing, and public aware-ness of the possibilities for specialized treatment for emotional disor-ders is expanding. Clinical psychologists in independent practice are rare at this moment, but it is easy to predict that this type of service will be prevalent in next two decades. This is probably a matter of how the Japanese national health insurance reform goes (Japanese Ministry of Health, Labor and Welfare 2000).

The variation among countries and therapists is large. Japan is unique in terms of freedom; practitioners and researchers alike consider this variation as a matter of course and feel it should be untouched because of their emotional disdain for external controls over their practice. The negative side of this freedom is the lack of accountability and quality control. Termination is not widely discussed in Japanese literature and not seriously considered. It has been left to the patient's discretion. The Japanese government decided to employ a DRG/PPS (diagnosis-related groups/prospective payment system) payment schedule for national health insurance for surgical operations. Mental health is largely left untouched, and it seems that advocates in mental health are avoiding discussing the change.

At this moment, Japanese practitioners have relatively independent decision-making power in comparison with American practitioners. On the other hand, increasing demand both for quantity and quality care, and the need for healthcare cost containment predict the independence will continue. Training CBT therapists and dissemination of proper information on emotional disorders and their treatment to the general public is one of the possible solutions to meet future change.

A classic trade-off in business concerns the trio of time, money, and quality. It is generally believed that only two of the three can be achieved at any given moment. Analyzing help-seeking behaviors and provider behaviors with principles of behavioral economics (Hursh 1984) would give us further insight.

References

American Psychiatric Association. (2000). *Diagnostic and statistical manual of mental disorders* Text Revision (DSM-IV-TR). (4th ed.) Washington DC, USA: American Psychiatric Press.

Asai, K. (1993). Japan. In D. R. Kemp (Ed.), *International handbook on mental health policy* (pp. 160–175). Westport, CT: Greenwood Press.

Deber, R., & Swan, B. (1999). Canadian health expenditures: where do we really stand internationally? *Canadian Medical Association Journal, 160* (12), 1730–1734.

Harai, H., & Haning, W. F. (2006). Comparison of substance abuse disorder treatment between Hawaii in America and Kyushu in Japan. Presented at the First World Congress of Cultural Psychiatry; Beijing, China.

Harai, H., Miyata, Y., Hashimoto, K., Okajima, M. (2005). Treatment outcome of obsessive compulsive disorder in a Japanese mental hospital – How does the system of health care provision affect empirically proven therapy? Presented at the Association for Advancement of Behavior Therapy, 39th Annual Convention; Washington, DC.

Healy, D. (1997). *The antidepressant era*. Cambridge, MA: Harvard University Press.

Hursh, S. R. (1984). Behavioral economics. *Journal of the Experimental Analysis of Behavior, 42* (3), 435–452.

Ikegami, N. (1994). Efficiency and effectiveness in health care. *Daedalus, 123* (4), 113.

Ito, H., Koyama, A., & Higuchi, T. (2005). Polypharmacy and excessive dosing: psychiatrists' perceptions of antipsychotic drug prescription. *British Journal of Psychiatry, 187,* 243–247.

Japanese Ministry of Health, Labor and Welfare. (2000). Part 1 Social Security and National Life. In *White paper of social security,* http://www1. mhlw.go.jp/english/wp_5/vol1/p1c1s1.html

Japanese Ministry of Health, Labor and Welfare. (2003). Annual survey of health care providers in 2003. In MHLW Statistical Database. http:// wwwdbtk.mhlw.go.jp/toukei/data/160/2003/toukeihyou/0004689/ t0099549/A0016_001.html

Nolte, E., & McKee, M. (2003). Measuring the health of nations: analysis of mortality amenable to health care. *British Medical Journal, 327* (7424), 1129.

Ozaki, S., Kikuchi, S., Wada, K., & Fukui, S. (2000). Lifetime prevalence of drug use in general population of Japan. In *Problems of Drug Dependence 1999, Proceedings of the 61st Annual Scientific Meeting of the College on Problems of Drug Dependence,* 276. Washington, DC: NIH.

SAMHSA (Substance Abuse and Mental Health Services Administration). (2000). Chapter 2. Illicit Drug Use. In Annual national household survey results.http://www.oas.samhsa.gov/NHSDA/2kNHSDA/chapter2. htm

Senba, T., Takayanagi, K., Kigami, G., Asai, K., Kominie, K., Kawasaki, S. & Orley, J. B. (1994). International comparative survey of mental health facilities' characteristics. *Rehablitation Research (Japanese), 79,* 5–10.

World Health Organization. (2005). *ICD 10 International Statistical Classification of Diseases And Related Health Problems: Tenth Revision.* Geneva: World Health Organization.

APPENDIX

Some examples from the Psychoanalytic Assessment/Evaluation (Toronto Institute of Psychoanalysis)

A   Identification Data   Date (d)____ (m)____ (y)____

B   Primary Diagnosis
    Instructions: Circle number to indicate patient's present level of functioning. (Descriptions should be used as guides rather than rigid criteria; score factor level according to your own evaluation of the patient's functioning.) Scores range from 1 (most impaired) to 5 (least impaired) or N/A.

C   Clinical Functioning: present ability to cope and lack of symptomatology—incapacitated/dysfunctional/moderate/mild/asymptomatic.
    1 _____ 2 _____ 3 _____ 4 _____ 5 _____

F   Life Circumstances: the degree that present personal (age, finances) and environmental (time, family, work) circumstances will support therapy at this time—poor/significant difficulties/questionable support/presently adequate support/favorable time to begin.
    1 _____ 2 _____ 3 _____ 4 _____ 5 _____

L   Affect Availability: the degree which patient is open and aware of feelings—unavailability (denial) of affects and memories/secretive/defensive/open/warm.
    1 _____ 2 _____ 3 _____ 4 _____ 5 _____

M   Motivation: the degree of self interest/commitment to understand and sufficient suffering to bring about a desire for change—poor/questionable factors / wish rather than realistic self-expectation/adequate self motivation / desire to do whatever is necessary.
    1 _____ 2 _____ 3 _____ 4 _____ 5 _____

N   Introspection: degree of psychological mindedness that includes self awareness, curiosity, intuition and capacity for insight—disinterest in introspection/questionable self reflection/adequate thoughtfulness/favorable self awareness/intuitive and insightful.

     1 _____ 2 _____ 3 _____ 4 _____ 5 _____

Q   Past Transferences: history of typical consistent attitudes towards parents, teachers, bosses, and former therapists, primarily—splitting/negative, resentful/ambivalent/benign/positive, grateful.

     1 _____ 2 _____ 3 _____ 4 _____ 5 _____

R   Object Relatedness: includes the degree of patient's social adaptation, friendships and intimacy potential—disinterested, chaotic or absent ties/exploitative or primarily self involved/inhibited or commitment concerns/able to form close friendships/successful at love and sensitive to others.

     1 _____ 2 _____ 3 _____ 4 _____ 5 _____

S   Patient Alliance: the degree of immediate positive feeling patient has towards therapy and therapist, includes facilitating transferences—overt mistrust/negative/guarded/benign cooperative/positive.

     1 _____ 2 _____ 3 _____ 4 _____ 5 _____

T   Therapist Alliance: the degree of the therapist's positive feelings regarding working with this patient—dread/negative/guarded/interested/positive.

     1 _____ 2 _____ 3 _____ 4 _____ 5 _____

INDEX